The Doctor & Sheikhs' Debate

M. H. Shojaeefard

Translated by:

S. Jeyran Main

The Doctor & Sheikh's Debate

Copyright © 2019 by M. H. Shojayeefard

Printed and bound in the United States by Ingram Sparks Self Publishing. All rights reserved. No part of this book may be reproduced or transmitted in any form or by any means, electronic or mechanical, including photocopying, recording, or by any information storage and retrieval system, without written permission from the author or publisher. Exceptions are permitted for quotations embedded in critical articles and reviews about this book.

Automotive Eng. Dept.

University of Science and Technology

Tehran, Iran

mhshf@iust.ac.ir

iust.ac.ir

Tel: 0098 21 77240360-63

Fax: 0098 21 77240364

For information about special discounts available for bulk purchases, sales promotions, fund- raising and educational needs, contact:

S. Jeyran Main

Tel: (1)-519-841-4300

jeyranmain.com

ISBN 978-1-988680-05-7 (Electronic)

ISBN 978-1-988680-04-0 (Soft Copy)

First Edition

Contents

Translator's Preface 1

Introduction 3

Ordinance of Pilgrimage 7

Day Nineteenth of Zyqadeh, Flying to Medina 9

Getting Acquainted with Sheikh Ibrahim Usman (Sheikh) 13

The Twentieth of Zyqadeh 21

    Proof of Brotherhood (Shias are Muslims) 21

        The One God 22

        The One Prophet 22

        The One Quran 23

        The One Qibla 23

        The One Salat (Pray) 24

        The One Hajj 24

    An Organised Discussion 25

    The Rules for the Debate and Discussion 26

    The Lack of Probity of Companions in Quran 27

    Every Day after the Morning Pray at Baqi 37

    Is the Prophet (s.a.w.a) Dead? 38

Day Twenty First of Zyqadeh 41

    Accuracy Verification of the Hadith's in Sihah al Sittah 42

    Mote' (Concubine) and Temporary Marriage 48

    The 1987 Mecca Incident 57

The Twenty Second of Zyqadeh 59

    There is No Difference between the Prophet Being Dead or Alive 60

    Crying for the Dead 65

    Blessing and Pleading to the Righteous Dead 72

    Pleading to Imam Bukhari's Grave 73

    Supplication in Shia'sm 74

- Day Twenty Third of Zyqadeh 91
  - Continuation of Supplication in Shia'sm 92
  - Combining the Zuhr, Asir and Maghrib, Isha Prayer 110
  - Supplication for Repentance 112
  - Pilgrimaging in Shia'sm and the license Permission for Sunni to Pilgrimage ... 115
  - Pilgrimaging and Its Ritual's Based on Alazhar 122
- The Confessions of Mohammad Ibn Abudl Wahab 125
- The Dynamics of Authority and Imitating in Shia'sm 126
- Day Twenty Fourth of Zyqadeh 133
  - Getting Acquainted with Sheikh Hamid Al Najdi 133
  - A Debate in Sheikh Hamid's House 134
  - Ablution in Islam 141
  - Call for Prayer in Islam 150
  - Amen and Taktuf (placing a hand on hand) 153
  - Loudly Reading "In the name of God the Beneficent, the Merciful (بسم الله الرحمن الرحيم)" While Praying 154
  - Reading a Full Surat in Salat 156
  - Tashahod (Confession of Faith) in Praying 160
  - Sijdah (Prostration) On Soil 164
- Twenty Fifth of Zyqadeh 171
  - Issue Regarding Ahl al Bayt 171
    - Who are the Ahl Al Bayt? 172
  - Why is Passing In front of Worshipers Prevented? Where does it originate from? ... 181
  - In My Room with My Roommates 184
  - Attention in Conducting Ordinances, Obsession and or Creating Concerns ... 184
- Day Third of Zihijjah 187
  - First Meeting with Sheikh Ibrahim in Mecca 187
  - The Situation with Human Sciences in Iran 188
- Day Fourth of Zihijjah 193
  - Islam and Politics 194

Day Sixth of Zihijjah 207
    Hazrat Mahdi in Ahl Sunnat's Books 207
    The Age of Imam Mahdi 209
Day Seventh of Zihijjah (Friday) 221
    1- The Difference between the Prophet and the Caliphas 222
    2- The Disagreement over the way the Caliphas were Chosen 225
    3- The Number of Caliphas after the Prophet 227
Day Eighth of Zihijjah 233
    4- The Companions Objection over Ali Not Being Chosen as Calipha 233
Day Ninth of Zihajjah (Arafa Day) 243
    The Arafa Supplication 243
Day Eleventh of Zihajjah 245
    5- Ali's Superiority over the Other Caliphas 249
Day Fifteenth of Zihajjah 253
    6- Consequences over Eliminating Ali from Being Chosen as Calipha after the Prophet 254
Day Sixteenth of Zihajjah 259
    7- The Prophet's Testimonial over Ali Being Calipha After Him 260
Day Seventeenth of Zihajjah (Eid Ghadir Night) 269
    8- Ghadir Khumm 269
    The Prophet's Remark: Whomever I am his Master, Ali is his Master 273
    The Companions Remarks after Ali Started as Calipha 290
    Why Is the Imam not Mentioned as Calipha In the Quran? 292
Appendix One: The Complete Speech of Ghadir in Arabic by The Messenger of God 300
The Translation of the Speech in English 309
    Praise and Glorification of Almighty Allah 309
    Divine Command of Ultimate Importance 311
    Formal Announcement of the Leadership and Mastership of Ali and the 12 Imams ... 312
    Allah's Messenger Publicly Appoints His Successor 314
    Emphasis on the Nation to Adhere to Imamat 315

Warning about the Plots of the Usurpers 316

The Devotees and the Enemies of Ahl Al Bayt 318

The Glad-Tiding of Reappearance of Imam Mahdi 319

Preparation for Seeking Allegiance (mentioning of Ahl Al Bayt) 320

The Nation's Reference for the Permissible and the Prohibited 320

Formal Seeking of Allegiance 322

List of Some of the Chain of Transmissions Mostly Used in the Software 325

Translator's Preface

In this book, M. H. Shojaeefard has exclusively written on various matters regarding the differences between the Shia and Sunni Muslims today. He has respectfully chosen to express the misunderstandings that are current in our day to day lives. He wishes to convey the information he has gathered within the many years of accomplished research to the reader.

The book is originally written in Farsi and converted to English by myself. In addition, there are, however, many Arabic references that I have faithfully tried to render and translate as well. In my belief, the object of a translator should ever be to hold the mirror up to his author. Undoubtedly, it is possible to have phrases and citations that have not been transferred to its best possible understanding. To prevent any confusion; if you stumbled upon any problem, please refer to the original Arabic words.

Inevitably, this book assumes that the reader has general knowledge about Islam and if that is not the case then our non-Muslim readers can always refer to other relevant Islamic books to clarify any questions they may have.

The translation of this book has been carefully agreed on and revised by the author and the editors.

I wish to send many thanks to my father, professor S. M. A. Boutorabi, and my beloved husband, C. R. Main, that have assisted me in editing this book. This book could not have finished if it had not been for their support, understanding, and patience.

I also wish to thank the author of this book for granting me the privilege of translating what I believe, a beautiful book in the path of true Islam and the Ahl al Bayt.

S. Jeyran Main

Sept 15, 2014

Introduction

When I was younger, and after graduating with my Technician Diploma from Abadan Oil Company Art School, I had a thought, how could we be sure that what we believe in is, in fact, the absolute truth and is the salvation of human being? In the old day's Marxism prevailed. Therefore, I decided to study Marxism. I concluded that it did not contain anything substantial to change the mind of an average thinking person. I also explored some of the new religious books and schools of thought, but I did not manage to find anything notable.

One of the leaders of the Baha'i Sect in the world happened to be our neighbor. I was also in contact with several other people who followed the Baha'ism. In addition, I spent a concise amount of time listening to them and lured to what they had to say. There were many Christian's in Abadan, and I was aware that the Christian faith is the most dominant faith in the world. I studied about their religion as well and concluded that even though their faith has a holy foundation, it did not continue with the Christianize monotheism. When I was studying in England several years later, I heard from many Christian scholars that the Holy Trinity was causing a setback with their youth.

After studying different schools and religions, I concluded that only Islam has a rational and scientific base. Thankfully, as a researcher in analyzing all the other faiths and their books, I did practice on the Islamic rules, and maybe that was the reason why the appearance of the other religions did not deceive me.

However, a question did cross my mind. Are our Sunni brothers that are the majority, closer to the true Islam? The answer to this question was a little harder because God, Quran, Qibla, the Prophet (s.a.w.a), and most of the prayers are the same. However, the political and cultural paths are different.

Therefore, to be able to understand the essence of the beliefs of our Sunni brothers, I learned Arabic and started reading their famous books in a specific one of their important ones named Sihah al Sittah. At the same time, for comparison, I also studied the Shias books as well.

Whatever I discovered in the Sunni books in regards to religious actions and alike were not so different from Shias. However, their efforts were various from what the essence of their books mandated. Additionally, regarding important matters, that was imperative when I was young and still are to this day now that I am older, is the role of religion in government and running the world. Unfortunately, this is contradicted in Sunni books, especially with the Quran's principles. This is even happening with a significant number of their Hadith.

Consequently, after studying our Sunni brother's books, I realized that the Ahl al Bayt's School (even though some Sunni followers believe that Shias act contradictory to their own rules) is the closest to the true Islam and the straight path. In other words, I have to say that it was reading the Sunni books that made me sense a much stronger belief to the Ahl al Bayt's School. After graduating with a Diploma in Mathematics, I entered the Iran University of Science and Technology, and because of the necessity, I felt in the University, I continued to research on that particular matter. In addition to my political and revolutionary activities against the Shah in specific the Islamic revolution, I felt the need to study even more on the matter.

Evidently, after the success of the Islamic revolution led by Imam Khomeini (On whom bid the mercy of God), scholars and young brave Sunni's that lived in Iran, declared their presence in the political ground and protected the sacred system of the Islamic Republic of Iran and followed the pure Mohammad way of Islam (free soul spirited living).

Currently following the 33 years of enlightenments in the shadow of the Islamic revolution of Iran and with the leadership of Hazrat Imam Khamenei, the Islamic world has woken. With the call of "God is the greatest," we have stood against the superpowers, and because of this, the Islamic countries have one by one released themselves from the domination of outsiders.

In my first visit to Hajj in 1982, I realized that I needed to work on my Arabic for conversing. This was because I saw many practices in Sunni religion that were contradicting their own rules, and I was not able to explain it to them adequately. In conclusion, I learned how to speak Arabic. It was an honor to go to Hajj many years later. I was able to talk with our Sunni brothers in specific their scholars, and this book is a report on some of those discussions.

For economic reasons, I will not go into too many details as to the way the discussions were recorded, filed, written, and published.

I managed to save single software on my mobile that contains roughly 7000 books about how our Sunni brothers think from the Masjid an Nabawi (s.a.w.a) in Medina. This software program is the essence of all the documents that are in this debate. All of the Hadith related to the papers given have been from this software and have been cited and translated in this book. For this particular reason, some of the writings have inflection. Even the book of "Characteristics of the faithful Ali Ibn Abitaleb" and parts of the book of "Kanzal Amaal (Treasure of the good-doers)" that describe the virtues of Ali have been copied and translated from this software. In the discussions, no document has been taken from the Ahl al Bayt's School. Much of the debate between the two parties have been removed due to the unimportance of the material, and many files have not been mentioned in this book. Nevertheless, it is possible to say them in my later published books if my honorable readers suggest it and if the files for that particular request are available. I need to mention that I did not include the Arabic material for the sections that had few differences, and therefore, I settled with the text content only.

The accountability of this discussion has no intention to covert our Sunni brothers and sisters to Shia'sm. I am trying to demonstrate to those beloved people that their beliefs could not be any further away from true Islam. I wish to explain how much the Ahl al Bayt's School is closer to the righteous path. God willing, with the emersion of Hazrat Vali e Asr the true Islam that is the genuine School of Ahl al Bayt will be declared without any uncertainty, and the whole world will be ruled by the highly honored.

I named this debate "The Doctor and the Sheikh's Debate" after the memory of reading the "Discussions of the Doctor and the Old man" book, written by the warrior for the faith and martyrdom of the honorable Hazrat Hojat al Islam val Muslamin Seyed Abdul Karim Hashemi Nedjad, 45 years ago.

I thank all the people that have assisted me in typing, editing, and publishing this book without mentioning any names and God willing their remuneration will be given by the Ahl al Bayt.

Mohammad Hassan Shojaeefard

Feb 11, 2012

Ordinance of Pilgrimage

We had registered many years ago to go to Mecca. Eventually, they announced our names for registration. I applied for registration for my wife and myself the first chance I acquired. In the first information meeting, they clarified the pilgrims accompanying us to Hajj. There were some Academic staff employers of the University and some from the public society. Even though I had been privileged enough to go to Hajj before this time, I had a different sense about the whole ordeal. Mainly because my wife was accompanying me and it was her first Tamattu Hajj.

Despite being familiar with the rituals of Hajj, I attended the information and training sessions with my wife. We were acquainted with new friends there. We bought some of the materials needed for Ihram at those meetings. It mostly was books and notes for introducing the philosophy of Hajj. There were ten sessions; however, we only went to four of them. We attended the first and last two sessions, which were 3 weeks away from our trip.

It was at the 9th session that four other people and I agreed to share one room. The women were in separate rooms from the men. One of the people was a military man working for the Iranian Revolutionary Guards of the Islamic Revolution. His name was Haj Abbas Niyazmand. The other was a professor at the University of Tehran, Dr. Mohammad Ahmadi and one other was the member of the board of directors for one of the biggest banks in Iran, Haj Ali Ghargham. The other person, named Haj Mohammad Karbalayi, worked in economics and trade. It was at the last sessions that the tour manager announced that one of our roommates was not coming. I asked the reason for his absence, and he said he wanted to give the cost of the trip to an ill young person to buy a kidney and replace it with the one that is not working. I was happy for the sacrifice he made for this brother and became saddened because Haj Abbas could not come with us. Nevertheless, he requested that the other women in our group to take care of his wife as she was still traveling with us.

I attempted, with the assistance of a couple of charitable people, to arrange the cost of purchasing the young man's kidney. We gave the money to Haj Abbas. This way would not be depriving us of his company and so he could accompany us on the trip and thankfully we were successful.

At the last information session, we received identical bags and luggage with signs and numbers of our tour group written on them and got ready for a trip that all the Muslims of the world wish to go on. From experience, I took my wife to buy the essential things that we needed for the trip.

We visited several different bazaar's and eventually filled two of the luggage's with Ihram material, personal clothes, snacks, and other food and presented it to the tour group.

Day Nineteenth of Zyqadeh, Flying to Medina

We managed to hand in our luggage two days before our flight. The flight time was for Saturday at eight in the morning from Tehran to Medina. We were in the airport at four in the morning to obtain our passports, tickets and all of the rest of our paperworks from the trip manager.

The children came to the airport with us to help, in particular, with carrying of the luggage, passports, tickets and other handheld items. They were all of the things that needed to be taken inside the airplane. We all waited for the airport to call out our flight at eight. However, it did not happen. Eventually, at 9:15, our plane was ready to fly. Iran had rented a 747 Saudi plane for Hajj expeditions.

Transporting a range of 100,000 people in a short period of one month for Hajj is not in the Islamic Republic of Iran airline's ability; therefore, they would rent the Arabian planes. The Arabian flight attendant would use hand motions and speak Arabic and English to some, to communicate with the pilgrims. This brought some tension between the flight attendant and the pilgrims.

Eventually, after two and a half hours of flight, our plane landed in Medina Airport. I could hear the sound of the pilgrims sending special blessings to the Prophet and his followers. It was in gratitude for arriving at Medina and being healthy and safe.

It took a very long time before they allowed us to leave the airplane. I asked one of the flight attendants the reason for the delay in which they replied that the other pilgrims had arrived into the terminal and that there was no space for them to sit until they gave the all clear.

Eventually, after what seemed to be another two hours of waiting in the plane, and continuous complaints of the passengers, the permission to leave the aircraft was given.

We had to walk into the terminal only to realize the reason for the delay. They were photographing and fingerprinting everyone that was landing. After several complaints from us, they did not fingerprint the people that were over fifty. This helped, immensely, in speeding up the process. We were done in half an hour.

After the picture taking and fingerprinting, it was time for the inspection of luggage. This was to prevent any forbidden substances imported. I had brought several books for reading and a computer in which they asked what the content of that was. My visit card showed that I was a professor at the university specialized in engineering. Therefore, they gave up turning the computer on and just asked in what university was I teaching engineering? I replied to the University of Science and Technology. They then asked if there was ample of Professors in Iran. I responded: yes. They asked if I was carrying any political or advertising books with me. I replied, no.

By the time I managed to escape from the border Officers questioning, I had realized that my wife was nowhere to be seen. She was not on the bus that was heading towards the hotel, nor was she anywhere else. No one seemed to have seen her. Eventually, after what appeared to be like twenty years for me, I found her. The physical inspection side for women had detained my wife. Fortunately, even though she had nothing in particular with her, she had still been inconvenienced. I released a sigh of relief and headed towards the bus that took us to the hotel with my wife. Our luggage was put on the bus, and apparently, everyone was waiting for us. Finally, we managed to head towards the hotel. It was on the Ali Ibn Abitaleb Street behind the Baqi. The hotel was newly built, and we were one of the first groups ever to enter it. The rooms were previously assigned, and the names of the people were tagged. It was a tradition for the group leader to meet and greet their team upon arrival and explain the rules and regulations for breakfast, lunch, and dinner. Once the keys for the rooms were distributed and the ceremony was finished, we headed towards the shrine with Haj Abbas for the Zuhr prayer immediately.

We found a spot outside the Mosque on the heated stones to pray in congregation. Once the prayer was over, we were content with just sending our salutations and blessings to the Prophet (s.a.w.a) from the end of the Mosque and come back with the ceremony.

We returned to the hotel. Our lunch was ready made, and we ate it and then decided to catch up on some sleep. Unfortunately, two men had already fallen asleep before us and were snoring so severely that it was almost impossible to sleep. We lingered outside of the room for two hours until they woke up. It then became apparent that Hajj Mohammad Karbalayi and Hajj Ali Ghargham have been suffering for years with this problem. For that reason, Hajj Abbas found a quiet spot by the pantry to take a nap. I, on the other hand, did not have such a severe problem with the issue as I had grown up sleeping with noise and not so very comfortable conditions, therefore, thankfully, my experience became very handy. Dr. Ahmadi was not coping very well under the circumstances. He had a severe problem with the noise, speaking and in general sleeping. We decided to have Dr. Ahmadi sleep in the room when we were all gone to the shrine and vice versa. In summary, Hajj Abbas slept in the pantry, Dr. Ahmad slept when we were not in the room, and I did not have a problem with the situation.

Eventually close to sunset and after resting for a little while we bathed (Ghusl) and headed towards the Prophet's (s.a.w.a) shrine and the Jannat al-Baqi. My wife accompanied me. We had agreed to go our separate ways once we arrived and only be together for specific things such as Bazaar shopping.

I explained the changes made over the thirty years to my wife. They had expanded and designed the Mosque with an open concept. All the old bazaars, religious artifacts, Bani Hashm's street, Imam Sadegh's house that had altered to a library, the Prophet's father, and Hazrat Abdullah's shrine were all ruined. Although there had been much loss to what used to be, the Prophet's (s a.w.a.) shrine had expanded and was much more significant. The other interesting fact was that contrary to thirty years ago where the police used to gamble and play cards in the tents around the entrance doors of the Mosque and the Prophet's (s.a.w.a) shrine, they had placed religious enforcement Officers and a couple of law enforcement Officers to protect them.

I entered the Mosque and read the pilgrimage to the Prophet (s.a.w.a) and some supplications accompanied by the pilgrimage of Hazrat Zahra, and then I began to get ready for the Maghrib Prayer. I had half an hour to spare before it started. I waited for a spot between the old part of the Mosque and the shrine (between the pulpit and sepulcher) very patiently and was rewarded as one person left and I took his spot.

I read some voluntary supplications, and then I sat down. An older man was sitting next to me, smiling. As soon as I finished my prayer, I looked at him and said, hi. He responded and continued smiling and started to speak to me in Arabic. He said that there was no other prayer after the Asir prayer until sundown. I was not sure how he knew that I understood Arabic. Naturally, most Arabs think that anyone visiting Medina and Mecca can speak Arabic. I replied with a smile and said that the Hadith he told was not entirely authentic. He laughed and said, but everyone else acts on this Hadith. Therefore, it cannot have any substance. I replied saying that in one of the Sihah Sittah books I had read that Imam Ali would read an extra two Sermon Salat after his Asir prayer. The older man asked if I remembered which book. I responded yes, the book of Musnad Ahmad, chapter 6, Page 105, Hadith number 101. Alternatively, in Lesan Al Mizan, chapter 6, Page 398, Hadith 1074 it is written that Abuzar had mentioned the Prophet (s.a.w.a) had said: There is no other prayer after the Asir prayer unless in Mecca. Therefore, if someone says that there is no prayer after the Asir prayer, there would be some that agree otherwise. For this particular reason, there are many Muslims that act on things that are not necessary as part of the mainstream Islamic discipline. In addition, many Muslims do not act on mandatory provisions. As I was talking away, the sound of Azan for the sunset started to sing. God is the greatest (Allāhu Akbar).

I am not sure why the Muezzin's in Saudi Arabia do not sound euphonious. None of the calls for prayer gives you that spiritual connection. There is one call for the prayer initially at the start of prayer time. After ten to twenty minutes, they sound the second call for prayer. This name for this action is Iqama. This is to create an excuse, so people have enough time to come to worship at the

Mosque as they hear the first call for prayer. The second call for prayer is when the Maghrib prayer starts. From the sound of the Imam leading the congregation of worship, I understood that it was Sheikh Ali Abdor Rahman Huthaify. This was because I had heard his tapes, reading the Quran.

Contrary to the Muezzin's in Saudi Arabia in specific their Mokaber's, the Imams that lead the congregation prayers are very euphonious. Once the Maghrib Prayer finished, numerous people left Al-Masjid an Nabawi. A young man that was sitting next to me went, and the older man stayed. I drew closer to the older man and said, hi again. He said hi back and asked me why I carry the deeds of the Hadith's with me. I replied it is because, in many other places including Mosques, I get to hear the same thing you said, therefore, by carrying proof with me, it is easy to support what I mean.

Getting Acquainted with Sheikh Ibrahim Usman (Sheikh)

Dr: May I ask your name?

Sh: My name is Sheikh Ibrahim Ibn Usman.

Dr: Wow, are you a Sheikh?

Sh: Yes.

Dr: Where are you from?

Sh: I have originated from Syria. However, I live in Egypt, where are you from?

Dr: Iran, what is your occupation?

Sh: I am a professor at the University in the section of the ordinance of Alazhar University in Egypt.

Dr: Bravo, what an honor. I am thrilled to meet your acquaintance.

Sh: I am happy too.

Dr: Are you alone, or are you with family?

Sh: I have two wives, and due to it being challenging to choose one to accompany me on this trip, I decided to come alone. I went with an Egyptian tour group.

Dr: When did you come to Medina?

Sh: We arrived this morning.

Dr: How many days will you be in Medina?

Sh: We will be in Medina for eight days, and then we will go to Mecca.

Dr: I arrived this morning to Medina as well. However, we will stay in Medina for 10 days and then we will go to Mecca

Sh: Mashallah, you asked me all the questions but did not say anything about yourself. You only said that you are an Iranian.

Dr: Please ask me any question you want, and I will reply.

Sh: What is your occupation?

Dr: I am a professor at the University.

Sh: I bet that you are in Theology or Arabic literature because you speak Arabic very well.

Dr: No, actually, I am a Mechanical Engineer.

Sh: So, you must be from Ahwaz, Khuzestan meaning you are an Arab.

Dr: No, actually, I am not from our Arabian Iranians either.

Sh: Then, where did you learn how to speak Arabic this way?

Dr: I liked the Arabian Language. I taught myself using books, radio, and television.

Sh: But you speak so well.

Dr: I hope that I can speak well enough for you to understand me well.

Sh: I understand you very well because you also speak a little to the book.

Sh: Which university do you attend?

Dr: The University of Science and Technology, Tehran.

Sh: Which department and section?

Dr: I am a professor in the Mechanical Engineering Department.

Sh: Do you have a Visit card?

Dr: Yes, here you are.

Sh: But here it says that you are the manager of the School of Automotive Engineering.

Dr: Yes, you are correct. I am a professor at the Mechanical Engineering Department and the manager of the Engineering School of Automotive Engineering.

Sh: Have you studied in Iran?

The Doctor & Sheikh's Debate

Dr: I studied my Bachelors in Iran; however; I spent my Master's and Doctorate in England.

Sh: Mashalla, so you can also speak English.

Dr: My English is better than my Arabic because I have obtained my education in that language.

Sh: How many years were you in England?

Dr: I was there for roughly four years.

Sh: I have also traveled to England for preaching.

Dr: Which city in England did you stay?

Sh: I stayed for a couple of days in London and a couple of days in Manchester.

Dr: Actually, I was between those two cities meaning Birmingham. You must have passed Birmingham, am I right?

Sh: Yes, but our stay was very short. It was just for the Zuhr and Asir prayers.

Dr: Which nationality of the Muslims living in England were you preaching? Majority of the Muslims in England are from Pakistan. They have very little Arabs.

Sh: Yes, but I was invited from some of the persistent Egyptians living in England.

Dr: How has your education been like?

Sh: I studied the basics of religion in Syria, and then I came to Saudi Arabia, Medina to continue my education and studied at Medina University. After 10 years of living in Saudi Arabia, I went to Egypt. I was young then, and I continued my education there and married again. I had some children, and now they are all independent.

Dr: I am Sorry if it took so long. Are you staying for the Isha Prayer, or will you be leaving?

Sh: I will be staying.

Dr: So, we still have time to continue.

Sh: Yes, but it is my time to ask questions.

Dr: Please go ahead.

Sh: Are you with family, or are you alone?

Dr: I am with my wife. Actually, in Iran, we do not have more than one wife. Of course, we still do have men that have two wives that are scholars like you. They are the old-fashioned type.

Sh: It is allowed to have up to four wives.

Dr: Yes, we allow such a thing. However, to manage four reasonably is very difficult.

Sh: Nevertheless, most Arabs have more than one wife.

Dr: I met many Arabs in England that only had one wife, especially Egyptians.

Sh: Yes, the University type ones frequently marry women from the university, which do not allow the second wife. Dr: But in Iran, it is different. Due to tradition, most of the men in Iran only have only one wife. They are very different with men from Arabian countries that normally have more than one wife.

Sh: I believe that what you say is correct because almost everyone looks up to his or her fathers and how they lived.

At this moment, someone asked if he could sit between the Sheikh and me because we were seated too comfortably and taking more space than we should. They usually don't allow people to sit this far apart when it is close to Iqama and especially the ones that arrive late and wish to be sitting closer up the congregational prayer lines. However, I asked him to sit either of our sides as we were talking, and he thanked us and agreed.

Sh: How many times have you come to Hajj.

Dr: This is my seventh time for Tamattu, and I have visited eight times for Umrah.

Sh: But this is my fifth time visiting from Egypt. I once visited Tamattu Hajj for my own. The other three times that I was invited from the Management of Guidance organization of Arabia as a temporary congregational Imam for Mosques in the Hajj period, and this time, I have visited as a guest.

Dr: What is the meaning of a temporary congregational Imam?

Sh: Many years ago, when Saudi Arabia had limited amount of congregational Imams, in the Hajj period, many people would arrive from different countries and spread into Medina and Mecca. They would gather in Mosques for congregational prayers and would ask many religious and lawful questions. The answer to their questions was complicated for the young congregational Saudi Imams who were partly also helpers. Therefore, in the two months of Zyqadeh and Zylhaj, the congregational Imams come from Egypt specifically for the large Mosques.

Dr: That is correct because I do happen to remember in my previous visits that some of the Mosques close to our hotel had Egyptian congregational Imams.

Sh: There is a very high chance that it would have been a temporary congregational Imam.

Dr: Typically, the Alazhar professors have different religious opinions from the Saudi Arabia scholars. Egyptians are mostly Shafi'ite while the Saudi Arabian scholars are Hanbali and especially the Imams chosen for the congregational prayers are from the government's religion, meaning they are Wahabi.

Sh: Naturally, for being the Imam of the congregation, they would invite scholars that are possibly Hanbali.

Dr: If they are not Wahabi, would that be a problem?

Sh: The Wahabis are the extreme version of the Hanbalis. This is because the Wahabis are the followers of Imam Ahmad Ibn Hanbal. They are called Salafi.

Dr: But the Alazhar does not usually agree with the Wahabis.

Sh: There would not be any disagreement because the governments used to have good relations with each other, and scholars would not quarrel.

Dr: May I ask you a question? Do you agree with the Wahabis or not?

Sh: Yes, I am Hanbali, and I agree with the majority of their sayings. However, they do have some extreme ways.

Dr: But they believe that every other Muslim following any other religion are faithless; however, you seem to be speaking to me as a Muslim, do you not see me as an infidel?

Sh: I am afraid I have to disagree with the way the Muslims from Iran think; however, I do not class them as infidels.

Dr: But in Iran, we do have Hanbali's. Why do you not agree with them?

Sh: I meant the Shias. They act against religion.

Dr: I am glad that this discussion has gotten here so far because I have some questions that I would like to ask of you.

Sh: I am not in favor of political questions; however, if you have any religious questions, and I know the answer, I would be happy to respond to it.

Dr: However, the Isha call of prayer is close by, and I do not believe we would get a chance. If you agreed, I would express my opinion after the Isha prayer.

Sh: That is very good. How many minutes do we have left before the Isha prayer?

Dr: I think I have roughly ten minutes. By that time, we can pray a two Sermon prayer for the blessing and happiness of our mother and father's soul it would be time for the Isha prayer.

Sh: Yes, yes, let us get to it.

Eventually, they call for prayer sung with the words of "God is the greatest," followed by the second call of prayer, and then everyone rose. As soon as we stood, two other people squeezed themselves into the line. There is so much pressure in the lines. It is almost impossible to stand straight and pray. There is only your face that is towards the Qibla and the strain on your shoulder is from both sides in a way that it turns you away from the Qibla.

The Isha prayer finished, and everyone was in such a rush to leave, especially people who had come for the Maghrib prayer and had stayed like us to pray the Isha Prayer. For this reason, the lines for the restrooms around the Al-Masjid an Nabawi are quite crowded after the Isha prayer rather than the Maghrib prayer.

Dr: You wish to leave, and I have agreed to meet my wife after the Isha prayer. When may I see you again to ask my questions?

Sh: Please allow me to see you before the Zuhr prayer tomorrow

Dr: Are you not coming for the Morning Prayer tomorrow?

Sh: No, because our hotel is far away, I only come for the Zuhr and Maghrib and Isha prayer.

Dr: That is not a problem. I will be waiting for you at ten in the morning, which is two hours before the Zuhr prayer in the Mosque.

Sh: That is good. Where would you want to meet?

Dr: After pointing at a column in the Mosque, I said, I would be waiting for you by the tented column situated outside the Mosque and has the name, Mohammad (s.a.w.a) written on it.

Sh: Very well. Have a good night.

Dr: Good night.

The Doctor & Sheikh's Debate

My wife was waiting for me in the Mosque. We both returned to the hotel. Many people had already had their dinner. We also went and had ours and returned to our individual rooms. Back in the room, the discussion was surrounding solutions for Haj Mohammad and Haj Ali snoring. Haj Mohammad was saying that it would help if one of us would move his head so the snoring noise would stop or to give him an additional pillow for under his head. Dr. Ahmadi suggested that three of us would stand on guard in turns to quiet down the snoring noise. Karbalayi decided to bring out some Yazdi sweets from his bag. Haj Abbas thanked him and said, "But this will not make up for the snoring."

Haj Ali said: "It is what it is, and there is nothing you can do about it, therefore, help yourselves with these sweets."

I said, "That in the case of traveling together especially to Hajj we have compromise and work together as a team. I believe that Dr. Ahmadi's solution isn't so bad."

Haj Abbas said: "There is another way. We could all go into spare rooms when it is time to sleep and rest there."

I disagreed and said that it would possibly create separation. Haj Abbas said: "If that is not possible, then I will go and sleep in the attic."

Eventually, the lights turned off after two hours. The sound of someone's snore the size of a tractor took over the room. Dr. Ahmadi placed cotton wool in his ears, but that did not stop the noise. Haj Abbas had gone to sleep in the attic leaving me, who was almost used to sleeping in noisy environments realized that in this trip, it came handy. This situation continued until the end of my, and I managed to sleep through it.

Before the morning call for prayer, I woke up. I did the Ordinal Bath for the Prophet's (s.a.w.a) blessing and the Imams of Baqi and headed to the Mosque for prayer. After the Morning Prayer, I went to the Imams Baqi and sent my blessings. The Imams of Baqi is the most important graveyard in the Islamic world. In this cemetery some of the Ahl al Bayt (Greetings to them), the Prophet's (s.a.w.a) wives, the martyrs of Uhud, the martyrs of Hurrah (Medina Martyrs in the Yazid's troop attack in year 63 A.H)

Many voices of blessings and the sound of the Baqi keepers, asking people not to read the blessings of books and not to cry and mourn for the dead could be heard…I visited the Baqi, went back to the hotel, and slept again.

I headed towards the Shrine at 9:30. I arrived fifteen minutes before ten. I read my blessings and waited for the Sheikh by the column agreed that we had agreed on. He arrived on time. However, I had a feeling that he must have also had something going on before our meeting at the Mosque.

The Twentieth of Zyqadeh

Dr: Dear Sheikh, good day

Sh: Good day to you, Doctor

Dr: Shall we have a seat somewhere?

Sh: We can sit wherever we want, however, if we go and sit close to the end of the Mosque where people gather to read the Quran together we shall be less interrupted.

Dr: Let's go then.

We sat closer to one of the columns situated where the Mosque had no roof and upon rain or in the day it would be covered by tents.

Dr: Dear Mr Sheikh Ibrahim you are an educated person from the university and so am I. Would you like to meet with me on a more organised schedule while we are here for Hajj so you could answer my religious questions? My field of practice is technical and I have come to Hajj quiet often, therefore I have accumulated many religious questions during my visits.

Sh: Yes, of course there is no problem with us meeting on a more organised basis so I could answer your questions.

Dr: If you agree, let's first clear a couple of small discussions so we do not get confused especially the conversations we had yesterday.

Proof of Brotherhood (Shias are Muslims)

Sh: Which conversation?

Dr: The part where you said that you didn't agree on the Iranian Muslims.

Sh: But this is in fact the essence of our discussion and not a small matter.

Dr: Very well, then let's clarify a few important matters first.

Sh: Very well.

The One God

Dr: Do you agree that Iranian and in specific Shias believe in God?

Sh: Yes, Shias believe in God however we could debate on that too.

Dr: Please allow us to just concentrate on the principle of accepting God. Do they believe in God?

Sh: Yes, they believe in God.

The One Prophet

Dr: Do Shias believe in the Prophet (s.a.w.a)?

Sh: Yes, they believe in the Prophet (s.a.w.a). However, there is still an issue where Shias at the end of their prayers mention "Khan al Amin" meaning Gabriel betrayed the secrecy and instead of bringing the revelation for Ali he brought it for Mohammad (s.a.w.a).

Dr: Have you read this in a Shia written book?

Sh: No, I haven't read them in Shia books. However, I have heard about it many times, and I have seen it in many books published in Saudi Arabia, Egypt, and Pakistan.

Dr: Have you met one common Shia that believes in such a thing?

Sh: I have not been in touch with many Shias; however, as an educated person from a university, please tell me if such a thing exists then I will accept it. In my opinion, it is highly unlikely for a Muslim to believe in such a thing.

Dr: I thank you so much for trusting, in my opinion.

Sh: But if such a thing does not exist amongst Shias, then how come they are accused of it?

Dr: Dear honorable Sheikh this is a tremendous accusation, not only for the Shias living in Iran but even amongst the Shias in the world there is not a single one that says such a thing.

Sh: Then how come this accusation has been spread?

Dr: You, yourself are saying that it is an accusation. It is not very hard to spread such a rumor, especially for government's that wish to destroy the way that Shias are portrayed.

Sh: In any case, I accept that such a thing does not exist because it is not something that Muslims would be proud of, and you are also saying that it is not valid.

Dr: Amongst the conversations as I said: there is not one case, it is not even mentioned in non-credible Shia books and if any Shia would hear such a thing they would be disgusted.

Sh: I have to say that I have neither seen it in any books or credible writings from Sunni followers that suggest the Shia faith say this thing.

The One Quran

Dr: The next question is, do Shias believe in the Quran?

Sh: Yes, Shias believe in the Quran but also understand that the Quran has been distorted. The revelations have been changed, and the correct Quran is Ali's Quran.

Dr: The Shia faith believes that Imam Ali assembled the verses and chapters of the same existing Quran in addition to some further explanation of some verses. However, to keep the unity he did not mention it and accepted the current existing Quran, and all the other Shia Imams accepted this Quran.

Sh: If such a discussion exists, then how come Ali did not propose his Quran.

Dr: Just as I said: Ali's Quran was the existing Quran with some further explanations that Ali decided to disregard to preserve the unity of Muslims. He preferred everyone to have one Quran.

Sh: So, you are saying that everyone believes in the same existing Quran?

Dr: Yes, it is good for you to know that the majority of Qurans writings are in the same handwriting of Usman Taha. Meaning not only that the Qurans are not different but, the types of manuscripts are the same as the other Muslim brothers. The majority of the published Quran books are from the handwritings of Usman Taha.

Sh: Thank the Lord, this news regarding the unity of the book is very good and exciting to me.

Dr: Please have a look at the small Quran that I am holding. It is published with Usman Taha handwriting. This Quran is published in Iran.

Sh: Very interesting, the Farsi translation is written across it.

Dr: Then you accept that we have the same Quran.

Sh: Yes, I accept.

The One Qibla

Dr: Do you accept that we have one united Qibla?

Sh: Yes, I do not have any doubt. Your Qibla is also Kaaba.

Dr: Thank the Lord; at least we agreed without arguing.

Sh: The sideline discussions weren't that serious. I just mentioned them as they were rumors and things that I had seen and read not anything substantially researched or proven to be correct.

Dr: Thank you for clarifying that it was a rumor and not a genuine affair.

Sh: We should now discuss the areas that we disagree upon.

Dr: We have many things that we disagree on so let's firstly prove our brotherhood then we can get on to the differences.

The One Salat (Pray)

Sh: Very well, let's start.

Dr: Do you agree that the principles of our prayers are the same? Last night you and I prayed the Maghrib and Isha together.

Sh: I have to acknowledge that I didn't believe it before; however, after several trips to Hajj, I concluded that the differences in praying between us are marginal and of minor importance. I was reassured when I saw several congregational prayers being held from the Iranian satellite channels, and thankfully, the congregational Imam would read all the worship words loudly. I realized that we truly have no severe difference, and it is a minor variation.

We realized at this point that one of the pilgrims that later on was discovered to be from Syria had been observing us and desired to join our discussion. He got up and came back with two cups of Zamzam Water taken from the dish of water from the Mosque and offered it to us. He wanted to sit and listen to us talk. We accepted the water and thanked him and because we didn't have time to talk about sideline matters we acted in a way to show that we weren't that eager to have him in the discussion and so he thanked us and left.

The One Hajj

Dr: Do you accept that we Shias have the same Hajj as other Muslims coming for Hajj?

Sh: Yes, due to Hajj being one of the rituals, there isn't much difference between us.

Dr: Do you accept that some of the differences between Shia and Sunni's are not more than the differences between Hanbali and Shafi'ies?

Sh: Yes, I have seen in Egypt that many discussions between Shafi'ies are the same as yours.

Dr: Will you allow me to see?

Sh: Please do so.

Dr: With explaining God, the Prophet (s.a.w.a), Quran, Salat, and Hajj being, all the same, can you accept that Shias are Muslims?

Sh: On a somber note, I accept that Shias are Muslims.

An Organised Discussion

Dr: Thank the Lord, if you agree, let's discuss some of the differences in their own place.

Sh: Yes, especially in regards to matters such as the differences between ablution (Wudu) or prostrating on the ground.

Dr: I even agree that we also discuss the minor differences.

Sh: But currently, we do not have much time to get to these discussions.

Dr: One of the characteristics of Hajj is these dialogues. Therefore, God willing within the duration of our whole Hajj we can spend at least two hours together to talk. This way, God prepared our hearts can come closer, and the truth can be clarified for both of us.

Sh: You mean, we have two hours of dialogue every day?

Dr: Do you not agree that scientific discussions have more oblation than non-obligatory things?

Sh: Yes, I am scared not to be able to commit two hours every day to this.

Dr: We can plan the whole thing. We aren't required to make it a necessary specific time or every day. If at any day we have any other engagement we can cancel the discussion and make up for it another day.

Sh: That is good, God willing he can help us so we could speak together for two hours every day.

Sh: Yes, however, I wish to confess.

Dr: Confess to what? Please do say.

Sh: When I was in Syria I believed Shias to be Muslims, but after going to Medina University and studying over here with the education the scholars were giving us I did not doubt that Shias were not Muslims. After many years of studying, I went back to Egypt, and I was in Alazhar, and there

I noticed that they acknowledge Shias to be Muslims. That's when I realized that Shias are Muslims; however; they have differences with the four other religions.

Dr: Well then, I have a couple of questions for you because my field is in Mechanics and you are a scholar in religion.

Sh: That is not a problem, please ask.

The Rules for the Debate and Discussion

Dr: Thank you. However, because we are educated from universities and my questions are embedded, therefore, let's agree on some rules and principles. For discussions or as the British say debates, there must be some regulations. With the understanding that we have from each other to the rules, it is better for us to comply with it.

Sh: Does asking and answering questions need regulations?

Dr: While driving on the street needs rules and regulations, do you not think it wise that a scientific and religious discussion would need boundaries?

Sh: Then you don't have any questions you wish to have a religious debate.

Dr: I have questions, but you could call it a discussion.

Sh: Agreed, evidently, questions and answers require rules.

Dr: What are your thoughts about this principle?

Sh: Firstly, let's talk using cited basis documents, meaning we have to cite an Islamic document. Secondly, let's not be biased towards our own beliefs. If we obtain the truth, we agree to it. What is your opinion?

Dr: These are very good. In addition to citing a legitimate chain of transmissions, let's rely on the most important ones such as the Quran. Anything that goes against the Quran is not acceptable.

Sh: Definitely, absolutely.

Dr: Please look at my mobile. It obtains single software that has been taken from the Library of the Al-Masjid an Nabawi (s.a.w.a). It is called Maktab Shamilah. It has roughly 7000 books from our Sunni brothers. Would you accept these books as documents for me to cite?

Sh: I need to know about the books. If any of the books were acceptable to me, then I will accept them. Now, which books are you using in this program?

Dr: My questions are based on these books.

Sh: Yes, the books that I see are all acceptable and reasonable.

Dr: But in regards to the Hadith I will be citing from the books in this software.

Sh: I know these books. If you show me the book, I can then see the Hadith.

Dr: If the Hadith or topic that we mention is acceptable, then let's not need to cite it.

Sh: It is axiomatic because these are topics that we both agree with.

Dr: Anywhere the Quran has no definitive answer and cites and documents are not strong enough; let's agree based on our judgment.

Sh: That is good.

Dr: We trust each other, meaning we accept that none of us will lie about anything.

Sh: If that were the case, then our debate would be baseless and pointless. I am sure that we both agree with each other's words.

Dr: Please allow me to ask the first questionSh: Please go ahead.

The Lack of Probity of Companions in Qurān

Dr: When I read the Quran, I notice some parts that require a great deal of attention.

Sh: For instance, which verses?

Dr:

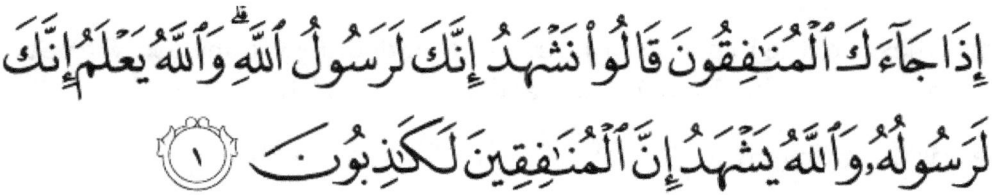

"When the hypocrites come to you, [O Muhammad], they say, "We testify that you are the Messenger of Allah." And Allah knows that you are His Messenger, and Allah testifies that the hypocrites are liars.
[Surat Al-Munāfiqūn (The Hypocrites)]"

Sh: Yes, the aim and purpose of the hypocrites are precise. The objective is for the attention of Abdullah Abe and his followers and supporters. He is very famous in the history of Islam.

Dr: You are absolutely correct. It has also been explained in the verses that they first believed in God and then became infidels. In later verses, it is mentioned that the hypocrites said: do not to spend time on those that are around the Prophet (s.a.w.a). They said that if we return to Medina, the dear to the hearts (themselves) will deport the debased (Meaning Muslims) from Medina. So, their destiny is, and the interpretations of the Quran clarifies that.

Sh: Yes, their stories are written in commentary books and history.

Dr: However, my problem understands verse 101 Surat at Tawbah that says:

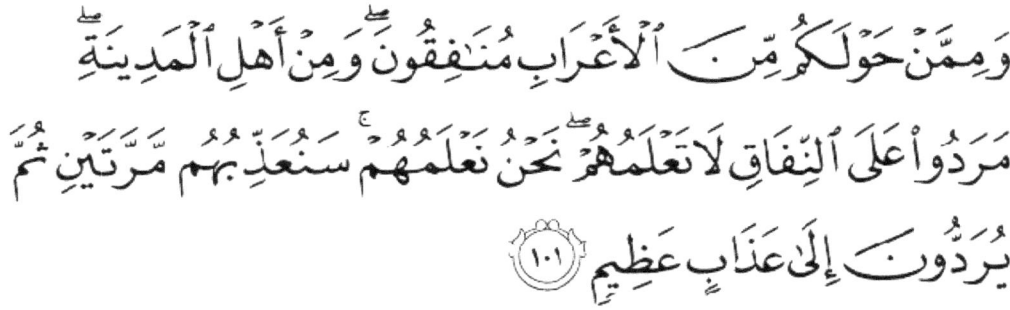

"And among those around you of the Arabs are hypocrites, and [also] from the people of Medina. They have become accustomed to hypocrisy. You, [O Muhammad], do not know them, [but] we know them. We will punish them twice [in this world]; then they will be returned to a great punishment."

Sh: What is the problem?

Dr: Firstly, these are the hypocrites that are surrounded the Prophet (s.a.w.a). Secondly, they are from Medina; thirdly, The Prophet (s.a.w.a) does not know them.

Sh: Where is the problem?

Dr: I do not have a problem with the actual verse. My question is in regards to the proof of this verse and its difference and contradiction with some of the Hadith that are in your books.

Sh: What are the problems, contradictions, and differences that our Hadith has with this verse?

The Doctor & Sheikh's Debate

Dr: You, in the majority of your books have Hadith that pronounces the Prophet (s.a.w.a) saying: "اصحابي كالنجوم بايهم اقتديتم اهتديتم" "My companions are like stars, whichever of them you use as a guide, you will be rightly guided," extracted by Rizin."

Sh: We both agree on this Hadith, so what contradiction is there with the verse?

Dr: Your scholars explain that the companions can be any person that has met the Prophet (s.a.w.a) or has not even set eyes upon him (is blind) and has believed in him and dies believing in him is classed as his companion. This is the case yet if he has met the Prophet during his youth and is adolescent.

Sh: That is correct.

Dr: But the subject matter is essential that in this Hadith, following any companion has been recommended and even more critical following any one of them will get you into heaven.

Sh: That is correct.

Dr: However, this verse says: "O Prophet (s.a.w.a), some of your companions are in the direction of hypocrisy, and you don't know them, God knows them, and they will come to great agony."

Sh: Where is the problem?

Dr: The Prophet (s.a.w.a) does not know many of the companions that he has met and is in his acquaintance. Therefore, he is not aware of their infidelity. These people will experience great agony on judgment day and are hypocrites. Now if some Muslims follow these companions that even the Prophet (s.a.w.a) is unaware of them to be hypocrites until they die, will they go to heaven?

Sh: There is a possibility that these hypocrite companions go to hell, but their followers will be going into heaven because it has been said: in the Hadith that, to whichever one we trust we will be guided.

Dr: This cannot be because in Quran Surat Al- Isra it says: "بإمامهم أناس كل ندعو يوم" " On judgment day, every group is followed by his own Imam." How can it possible for an Imam to go to hell and his followers to go to heaven.

Sh: But many of the books have known and accepted this Hadith to be true.

Dr: Is Hadith more important than the Quran? We agreed that when it comes to comparing between Quran and Hadith, we base the Quran as the base.

Sh: I accept. However, if we say that some of the companions that we do not know are hypocrites, then all of the companions are then questionable.

Dr: In what way do they become questionable?

Sh: Since the hypocrites have not been identified, then the conclusion sways towards the possibility of any of the companions to be a hypocrite.

Dr: I believe that this verse does not accuse all of the companions. It just says that not all of the companions are good human beings.

Sh: If that is the case, then there will be no proof left to say that the companions were impeccable and for people to be guided by them.

Dr: My debate is precisely this. Now allow me to read you another verse.

Sh: Please do so.

Dr: Verse 11, Surat Al Jumuah says:

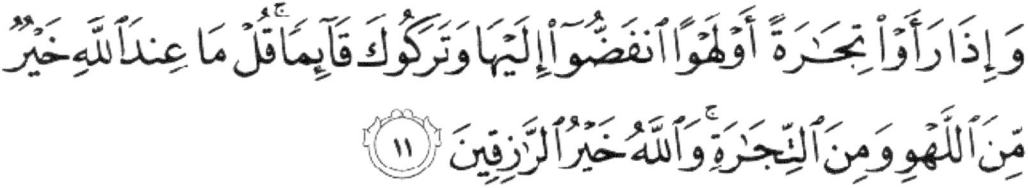

But when they saw a transaction or a diversion, [O Muhammad], they rushed to it and left you standing. Say, "What is with Allah is better than diversion and than a transaction, and Allah is the best of providers."

Dear Sheikh, the Prophet (s.a.w.a) stood to perform the prayer on Friday. The sound of the drums was made to announce the arrival of the trade caravan. These companions that were supposed to be the number one believer and were praying leave the Prophet's (s.a.w.a) side as soon as they hear the drums. In the commentary of Siuti and Dur Al Mansour's book, it says that only twelve of the companions stayed with the Prophet (s.a.w.a) after hearing the arrival of the trade, caravan in Shaam and prayed behind him. Do you believe that such companions are worthy of guiding people? Can one believe in them and be guided by them?

Sh: It is evident that the importance of the companions is relative; not all of them are the same.

Dr: But the Hadith does not say this. It means that to whichever one we follow, we will be guided.

Sh: If we agree with such a debate, then how are we able to distinguish the hypocrite companions from the non-hypocrites?

Dr: We seek refuge in God (بــالله نعــوذ); we are not trying to accuse all of the companions to be hypocrites. However, we have to change the way we view our companions.

Sh: How should we perceive them?

Dr: Let's be like many of your scholars and say because the Quran is the base, and this verse 101 Al Surat at Tawbah is firm and correct. Then this Hadith is wrong, and we conclude that not all of the companions are to be trusted and are not competent to lead a community.

Sh: Using what argument can we say the Quran has the authority? It has been centuries that we have spoken about the importance, and the integrity of the companions and no one has made any complaints.

Dr: Even though the authority of the Quran is sufficient but have a look at history at the beginning of Islam and pay attention to some of these examples. Differences between Companions, the Reason for their Probity

Sh: In fact, the history of the beginning of Islam is an excellent example in portraying the importance of the companions.

Dr: First example: at the beginning of Islam a newly converted Muslim that has gone to Medina sees that some of the well-known companions have surrounded one of the other companions, that also happens to be Calipha (meaning Usman) and they aim to kill him. In your opinion, does the Muslim that joins the line of the ones following Usman, guided or if he joins the line of the followers that are against Usman?

Sh: Shall I respond?

Dr: Please do so.

Sh: He should listen to the Calipha and go towards him.

Dr: Then this will be acting against the Hadith. Because the Hadith says that every companion has the ability to be followed and is able to guide.

Sh: Well, there are other cases too.

Dr: Yes, please pay attention to the other cases.

Sh: Very well.

Dr: Second example: One Muslim has gone to the Battle of Jamal. He sees that the Prophet's wife (Aisha) and several other famous companions of the Prophet (s.a.w.a) are on one side and the other side, some of the other companions including the Calipha are amongst them (meaning Ali), and they are fighting. If this Muslim joins the line of the Prophet's wife division and some of the other companions, is he guided? Alternatively, if he joins the line of Ali in which some of the other famous companions are? Based on your Hadith, whichever way he goes, he will go to heaven.

Sh: If there is another case, please state it. I will respond afterward.

Dr: Third example: One Muslim has gone to Siffin (two rows) and sees that some of the Prophet's (s.a.w.a) companions are led by Muawiyah on one side and the other side some of the other companions such as Ammar Yasir lead by Ali are fighting. Does this Muslim go to heaven if he joins any of the hands of the battle?

Sh: The answer, the truth is this, that these people had Ijtihad. We won't argue the genuine reason for the differences between the companions at the beginning of Islam, so we don't get to deal with such problems. We say whatever they did, they were the genuine companions, and we cannot understand their real reason for their actions.

Dr: Dear Sheikh, I am an engineer. I have studied mathematics and logic. I cannot accept such a response and disregard my question.

Sh: We cannot interpret Hadith with History?

Dr: I didn't say let's interpret the Hadith. Please guide me. Interpret the verse for me and then give me the hypocrite based on the verse and tell me: How is this Muslim that is in each of the three examples explained to do? I gave you three different timelines and three different places with six different groups of companions. Guide me with which side he should go.

Sh: God rewards anyone who joins any of the groups with the intention of good will.

Dr: Are you suggesting then that we have several straight paths?

Sh: How do you mean?

Dr: One straight path is Usman and the companions surrounding him, another straightway are the companions against him, in Jamal one of the following ways, Aisha and the companions surrounding her, another straight path is Ali and the companions surrounding him and in Siffin is another straight path and Muawiyah and his surrounding companions.

Sh: I agree that we can only have one straight path, but what do we do in regards to the Hadith? It is the Prophet's (s.a.w.a) words.

Dr: The problem is this. The Hadith is not from the Prophet (s.a.w.a).

Sh: We believe it is.

Dr: If I bring you several cited references from your important people that say that this Hadith is not authentic will you accept it?

Sh: If you cite me them yes, I will accept.

Dr: Thankfully in the software on my mobile I have, the Maktab Shamlah that almost has all of the old and new books of our Sunni brothers and all of its references are there too. Here you go. In this cite they have said that the authenticity of this Hadith is weak and it even says that the Hadith is false. Please look at the several Hadith below.

References about the Weakness of the Hadith Regarding the Justice of Companions

1- Sharh Al Shifa, Qazi Ayyaz, volume II, page 91, says that this Hadith has no chain of transmission.

2- Ibn Abd al Berr in his book "Istiyab" means there is a train of transmission for this Hadith.

3- Ibn Abd Hamid in his book named "Mosnad" says from Abdullah Ibn Omar that this Hadith does not exist.

4- Ibn Oday in his book titled "Kamel" agrees with Abdullah Ibn Omar says there is no proof.

5- Bayhagi says that the chain of transmission is weak because the chain of the Hadith reaches Harith bin Ghazin (anonymous case) and Hamza Abi Hamza saying they both are fraudsters.

6- Ibn Hazm says that this Hadith is a lie.

Sh: I had seen that some had declared that this Hadith could have been weak but not to the extent of how you showed me in detail.

Dr: It wouldn't be so bad if we went and asked that scholar that is teaching seminar students over there and ask him about this Hadith.

Sh: Do you know him?

Dr: Yes, in my previous Amra trip I saw him and asked questions about him. They said that he is the chancellor of the Medina University.

Sh: Yes, that is correct. He is the chancellor of the Medina University. Although when I was studying here, he was just a professor. He is now the President. I feel embarrassed to ask him such a question.

Dr: Then I will go and ask him, but please accept the answer I come back with.

Sh: We seek refuge in God (بـــالله نعـوذ) we agreed from the start to accept each other's words and truthfulness.

Dr: Thank you, please wait here until I return because this man's meeting seems to be over as people are leaving.

I rushed to the man (President of Medina University) and said: to him that I had a question. He said: for me to ask his students. I said: no, I am a professor at the University and wish to ask you directly because you are the President of a University. He said: ask away then.

I asked him, do you believe this Hadith to be true or not?

اصحابی کالنجوم بایهم اقتدیتم اهتدیت

He said: no, this Hadith is weak and scholars in specific religiously educated people do not pay much attention to it. The Prophet (s.a.w.a) has had 120000 companions. Without a doubt, it is not possible to follow all of them. For that particular reason, the Hadith is weak. Then he lowered his voice and said: some even believe it to be a lie. I returned to Sheikh Ibrahim.

Dr: Dear Sheikh, do you want to know how the President of the Medina University responded?

Sh: What did he say?

Dr: He said that the Hadith is weak, and scholars in specific the university ones do not pay much attention to it. He also mentioned that some also believe it to be a lie. Even if he had shown me any documents or made any arguments, especially the Quran, not all companions agree so it wouldn't have helped. Now look at this Hadith:

(Musnad Ahmad, Volume 46, Page 442, 21890)

The Doctor & Sheikh's Debate

حَدَّثَنَا ابْنُ نُمَيْرٍ عَنْ شَرِيكٍ حَدَّثَنَا أَبُو رَبِيعَهْ عَنِ ابْنِ بُرَيْدَهْ عَنْ أَبِيهِ قَالَ: قَالَ رَسُولُ اللَّهِ صَلَّى اللَّهُ عَلَيْهِ وَسَلَّمَ إِنَّ اللَّهَ عَزَّوَجَلَّ يُحِبُّ مِنْ أَصْحَابِي أَرْبَعَهْ أَخْبَرَنِي أَنَّهُ يُحِبُّهُمْ وَأَمَرَنِي أَنْ أُحِبَّهُمْ قَالُوا مَنْ هُمْ يَا رَسُولَ اللَّهِ قَالَ إِنَّ عَلِيًّا مِنْهُمْ وَأَبُوذَرٍّ الْغِفَارِيُّ وَسَلْمَانُ الْفَارِسِيُّ وَالْمِقْدَادُ بْنُ الْأَسْوَدِ الْكِنْدِيُّ

"The Prophet (s.a.w.a) said: Indeed, the almighty God is fond of four of my companions and told me to like them too. They asked O' Messenger of God who are these people? He replied: Ali is amongst them and Abu Dharr Gheffari, Salman Farsi and Miqdad Ibn Asvad Kendi."

Sh: We do have other Hadith regarding these companions but not with such strong content.

Dr: That verse from the Quran and this Hadith indicates that not all of the Prophet's companions are to be trusted, and some of them are the faithful followers.

Sh: Now that the President of the Medina University also agreed, I do not have anything else to say. However, there are many unsolved cases regarding the companions that it's best not to debate them here.

Dr: I suggest it is best for us to accept the truth and then resolve the cases from using other methods.

Sh: The pray time is close. Please allow us to conclude this detailed debate that ended to your advantage and discuss another case later.

Dr: Allow me to make a joke. In my opinion, the debate turned to your advantage because I already knew about the conclusion, but you came to realize the truth.

Sh: [chuckled] yes, you are right. However, it will take me some time to deal with the understanding of this revelation. It has been years that I believed that all the companions were righteous and to be followed, and today, things changed. I have to be honest with you, instead of dealing with the problems caused by the companion's actions from the beginning of Islam; we always justified it by saying that we do not wish to interfere and they had Ijtihad. In reality, we would erase the problem rather than to deal with it.

Dr: May God bless you with more success with the additional detail you gave me it is clear that not only did you honor the promise we made to each other but you also showed that you are a researcher that is not biased. Let's go for prayer (Salat). Goodbye.

Sh: Goodbye.

We moved ahead for prayer. We met several familiar Iranians, but they didn't have enough room for me to sit next to them, so I eventually went and found a suitable spot to pray. The first and second calls for prayer were called and the pray started. If there were no congregational Zuhr and

Asr prayers in Al-Masjid an Nabawi (s.a.w.a) and Sacred Mosque it would be spiritless. Because all you can hear from the congregational Imam is the sound of him saying Takbir (Allahu Akbra). If you are not in sync with the people in line, you would not know which part of the prayer the Imam is reading. In Iran, when the Zuhr and Asr congregational prayer is happening, alongside the Hamd and Surah, they also read out the other parts (Ruku, Sajdah, Tajlis, and Tasleem) loudly.

For this reason, there is a connection felt between the person praying and the Imam. I have to add that this case is also happening for the morning and Maghrib and Isha prayers too. In Saudi Arabia apart from the Hamd and

Surah, you only hear a couple of Takbirs. However, in the congregational prayers held in Iran just like "In the name of God the Merciful," they also read out the verses of prayers in the Zuhr and Asr prayers. The person praying even knows when the Hamd finishes and Surah begins, and from this point of view, the congregational prayers in Iran and general Shias is more alive.

The second thing that used to be an issue but has been slightly fixed is that between 1981-1986, as soon as the second call for prayer is done anyone that was any part of Medina would join the congregational Imam for the Al-Masjid an Nabawi. I remember the shopkeepers around Baqi would join the prayer from in their shops, and some that wouldn't reach the Mosque would stand for prayer even 100 meters ahead of the Imam and Al-Masjid an Nabawi and start praying. This situation has been remedied by the Iranian scholars many times, and also currently there are signs placed indicating that any prayer done past the lines is not acceptable. Even still, some do not listen to it and still stand for worship. Eventually, I read my prayer, and after chit chatting with some of the Iranians, I exited the Mosque.

The pilgrims would get themselves back to the hotel using the bus and taxi, but because my hotel was close, I could walk back.

We had lunch, and everyone returned to their rooms and preparations for tea and chatting was on its way. Dr. Ahmadi was a psychologist and said that he met many pilgrims today and was exceedingly happy. Enthusiasm, love, and excitement were clearly seen in his eyes as he felt that all of his sins were brushed off his shoulders after he had left the Al-Masjid an Nabawi, and he felt victorious. Karbalayi said that he did not feel such a way, especially among the easterners who would smile and didn't seem to show any particular feeling. Dr. Ahmadi responded: you have to pay more attention as I believe that everyone has such an attitude. I spent much attention, and the people who seem to be like that are people who work here and are the local Arabs in Medina.

Other different discussions were being made. I asked Karbalayi and Ghargham to wait until everyone else is sleeping and obeying this rule at least at noon times. Ghargham told me that he had already slept enough in the morning. I took a short nap and headed towards the Al-Masjid an Nabawi for the Maghrib prayer. Of course, going to the Mosque is always accompanied by the pilgrimage to visit the Prophet (s.a.w.a) and Hazrat Zahra.

After the Isha prayer, I went to the bazaar with my wife so we could buy some souvenirs and a black veil. The shop keepers greet you much more helpful when they see that you can speak Arabic, and because of my accent they think that I am an Iraqi. After two hours of shopping around, we returned to the hotel and slept.

Every Day after the Morning Pray at Baqi

Whenever the morning prayer has finished the doors to Baqi are opened. The women are not allowed in, and the men have only an hour and a half to pilgrim the graves. The people that are buried in Baqi are as followed:

1- Imam Mujtaba

2- Imam Sajjad

3- Imam Baqir

4- Imam Sadiq

5- Abbas, The uncle of the Prophet (s.a.w.a)

6- The Prophet's (s.a.w.a) wives

7- Fatimah bint Asad, Mother of Ali

8- Omolbanin, wife of Ali and mother of Hazrat Abbas

9- Safiyah, Prophet's (s.a.w.a) aunt

10- Atekeh, Prophet's (s.a.w.a) aunt

11- Halimah Sadia, Prophet's (s.a.w.a) nurse

12- Ibrahim, Prophet's (s.a.w.a) son

13- Aqeel (Moslem's father) and Imam Ali's brother

14- Martyrs of Ohod (They were injured and died in Medina)

15- Herrah Martyrs (They martyred from the attack of the Yazid's soldiers in Medina)

16- Ali Ibn Jafar (Imam Sadeq's son was brought from an Orayz village to Baqi in Medina, and Sheikh Omri (The leader of Shias) said that I saw the body when they moved him and the body was completely intact. Meaning after 1300 years, the body had not deteriorated.)

17- Ismail Ibn Jafar (Imam Sadiq's son)

18- Othman Ibn Mazon. He is the first person who was buried in Baqi and was one of the good companions of the Prophet (s.a.w.a) and Ali

19- Othman Ibn Affan (The third Calipha that was moved from another graveyard to Baqi in the Muawiyah period.)

I read the permission to enter pray and entered Baqi. In Baqi, everyone is busy praying. Everyone is sitting in a corner and mumbling supplications. Most of the pilgrims are Iranian, even though there are visitors from other countries. The Saudi Arabian government has even brought some Afghanis' so they can talk to the Iranian pilgrims. They also kept suggesting for everyone to close the books of supplication and the books of pilgrims. These Imams are dead and that we should not worship the dead and not do idolatry. We should send our regards and leave. Many try to explain to them, and many recommend that it's pointless trying to argue with them. Amongst the Officers in Baqi, there was one Arab that did not know Persian and seemed to be in charge of the others. He kept saying that this is polytheism and we are putting a distinction partner to God, and we should now supplicate even if it is the Prophet (s.a.w.a). The dead body of the Prophet (s.a.w.a) is no different from anybody else's.

Is the Prophet (s.a.w.a) Dead?

I went towards the man and apologized, said: Hello and added that I had a question. He said: please ask away. I asked: In your opinion, and based on your beliefs is the status of the Prophet (s.a.w.a) higher or the martyrs? He replied: The Prophet (s.a.w.a). I asked, but the Lord in verse 169 of Surat Ale Imran says:

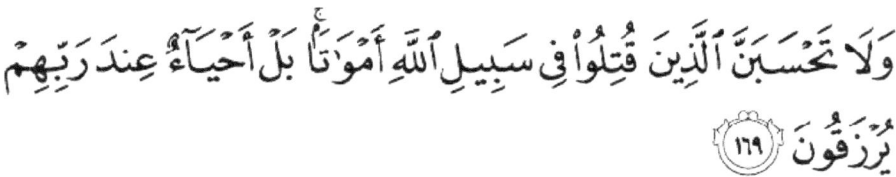

The Doctor & Sheikh's Debate

"And never think of those who have been killed in the cause of Allah as dead. Rather, they are alive with their Lord, receiving ordinance"

This verse in the Quran is clearly stating not to class martyrs as dead, but they are alive. Do you perceive the martyr's as dead when you perceive the Prophet (s.a.w.a) alive? He responded: they are active in limbo. I replied, but the Quran does not say that. It says: "رزقونی بهم عندر ای‌اح" "they are with their Lord receiving ordinance." Do you think that they wouldn't give this ordinance to the Prophet (s.a.w.a) too?

He said: I do not have the answer to these questions. If you wish we can go to the underground of Baqi and speak to our scholars. I told him that I am ready to go with him but if he is not sure and has limited information not to say these people who possibly know even less than him incorrect information.

I went underground of Baqi accompanied by the Officer and one Afghani. We asked for about an hour, but they just jumped from one branch to another and spoke unrealistically and irrationally. For this reason, I said: to them that I thought that underground in Baqi the scholars would have the answers, but I see that you guys are no different from the ones upstairs by the graves.

In the end, the Arab soldier said: we are not quite sure why you are not allowed to read pilgrims. We do not know why you are not allowed to read a prayer from over the books. We are not sure why you cannot come close to the graves. We do not know; we do not see, we do not know; these rules come from the government. The end! The end! The end!

I responded by saying well; you should have just said that from the start and not wasted our time. I said: goodbye to them and left the place and headed towards the hotel to have some breakfast.

Day Twenty First of Zyqadeh

It was ten o'clock, and we met as we had agreed.

Dr: Hello, peace be upon you.

Sh: Good morning, peace be upon you.

Dr: It truly is a tremendous honor that I can be here with you.

Sh: It is a happy time for me, too, but I have a request.

Dr: Go ahead.

Sh: I think that two hours in the morning is a bit problematic. If it is possible for us to change the time and at least make it once every other day, it would be more suitable.

Dr: I agree, for example, let's have tomorrows debate after Zuhr prayer, and then you come to my hotel for lunch. It would be my treat, and I could introduce you to my friends, and we can continue the debate there. In my opinion, after Zuhr prayer and lunch is the best time as there aren't many group activities as everyone is taking a rest.

Sh: I agree. So, from tomorrow, we agree to meet up after Zuhr pray, and then we go back to your hotel for one day and to my hotel the next.

Dr: I agree but for today let's have a talk or do you wish to postpone it to Zuhr pray.

Sh: No, I have come to talk today. It is best to take advantage of the situation. Let's find a place to sit.

We sat where we had been sitting yesterday. Several other people were sitting there too, so we moved to another corner and rested there. Before starting to debate we drank some Zamzam water. As I was drinking the water, I was told by a Saudi Sheikh to hold the cup with my right hand and not the left. I apologized and did as I was told and then told the Sheikh that it is always good to obey the traditions however this Sheikh that is stuck on such a small detailed thing is oblivious to things that are happening in Palestine, Gaza, Lebanon, Iraq, and Afghanistan. These people remind me of the Hojatiyeh Groups in Iran. Instead of opposing against the Shah, they were fighting over Pepsi Cola.

Dr: You told me you were going to go over the companion debate. How did that go?

Sh: I thought a lot about it. I could not quickly deconstruct my thirty years of beliefs, and neither could I find answers to your professional accounts.

Dr: But the difference between a researcher and an ordinary person is that once he comes to a truth that could be brutal and bitter, he would still accept it.

Sh: No, no, I didn't say that I don't accept it. I meant that altering all my past beliefs requires some time.

Dr: I think that this case is going to be the base of most of our debates.

Sh: How come?

Dr: Many of our issues would be resolved if we agreed that all of the companions were not competent to be guided from, and not all were to be trusted.

Accuracy Verification of the Hadith's in Sihah al Sittah

Dr: Today, I intend to ask you a mathematical and statistical question.

Sh: What do you mean mathematics and statistics?

Dr: I mean statistical and mathematical questions about religion.

Sh: Doctor, please do not debate using mathematics because I have not studied that.

Dr: It is not so much about mathematics. It is only using numbers to compare.

Sh: Go ahead then.

Dr: All the Hadith that are available in your books and some of the most important ones are in the six books that are called the Sihah al Sittah. In your opinion, do you think that they are correct?

Sh: You fired the companions from being guided yesterday. Is it time for the books today?

Dr: I didn't drop all of the companions to be guided from, but just concluded that not all of them are. This is not to mean that all of the companions are, we seek refuge in God (بـالله نعـوذ), hypocrites. This is only because of the Quran saying that the Lord has spoken about some of the companions not to be trusted and for the Prophet to keep away from the ones he doesn't know much as they are hypocrites.

The Doctor & Sheikh's Debate

Sh: I was humorous. I am pleased about the discussion we had yesterday and did not get offended. I was pleased that from using reasoning, we achieved the truth and also got upset as I started questioning why we have spent forty years reading verses and not paying attention to the details in them.

Dr: Well, today I wish to ask you about the books of Hadith.

Sh: Please ask away.

Dr: I will repeat the question. Do you think that all of the Hadith in the Sihah al Sittah to be genuinely correct?

Sh: Of course, Hadith from Sahih Bukhari and Sahih Muslem are mostly sought after especially the ones that are in those books. Some odd weak ones can be in there too.

Dr: What do you think is the ratio of the weak to the correct?

Sh: I have not researched that in precision, but I do know that there are very few weak Hadith in those two books.

Dr: Do you mean all the six books of Sahih al Sittah or just Sahih Bukhari and Sahih Muslem?

Sh: No, they are just examples. For instance, Ahmad Hanbali's Mosnad is very famously credited, and his Hadith's are entirely like a chain of transmission.

Dr: Who are these Hadith from specifically? I mean, who are these narrators?

Sh: These documents are to go back to the Prophet and to be either his words or actions.

Dr: Would you remember how many Hadith you have in your Sihah al Sittah books?

Sh: No, I don't remember. I have not even paid attention to it. There are many repetitive Hadith in them. I mean many of the Hadith have been repeated in different books.

Dr: Then, please allow me to ask my mathematical question.

Sh: Please go ahead.

Dr: If it is possible, please tell me roughly how many Hadith we have for the four Caliphas in the Sihah al Sittah (six books)?

Sh: I do not know.

Dr: But you do know how many years were the Caliphas with the Prophet?

Sh: Yes, from what is clear, Abubakr 23 years, Umar 18 years, Usman 19 years and Ali 23 years.

Dr: You are entirely correct. How many years was Abu Huraira with the Prophet?

Sh: I am not sure exactly. However, it shouldn't be more than four to five years.

Dr: Did you know that Abu Huraira converted to Islam in 7 AD and was with the Prophet until the 10 AD when the Prophet died. This means that he was in a total of 3 years with the Prophet. He also was on trips within these three years too.

Sh: That is correct; you are right.

Dr: Now let's see how many Hadith do Abubakr and Umar, and Usman and Ali (God bless them) have in these books.

Sh: Have you calculated?

Dr: I have not personally calculated them. However, I found one reliable research book and noticed that it had gathered all of the Hadith that were about the closest companions of the Prophet from the Sihah al Sittah. It was the cause of my questioning.

Sh: How many are there from the four Caliphas?

Dr: Abubakr 142, Umar 527, Usman 146, Ali 537.

Sh: That is weird. That does not sound a lot. However, my expectations were the same.

Dr: But Abu Huraira, meaning the companion that only spent three years with the Prophet, has 5374 Hadith from the Prophet. Could you please tell me how the Prophet could have spoken so much in the presence of this man but not to the four Caliphas?

Sh: Again, you put your finger on a hurtful subject.

Dr: I am just asking.

Sh: You are right, but it has been a very long time that this issue has been on my mind. Why is there so many Hadith from Abu Huraira but not from other people such as Aisha (mother of the faithful), who was the Prophet's Wife? She even lived in the same house as the Prophet and slept in the same bed as him, but she still does not quote this many Hadith's.

Dr: Would you know what reason they have given you?

Sh: I have never heard a convincing response. Unless they could say that Abu Huraira was very much inclined to ask questions and quote Hadith.

Dr: Do you still think that after knowing the statistics and accepting that he has quoted this many Hadith's, it was all due to his enthusiasm?

Sh: It is a very contemplative debate.

Dr: In my opinion, if we spend some time based on these statistics working on the Hadith that Abu Huraira has said: we could resolve many of the differences that Shia and Sunni's have.

Sh: It is not unlikely, however, based on the topic we have been talking about; if we start doubting the truthfulness of Abu Huraira's Hadith with this debate there wouldn't be much left on the Sihah al Sittah to debate on.

Dr: Well, we come across two real scenarios, and they are both correct.

1. Compared to the Caliphates with the substantial amount of Hadith that Abu Huraira has there is a severe amount of room to contemplate.

2. The majority of the Hadith from the Sihah al Sittah is from Abu Huraira.

Sh: This is a very harsh truth, and it is hard to accept. However, not accepting it goes against science and reason disregards a revelation too.

Dr: A brief look at Abu Huraira's Hadith demonstrates that the majority of the Hadith were based on the needs of the Calipha especially in the time of Muawiyah and were made from Abu Huraira's mind.

Sh: Unfortunately, Abu Huraira's Hadith have much opposition.

Dr: Whatever they are, it has to be said that these Hadith have changed the destiny of Islam.

Sh: That is possibly true, but it is tough to distinguish between Abu Huraira's Hadith that are correct and incorrect.

Dr: There is no reason for that. That is because in comparison to the four Caliphas and the Prophet; 3 years of Abu Huraira's time has been rough with the Prophet compared to the 23 years Abubakr spent with the Prophet. Therefore, 3/23 of his Hadith are true. This means that 142 x 3/23 = roughly 20 of Abu Huraira's Hadith are, which should not have a significant effect on people's religious belief.

Sh: Yes, 20 Hadith does not have a significant effect. However, if our religious students come across such statistics, then all of the Sihah al Sittah's Hadith would go under question.

Dr: It seems that it would not make a difference how much it is questioned. What is important is that Islam, the Quran, and the Prophet do not go under question. Many of Abu Huraira's Hadith have our youth and astute scholars questioning.

Sh: I am in total agreement.

Dr: Now that we have come this far, it wouldn't be so bad if we went through some of your books regarding the credibility of Abu Huraira's Hadith.

Sh: I have seen some things regarding this.

Dr: These that I show you are more than just things. Please pay attention to the program on my mobile.

1- In Al Tabaqat al Kebri, volume 4, page 335; and Sir Aalaam al Nabla, volume 2, page 612; and Ansab al Shiraf, volume 3, page 414; Aghd al Gharid, volume 1, page 13 says that Abu Huraira was stealing from the "Beytul Mal" (treasury). Omar Ibn al Khattab said: "سرقت ،کتابــه عدو و یاعــدوالله المال " "O enemy of God and enemy of his book, you have stolen what belongs to God".

2- In Sir Aalaam al Nabla, volume 2, page 604 and 605 and Hakim in mashtrd, volume 3, page 582, Hadith 6160 says, Aisha said: to Abu Huraira:

ما رأینــا؟ ما الا رأیت هل و ســمعنا؟ ما الا ســمعت هل بـها النـبـي عن بـها تـحـدث انـك ،تبلغنــــــا الــتي الاحــادیــث هذه ما هذه الاحادیث التي تبلغنا، انك تحدث بها عن النبي هل سمعت الا ما سمعنا؟ وهل رأیت الا ما رأینا؟

"What are these Hadith you are telling us? Are you quoting these from the Prophet? Have you heard something other than what we have heard? Or have you seen something we haven't seen?"

3- In Sir Alaam al Nabla, volume 2, page 604 and 605, Marvan Ibn Hokm said: to Abu Huraira:

ان الناس قد قالوا: أكثر الحدیث عن رسول الله وانما قدم قبل وفاته بیسیر

"People are saying: All these Hadith's that you are quoting is not proportional to the short period of time you were with the Prophet before he died"

4- In Al Matalib Al Aliyah, volume 9, page 205 it says: Abu Huraira sometimes would say: "حدثنى خلیلى ابوالقاسم" My friend the Prophet gave me some Hadith however, Ali forbid him from speaking and said: "متى كان (رسول الله) خلیلا لك" "When was the Prophet friends with you?"

5- In Al Matalib Al Aliyah, volume 9, page 205, Fakhr Razi says:

ان كثيراً من الصحابه طعنوا في ابي هريره وبيناه من وجوه: أحدها: انّ ابا هريره روى انّ النبي قال: من اصبح جنباً فلا صوم له. فرجعوا الي عائشه وام سلمه، فقالتا: كان النبي يصبح ثم يصوم. فقال: هما اعلم بذالك. انبأني بهذالخبر الفضل بن عباس، واتفق انّه كان ميتاً في ذالك الوقت

Considerable amounts of companions were insulting Abu Huraira and were questioning the accuracy of his Hadith. Among the ones: Abu Huraira quoted from the Prophet that he has said: If anyone had intercourse in the morning and was sexually induced impurity (Junub), he cannot fast. So, people referred back to Aisha and Umul Salamah and they both said: The Prophet was Junub and was still fasting. Abu Huraira then said: you would be wiser in knowing this but Fazl Ibn Abbas had told me otherwise. As a matter of fact, Fazl Ibn Abbas happened to be dead at that time.

6- In Al Matlab Al Aaliyah, volume 9, page 205, Ibrahim Nakhai says:

"كـان اصحابنا يدعون من حديث ابي هرير "

"Our friends would ignore any Hadith from Abu Huraira."

7- In Tarikh Ibn Asaker, volume 19, page 122 it says:

"ما كانوا يأخذون من حديث ابي هريره الا ما كان من حديث جنه او نار"

"From the Hadith Abu Huraira would quote there was nothing but Hadith from heaven and hell (they wouldn't believe it)"

Sh: Dear Doctor, I think that is sufficient. These were important even though that one analysis of statistics was enough to reject Abu Huraira's Hadith's.

Dr: Thank the Lord for this subject is now cleared. Do I have time to ask you another question?

Sh: There is time, but why are you the one always asking questions? Please allow me to ask a question this time.

Dr: That would make me happy. Please ask away, but bear in mind that I am just specialized in Engineering and Technical things, not religious affairs and you are a religious scholar.

Sh: I consider you someone who is a professional in religious affairs and permit myself to ask you regarding Shia affairs, God willing something can be also clearer for me too.

Dr: The truth is that I am not proficient in religious affairs; however, I have educated myself, so I can defend myself in what I believe in.

Sh: The information you are giving me is fascinating to me. So I will ask away.

Dr: Please go ahead.

Sh: To disregard Abu Huraira's Hadith, you referred to the four Caliphas. Do you honestly accept them as the Prophet's Calipha?

Dr: If it is okay with you, I would rather have this topic discussed at a later date when we have more time. This is because prayer time is close, and we can finish talking something shorter.

Sh: That is not a problem; however, you will have to explain this question of mine at a more convenient time.

Dr: Definitely, because I want to have a thorough discussion with you regarding it.

Mote' (Concubine) and Temporary Marriage

Sh: I will ask a small question. Why do you permit temporary marriage, which is classed to be one kind of adultery, and defend it vigorously?

Dr: Firstly, temporary marriage is not adultery.

Sh: Why is it not classed as adultery? If a woman is sexually available for someone daily, besides adultery what another kind could it be called?

Dr: Then it wouldn't be so bad if I explained what temporary marriage means. Dear Sheikh, you are aware of how permanent marriage is commenced. A couple of sentences are read which are called the "Formula Contract," and after that is read the unlawful couple are lawful. Sh: That is correct. This happens in permanent marriages and there are some conditions associated with it.

Dr: The same conditions apply for temporary marriages too. I mean that two people have to read a formula contract so they can be lawful to each other. If the formula contract is classed as adultery then all women and men are conducting adultery and temporary marriage is also classed as adultery.

Sh: But there is a crucial difference between a permanent marriage and a temporary one.

Dr: Can you tell me what the differences are?

Sh: The first difference is that Islam forbids it. Secondly in a temporary marriage a woman can be with a different man on a daily basis.

Dr: We will discuss the part regarding Islam's permission on a later date however, regarding you saying that a woman can sleep with a different man daily is completely wrong. Because once a woman is under a temporary marriage she has to wait an "Eddeh" (waiting period) amount in order to marry again therefore she cannot possibly have a temporary marriage on a daily basis.

Sh: This is not what has been transferred to us.

Dr: It cannot be any other way. If it is not like this we then class it as adultery.

Sh: Secondly, there is nothing associated to it.

Dr: There are many rules associated to it.

Sh: Like what?

Dr: Firstly, there must be an agreed upon expiry date. Secondly, once the temporary marriage duration is over regardless of it being one day or one month or one year they all have to wait a total of one "Eddeh" (waiting period) in order to conduct a temporary or permanent marriage. Thirdly, a woman does not receive any inheritance. However, if a child is produced from this marriage, the child will have the right to inheritance just like any other child. Even if the child is born after the temporary marriage is over he will still have a right to inheritance. The woman can ask for alimony once she is pregnant because she cannot re-marry during her pregnancy. Fourthly, during the temporary marriage the women is as if she is treated as if she is permanently married with the difference that she receives her dowry straight away and she has no alimony.

Sh: There are more conditions to it.

Dr: Yes, I believe there are four or five more left and you can see that it is not as easy as you thought it was.

Sh: I accept that there are conditions for a temporary marriage.

Dr: Now let's look and see if Shias invent the temporary marriage or if the brief marriage was happening during the Prophet's lifetime or it was removed from the true Islam at the time when everything was followed by his companions or Caliphas only.

Sh: Based on our jurisprudence, temporary marriage is not permitted in Islam.

Dr: Temporary marriage was an Islamic affair that existed during the Prophet's time, and Umar's orders forbade it. So, we cannot say that people were conducting adultery in the Prophet's time.

Sh: Temporary marriage was not proposed, as you are saying, in this detail during the Prophet's time. Even if we agree that it existed at his time, it has been forbidden after him, and therefore it is an unlawful act.

Dr: Actually, temporary marriage is there to prevent adultery. Usually, the person who is after a brief marriage is someone whom does not wish to do anything unlawful and is not in a position to permanently marry so instead of conducting something that is forbidden he sways towards a lawful act.

Sh: But this is not common amongst any other Muslims except the Shias.

Dr: We can't say that due to other religions not using the temporary marriage that it is unlawful.

Sh: This subject is reprobated amongst all Muslims.

Dr: Do you accept that based on the Hadith in the Sihah al Sittah any innovation is perdition?

Sh: Yes, of course, it is.

Dr: Can we ever say that innovation is good?

Sh: Yes, for instance, the two innovations that Umar said: he has made.

Dr: Don't you think that this matter is against the Hadith that the Prophet has said:

"كل بدعه ضلالت"

"All innovations are deviations?"

Sh: Umar was also the Prophet's Calipha. His words are needed to be followed.

Dr: Even if it's against what the Prophet says?

Sh: No, not against what he says.

Dr: Dear Sheikh, please have a look at my mobile. Muslem in Sahih has said: in his Kutub al Hajj - Chapter Jawaz Al Matah, volume 2, page 897 says that Umar has said:

"متعتان كانتا علي عهد رسول الله و انا انهي عنهما و اعاقب عليهما متعه النساء و متعه الحج"

"There are two temporary marriages that existed in the time of the Prophet and I have forbidden them. One is the temporary marriages of women and other is Mutat al Hajj"

The Doctor & Sheikh's Debate

The same thing has been cited again in the following books: In Tafsir Razi, volume 5, page 158; Jame Al Ahadis, Musnad Umar Khatab, volume 26, page 358; Kanzal Amaal, number 45722 and 31433 also mentions it. Musnad Ahmad, volume 1, page 351, Hadith 347; Musnad Ahmad, volume 39, page 4, Hadith 13955; interpretation of Razi, Surat Al Nisa, volume 1, page 14/9 and Musnan Beyhaghi, Number 13948 and in the list below it has been mentioned in your books.

Sh: Yes, this is a famous Hadith, and we both agree on it.

Dr: In your opinion, would it be okay for a Calipha to forbid something lawful in the time of the Prophet and make it unlawful?

Sh: To be honest with you, no, it is not okay.

Dr: Now, the other case that hasn't even been discussed as part of the innovations. In Sahih Bukhari 1/228 and Muslem 1/539 and other Hadith, we have that the Prophet was reading the Supererogatory Ramadan (Taravih) prayer in a house. Some of his companions were praying with him. The Prophet noticed something, and he exited the place and said: I have heard about your works. People you can read the non-compulsory prayers at your home, as the best prayer is a man's prayer in their own home.

"انّ افضل الصلوةَ، صلوةَ المرء في بيته"

"The best Salat (non-compulsory) is the one that is read at home"

Sh: Well this is correct but after the Prophet died Umar has said that the Taravih prayer has to be read in the congregation.

Dr: Do you mean that there is no problem with him speaking against the Prophet's wishes?

Sh: Well it would have been if they weren't praying in congregation.

Dr: If two Caliphas spoke against each other's opinions' which one should we accept?

Sh: But the other four Caliphas have not spoken against his words either.

Dr: What if they had spoken against his words.

Sh: Each is to be obeyed in its own time.

Dr: That is okay then. Umar said that the Taravih prayer is to be read in the congregation and they all did. Then Ali came and said: it is incorrect to read it in the congregation, but no one has listened to him until this day. This was when it was a Hadith said: by him, stating that the Supererogatory prayer is to be done individually in your own home.

Sh: Maybe this is a particular case because of the tremendous respect people have for Umar.

Dr: Do you mean that respect takes over a religious rule?

Sh: No, no, they must obey Ali's words.

Dr: But they didn't.

Sh: That is because Ali did not insist.

Dr: So now if someone prayers the Taravih prayer individually, it is okay.

Sh: Yes, that is correct.

Dr: Calipha has said: to read it in the congregation, but now you are saying that some can read it individually. This means that the word of Calipha Umar is not probative validity.

Sh: For a non-compulsory prayer, it is not probative validity.

Dr: Then how come temporary marriage has been prohibited. Is that out of respect?

Sh: That is a different matter.

Dr: How can that be any different? In fact, in the case of the Taravih prayer, it is a personal affair while in the temporary marriage case, it is a social affair. Moreover, according to Ali, the fourth Calipha, if the brief marriage were not deemed unlawful in Islam, in the Islamic world, adultery would not have happened.

Sh: Yes, if temporary marriage with the conditions mentioned were permitted, adultery would be reduced substantially.

Dr: Now you accept that temporary marriage was lawful during the Prophet's time.

Sh: Yes, it was deemed unlawful after the Prophet because we have a Hadith:

"حلال محمد حلال الي يوم القيامه و حرام محمد حرام الي يوم القيمه"

"Whatever deemed lawful to Mohammad is lawful till judgement day and whatever deemed unlawful is unlawful till judgement day."

The Doctor & Sheikh's Debate

Dr: Okay, then we refer back to your books and go through the Hadith that shows the temporary marriage was permitted in the Prophet's time and Umar forbid it in his time.

Sh: You are so determined and sure of what you are saying. If we had this many reference as proof, our scholars would not have spoken so against it.

Dr: We shall look into the computer program.

1- In Sahih Muslem, Book of Marriage (Kitab Anikah), Chapter number 13, Hadith number 1023/2 it says: Jabir Ibn Abdullah was conducting Umrah. We entered his place, and people were asking questions regarding issues and then mentioned the temporary marriage. He said: We would perform temporary marriages with some food such as dates and flour in the time of the Prophet and Abubakr until Umar banned it because of Amr Ibn Hurayth actions. This information has also been mentioned in Ahmad Musnad in 380/3, Hadith numbers 439 -438-429.

Sh: This information that you are giving me is correct.

Dr: Then if it is correct, how come we insist on what God and the Prophet have permitted lawful?

Sh: We say that the Prophet's Calipha is same as the Prophet and when he gives an order we should obey it.

Dr: That is correct. That is the case when what the Calipha is saying is not against the Prophet's or especially what God is saying.

Sh: When did God give a direct order, you just told me now that it was permitted in the time of the Prophet.

Dr: God in Surat an Nisa says: "فَمَا اسْتَمْتَعْتُمْ بِهِ مِنْهُنَّ فَآتُوهُنَّ أُجُورَهُنَّ" meaning: "**pay the women after you are temporary married to them**" that is mandatory. This verse from the Quran says that they should pay and enjoy. We also have Hadith from Jaber saying that we would temporary marriage with a hand full of dates and flour.

The critical fact is that we believe that just like other verses where the start and end are clarified, here it has not been necessary to be specified. This is just like where there is no mention of a formula contract for the permanent marriage. Therefore, in this situation, a formula contract needs to be read just like the lifelong marriage, and then after the temporary marriage finishing the conditions need to be abided.

Sh: Seems like this verse has been abrogated.

Dr: No, that is not the case. That is because you can see from the computer program on my mobile that in the Books of Jam al-Bayan, Al Tabari, under the interpretation of this verse number 9042 it says:

محمد بن مثنى، حدثنا محمدبن جعفر حدثنا شعبه عن الحكم، سألته عن هذه الايه

امنسوخه هي قال لا. قال الحكم وقال علي

لولا انّ عمر (رضي الله عنه) نهي عن المتعه مازني الا الشقي

I asked Muhammad Ibn Muthanna whom had asked Muhammad Ibn Jafar, whom had asked Shobe whom had asked Al Hokm regarding this verse being abrogated or not. He said: no. Al Hokm said that Ali said: if Umar had not forbidden temporary marriage, there would have been no adultery happening unless they were despicable

Ibn Ashur in "Al Tahrir and Al Tanvir" says that Ibn Abbas said:

"ولم ينزل بعدها تنسخها"

"After that there was no other to abrogate it"

In Tafsir Neishabouri and in Al Moharar Al Vajiz, chapter 24, section 2 page 104 Ibn Attia quotes that Aisha said:

ولا زوجيه مع الاجل ورفع الطلاق ولعده والميراث وكانت ان يتزوج الرجل المرأةَ بشاهدين واذن الولي الى اجل مسمى و على ان لا ميراث بينهما و يعطيها ما اتفقا عليه فاذا نقضت مده فليس له عليها سبيل و تستبريء رحمها لان الولد لاحق قبه بلاشك فان لم تحمل حلت لغيره

"Permanent marriage does not just conduct with a set amount of time or by taking away divorce, setting a delay time between marriages and inheritance. A woman can marry a man with two witnesses and with permission of her father but for a certain amount of time and not inherit anything from him based on a mutual agreement. Once the set time is over they have no obligations to each other and they are free. If she is not pregnant she is lawful to marry again."

Sh: These are the same conditions that you had mentioned before.

Dr: These are the conditions from your own books. Quoted from Aisha that is a woman and should be sensitive regarding temporary marriages.

The Doctor & Sheikh's Debate

Sh: Since you are so defensive towards temporary marriages, how many have you had?

Dr: I am married and haven't had the need to temporarily marry. Because I believe that temporary marriage is for people who do not have the ability to permanently marry and also being allowed to do something is very different to it being compulsory.

You also have quotes in your books from the Calipha that was appointed after Umar. Ali, the fourth Calipha says:

"لولا ان عمر نهي عن المتعه ما زني الا شقي"

Or in Jame Tabari page 179 it says that there were quotes existing in the verses of the Quran: "منهن الاي اجل مسمى"

Ibn Abbas would read it that way and Mujahid says that everyone would act opposite to the verse.

In the Tafsir of Ibn Kasir Volume 2, page 170. Abdullah Ibn Masoud says that he was with the Prophet on an expedition. Due to our wife's were not with us we wanted to release ourselves, and the Prophet forbade us and said that we have to marry the woman temporarily with a set duration then Abdullah Ibn Masoud said:

"يا أَيُّهَا الَّذينَ آمَنُوا لا تُحَرِّمُوا طَيِّباتِ ما أَحَلَّ اللَّهُ لَكُم وَ لا تَعْتَدُوا إِنَّ اللَّهَ لا يُحِبُّ الْمُعْتَدينَ"

(Maidah 87)

Sh: These cases exist, but the public did not act on it, and they are unaware that even Aisha has a Hadith regarding this topic, and it is not classed as adultery.

Dr: However, the actions of the public cannot deny the truth that exists; that is why I brought a reference from Aisha.

Sh: It is essential. Because quoting a Hadith from her was very unlikely.

Dr: God willing, you accept that Islam is a religion that has placed a solution for every problem a person has in any different situation.

Sh: Yes, definitely "نحن نريد بكم اليسرولانريد بكم العسر", "we wish your freedom and not your hardship"

Dr: Well, why shouldn't God place the right solution for some people who have problems getting permanently married. The same God that allows a human being to eat a dead person's body in an emergency case would not think about this great instinct that is the attention of people?

Sh: This last sentence is significant that God has thought about every situation his people may fall under.

Dr: Currently, most of the Islamic university students going to western countries are conducting adultery to resolve their sexual needs, or they permanently marry Christians when they would fix the problem by temporarily marrying.

Sh: That is correct. This topic is currently being discussed amongst our bright minded and educated people from Arabian countries that majority of those that marry with western. women do not have a successful living. Those western women dramatically draw their husbands towards the west.

Dr: No one can deny the attention; God and the Prophet give humans. However, they say that Umar forbid it and said that his new idea was better. In conclusion, if these reasons did not exist and all the information mentioned had not happened and the sole reasons as to Umar preventing it from happening we would have indeed had temporary marriages as lawful.

Sh: Yes, "و من اصدق من الله و رسوله", "**And who is more honest than the Prophet and his God**" when we have a strict verse from the Quran and no other verse to abrogate it, with all these discussions and in addition to the question that can a Calipha of the Prophet speak against him or not? It must be accepted and you are right. Those scholars that believe that temporary marriage is allowed are right.

Dr: Thank the Lord that this case cleared and that we are the followers of the verses of the Quran and the Prophet's tradition. I am thankful that you accept an issue when you come to the actual realization of the matter.

Sh: We should accept the truth because this is important for the judgment day of every person. If we came to the truth about a matter and dismissed it, how could we answer back to the Lord? There are an interpretation and explanation in the word "Motaghin" in verse "Lel Mutaghin," and that is to accept the truth. The Quran can be your guidance only if you can be acceptable towards the fact.

Dr: You are entirely correct, and I am so thankful to God that you accept these explanations.

Sh: With all of these reasoning's, Hadith, and verses, how could I disagree with such a clear revelation?

Dr: Thank you, praying time is close. God willing, we meet again tomorrow, after the Zuhr pray in front of the door of Gabriel.

Sh: God willing, God is with you.

The 1987 Mecca Incident

I went back to the hotel after praying and joined my friends in having lunch and a short discussion over the incident on the year 66 in Mecca. Haj Abbas was explaining the story of how the Iranian pilgrims had the intentions of proving their renunciation of the infidels by marching quietly. This event would happen every year on the 6th of Zihijjah in Mecca. I witnessed in year 60 and 61 this happening and the vital role it had in convicting America and Israel. Haj Abbas explained that in year 66, after the speech was done at the ceremony just like it's done every year. The pilgrimages started to walk towards Masjid Al Haram.

I was in the middle of the rows, and when the crowd got closer to the bridge of Hyun, the security Officers of Saudi Arabia started hitting the Iranian Pilgrims and several non-Iranian Pilgrims with stones, pieces of wood and anything they else could get a hold of. From the other side, the people behind the protestors were unaware of what was happening in the frontline, and so they were pushing ahead. Therefore, the people at the frontline were under pressure from both sides. One side was the pressure from the security Officers of Saudi Arabia with their stones, wood, and on another hand, there was the pressure of the pilgrimages from behind. Once they heard the gunfire, many of them started to run away. The women were mostly left under the stampede of the crowd. Blood filled the street, and the dead bodies were piled on top of each other. Haj Abbas said that although he was in the army and military and had strong stamina still endured defeat and fell on the ground and passed out for a couple of minutes. Many dead bodies around me had suffered due to the pressure of the crowd, he said. I got up with all my strength and managed to help get up several women that were still alive but injured from the grounds and headed towards the hotel, he added. As I was heading towards the hotel, I was passing all the dead bodies, and it made me feel sick. I could not come to terms with the trauma. We would bring back the bodies of the martyrs at least in war, but here, I was not able to do anything. All I could do was morn and cry, not just because of the incidents but for myself feeling so helpless. I remember thinking to myself how God was going to answer back to such behavior. Then I realized that God already paid those killers of Karbala after years by the hands of Mukhtar.

When was he going to respond to the actions of the Saudi Arabians? I convinced myself with eyes full of tears that there was nothing I could do, and there wasn't. I eventually got to the hotel. Everyone was mourning the loss. Due to this incident, over 450 innocent Iranian pilgrims were given the honorable title of martyrs in the land of holy Mecca and the month of unlawfulness (Zihijjah) by order of American and Israel's puppets.

The details of the day which Haj Abbas was reciting are not easy to write, and I have no tolerance in hearing the story again never mind writing it.

At this moment, the tour manager started citing a strange occurrence that had happened with the Saudi Arabians and was a demonstration of their irreligion.

He said that after the year 1993 meaning after 5 years the pilgrims came to Mecca again. One of the Iranian women had gone to the Mecca organizers and had said that she was present at the year 66 Mecca incident and that she was injured. She had headed towards one of the homes that were close to the Bridge of Hjun seeking refuge. After the killing of the people was finished she had requested to leave and to go back to the hotel, but the Sheikh that was living in the house and had several wives had refused and abducted her. He did not let her leave the house until the whole Hajj ceremony was finished. After the end of the Mecca ceremony, he forcibly made her his wife and forbade her to call or go anywhere. He forced her to have three children without her consent. However, this year that Iranian's were able to come to Mecca she was able to run away from the house and had come to me asking to rescue her as she was already married in Iran and had children of her own.

Our tour leader said that, with the immense help of everyone, they had tried to arrange a passport for her to leave accompanied by the other woman back to Iran and they had sent her out of Jeddah.

She was now imagining how her family, husband, and children were thinking of her return after five years. Not knowing anything about her whereabouts and thinking that she had passed away in the Mecca killing incident. It was good that they were at least informed of her abduction, and she was wise enough to run away. There might have been several incidents such as this one. In any way, this news alongside the other was a catastrophe of its own and will always remain a portrait of the Saudi Arabians pure dark nature.

After hearing all the stories, I had no desire to do anything else but to just put my head down and to sleep and if possible rest for a couple of minutes.

Once I woke up, I started talking about the time when I was in England and that I had assembled some proper proceedings while being there. Such as started up a protesting rally in London in which as usual I was with the microphone shouting slogans against the Saudi Arabian's, Americans and Israeli's. The heat of passion felt amongst the people than at the rally was even more than the ones held when I was at war.

Eventually, after hearing more upsetting stories, I had a stronger tea and headed towards the Mosque for the Maghrib prayer and then came back had dinner and then went to the Bazaar with my wife.

The Twenty Second of Zyqadeh

I read the Zuhr prayer and lingered for a while before the time got close to my meeting. During this time, someone came and asked me if I was an Iranian. I replied yes, how can I help you? He said: I am a Muslim and I am very proud of Iran standing against the United States of America as a Muslim country and that it has proved that God is greatest. Just as I was about to continue the conversation, the shrine police started to drive out the worshippers. This was because it was the women's turn to have a chance of praying by the Prophet's Shrine. Unfortunately, they had not organized a decent plan for this. They only allowed one and a half hours in the morning and one and a half hours in the afternoon for all the women to visit the Prophet's shrine. I have heard exciting things once it is their turn as well. My wife told me that they divide the women based on the country they have come from. For instance, for every country that has a hundred women pilgrims, they are only allowed 10 minutes to pray by the shrine. They also discriminate by race as well. For instance, they give more time to the Arabs and Egyptians. They offer less time to people from Africa and even less to Iranians.

I had a small conversation with the Egyptian professor and then said: goodbye to him. He requested to meet me again, but I said that it was not possible and to get away from the shrine police. I exited the Mosque and saw Sheikh waiting for me by the door of Gabriel (Baab Gabriel).

Dr: Greetings and in the hope that God accepts all your efforts.

Sh: Greetings to you as well and the same to you God willing.

Dr: Our hotel is this way. Please come and let's go to my hotel.

Sh: It appears that your hotel passes the graveyard of Baqi. Did you know that this graveyard was made after Islam?

Dr: That is true. Apparently, they call it Jannat ul Baqi. In your opinion, is this place not the most important graveyard in the Islamic world?

Sh: Yes, this is the most famous graveyard in the Islamic world.

Dr: It is by sure famous, but I said: most important because being famous does not necessarily imply that it is important.

Sh: Medina is the most famous Islamic city in the world, and this graveyard is the most famous graveyard in this city.

Dr: In my opinion, the importance of it is because of the highly honored people that are buried in this graveyard. If these people were buried in any other city or country, that cemetery would have been the most important. Sh: Any important person, once dead is possible to have his soul moved to good places but his body does not necessarily matter where it is. Wherever it is it wouldn't make a difference.

There is No Difference between the Prophet Being Dead or Alive

Dr: Do you honestly believe that all dead bodies are the same once the soul has left them?

Sh: Yes, "إِنَّكَ مَيِّتٌ وَ إِنَّهُمْ مَيِّتُونَ" "Therefore the Prophet is dead just like everybody else."

Dr: But the Quran speaks differently to what you are saying.

Sh: How come? I have read in the Quran that God says, you, just like everyone else, will die.

Dr: But this is only one verse of the Quran. There are other verses. This verse only gives the news of the death of the Prophet that no one is denying. However, other verses are stating that death by martyr is not death but a continuation of life and is different from everyone else.

Sh: Which verse has made this distinction?

Dr: Verse 169, Surat Al Imran cites:

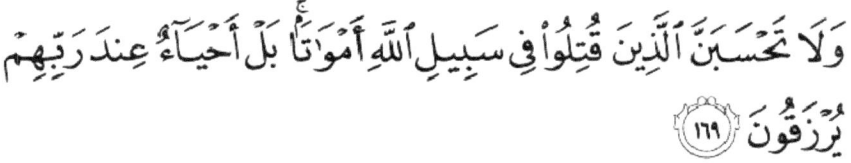

"And never think of those who have been killed in the cause of Allah as dead. Rather, they are alive with their Lord, receiving ordinance"

Based on the Quran's, the martyrs are alive and are rewarded by the Lord.

Sh: Yes, this is the limbo life that martyrs have.

The Doctor & Sheikh's Debate

Dr: Apparently, the discussion is not about life in limbo. There is no reward in limbo; these people are receiving ordinances.

Sh: Do you imply that the martyrs are living?

Dr: Who am I to say? I have read the Quran and God's own words. If you do not believe in this matter, please give me reasons. I am not claiming anything; God is.

Sh: Maybe, in this case, the Quran is giving an example for metaphorical expressions meaning the martyrs are like the living and are rewarded by God.

Dr: If we agree with what you are saying, then that means the martyrs are like the living being rewarded but in a different situation.

Sh: Yes, surely.

Dr: But at least the difference between the martyrs and people is that based on the interpretation of the Quran. Their living is in a different condition, and it isn't like the actual life.

Sh: I didn't say that they are not alive. I said that maybe they are similar and like the actual living.

Dr: So, let's agree that based on what the Quran is saying they are alive even though they are not living like the people who have not experienced death yet. Moreover, they are receiving ordinance by God for sure.

Sh: I accept that between what we are assuming and what the Quran says, the Quran is a much stronger candidate. Even though we are not familiar with the living, they are talking about.

Dr: Now, I have a question. Is the Prophet's rank higher or the martyr?

Sh: Most definitely the Prophet's. Because we have in verse 69 Surat Al Nisa:

وَمَن يُطِعِ ٱللَّهَ وَٱلرَّسُولَ فَأُو۟لَٰٓئِكَ مَعَ ٱلَّذِينَ أَنْعَمَ ٱللَّهُ عَلَيْهِم مِّنَ ٱلنَّبِيِّـۧنَ وَٱلصِّدِّيقِينَ وَٱلشُّهَدَآءِ وَٱلصَّٰلِحِينَ وَحَسُنَ أُو۟لَٰٓئِكَ رَفِيقًا ۝

> "And whoever obeys Allah and the Messenger - those will be with the ones upon whom Allah has bestowed favor of the Prophet's, the steadfast affirmers of truth, the martyrs and the righteous. And excellent are those as companions."

Dr: So, for sure, the Prophet must have at least been classed as the living kind just like what the martyrs are experiencing because, in this verse, even the righteous are ahead of the martyrs.

Sh: Yes, you are correct.

Dr: Who is in this graveyard? Is it the martyrs of Uhud, the martyrs of Hurrah?

Sh: Yes.

Dr: The Prophet's families (Ahl al Bayt) are more important than the martyrs are. Are they there too?

Sh: Yes, there are people from the Ahl al Bayt there too.

Dr: Then the importance of this graveyard is because of these people and not because of the city of Medina. Medina does have other cemeteries as well.

Sh: You are right. I wish to ask your opinion regarding the Iranians that come over to the graveyard, cry, and mourn seeking help from the Ahl al Bayt.

Dr: Now that we have arrived at the hotel, let us talk about this discussion later and have some lunch together.

We headed towards the restaurant of the hotel to have lunch. Everyone wanted to meet with the Sheikh and to say hi, even though he was not wearing his spiritual clothing and appeared as a normal Arab. We had lunch, and I apologized to the Sheikh because they would give only one kind of food for everyone. They also had meals for people who did not want to have fried or fatty food. However, it seemed that Sheikh was happy with our food because he praised it after lunch.

Sh: The food was very delicious. Are the cooks Iranian?

Dr: Yes, they prepare food for all the Iranians and then distribute it accordingly.

Sh: Do you mean that they prepare food for all of the Pilgrim Iranians in one place?

Dr: Yes, averages of 40,000 dishes are in Medina distributed for every breakfast, lunch, and dinner. In Mecca, the amount goes up to 100,000.

The Doctor & Sheikh's Debate

Sh: Are we staying here in the restaurant, or are we going to your room?

Dr: No, we will go to my room because I know that all of my roommates have gone to rest and the two others have gone to the shrine. (Ghargham and Karbalyi were the snorers so they would go to the shrine after lunch, as a result, the others would be able to rest.)

Sh: Very well let us go.

We went to my room. We sat behind a small table provided by the hotel, and I brought tea, Persian sweets and Persian nuts.

Sh: We just had lunch. How are we able to eat these sweets?

Dr: They have a phrase where they say salt first and then halouaa afterward.

Sh: Yes, you are correct, but I will be a bit cautious because my blood sugar is higher than it should usually be. It is tough to resist eating these delicious sweets.

Sh: I am the same. I even eat glucose tablets.

After speaking about the hotel and my roommates, especially the two that were the snorers we talked about Iranian snacks and the combination of their sweets. Dr. Ahmadi arrived and said a few words in Arabic to the Sheikh. He greeted him, and then the Sheikh asked if he was the one that snored. I said, no, they have gone to the Shrine. I told Dr. Ahmadi to rest and that we would keep the volume low so we would not bother him. Dr. Ahmadi said that he will sit in a corner and will not intervene in our discussion as he was not fluent in Arabic and that if it was a problem he could go. I asked him to stay and that it was not a problem and I was sure he would understand quite a bit of our discussions.

Sh: So, let us start. If it is possible, please respond to the question I had yesterday. Then what is your opinion about the Caliphas?

Dr: Before we start this discussion, do you have any questions regarding temporary marriages?

Sh: No, it was fascinating to me. When Aisha had accepted the temporary marriage, and she is a woman, then it is obvious for me where I stand.

Dr: Let's pay attention to the fact that Aisha died forty years after Umar and that she spoke against his saying.

Sh: Yes, I agreed to it now let's go back to my previous question.

Dr: You have an incredible amount of interest to hear the answer to your question, don't you?

Sh: Yes, it is imperative because I wish to know your personal opinion on this matter.

Dr: Can you ask the question again clearly so I can respond accordingly.

Sh: My question is this: What is your opinion regarding the Caliphas? Do you accept them as Caliphas, too or not?

Dr: I look at the case of what happened after the Prophet in different ways.

Sh: How do you see it?

Dr: Dear Sheikh if you would agree, let's discuss this when we have talked about everything else leading up to this question. The debate over the Calipha itself, leadership (Imamat) and Faqih (Jurist), all have very fundamental matters that need to be covered. Even though their importance is very high, but we need to discuss things like the eligibility of all of the Prophet's fellowship. This was covered and dealt with, or similar matters to it need to be spoken about. That would make it so much easier to answer your question. Sh: Doctor, you are trying to run away from starting this important discussion.

Dr: Honestly, I am not trying to run away. I like getting to the branches and leaves of the matter before getting into the roots and essence of it.

Sh: Very well. I am your guest so that I will surrender.

Dr: Come on; please don't see it this way. You are very welcome here, and we agreed to agree on all the topics we discuss.

Sh: True, I agree so if you are okay, we could continue the discussion the topic regarding Baqi and how the dead people are being portrayed.

Dr: That is good.

Sh: I have seen it several times that Shias come to pilgrimage and cry instead of pray when they are close to the Ahl al Bayt's graveyard. Even when I was in Syria, I saw that the Shias were weeping and mourning in the presence of Seyedeh Zainab and Seyedeh Ruqayyah, someone that has passed away 1,000 years ago. Why is there a need to cry for them? They should send their regards, read the Al Fatihah supplication and leave.

Dr: If you agree, let's have a debate here regarding several things.

Sh: Debate about what?

Crying for the Dead

Dr: Crying for the dead, visiting the graves, building a structure over graves and or amending them, kissing and blessing their shrines and imploring to them.

Sh: That is a lot now. In my opinion, discussing the graves is possible, but considering restoring someone that is not God has nothing to do with the graves and is a colossal mistake. Therefore, let's separate the two. Let's talk about the topics concerning the cemeteries another time.

Dr: I agree, which one do would you like us to continue with? (From now I won't be mentioning referring to the program on my mobile as I carry it everywhere and see to it every time I say a Hadith)

Sh: Let's discuss the crying only because we have a Hadith that cry disturbs the dead person, and everyone has cited it.

Dr: That is correct. I have this Hadith on my mobile. The truth is that some of the people that have cited this are either nonexistent or unreliable. For instance, Ahmad Ibn Hanbal in the book of Tahzib Al Kamal (refinement of perfection in the names of men), section 16, page 70 says that Isaac Ben Sayar who has also been one of the people that has talked about the same.

thing (go and calm them down) has called it false and has said that he would portray the weak Hadith to be strong but in Imstadrak Al Sahiheyn, section 1, page 381 and also Musnad Ahmad section 2, page 444 says that one day the Prophet and Umar were at a funeral and the women were crying. Umar forbid them to cry and the Prophet said:

"يا عمر دعهن فان العين دامعه و النفس مصابه و العهد قريب"

"Umar leave them be, they are teary eyed due to the trauma and the sudden distance and separation that has recently happened for them"

Sh: But Ibn Umar has mentioned this Hadith again, afterward right?

Dr: If you read the Hadith ultimately you see that Aisha rejected his opinion in the presence of the Son of Umar (Abdullah Ibn Umar) and completed the Hadith that the truth was not this.

Sh: But subsequently, there are plenty of people that have cited this Hadith and similar Hadith regarding not crying over the dead.

Dr: Even if what you say is the truth and these sayings are from Umar, it would not have any authority. The most important reason is based on the fact that the Prophet told him to leave them as they are.

Sh: This is correct that a Calipha has no authority to deny what the Prophet has previously said: to be, but we cannot accept the Caliphas saying to be similar to other followers.

Dr: If you accept this one thing, then all other issues would be solved and that is that spoken words of the Calipha or the Prophet's followers have no authority over the Prophet's words.

Sh: These people are not talking from their own opinions. They are reciting the Prophet's and God's words.

Dr: But if they spoke from their own opinions and it was against what God and his Prophet were saying, what do we do then?

Sh: We don't accept them.

Dr: You accepted this matter when it came to temporary marriage and Mutat Al-Hajj and Taravih Prayer even though Umar had spoken against it and said that these two matters were lawful in the time of the Prophet, but I will ban them. The Taravih prayer was also an individual supplication pray in the time of the Prophet, and it was advised to read non-compulsory prayers in the comfort of our own homes, but Umar changed that too.

Sh: Doctor you are referring to something that has already been covered and agreed upon. Please do not repeat it again I accepted the temporary marriage case and accepted that I believe in your opinion.

Dr: The discussion we had before was a fundamental debate. I want to remind you that the prominent reasons as to why our Sunni brothers and we Shias all have differences. This is because of the actions of the companions, the Prophet, and the manners of our Caliphas.

Sh: Do you have at least one cite to say that the Prophet himself cried for the death of someone?

Dr: As a matter of fact, I do. I have three documents stating that the Prophet cried for the death of a person.

Sh: Please tell me then as that is more important than the previous Hadith we discussed.

Dr: Firstly, in Musnad Al Tayaalisi, section 4, page 389, Hadith 1515 and 1531. Also in Mustadrak Al Sahiheyn section 1, page 514 says that Aisha said: when Usman Mazon died the Prophet opened up and cried so much that tears ran across his cheeks. In document 1531 Umar Ibn Hamid says that the Prophet firstly kissed Usman Mazon's face and then cried so much that tears ran across his cheeks.

Sh: I have not seen this Hadith.

The Doctor & Sheikh's Debate

Dr: Here you are. It says in Maktab Al Shamlah.

Sh: This Hadith is essential.

Dr: Secondly, the crying over Ibrahim, his son, which has been covered in many, books such as Sunan Ibn Majah section 5, page 69, Hadith 1578. In Sahih Al Bukhari section 3, page 172 and 173. In Shahih Al Muslem section 4, page 1807 and section 5-page 1808 that when Ibrahim died the Prophet "So he kissed him (Ibrahim) and smelt him and Ibrahim had passed away,"

"فقبله وشمه وابراهيم تجود بنفسه"

Then people complain and the Prophet says:

"ان العين تدمع وان القلب يخشع ولا تقول الا ما يرضي ربنا وان لفراقك يا ابراهيم لمحزونون"

"Eyes cry and the heart breaks and nothing can be said: against what God's will is and O' Ibrahim we are very distressing in your absence".

People then continued to complain that you had told us not to cry over the dead.

The Prophet then said:

" اني لم انه عن البكاء ولكن نهيت عن صوتين احمقين فاجرين، صوت عندنعمه لهو ولعب مزامير شيطان وصوت عندالمصيبةٌ ولطم وجوه وشق جيوب",

"I never forbid you to cry. I told you all not to make two brainless noises, one was when it is as you are very happy and you laugh out loud, talking, making sounds like Satan. Second, the sound that comes from weeping, self harming over sadness and ripping ones clothes."

Sh: I have heard about that but the last part.

Dr: Thank the Lord. The last part is also in Bukhari and Muslim.

Sh: Please tell me the other case that you mentioned.

Dr: The other case is when Hamza was martyred. It has been mentioned in Subule Al Huda Va Al Rashad, section 4, page 222. Al Tabarani says:

"فلما راي جثته بكي شهق. وخاف علي صفيةٌ بنت عبدالمطلب فوضع صدره علي صدرها فاسترجعت و بكت ,

"When the Prophet saw Hamza's body he cried loudly and was hesitant of seeing Safiyah (Hamza's sister). He put his chest on Hamza's chest and read the verse Esterja and cried."

Sh: Yes, yes that is correct.

Dr: There is more.

Sh: There is more?

Dr: Many more. For instance, when Sad Ibn Muadh was martyred, the Prophet cried and said: for everyone to tell his story so they cry for him too. When Jafar and Zeyd passed away the Prophet cried and said that they were my brothers and close friends and talking companions.

In the interpretation of Ibn Kasir section 2, page 329 regarding crying Malik Ibn Anas said: to Sad Ibn Miad (Sa'ad Ibn Ma'az grandchild) that: I came upon Anas Ibn Malik and he asked who I was. I replied: I am Waaqid Ibn Saadbn Ma'az. He said: You look like him. Then he cried and said: may God bless his soul. Sa'ad was one of the greatest men and highly honored.

Sh: This is very interesting. There are so many cases.

Dr: I have one from Abubakr.

Sh: Please do so.

Dr: Ibn Kasir section 4, page 480. Musnad Ahmad section 4, page 362 and Bukhari section 4, page 463 and 2256 from Aisha's saying she claims: When the Prophet passed away Abubakr entered the Mosque came inside Aisha's house

"فكشف عن جهه ثم اكب عليه فقبله و بكي"

"He opened up to see the Prophet's face, places his head next to him and kissed him and cried."

Sh: Okay so we can agree that once someone is martyred or has died it is okay to cry. But what of crying after the person has died and buried and crying over the grave?

Dr: I have proof from the Prophet himself.

Sh: It seems that you have gathered all the evidence.

Dr: I have not gathered them. They are all in this software as soon as I type in the subject matter.

Sh: Please go ahead; this is very good.

Dr: There are documents from the Quran, such as the crying of Jacob or the sorrow of the Prophet, which are all correct.

The Doctor & Sheikh's Debate

Sh: That is correct. What about crying after death? Jacob cried due to being separated from Joseph.

Dr: In Sunan Ibn Majah 1620 and Hakem in Almstdrick in the Mustadrak Al Sahiheyn 3250 says on behalf of Abdullah Ibn Masoud that the Prophet would look upon the graves and we were all with him. He then asked us to sit. He then cried loudly, and the others joined him, crying. We then saw Umar asked the Prophet the reason why he had cried and caused sadness for everyone else. The Prophet said: Was it my crying that made you cry? He replied, yes. The Prophet said: this grave that you see me crying upon is my mother's grave Aminah Bint Wahb.

Sh: Wow, this is in Almstdrick?

Dr: Yes, please come and have a look. Can you see that the Prophet is crying over his mother's grave after fifty years?

Sh: This is correct. This is an important case that our scholars have never mentioned. They haven't put these Hadith next to each other and talked to people about them.

Dr: Recently they have. For instance, look at this part of the software.

Albarzakh Thesis of Dr. Sheikh section 1, page 190- 227 has done the same thing. However, Dr. Alfatih Alhabr Umar Ahmad has also written a book called Hayat AlBarzakh in the Sihah Sittah, which is fascinating research and is written in my university. He proves that based on the Prophet's order, crying for a dead person is permitted.

Besides, there are more than 50 cases in the software of the same thing being mentioned for instance there is a section that Hoghogh Mostafa that says the same something in chapter 6, page 41 that Fatawa Alazhar section 8, page 108, Bab Al Ziyarat Al Rasool.

Now the part regarding honoring the Prophet (s.a.w.a) grave, in Ibn Kabir section 2, page 21 in door of Hoghogh Al mostafa cites:

Malik Ibn Anas said: to Calipha Abu Jafar Mansour:

"لاتر فعو صوتكم فوق صوت نبي فانّ حرمته ميتًا كحرمته حياً"

"Do not raise your voice in front of the Prophet because his honor and respect are to be kept even when he is dead as when he is passed away he is as if he was alive" Abu jafar asked

يا ابا عبد الله (مالك) استقبل قبله ام استقبل(قبر) رسول الله. مالك قال: لم تصرف وجهك عنه وهو وسيلتك ووسيله ابيك آدم الي الله يوم القيامه بل استقبله و فاستشفع به فيستشفعه الله

> **"When going to his pilgrimage shall I face towards the Qibla or face Malik? He replied: Do not face away from his grave because he is the means for you, concubine with Adam in the presence of God at Judgment day."**

Sh: This is a strange Hadith; what were its sources?

Dr: Here in my mobile you can see them all there are roughly 30 sources for it.

Sh: Malik has said: a significant thing.

Dr: Malik has said: what Islam is saying. We are also saying what Islam is saying.

Sh: But other religions do not say that we could face the grave.

Dr: Actually, others say the same thing too. Please look at my mobile. Based on here Fatwa from Ibn Teymiyah section 1, page 12 states:

Malik and Shafia and Ahmad Ibn Hanbal all said that when coming to pilgrimage the Prophet facing towards the shrine. However, Abu Hanifah says: meet the Qibla, not the shrine. In Fatwa Alazhar section 8 page 108, the same topic has been announced: from Ibn Teymiyah.

Sh: But practically everyone faces the Qibla.

Dr: This is because the authorities do not allow for everyone to face any other way or else we would see that everyone standing at the head of the Prophet's grave would be facing against the Qibla and be facing the shrine. Therefore, everyone understands what Malik, Shafia, and Ahmad are saying. Of course, it would make more sense because if someone were to stand at the head of the Prophet's grave and send his regards then face his back to it and look towards the Qibla, it would be entirely out of reason.

Sh: Dear Dr., I accept that crying over a dead person is acceptable and that we could face the chamber when going to pilgrimage.

Dr: I am not saying this. It is all based on the sources in the books stored on my mobile. All I am trying to say is that for you to act just like your books and Hadith's say, which by the way are not contradicting with what the Quran says.

Sh: And I am saying that I accept.

Dr: Now in continuation of the case please pay attention, Malik said: To Abu Jafar when you go to the Prophet's grave to ask for forgiveness. Meaning you can go to a dead person asking refuge.

The Doctor & Sheikh's Debate

Sh: Yes, that is correct. That was an essential content. Us scholars have never referred to these books and have not been paying attention to them. We go by with what has been said: Around without relating to its source and its validity.

Dr: Well, we have limited your job.

Sh: Yes, you are correct; this is very good. May God bless you.

Dr: Please look, Samhoodi says in Vafa Al Vafa, page 1361: Hafiz Abu Abdulla Mohammad Ibn Musa Ibn Al Numan said: based on a source from Ali Ibn Abitaleb a.s that three days had passed from burying the Prophet (s.a.w.a) that an Arab came from a trip outside of Medina. He placed the Prophet's grave soil on his head and said:

" يا رسول الله قلت فسمعنا قولك و وعيت عن الله سبحانه ما و عينا عنك و كان فيما انزل عليك ولو انهم اذ ظلموا انفسهم
"جاوك فاستغفرواالله و قد ظلمت وجئتك تستغفر لي"

"O Messenger of God, you told us and we heard you. You obtained from God what we obtained from you. From all the things that have been given to you there is this verse of the Quran: Whenever anyone has wronged to himself and then come to you and ask God for his forgiveness. You will ask forgiveness on your behalf. I have come to you so you could ask for my forgiveness and ..."

At the end of the book, Vafa Al vafa le Akhbar daar al mustafa, door number 8, the author has cited many events that provide evidence that asking forgiveness and pardon and asking for requests from the Prophet have all been a continuous repetitive action for the Muslims. He even writes: Imam Mohammad Ibn Musa Ibn Numan regarding a book named Mesbah Alzalem fi Al Mostaqisin Bekheyr al Anaam has said: the same thing.

Sh: It is fascinating that asking for forgiveness and pardon can still be continued to be asked after the person has passed away.

Dr: Yes, and this is the answer to those who say not to seek help from people that have passed away.

At this moment some pistachio and Persian sweets on the table were offered to Sheikh, and he took some. He pointed at the Persian sweets.

Sh: These are very delicious.

Dr: I am not sure about Egypt but they are not comparable to Syrian sweets.

Sh: Egypt has good sweets but they are not comparable to Syrian sweets.

Dr: Syrian and Lebanon sweets are extremely delicious to eat.

Sh: What was the sweet that I had? Gaz? It is very delicious. It does come close to Syrian sweets and it is less sweet. It is good for old folks like me. Syrian sweets are very sweet.

Blessing and Pleading to the Righteous Dead

Dr: Regarding pleading to the Prophet's grave (s.a.w.a) there are advocates that I could mention as well.

Sh: We do not permit blessing or pleading to the dead.

Dr: The Quran permits you to plead to the living, and the best example is Joseph's shirt.

Sh: Yes, when the Prophet was living, they would do blessings on the water that the Prophet would do ablution on. We do not have anything for the dead.

Dr: We do have cases after death too.

Sh: Where?

Dr: One apparent source is in Sobol al Hoda and Alreshad, section 12, page 347, ba'ab number 8. We also have another source in Sunan Darmi, section 1, page 56, and Ibn Jawzi section 12, page 357 from Abu Aljovza. He talks about pleading to the Prophet's honorable grave requesting for rain:

٩٢ ـ حدثنا أبو النعمان ثنا سعيد بن زيد ثنا عمرو بن مالك النكري حدثنا أبو الجوزاء أوس بن عبد الله قال : قحط أهل المدينة قحطا شديدا فشكوا إلى عائشة فقالت انظروا قبر النبي صلى الله عليه و سلم فاجعلوا منه كوا إلى السماء حتى لا يكون بينه وبين السماء سقف قال ففعلوا فمطرنا مطرا حتى نبت العشب وسمنت الإبل حتى تفتقت من الشحم فسمي عام الفتق

قال حسين سليم أسد: رجاله ثقات"

"Aus Ibn Abdullah said: Medina was suffering from food and drought shortage and people were extremely deprived on resources so they complained to Aisha and Aisha said: to face the Prophet's (s.a.w.a) grave and to make a hole on the roof of the house where his grave buried was so there wouldn't be a gap between the grave and the sky. Aus Ibn Abdullah said: we did this and rain came upon us. There was so much rain that all the grasses became green, the camels became large and fattened so much so that they called that year the year of plenty. Hussain Salim said that they were sure of the Hadith."

Sh: This is very interesting, this pleading after the Prophet's death. This is a good example for what you are trying to prove.

The Doctor & Sheikh's Debate

Dr: Please look again. Hafiz, in the book of Fatho Al bary section 2, page 495 and Author Ibn Abi Shaybah section 12 pages 32 says:

روى بن أبي شيبة ْ بإسناد صحيح من رواية ْ أبي صالح السمان عن مالك الداري وكان خازن عمر قال أصاب الناس قحط في زمن عمر فجاء رجل إلى قبر النبي صلى الله عليه و سلم فقال يا رسول الله استسق لامتك فإنهم قد هلكوا فأتى الرجل في المنام فقيل له ائت عمر الحديث....وقد روى سيف في الفتوح أن الذي رأى المنام المذكور هو بلال بن الحارث المزني أحد الصحابة ْ

"Ibn Abi Shaybah with true documents from Abi Saleh Alsaman Malikdar that was the holder of Umar's warehouse says that in the time of Umar there happened to be shortage of food. A gentleman came upon the Prophet (s.a.w.a) grave and said: O' Messenger of God feed your Ummah as they are perishing. The Prophet came upon the gentleman when he was asleep and asked him to go to Umar and ...."

Sh: This is also very interesting.

Dr: Yes, so we did have pleading at the time of the Caliphas. Even though we believe that the Prophet's state is the same dead or alive.

Sh: That is correct. In Alazhar this kind of pleading is acceptable after death but I am educated from Saudi Arabia and accept these things rarely. In Egypt this is completely acceptable.

Dr: In the Quran, Surat Al Maidah "وابتغو اليه الوسيله" it says use means of nearness to God as that is the meaning of pleading.

Pleading to Imam Bukhari's Grave

Sh: I accept, having said that I did not initially have any problem with pleading.

Dr: Dear Sheikh, this was regarding the Prophet's grave. Come and read about the Sunni Muslims that lived in Samarkand many years ago regarding Ibn Teymiyah and the way he thought even though this was practiced many other places too.

Sh: Please go ahead.

Dr: Pleading to Imam Bukhari's grave in Khartang Samarkand.

Sh: This should be interesting.

Dr: Look here in Siyar E'lam Nabala section 12, page 469, Tarikh Al Islam Zahabi section 19, page 273 and in Tabaghat Al Shafiah Al Kobra section 2, page 234 cites:

قال أبو علي الغساني: أخبرنا أبو الفتح نصر بن الحسن السكتي السمرقندي: قدم علينا بلنسيةْ عام أربعةْ وستين وأربع " مئةْ.

قال: قحط المطر عندنا بسمرقند في بعض الاعوام، فاستسقى الناس مرارا، فلم يسقوا.

فأتى رجل صالح معروف بالصلاح إلى قاضي سمرقند، فقال له: إني رأيت رأيا أعرضه عليك.

قال: وما هو ؟ قال: أرى أن تخرج ويخرج الناس معك إلى قبر الامام محمد بن إسماعيل البخاري، وقبره بخرتنك، ونستسقي عنده، فعسى الله أن يسقينا.

قال: فقال القاضي: نعم ما رأيت.

فخرج القاضي والناس معه، واستسقى القاضي بالناس، وبكى الناس عند القبر، وتشفعوا بصاحبه، فأرسل الله تعالى السماء بماء عظيم غزير، أقام الناس من أجله بخرتنك سبعةْ أيام أو نحوها، لا يستطيع أحد الوصول إلى سمرقند من كثرةْ المطر وغزارته، وبين "خرتنك وسمرقند نحو ثلاثةْ أميال

"Abu Ali Ghassani says that Abulfath Nasr has information from Hassan Sakti Samarkandi that lived in year 1085. He said: in Samarkand in some of the years there would be shortage of rain. People would request for rain but it wouldn't rain. An honorable man that was very well known came to the judge of Samarkand and said: I have a suggestion for you. The judge said: what is your suggestion? He replied my suggestion is for you to exit the city with the people and head towards the Grave of Imam Muhammad Ibn Ismail Bukhari. His grave is in the city of Kartang we can go there and plead for rain by his grave and God willing rain will come."

The judge accepted, and therefore the judge gathered the people and exited the city and pleaded for rain and cried at Imam Bukhari's grave and asked for intercession. Then God sent rain upon them. There was so much rain that people had to stay in Kartang for eight days before they were able to return to Samarkand even though the distance was not more than three miles."

Sh: This was very interesting that they pleaded to Bukhari's grave, and it mentions the word intercession.

Dr: If you pay attention to your books there are many similar quotes.

Sh: I think that it is sufficient. Let's move on to another debate.

Suddenly Sheikh paid attention to two books on the table in front of him and asked:

Supplication in Shia'sm

Sh: What is this book of Mafatih Al Jinan?

Dr: One of our scholars that have been dead for a very long time has gathered all of the supplications that the Prophet and the Ahl al Bayt have recommended us to read in one book and has called it Mafatih Al Jinan.

Sh: Yes, I had heard of it before but had never seen it. You have much respect for the book. They say that even as much as the Quran or even more.

Dr: Yes, we have high respect for the book but not as much as the Quran. We consider the Quran to be the word of God and so we say if you wish to have God talk to you read the Quran and if you want to to speak with God read the supplication.

Sh: We have prayers too but not to the extent like this book.

Dr: This book contains parts of the supplications that we read every year. We do have other books too. For instance, we have another book called Sahifa Sajjadiya that has an exciting supplication in it.

Sh: Do you mean that people read these supplications daily?

Dr: Not every day. However, some parts can be read on some days and others on other days. Mostly they are for specific days or occasions. For instance, some supplications are for when you have finished reading the daily prayers. Some of the supplications are for Friday nights, some for days and some for nights of different occasions such as Rajab, Shaban, Ramadan or special days like Arafa.

Sh: Which one do you personally read?

Dr: I also read some of the supplications written in here but there some, in particular, that is very moving.

Sh: Please show me. I wish to see those parts.

Dr: Sure, here you go. For instance, there is a supplication called Kumeyl that Ali taught Kumeyl:

اللَّهُمَّ اغْفِرْ لِيَ الذُّنُوبَ الَّتِي تَهْتِكُ الْعِصَمَ

اللَّهُمَّ اغْفِرْ لِيَ الذُّنُوبَ الَّتِي تُنْزِلُ النِّقَمَ

اللَّهُمَّ اغْفِرْ لِيَ الذُّنُوبَ الَّتِي تُغَيِّرُ النِّعَمَ

اللَّهُمَّ اغْفِرْ لِيَ الذُّنُوبَ الَّتِي تَحْبِسُ الدُّعَاءَ

اللَّهُمَّ اغْفِرْ لِي كُلَّ ذَنْبٍ أَذْنَبْتُهُ وَكُلَّ خَطِيئَةٍ أَخْطَأْتُهَا

اللَّهُمَّ إِنِّي أَتَقَرَّبُ إِلَيْكَ بِذِكْرِكَ وَأَسْتَشْفِعُ بِكَ إِلَى نَفْسِكَ

وَ أَسْأَلُكَ بِجُودِكَ أَنْ تُدْنِيَنِي مِنْ قُرْبِكَ وَ أَنْ تُوزِعَنِي شُكْرَكَ وَ أَنْ تُلْهِمَنِي ذِكْرَكَ

اللَّهُمَّ إِنِّي أَسْأَلُكَ سُؤَالَ خَاضِعٍ مُتَذَلِّلٍ خَاشِعٍ

أَنْ تُسَامِحَنِي وتَرْحَمَنِي وتَجْعَلَنِي بِقِسْمِكَ رَاضِياً قَانِعاً وَ فِي جَمِيعِ الأَحْوَالِ مُتَوَاضِعاً

"O Allah! Forgive me my such sins as would affront my continence O Allah! Forgive me my such sins as would bring down calamity

O Allah! Forgive me my such sins as would change divine favours (into disfavours) O Allah! Forgive me my such sins as would hinder my supplication

O Allah! Forgive me such sins as bring down misfortunes (or afflictions) O Allah! Forgive my such sins as would suppress hope

O Allah! Forgive every sin that I have committed and every error that I have erred O Allah! I endeavour to draw myself nigh to Thee through Thy invocation And I pray to Thee to intercede on my behalf And I entreat Thee by Thy benevolence to draw me nearer to Thee And grant me that I should be grateful to Thee and inspire me to remember and to invoke Thee

O Allah! I entreat Thee begging Thee submissively, humbly and awestricken to treat me with clemency and mercy, and to make me pleased and contented with what Thou hast allotted to me and cause me to be modest and unassuming in all circumstances"

Sh: This is so interesting, very interesting. This shows the different kind of sins that we have.

Dr: Yes, please have a look at this too. There is a prayer in the name of "Monajat Shabaniyah" that is read mostly in the month of Shaaban.

واسْمَعْ دُعَائِي إِذَا دَعَوْتُكَ واسْمَعْ نِدَائِي إِذَا نَادَيْتُكَ

وأَقْبِلْ عَلَيَّ إِذَا نَاجَيْتُكَ فَقَدْ هَرَبْتُ إِلَيْكَ ووَقَفْتُ بَيْنَ يَدَيْكَ مُسْتَكِيناً لَكَ مُتَضَرِّعاً إِلَيْكَ

رَاجِياً لِمَا لَدَيْكَ ثَوَابِي وتَعْلَمُ مَا فِي نَفْسِي وتَخْبُرُ حَاجَتِي وَ تَعْرِفُ ضَمِيرِي

وَ لاَ يَخْفَى عَلَيْكَ أَمْرُ مُنْقَلَبِي وَ مَثْوَايَ

وَمَا أُرِيدُ أَنْ أُبْدِئَ بِهِ مِنْ مَنْطِقِي وأَتَفَوَّهَ بِهِ مِنْ طَلِبَتِي وَ أَرْجُوهُ لِعَاقِبَتِي

وقَدْ جَرَتْ مَقَادِيرُكَ عَلَيَّ يَا سَيِّدِي فِيمَا يَكُونُ مِنِّي إِلَى آخِرِ عُمْرِي

مِنْ سَرِيرَتِي وعَلاَنِيَتِي وبِيَدِكَ لاَ بِيَدِ غَيْرِكَ زِيَادَتِي وَ نَقْصِي وَ نَفْعِي وَ ضَرِّي

The Doctor & Sheikh's Debate

In the Name of Allah, the most Beneficent, the most Merciful

My Lord, bestow Your blessings on Muhammad and his descendants; respond to my prayer when I pray to You; listen to my call when I call You; and turn to me when I make my submission to You in confidence. I have come running to you and am standing before you imploring you in humility and hoping to get the reward you have for me. You know what is in my heart, and you are aware of what I need. You know my mind and are not unaware of my future and of my present, of what I want to begin my speech with; of the request I would utter, and of the hopes I have in regard to my ultimate lot.

My Lord, whatever you have destined for me up to the end of my life, whether concerning the open aspect of my life or the hidden aspect of it, is bound to come. What is to my advantage and what is to my disadvantage - all my losses and gains are in your hand, not in the hand of anybody else.

My Lord, if you deprive me, who else will provide me; and if you let me down, whom else will help me?[1]

Sh: This is the most perfect divine unity.

Dr: You are precisely correct.

Sh: So, they say that you believe that everything is in the hands of the Imams

Dr: We have retrieved these prayers from the Imams themselves. We place the Imams as mediator of emanation in the presence of God.

Sh: Which are the prayers that you personally read?

Dr: The morning supplication which is non-compulsory to be read after the compulsory Morning Prayer. Please look at these:

إِلَهِي إِنْ لَمْ تَبْتَدِئْنِي الرَّحْمَةُ مِنْكَ بِحُسْنِ التَّوْفِيقِ فَمَنِ السَّالِكُ بِي إِلَيْكَ فِي وَاضِحِ الطَّرِيقِ

وَ إِنْ أَسْلَمَتْنِي أَنَاتُكَ لِقَائِدِ الْأَمَلِ وَ الْمُنَى فَمَنِ الْمُقِيلُ عَثَرَاتِي مِنْ كَبَوَاتِ الْهَوَى

وَ إِنْ خَذَلَنِي نَصْرُكَ عِنْدَ مُحَارَبَةِ النَّفْسِ وَ الشَّيْطَانِ فَقَدْ وَكَلَنِي خِذْلَانُكَ إِلَى حَيْثُ النَّصَبُ وَ الْحِرْمَانُ

إِلَهِي أَ تَرَانِي مَا أَتَيْتُكَ إِلَّا مِنْ حَيْثُ الْآمَالُ أَمْ عَلِقْتُ بِأَطْرَافِ حِبَالِكَ إِلَّا حِينَ بَاعَدَتْنِي ذُنُوبِي عَنْ دَارِ

1- Abbas Qummi.

(صِرْبَهْ) الْوِصَالِ

* * *

فَبِئْسَ الْمَطِيَّةُ الَّتِي امْتَطَتْ نَفْسِي مِنْ هَوَاهَا فَوَاهاً لَهَا لِمَا سَوَّلَتْ لَهَا ظُنُونُهَا وَ مُنَاهَا وَ تَبّاً لَهَا لِجُرْأَتِهَا عَلَى سَيِّدِهَا وَ مَوْلَاهَا

إِلَهِي قَرَعْتُ بَابَ رَحْمَتِكَ بِيَدِ رَجَائِي وَ هَرَبْتُ إِلَيْكَ لَاجِئاً مِنْ فَرْطِ أَهْوَائِي وَ عَلَّقْتُ بِأَطْرَافِ حِبَالِكَ أَنَامِلَ وَلَائِي

If Thy deliberateness would turn me over to the guide of hope and wishes, then who will annul my slips from the stumbles of caprice? If Thy deliberateness should turn me over to the guide of hope and wishes, then who will annul my slips from the stumbles of caprice? If Thy help should forsake me in the battle with the soul and Satan, then Thy forsaking will have entrusted me to where there is hardship and deprivation. My God, does Thou see that I have only come to Thee from the direction of hopes or clung to the ends of Thy cords when my sins have driven me from the house of union?

So, what an evil mount upon which my soul has mounted - its caprice! Woe upon it for being seduced by its own opinions and wishes! And destruction be upon it for its audacity toward its Master and Protector! My God, I have knocked upon the door of Thy mercy with the hand of my hope, fled to Thee seeking refuge from my excessive caprice and fixed the fingers of my love to the ends of Thy cords [2]

Sh: This supplication is also recommended by Ali

Dr: Yes.

Sh: How come these supplications are not mentioned in any of our books?

Dr: Unfortunately, there are very few supplications in your books. Please pay attention to the excerpt here. This is the one that Ali Ibn Hussein has taught to Abu Hamza Thumali:

بِكَ عَرَفْتُكَ وَ أَنْتَ دَلَلْتَنِي عَلَيْكَ وَ دَعَوْتَنِي إِلَيْكَ وَ لَوْ لَا أَنْتَ لَمْ أَدْرِ مَا أَنْتَ

"Through you have I know you And You guided me to you and called me towards you, if it were not for you, I would not have known what you are"

الْحَمْدُ لِلَّهِ الَّذِي أَدْعُوهُ فَيُجِيبُنِي وَإِنْ كُنْتُ بَطِيئاً حِينَ يَدْعُونِي

---

[2] Abbas Qummi.

The Doctor & Sheikh's Debate

"All praise is due to Allah, upon whom I call, and He responds to me, even though I am slow (in responding) when He calls on me"

والْحَمْدُ لِلَّهِ الَّذِي أَسْأَلُهُ فَيُعْطِينِي وَإِنْ كُنْتُ بَخِيلاً حِينَ يَسْتَقْرِضُنِي

"All praise is due to Allah, whom I ask, and He gives me, even though I am stingy when He asks me (to give for the sake of God)"

والْحَمْدُ لِلَّهِ الَّذِي أُنَادِيهِ كُلَّمَا شِئْتُ لِحَاجَتِي وأَخْلُو بِهِ حَيْثُ شِئْتُ لِسِرِّي بِغَيْرِ شَفِيعٍ فَيَقْضِي لِي حَاجَتِي

"All praise is due to Allah, upon whom I call for my needs whenever I wish, and with whom I converse in confidence whenever I want, without any intercessor, and he grants my need"

والْحَمْدُ لِلَّهِ الَّذِي لاَ أَدْعُو غَيْرَهُ ولَوْ دَعَوْتُ غَيْرَهُ لَمْ يَسْتَجِبْ لِي دُعَائِي

"All praise is due to Allah - I do not call on other than Him, and if called on other than He, they would not answer my prayers"

Sh: These supplications are a testament to completed unification of God.

Dr: But your friends, in Al Masjid an Nabawi and in Masjid al Haram consider us as gentiles because of reading these prayers and calling for God.

Sh: We seek refuge in God (Naouza Bellah), these are higher than the honor of martyrs.

Dr: Yes, but unfortunately the officials responsible for spreading the word of Islam in Masjid an Nabawi and Masjid al Haram without even looking at these supplications accuse us readers as infidels.

Dr: Please look at these passages:

وَ مَا أَنَا يَا رَبِّ وَ مَا خَطَرِي هَبْنِي بِفَضْلِكَ وَ تَصَدَّقْ عَلَيَّ بِعَفْوِكَ

"What am I? O Lord! What important do I have? Grant me through Your benevolence, and be charitable to me by means of Your pardon"

أَيْ رَبِّ جَلِّلْنِي بِسَتْرِكَ واعْفُ عَنْ تَوْبِيخِي بِكَرَمِ وَجْهِكَ

"O My Lord! Cover me with your protective covering, and pardon me from reproach, by the Honour of Your Face"

فَلَوِ اطَّلَعَ الْيَوْمَ عَلَى ذَنْبِي غَيْرُكَ مَا فَعَلْتُهُ وَ لَوْ خِفْتُ تَعْجِيلَ الْعُقُوبَةِ لاَجْتَنَبْتُهُ

"For anyone other than You was aware of my sin today, I would not have performed it, And if Had I anticipated a quick punishment, I would have avoided it"

لَا لِأَنَّكَ أَهْوَنُ النَّاظِرِينَ (إِلَيَّ) وَ أَخَفُّ الْمُطَّلِعِينَ (عَلَيَّ)

"Not because You are the least important of those who watch over me, or because You are the least weighty of those who observe me"

بَلْ لِأَنَّكَ يَا رَبِّ خَيْرُ السَّاتِرِينَ وَ أَحْكَمُ الْحَاكِمِينَ (وَ أَحْلَمُ الْأَحْلَمِينَ) وَ أَكْرَمُ الْأَكْرَمِينَ

"But because You, O my Lord, are the Best Concealer, The Most Wise, The Most Generous"

سَتَّارُ الْعُيُوبِ غَفَّارُ الذُّنُوبِ عَلَّامُ الْغُيُوبِ تَسْتُرُ الذَّنْبَ بِكَرَمِكَ وَ تُؤَخِّرُ الْعُقُوبَةْ بِحِلْمِكَ

"The Concealer of defects, the Forgiver of sins, the Knower of the unseen, you conceal the sin out of Your Magnanimity and put off punishment out of Your Forbearance"

Sh: I am astonished by all the arguments it has brought for God. This supplication answered my forty years question that why do we not sin in front of a five-year-old innocent child. However, if no one would be not around, we would not consider that God is still there with us. However, this supplication says that if I sin when you are about is because you are my covering star.

Dr: Please see this passage too.

اللَّهُمَّ إِنِّي كُلَّمَا قُلْتُ قَدْ تَهَيَّأْتُ وَ تَعَبَّأْتُ (تَعَبَّيْتُ) وَ قُمْتُ لِلصَّلَاةْ بَيْنَ يَدَيْكَ

"O Lord! I, whenever I thought I was prepared and ready and rose to pray before you and called upon you"

وَنَاجَيْتُكَ أَلْقَيْتَ عَلَيَّ نُعَاساً إِذَا أَنَا صَلَّيْتُ وَسَلَبْتَنِي مُنَاجَاتَكَ إِذَا أَنَا نَاجَيْتُ

"You cast a sleepiness on me as I prayed and denied me (the opportunity) of conversing with You as I called upon You"

مَا لِي كُلَّمَا قُلْتُ قَدْ صَلَحَتْ سَرِيرَتِي وَ قَرُبَ مِنْ مَجَالِسِ التَّوَّابِينَ مَجْلِسِي

"What is the wrong with me? Whenever I think that my soul has become righteous, and my gatherings are close to the gatherings of the repentant"

عَرَضَتْ لِي بَلِيَّةٌ أَزَالَتْ قَدَمِي وَحَالَتْ بَيْنِي وَ بَيْنَ خِدْمَتِكَ

"A misfortune would befall me, making me stumble, and forming a barrier between me and your service"

سَيِّدِي لَعَلَّكَ عَنْ بَابِكَ طَرَدْتَنِي وَ عَنْ خِدْمَتِكَ نَحَّيْتَنِي أَوْ لَعَلَّكَ رَأَيْتَنِي مُسْتَخِفّاً بِحَقِّكَ فَأَقْصَيْتَنِي

"My Seyed, perhaps You have turned me away from Your Door, and You have cast me aside from Your service, Perhaps You found me taking your right upon me lightly, so you cast me aside, or perhaps you saw me turning away from You and so You turned away from me"

أَوْ لَعَلَّكَ رَأَيْتَنِي مُعْرِضاً عَنْكَ فَقَلَيْتَنِي أَوْ لَعَلَّكَ وَجَدْتَنِي فِي مَقَامِ الْكَاذِبِينَ (الْكَذَّابِينَ) فَرَفَضْتَنِي

"Or perhaps You saw me ungrateful for Your belssings so You deprived me"

أَوْ لَعَلَّكَ رَأَيْتَنِي غَيْرَ شَاكِرٍ لِنَعْمَائِكَ فَحَرَمْتَنِي أَوْ لَعَلَّكَ فَقَدْتَنِي مِنْ مَجَالِسِ الْعُلَمَاءِ فَخَذَلْتَنِي

"Or perhaps You saw me missing from the gatherings of the scholars and so You humiliated me"

أَوْ لَعَلَّكَ رَأَيْتَنِي فِي الْغَافِلِينَ فَمِنْ رَحْمَتِكَ آيَسْتَنِي

"Or perhaps You saw me among the oblivious, so You made me despair of Your Mercy"

أَوْ لَعَلَّكَ رَأَيْتَنِي آلِفَ مَجَالِسِ الْبَطَّالِينَ فَبَيْنِي وَ بَيْنَهُمْ خَلَّيْتَنِي أَوْ لَعَلَّكَ لَمْ تُحِبَّ أَنْ تَسْمَعَ دُعَائِي فَبَاعَدْتَنِي

"Or perhaps you saw me comfortable in the gatherings of the promoters of falsehood so you let me be, among them, or perhaps you did not like to hear my supplications, so you distanced me"

أَوْ لَعَلَّكَ بِجُرْمِي وجَرِيرَتِي كَافَيْتَنِي أَوْ لَعَلَّكَ بِقِلَّةِ حَيَائِي مِنْكَ جَازَيْتَنِي

"Or perhaps you have recompensed me for my sins and transgressions, or perhaps you have recompensed me for my lack of shyness before you"

فَإِنْ عَفَوْتَ يَا رَبِّ فَطَالَمَا عَفَوْتَ عَنِ الْمُذْنِبِينَ قَبْلِي لِأَنَّ كَرَمَكَ أَيْ رَبِّ يَجِلُّ عَنْ مُكَافَاةِ الْمُقَصِّرِينَ

"If you forgive me, O Lord, then you have forgiven sinners like me for a long time, because your magnanimity, My Lord, is too Exalted than to recompense those with shortcomings"

Sh: This teaches you the understanding of one's sins specifically the ones that we don't even consider to be sins. This prayer is very good for the Arabian people living in Arab countries. This makes them aware as they run away from scholars they get to know that it is a sin and that God does not permit them to his door because of it. I sincerely enjoyed this. Please tell me if there is any other passage that you would like me to know about.

Dr: Please have a look at another argument made:

وَ إِنْ كُنْتَ لاَ تُكْرِمُ إِلاَّ أَهْلَ الْوَفَاءِ بِكَ فَبِمَنْ يَسْتَغِيثُ الْمُسِيئُونَ

"If You honour none but those who loyal to You, then whose shelter will the evildoers seek?"

إِلَهِي إِنْ أَدْخَلْتَنِي النَّارَ فَفِي ذَلِكَ سُرُورُ عَدُوِّكَ وَإِنْ أَدْخَلْتَنِي الْجَنَّةَ فَفِي ذَلِكَ سُرُورُ نَبِيِّكَ

"My Lord, If You make me to enter the Hell- Fire, in this is the happiness of Your Prophet"

وأَنَا واللَّهِ أَعْلَمُ أَنَّ سُرُورَ نَبِيِّكَ أَحَبُّ إِلَيْكَ مِنْ سُرُورِ عَدُوِّكَ

"And I take an oath by Allah, that I know that the happiness of Your Prophet is more beloved to You than the happiness of Your enemy"

Sh: These supplications position God in a way that he would open his forgiveness to the prayer and puts him on the spot. He would never grant the happiness of Satan and would make his Prophet pleased instead.

Dr: This is a very interesting supplication from the father of Imam Sajad whom is Imam Hussein in the name of Arafa

Sh: Hang on where is that?

Dr: This is the prayer that Imam Hussein Ibn Ali read on the day of Arafa

أَنْتَ الَّذِي مَنَنْتَ أَنْتَ الَّذِي أَنْعَمْتَ أَنْتَ الَّذِي أَحْسَنْتَ أَنْتَ الَّذِي أَجْمَلْتَ

"You are He who was gracious, You are He who blessed, You are He who did good, You are He who was kind,'

أَنْتَ الَّذِي أَفْضَلْتَ أَنْتَ الَّذِي أَكْمَلْتَ أَنْتَ الَّذِي رَزَقْتَ أَنْتَ الَّذِي وَفَّقْتَ

"You are He who was bounteous, you are He who perfected, you are He who provided, you are He who gave success"

أَنْتَ الَّذِي أَعْطَيْتَ أَنْتَ الَّذِي أَغْنَيْتَ أَنْتَ الَّذِي أَقْنَيْتَ أَنْتَ الَّذِي آوَيْتَ أَنْتَ الَّذِي كَفَيْتَ

The Doctor & Sheikh's Debate

"You are He who bestowed, you are He who enriched, you are He who contented, you are He who sheltered, you are He who sufficed"

أَنْتَ الَّذِي هَدَيْتَ أَنْتَ الَّذِي عَصَمْتَ أَنْتَ الَّذِي سَتَرْتَ أَنْتَ الَّذِي غَفَرْتَ

"You are He who guided, you are He who preserved (from sin), you are He who covered (my sins), you are He who forgave"

أَنْتَ الَّذِي أَقَلْتَ أَنْتَ الَّذِي مَكَّنْتَ أَنْتَ الَّذِي أَعْزَزْتَ أَنْتَ الَّذِي أَعَنْتَ

"You are He who overlooked, You are He who established (in the earth), You are He who exalted, You are He who aided"

أَنْتَ الَّذِي عَضَدْتَ أَنْتَ الَّذِي أَيَّدْتَ أَنْتَ الَّذِي نَصَرْتَ أَنْتَ الَّذِي شَفَيْتَ

"You are He who supported, You are He who confirmed, You are He who helped, You are He who healed"

أَنْتَ الَّذِي عَافَيْتَ أَنْتَ الَّذِي أَكْرَمْتَ تَبَارَكْتَ وَ تَعَالَيْتَ

"You are He who gave well being, You art He who honoured, Blessed and Exalted are You"

فَلَكَ الْحَمْدُ دَائِماً وَ لَكَ الشُّكْرُ وَاصِباً أَبَداً

"So, to You belongs the praise everlastingly"

ثُمَّ أَنَا يَا إِلَهِي الْمُعْتَرِفُ بِذُنُوبِي فَاغْفِرْهَا لِي

"Then I, my Lord, am the one confessing my sins, so forgive them for me"

أَنَا الَّذِي أَسَأْتُ أَنَا الَّذِي أَخْطَأْتُ أَنَا الَّذِي هَمَمْتُ أَنَا الَّذِي جَهِلْتُ أَنَا الَّذِي غَفَلْتُ

"I am he who did evil, I am he who made mistakes, I am he who purposed (to sin), I am he who was ignorant, I am he who was heedless"

أَنَا الَّذِي سَهَوْتُ أَنَا الَّذِي اعْتَمَدْتُ أَنَا الَّذِي تَعَمَّدْتُ أَنَا الَّذِي وَعَدْتُ

"I am he who was negligent, I am he who relied (upon other than you) I am he who premeditated, I am he who promised"

وَأَنَا الَّذِي أَخْلَفْتُ أَنَا الَّذِي نَكَثْتُ أَنَا الَّذِي أَقْرَرْتُ أَنَا الَّذِي اعْتَرَفْتُ بِنِعْمَتِكَ عَلَيَّ وَعِنْدِي وَأَبُوءُ بِذُنُوبِي

"And I am the one who went back on his promise, I am he who broke my allegiance, and I am he who acknowledged Your blessings upon me and with me, and then returned to my sins, so forgive me for them"

فَاغْفِرْهَا لِي يَا مَنْ لاَ تَضُرُّهُ ذُنُوبُ عِبَادِهِ وهُوَ الْغَنِيُّ عَنْ طَاعَتِهِمْ

"O He who is not harmed by the sins of His servants, and is Needless of their obedience"

Sh: This is supplication from Hussein Ibn Ali.

Dr: Yes, please look. The youth, scholars, and Muslim university educators should be aware of these passages of supplication.

Tears came from Sheikh's eyes, and he tried to hide them. As he dried them, he said, If Hussein Ibn Ali says these things to the Lord then what should we be saying. Now I understand why in the Prophet's shrine and in Masjid an Nabawi people have this book in their hands and are reading it.

Dr: These are just parts of the supplications. Please look at this passage from the supplication.

إِلَهِي أَغْنِنِي بِتَدْبِيرِكَ لِي عَنْ تَدْبِيرِي وبِاخْتِيَارِكَ عَنِ اخْتِيَارِي وَ أَوْقِفْنِي عَلَى مَرَاكِزِ اضْطِرَارِي

"My Lord, make me needless of my plans for me through Your plans for me, (and make me needless) of my choices for myself through Your choices for me, and make me stop at the points of emergency"

إِلَهِي أَخْرِجْنِي مِنْ ذُلِّ نَفْسِي وَ طَهِّرْنِي مِنْ شَكِّي وَ شِرْكِي قَبْلَ حُلُولِ رَمْسِي

"My Lord, free me from the degradation of myself, and purify me from my doubt and polytheism, Before the time of my death"

Sh: This teaches you theology and knowledge about yourself. God is greatest! God is greatest!

Dr: Please look at this Sahifa Sajjadiya. Look at the supplications in them. Just look at this part of the supplications named: "Makarem al-Akhlaq"

وَ اجْعَلْ يَقِينِي أَفْضَلَ الْيَقِينِ وَ انْتَهِ بِنِيَّتِي إِلَى أَحْسَنِ النِّيَّاتِ وَ بِعَمَلِي إِلَى أَحْسَنِ الْأَعْمَالِ

"Make my certainty the excellent certainty and take my intention to the best of intentions and my works to the best of works!"

اَللَّهُمَّ وَفِّرْ بِلُطْفِكَ نِيَّتِي وَ صَحِّحْ بِمَا عِنْدَكَ يَقِينِي وَ اسْتَصْلِحْ بِقُدْرَتِكَ مَا فَسَدَ مِنِّي

The Doctor & Sheikh's Debate

"O God, complete my intention through Thy gentleness, rectify my certainty through what is with Thee, and set right what is corrupt in me through what is with Thee and set right what is corrupt in me through Thy power!"

اَللَّهُمَّ صَلِّ عَلَى مُحَمَّدٍ وَ آلِهِ

"O God, bless Muhammad and his Household"

وَ اكْفِنِي مَا يَشْغَلُنِي الِاهْتِمَامُ بِهِ وَ اسْتَعْمِلْنِي بِمَا تَسْأَلُنِي غَداً عَنْهُ وَ اسْتَفْرِغْ أَيَّامِي فِيمَا خَلَقْتَنِي لَهُ

"Spare me the concerns which distract me, employ me in that about which Thou wilt ask me tomorrow, and let me pass my days in that for which Thou hast created me!"

وَ أَغْنِنِي وَ أَوْسِعْ عَلَيَّ فِي رِزْقِكَ وَ لاَ تَفْتِنِّي بِالنَّظَرِ وَ أَعِزَّنِي وَ لاَ تَبْتَلِيَنِّي بِالْكِبْرِ

"Free me from need, expand Thy ordinance toward me, and tempt me not with ingratitude exalt me and afflict me not with pride!"

وَعَبِّدْنِي لَكَ وَ لاَ تُفْسِدْ عِبَادَتِي بِالْعُجْبِ

"Make me worship Thee and corrupt not my worship with self-admiration!"

وَأَجْرِ لِلنَّاسِ عَلَى يَدِيَ الْخَيْرَ وَ لاَ تَمْحَقْهُ بِالْمَنِّ وَ هَبْ لِي مَعَالِيَ الْأَخْلاَقِ وَ اعْصِمْنِي مِنَ الْفَخْرِ

"Let good flow out from my hands upon the people and efface it not by my making them feel obliged, Give me the highest moral traits and preserve me from vain glory"

اَللَّهُمَّ صَلِّ عَلَى مُحَمَّدٍ وَآلِهِ وَ لاَ تَرْفَعْنِي فِي النَّاسِ دَرَجَةً إِلاَّ حَطَطْتَنِي عِنْدَ نَفْسِي مِثْلَهَا

"O God, bless Muhammad and his Household, raise me not a single degrees before the people, without lowering me its like in myself"

وَ لاَ تُحْدِثْ لِي عِزّاً ظَاهِراً إِلاَّ أَحْدَثْتَ لِي ذِلَّةً بَاطِنَةً عِنْدَ نَفْسِي بِقَدَرِهَا

"Without an inward abasement in myself to the same measure!"

Sh: Doctor is this supplication or Psychology? Indeed, God knows where to place his words. These supplications are like oceans of cognition. Doctor, may I take this book of Mafatih and Sahifa Sajjadiya?

Dr: Sure, you can take them, however, please pay attention to one thing, and that is Sahifa Sajjadiya contains many exciting and enjoyable supplications, but in the Mafatih there is a chance that you come upon cases that people have never even once read in their entire lifetime. Moreover, these supplications might not be your taste, and you may not like them. Therefore, I suggest you take the selected version of the book of Mafatih, which would be more suited for you.

Sh: But I wish to view all of the supplications.

Dr: With knowing that you have limited time, it would be ideal for taking the selected book of the supplication.

There are No Imprecations upon the Caliphas

Sh: These supplications that you showed me are an indication of speaking to God, but I have heard that in the book of Mafatih, there are imprecations towards to the Caliphas and cursing towards them too.

D: Is that why you wanted to take this book away with you?

Sh: No, No, but do you have any explanation about that?

Dr: Yes, firstly we do not have direct imprecations towards any Caliphas unless those that was cursed by the Calipha themselves.

Sh: That must class Muawiyah as Ali had cursed him.

Dr: Yes, and unfortunately this had become a common doing as based on the history cited, once a congregational Imam forgot to curse imprecate Ali and once he remembered he stopped in the middle of his way and instead sent 100 imprecations towards him and where he stood was later made as a Mosque. It is a Mosque for imprecations. Therefore, cursing Muawiyah is commonly known and is being done as he called for the Caliphas to be done so. We also have one thing from all the Muawiyah's sayings, and that is to imprecate him as that was his wish. I have to add that those who killed the Prophet's daughter and martyred her as are also among the cursed people.

Sh: But they have said: they have also imprecated the Calipha too.

Dr: There is a part where they might have thought that it was referred to them but it isn't. That is the supplication for Ashura that says:

"اللهم العن اول ظالم ظلم حق محمد وآل محمد"

"Then the second, third and forth are mentioned and then Yazid is named. Some say that the three named are the three Caliphas and the fourth is Muawiyah."

The Doctor & Sheikh's Debate

Sh: Well, this is bad to insult the Caliphas that are honorable and respected by Muslims.

Dr: not us.

Sh: Well, everyone knows this to be false. No one names their son after Muawiyah.

Dr: This is entirely correct, and that's why we do not curse the Caliphas.

Sh: So, what is meant but the first, second, and third then?

Dr: We do not know who is meant for in particular even although based on many of the scholar's opinions this part accompanying the part where the blessings are sent before that is deemed to be not as part of the original supplication.

Sh: Then how come has it been written in this book.

Dr: The versions of supplications are different. The book of Mafatih has brought the latest of the translations.

Sh: Then, why do you write them up and recite them?

Dr: Because it doesn't say whom. It is not clear who is meant by them. What difference does it make if we say that it is meant for the first Calipha and then Forth for Muawiyah? We are cursing him in the open there is no reason why should we do that is hidden. However, this passage has been added regarding people that did injustice to the Ahl al Bayt.

Sh: They should remove it from the supplications to prevent sensitiveness towards the matter.

Dr: I am not in charge of publishing for the country, but the question remains how come Muawiyah was able to curse Ali, and that was not removed even though his imprecation was in daylight, bright and in public.

Sh: We say that Muawiyah made a mistake, and that is about the past.

Dr: Very well, let's discuss the current situation. Please stop the police around Masjid Al Haram and around the Prophet's shrine that is naming Muslims in specific the Shias as infidels in the open. Whenever they stop openly calling us infidels, then we will advise them not to read these passages loudly.

Sh: These things are not under my control.

Dr: Are the authority of the publishers under my control so that I could ask them to remove this part of the book that is not even clear to be insulting anyone in particular or are people under my control to ask of them not to read it?

Sh: Then we are both the same in being unable to prevent people from doing these things.

Dr: Yes, but there is one difference, and that is this. You are unable to prevent something that is publicly unlawful, and that is to call a Muslim to be an infidel, but I am helpless in preventing a matter that is unclear to be of any sin.

Sh: But let me make something known regarding Shias being any different to other Muslims. This is what the Wahabis are doing in the Islamic world, and it is not a representative of what other religious schools believe in or follow. By the way, it is getting late, and I need to leave. Which book shall I take in the end?

Dr: Take the Sahifa Sajjadiya and the selected version of the Mafatih Al Jinan, so there is no sensitiveness in the hotel you are staying at. If there is no doubt in raising any sensitiveness, then you can take the full book if you wish.

Sh: Very well, then God willing I will see you after the Zuhr prayer tomorrow, and we will go to my hotel.

Dr: Don't you think that there is much more convenient? This is because I have this application on my mobile, and I will not be causing the rest of the travelers any sensitiveness. The other reason is if we sit and discuss where they might want to intrude and involve themselves in our discussion as they are Arabs and know how to speak Arabic.

Sh: But this way, I would be a burden on you every day.

Dr: We have an expression in Farsi that we say we are not a burden you are a delight.

Sh: Then, we shall meet again tomorrow after the Zuhr's prayer in front of the Door of Gabriel.

Dr: Good willing.

Sheikh left taking with him some pistachio, Persian sweets and the two books. I began to get ready to sleep before the Maghrib prayer, although Mr. Karbalyi and Ghargham were back from the shrine and were hardly going to let me do that.

The Doctor & Sheikh's Debate

After resting for a while, I got ready for the Maghrib prayer. I went to the Mosque. Sheikh was sitting with a distance from me. I rose to read the pilgrimage for the Prophet as I faced towards the chamber an Officer came close to me and said, Close the book, stand towards the Qibla and not the chamber. I replied I am doing this based on Ahmad and Malik and Shafia Fatwa's order). The Officer said: They do not say this. I replied, yes, they do. The book of Ibn Taymiyyah (Which is the gathering of all Fatwas) has even sited it. He replied that you are a liar. There is no such thing. I answered you are mistaken because I have proof. He said it does not exist. He began cursing and imprecating me. At this moment, Sheikh Ibrahim rose and said, this person is telling the truth. The Officer said: Where are you from? Sheikh replied, From Egypt. The Officer said: Have you seen it with your own eyes stating that you can pray to face the chamber? Sheikh replied, Yes, I have seen it myself. The Officer said, but they have told us to do such a thing is not allowed. This is a government order. Sheikh replied, yes, but there is no need to accuse someone of falsehood. It is allowed to read the Prophet's prayer while facing his shrine. I thanked the Sheikh and prepared myself to pray for the Maghrib prayer.

After the Maghrib prayer, I met a religious student from Oman, and we started talking. The student was from School of Medina. He said: What are you reading? I replied: I am reciting the supplications after the pray. He said: What are they? I responded: Firstly, chanting and then the supplications that are read after the pray. He asked: What do you say after the pray? I said: Firstly, we do chant: 34 times God is greatest, 33 times praise to God, 33 times Hallelujah (السبحان الله , السبحان, الحمدالله) and then I read many supplications for instance after the morning prayer we read:

بِسْمِ اللَّهِ وصَلَّي اللَّهُ عَلَى مُحَمَّدٍ وآلِهِ

وَ أُفَوِّضُ أَمْرِي إِلَى اللَّهِ إِنَّ اللَّهَ بَصِيرٌ بِالْعِبَادِ فَوَقَاهُ اللَّهُ سَيِّئَاتِ مَا مَكَرُوا

"In the Name of Allah, May Allah bless Muhammad and his Household, "I confide my cause to Allah" Surely; Allah is Seer of His slaves. So, Allah warded off from him the evils which they plotted"

لاَ إِلَهَ إِلاَّ أَنْتَ سُبْحَانَكَ إِنِّي كُنْتُ مِنَ الظَّالِمِينَ

"There is no God save You. Be You Glorified! Lord I have been a wrongdoer"

فَاسْتَجَبْنَا لَهُ ونَجَّيْنَاهُ مِنَ الْغَمِّ وكَذَلِكَ نُنْجِي الْمُؤْمِنِينَ

"Then, we heard his prayer and saved him from the anguish. Thus, do We save the believers"

حَسْبُنَا اللَّهُ ونِعْمَ الْوَكِيلُ فَانْقَلَبُوا بِنِعْمَةٍ مِنَ اللَّهِ وفَضْلٍ لَمْ يَمْسَسْهُمْ سُوءٌ

"Allah is Sufficient for us! Most Excellent is He in whom we trust. So, they returned with grace and favor from Allah, and no harm touched them."

مَا شَاءَ اللَّهُ لاَ حَوْلَ ولاَ قُوَّةَ إِلاَّ بِاللَّهِ

"There is neither strength nor power save with Allah"

مَا شَاءَ اللَّهُ لاَ مَا شَاءَ النَّاسُ

"Only that which Allah, but not people will shall come to pass"

مَا شَاءَ اللَّهُ وَ إِنْ كَرِهَ النَّاسُ

"Only that which Allah wills shall come to pass even if people detest it"

حَسْبِيَ الرَّبُّ مِنَ الْمَرْبُوبِينَ حَسْبِيَ الْخَالِقُ مِنَ الْمَخْلُوقِينَ

"Sufficient for me is the Lord against the Lorded; Sufficient for me is the Creator against the creatures"

حَسْبِيَ الرَّازِقُ مِنَ الْمَرْزُوقِينَ حَسْبِيَ اللَّهُ رَبُّ الْعَالَمِينَ

"Sufficient for me is Allah, the Lord of the Worlds"

حَسْبِي مَنْ هُوَ حَسْبِي حَسْبِي مَنْ لَمْ يَزَلْ حَسْبِي

"Sufficient for me He who is sufficient for me, Sufficient for me is He Who has been always sufficient for me"

حَسْبِي مَنْ كَانَ مُذْ كُنْتُ لَمْ يَزَلْ حَسْبِي حَسْبِيَ اللَّهُ لاَ إِلَهَ إِلاَّ هُوَ

"Sufficient for me is He Who had been since eternity and still sufficient for me, Allah suffices me. There is no good save Him"

عَلَيْهِ تَوَكَّلْتُ وَ هُوَ رَبُّ الْعَرْشِ الْعَظِيمِ

"In him have I put my trust, and He is the Lord of the Tremendous Throne"

The religious student said: So, they say that you praise Ali to be higher than they praise the Lord, but here there is nothing of that at all. I replied there are many of these sayings.

The religious student seemed gobsmacked. He asked if I could give him the book of supplication. I answered: Unfortunately, I only have one copy of this and need it until I finish my Hajj pilgrimage. Nevertheless, I can copy some of the parts for you and bring it. He thanked me, and the Isha prayer started. Unfortunately, I never saw the student ever again.

Day Twenty Third of Zyqadeh

As usual, I went to Baqi's graveyard after the morning prayer. Afterward, I went back to the hotel, had some breakfast, and then slept for a while. I went to the Mosque for the Zuhr prayer. After reading the Zuhr pray, Mr. Haj Abbas that had accompanied me waited for the Sheikh. The Shrine police told us to move as it was getting crowded. Eventually, we moved around so many times until we managed to see Sheikh and we headed towards the hotel.

Sh: The weather is perfect. It isn't that warm and God willing it will stay that way for Arafa and Mena.

Dr: God willing it will stay that way; however, if it rains, it would not seem that it would get any better.

Sh: By the way, did you get into any trouble last night?

Dr: With you coming into my defense there weren't any problems. However, if you were not there, I would have most definitely been taken into the custody of Masjid an Nabawi.

Sh: I think they only warn as I don't believe they have a specific place to keep anybody.

Dr: That is not true. Last night one of my colleagues was taking photos of his family outside of the Shrine, and while he was taking the picture a woman passes by, in front of him. Her face also got captured in the image. They took the poor photographer, and they were going to cut all of his hair off. I went and mediated, and eventually, they took a written promise from him that he will never make a photo of an unlawful woman again. We were there for four hours. The exciting part was here that the Officer that was also witnessed to what had happened and had reported the issue was trying to release him. (Because I swore that he was not lying about taking the photo of the woman). However, the Officer higher ranked than him would not accept.

Sh: It was not the photographer's fault. Did the woman of whom the photo was accidentally taken make any complaints?

Dr: No, she didn't make any complaint but the Officer that saw this happen complained.

Sh: For what excuse did they arrest him for?

Dr: That is because he took a photo of a woman that was not lawfully his.

Sh: God helps us with these extremists.

Dr: You think this is big? These men consider everyone as infidels and polytheist.

Sh: We seek refuge in God (بِـــالله نعــوذ), even if Ibn Teymiyah was here he wouldn't have behaved this way.

Dr: I believe these men are his students because these doings come from his book.

Sh: But acting on them and actually calling them infidels and polytheist is not right.

Dr: Normally, ignorant followers act worse than their kind.

Sh: Yes, that is correct.

Dr: For instance, Ibn Teymiyah, who considers himself as one of Ahmad Hanbal's followers is against several of Fatwa's that Ahmad Hanbal has said: himself. This is done in a way that even his brothers started being against him. Most of his Fatwa's were against the majority of the four Imams (Malik, Ahmad, Shafia, Abu Hanifah).

Sh: Yes, there were many objections towards him, but he also did innovate many new things.

Dr: In religion commonly, innovations are mostly troublesome rather than reinforcement for faith.

At this point, we arrived at the hotel. We had lunch, and on that day some of my hometown people had come to see me from Jahrom. I thanked them and requested Sheikh to eat at the table by my hometown people. He accepted, and we ended up having many various conversations. Luckily, they talked about their childhood memories and high school experiences in specific their Quran citing classes that happened every night. They left us after lunch, and we headed towards my room so we could start our debate. We had some tea and Persian sweets and then began.

Continuation of Supplication in Shia'sm

Sh: Last night, I read the supplications in the book. It was exciting for me. I have bookmarked some of the pages and brought the book with me. Please have a look at these passages. I am not sure if you have paid as much attention to these parts like the other ones you were mentioning yesterday. For instance, this is supplication that is the Sunday supplication.

Dr: Yes, it is fascinating.

Sh: By the way, how do they come up with the names of the supplications.

The Doctor & Sheikh's Debate

Dr: The name of the supplications does not have a substantial important base. Sometimes they come after the name of the people that said: The supplication or has taught them the supplication. For instance, Kumail or Abu Hamza Thumali is another example. Some of them are based on the name of the day, for example, the Morning supplication that is for the mornings. Some of the names come from the content of which it was for. An example of that is Makarem Al Akhlagh and Aliya Al Mazamin. Some of the supplications have been named based on the first word that the supplication starts with, for instance, Iftitah supplication or the Sabah supplication like we saw just before. Some of the supplication's names have been set officially. But their names whether it is official or not is not important. What is important is the content of them.

Sh: That is correct but I wanted to focus today's debate on the supplications that clarify the relationship of man with God. From one side a person gets fearful and from the other side gets closer to God and feels more hopeful.

Dr: I agree as well. Let's talk about the supplications.

Sh: Firstly, the supplications that are referring to the days of the week. Can we have a look at Sunday and Tuesday supplication? This is the Sunday supplication. Please look at the first part of the supplication.

بِسْمِ اللَّهِ الَّذِي لاَ أَرْجُو إِلاَّ فَضْلَهُ ولاَ أَخْشَى إِلاَّ عَدْلَهُ

"In the Name of Allah, the All compassionate, the All merciful, In the name of Allah, from whom I hope for nothing but bounty, I fear nothing but justice"

ولاَ أَعْتَمِدُ إِلاَّ قَوْلَهُ ولاَ أُمْسِكُ إِلاَّ بِحَبْلِهِ

"I rely upon nothing but His word and I cling to nothing but His Rope"

بِكَ أَسْتَجِيرُ يَا ذَا الْعَفْوِ والرِّضْوَانِ مِنَ الظُّلْمِ والْعُدْوَانِ

"In You do I seek sanctuary- O Possessor of pardon and good pleasure - from wrong and enmity"

ومِنْ غِيَرِ الزَّمَانِ وَ تَوَاتُرِ الْأَحْزَانِ وَ طَوَارِقِ الْحَدَثَانِ

"From the vicissitudes of time, from recurrence of sorrows, from the striking of mishaps"

ومِنِ انْقِضَاءِ الْمُدَّةِ قَبْلَ التَّأَهُّبِ وَ الْعُدَّةِ وَ إِيَّاكَ أَسْتَرْشِدُ لِمَا فِيهِ الصَّلاَحُ وَ الْإِصْلاَحُ

"And from the expiration of the term before preparation and readiness, From You do I seek guidance to that wherein is righteousness and setting aright"

وبِكَ أَسْتَعِينُ فِيمَا يَقْتَرِنُ بِهِ النَّجَاحُ وَ الْإِنْجَاحُ

"From You do I seek help in that which is linked to success and favorable response"

وإِيَّاكَ أَرْغَبُ فِي لِبَاسِ الْعَافِيَةْ وَ تَمَامِهَا وَ شُمُولِ السَّلَامَةْ وَ دَوَامِهَا

"From You do I desire for the garment of wellbeing and its completion"

Sh: If a person only reads this once a week he will have cleansed his soul so well with it and from so many prospective: Firstly, God will be his only reliance. After all the badness, and cruelty, even Satan seeks help from God and then requests to be at his service and asks for his forgiveness and in the end asks God for a brighter future.

Dr: Most of the supplications that have come to us have really perfect content.

Sh: Please have a look at Tuesday's supplication.

الْحَمْدُ لِلَّهِ والْحَمْدُ حَقُّهُ كَمَا يَسْتَحِقُّهُ حَمْداً كَثِيراً

"In the Name of Allah, the All- beneficent, the All- merciful. All praise be to Allah; and praise is His right, since He deserves it, abundant praise!"

وأَعُوذُ بِهِ مِنْ شَرِّ نَفْسِي إِنَّ النَّفْسَ لَأَمَّارَهْ بِالسُّوءِ إِلاَّ مَا رَحِمَ رَبِّي

"I seek refuge in Him from the Evil of my soul, for surely, the soul commands to evil except as my Lord have mercy."

وأَعُوذُ بِهِ مِنْ شَرِّ الشَّيْطَانِ الَّذِي يَزِيدُنِي ذَنْباً إِلَى ذَنْبِي

"I seek refuge in Him from the evil of Satan who adds sins to my sins"

وَ أَحْتَرِزُ بِهِ مِنْ كُلِّ جَبَّارٍ فَاجِرٍ وَ سُلْطَانٍ جَائِرٍ وَ عَدُوٍّ قَاهِرٍ

"I seek protection with Him from every wicked tyrant, unjust sovereign and conquering enemy"

اللَّهُمَّ اجْعَلْنِي مِنْ جُنْدِكَ فَإِنَّ جُنْدَكَ هُمُ الْغَالِبُونَ

The Doctor & Sheikh's Debate

"O Allah, place me among Your troops, for Your troops they" are the victors

وَ اجْعَلْنِي مِنْ حِزْبِكَ فَإِنَّ حِزْبَكَ هُمُ الْمُفْلِحُونَ

"And place me in Your party, for Your party- they are the ones who prosper"

واجْعَلْنِي مِنْ أَوْلِيَائِكَ فَإِنَّ أَوْلِيَاءَكَ لاَ خَوْفٌ عَلَيْهِمْ ولاَ هُمْ يَحْزَنُونَ

"And place me among Your friends, for Your friends- no fear shall be upon them, nor shall they experience sorrow"

اللَّهُمَّ أَصْلِحْ لِي دِينِي فَإِنَّهُ عِصْمَةُ أَمْرِي

"O Allah, set right for me my religion, for it is the preserving tie of my affair"

وأَصْلِحْ لِي آخِرَتِي فَإِنَّهَا دَارُ مَقَرِّي وَ إِلَيْهَا مِنْ مُجَاوَرَةِ اللِّئَامِ مَفَرِّي

"Set right for me my hearafter, for it is the abode of my permanent lodging, and to it I flee from the neighborhood of the vile!"

وَ اجْعَلِ الْحَيَاةَ زِيَادَةً لِي فِي كُلِّ خَيْرٍ وَ الْوَفَاةَ رَاحَةً لِي مِنْ كُلِّ شَرٍّ

"Make life an increase for me in every good, and death an ease for me from every evil!"

اللَّهُمَّ صَلِّ عَلَى مُحَمَّدٍ خَاتَمِ النَّبِيِّينَ وتَمَامِ عِدَّةِ الْمُرْسَلِينَ

"O Allah, send blessings to Muhammad, the Seal of the Prophets, and the completion of the number of the envoys"

وعَلَى آلِهِ الطَّيِّبِينَ الطَّاهِرِينَ وَ أَصْحَابِهِ الْمُنْتَجَبِينَ

"And upon his Household, the good, the pure, and upon his Companions, the distinguished"

Sh: Why does it say to send praise to the distinguished chosen by the Prophet?

Dr: Due to the same reason we concluded on the fact that not all of the Prophets followers were a worth blessing. So, we only praise the good ones.

Sh: This is interesting; I will praise the ones that are chosen too.

Dr: Just like I said: yesterday, Imam Khomeini recommended before the revolution to read this supplication every day.

Sh: God bless his soul. He was very right because it starts with praising the Lord, and then it talks about one's soul and selflessness, and then it seeks refuge to God. It asks to be a soldier of his group and to be his friend as they are the ones that are successful, with no fear and are prosperous. This is an excellent supplication for fighters in the path of the Lord.

Dr: Whenever I feel down and not worthy, I read this supplication.

Sh: This one is also very interesting to me:

اللَّهُمَّ ارْزُقْنَا تَوْفِيقَ الطَّاعَةْ وبُعْدَ الْمَعْصِيَهْ وَ صِدْقَ النِّيَّهْ

"O Allah reconcile us from the separation of our sins and keep our intentions pure"

وَ عِرْفَانَ الْحُرْمَهْ وَ أَكْرِمْنَا بِالْهُدَى وَ الِاسْتِقَامَهْ

"Give me whatever truth and loyalty is accountable in your presence. Please guide me towards being stronger in the path of your faith and dignity"

وَ سَدِّدْ أَلْسِنَتَنَا بِالصَّوَابِ وَ الْحِكْمَهْ وَ امْلأْ قُلُوبَنَا بِالْعِلْمِ وَ الْمَعْرِفَهْ

"Fill our words with the truth and goodness and oblation. And fill my soul with the knowledge and wisdom"

وطَهِّرْ بُطُونَنَا مِنَ الْحَرَامِ وَ الشُّبْهَهْ وَ اكْفُفْ أَيْدِيَنَا عَنِ الظُّلْمِ وَ السِّرْقَهْ

"Prevent us from eating anything unlawful (Haram) and prevent our hands from ever thieving and dishonesty"

وَ اغْضُضْ أَبْصَارَنَا عَنِ الْفُجُورِ وَ الْخِيَانَهْ وَ اسْدُدْ أَسْمَاعَنَا عَنِ اللَّغْوِ وَ الْغِيبَهْ

"Close our eyes from seeing anything wrong and treason and shut our ears from hearing useless conversations and talking behind people's backs"

وَ تَفَضَّلْ عَلَى عُلَمَائِنَا بِالزُّهْدِ وَ النَّصِيحَهْ

"Give blessing and goodness in his deeds on our scholars and scientists"

وعَلَى الْمُتَعَلِّمِينَ بِالْجُهْدِ وَ الرَّغْبَهْ وَ عَلَى الْمُسْتَمِعِينَ بِالِاتِّبَاعِ وَ الْمَوْعِظَهْ

"Bestow seriousness and happiness and wish the listeners to follow and act out of advice"

وَ عَلَى مَرْضَى الْمُسْلِمِينَ بِالشِّفَاءِ وَ الرَّاحَةِ وَ عَلَى مَوْتَاهُمْ بِالرَّأْفَةِ وَ الرَّحْمَةِ

"Provide cure for the ill and comfort for all of the Muslims that have passed away and mercy them"

وَ عَلَى مَشَايِخِنَا بِالْوَقَارِ وَ السَّكِينَةِ وَ عَلَى الشَّبَابِ بِالْإِنَابَةِ وَ التَّوْبَةِ

"Bestow poise and dignity to our elderly and repentance and atonement to our youth"

وَ عَلَى النِّسَاءِ بِالْحَيَاءِ وَ الْعِفَّةِ وَ عَلَى الْأَغْنِيَاءِ بِالتَّوَاضُعِ وَ السَّعَةِ

"Teach our women modesty and chastity and provide them with eminence"

عَلَى الْفُقَرَاءِ بِالصَّبْرِ وَالْقَنَاعَةِ

"Provide the poor with patience and contentment"

وَعَلَى الْغُزَاةِ بِالنَّصْرِ وَالْغَلَبَةِ وَ عَلَى الْأُسَرَاءِ بِالْخَلَاصِ وَ الرَّاحَةِ

"Offer our soldiers conquest and victory and provide our prisoners freedom and relaxations"

وَ عَلَى الْأُمَرَاءِ بِالْعَدْلِ وَ الشَّفَقَةِ وَ عَلَى الرَّعِيَّةِ بِالْإِنْصَافِ وَ حُسْنِ السِّيرَةِ

"Provide justice and compassion to our governors provide them with kindness, fairness and good character"

وَ بَارِكْ لِلْحُجَّاجِ وَ الزُّوَّارِ فِي الزَّادِ وَ النَّفَقَةِ

"Bestow food and ordinance to our Islamic pilgrimage and provide blessing on their finances"

وَ اقْضِ مَا أَوْجَبْتَ عَلَيْهِمْ مِنَ الْحَجِّ وَ الْعُمْرَةِ بِفَضْلِكَ وَ رَحْمَتِكَ يَا أَرْحَمَ الرَّاحِمِينَ

"Now that you have given Haj and Umra to them please give them grace and mercy O most merciful of the universe"

Dr: This supplication is regarding the awaited Mahdi.

Sh: But it is a crucial supplication. It clarifies everyone's duty based on their position. The supplication for the month of Rajab was interesting as well:

بِسْمِ اللَّهِ الرَّحْمَنِ الرَّحِيمِ

يَا مَنْ أَرْجُوهُ لِكُلِّ خَيْرٍ وَ آمَنَ سَخْطَهُ عِنْدَ (مِنْ) كُلِّ شَرٍّ

يَا مَنْ يُعْطِي الْكَثِيرَ بِالْقَلِيلِ يَا مَنْ يُعْطِي مَنْ سَأَلَهُ

يَا مَنْ يُعْطِي مَنْ لَمْ يَسْأَلْهُ وَ مَنْ لَمْ يَعْرِفْهُ تَحَنُّناً مِنْهُ وَ رَحْمَةً

أَعْطِنِي بِمَسْأَلَتِي إِيَّاكَ جَمِيعَ خَيْرِ الدُّنْيَا وَ جَمِيعَ خَيْرِ الْآخِرَةِ

وَ اصْرِفْ عَنِّي بِمَسْأَلَتِي إِيَّاكَ جَمِيعَ شَرِّ الدُّنْيَا وَ (جَمِيعَ) شَرِّ الْآخِرَةِ

فَإِنَّهُ غَيْرُ مَنْقُوصٍ مَا أَعْطَيْتَ وَ زِدْنِي مِنْ فَضْلِكَ يَا كَرِيمُ

"In the name of Allah, the Beneficent, the Merciful

O Allah, bless Muhammad and his household.

O He from whom I can hope for all goodness And I am safe from His anger at every evil.

O He who gives a lot in exchange of a little.

O He who gives to one who asks Him.

O He who gives to one who does not ask Him and does not know Him,

Out of His affection and mercy.

Give me, for my request is only to You alone, All the good of this world and all the good of the Hereafter.

Keep away from me, for my request is only to You alone, All the evil of this world and the evil of the Hereafter. For indeed it is not diminishing what is given by You. Increase (for) me from Your bounty, O The Generous."

On the other hand, this part of the supplication that is specified for the month of Shaban:

إِلَهِي هَبْ لِي قَلْباً يُدْنِيهِ مِنْكَ شَوْقُهُ وَ لِسَاناً يُرْفَعُ إِلَيْكَ صِدْقُهُ وَ نَظَراً يُقَرِّبُهُ مِنْكَ حَقُّهُ

فَلَا تُخَيِّبْ ظَنِّي مِنْ رَحْمَتِكَ وَ لَا تَحْجُبْنِي عَنْ رَأْفَتِكَ

إِلَهِي أَقِمْنِي فِي أَهْلِ وَلَايَتِكَ مُقَامَ مَنْ رَجَا الزِّيَادَةَ مِنْ مَحَبَّتِكَ

إِلَهِي وَ أَلْهِمْنِي وَلَهاً بِذِكْرِكَ إِلَى ذِكْرِكَ وَ هِمَّتِي فِي رَوْحِ نَجَاحِ أَسْمَائِكَ وَ مَحَلِّ قُدْسِكَ

إِلَهِي بِكَ عَلَيْكَ إِلَّا أَلْحَقْتَنِي بِمَحَلِّ أَهْلِ طَاعَتِكَ وَ الْمَثْوَى الصَّالِحِ مِنْ مَرْضَاتِكَ

The Doctor & Sheikh's Debate

فَإِنِّي لاَ أَقْدِرُ لِنَفْسِي دَفْعاً وَ لاَ أَمْلِكُ لَهَا نَفْعاً

حَجَبَهُ سَهْوُهُ عَنْ عَفْوِكَ

إِلَهِي هَبْ لِي كَمَالَ الاِنْقِطَاعِ إِلَيْكَ وَ أَنِرْ أَبْصَارَ قُلُوبِنَا بِضِيَاءِ نَظَرِهَا إِلَيْكَ

حَتَّى تَخْرِقَ أَبْصَارُ الْقُلُوبِ حُجُبَ النُّورِ فَتَصِلَ إِلَى مَعْدِنِ الْعَظَمَةْ وَ تَصِيرَ أَرْوَاحُنَا مُعَلَّقَةْ بِعِزِّ قُدْسِكَ

إِلَهِي وَ اجْعَلْنِي مِمَّنْ نَادَيْتَهُ فَأَجَابَكَ وَ لاَحَظْتَهُ فَصَعِقَ لِجَلاَلِكَ فَنَاجَيْتَهُ سِرّاً وَ عَمِلَ لَكَ جَهْراً

"My Lord, provide me with a heart, the passion of which may bring it near You, with a tongue the truth of which may be submitted to You, and with a vision the nature of which may bring it close to You.

My Lord, whoever gets acquainted with You, is not un-known; whoever takes shelter under You, is not disappointed; and one to whom You turn, is not a slave. One who follows Your path is enlightened; and one who takes refuge in You, is saved.

My Lord, I have taken refuge in You. Therefore do not disappoint me of Your Mercy and do not keep me secluded from Your Kindness.

My Lord, place me among Your friends in the position of one who hopes for an increase in Your love.

My Lord, inspire me with a passionate love of remembering You so that I may keep on remembering You, and by Your Holy Name and Pure Position cherish my cheerful determination into a success.

My Lord, I invoke You to admit me to the place reserved for those who obey You, and to attach me to the nice abode of those who enjoy Your good pleasure... I can neither defend myself nor do I control what is advantageous for me.

My Lord, I am Your powerless sinning slave and Your repentant bondman. So do not make me one of those from whom You turn away Your face, and whom his negligence has secluded from Your forgiveness.

My Lord, grant me complete severance of my relations with everything else and total submission to You. Enlighten the eyes of our hearts with the light of their looking at You to the extent that they penetrate the veils of light and reach the Source of Grandeur, and let our souls get suspended by the glory of Your sanctity.

My Lord, make me one of those whom You call and they respond; when You look at and they are thunderstruck by Your majesty. You whisper to them secretly and they work for You openly."

Dr: Dear Sheikh, are you a gemologist?

Sh: How come?

Dr: Imam Khomeini has mentioned this part of the supplication that is regarding Shaban several times. It is as part of a supplication that has concepts that it is tough to understand. For instance, what does "Thunderstruck by Your majesty" mean?

Sh: Actually, I was about to ask you regarding some of the meaning of these supplications.

Dr: We should be asking you.

Sh: When Imam Khomeini is contemplating on them who am I to say anything?

Dr: Then my position in this matter is quite clear my field is in Mechanics.

Sh: This supplication called Iftitah is also enjoyable. Especially the beginning of it:

اللَّهُمَّ إِنِّي أَفْتَتِحُ الثَّنَاءَ بِحَمْدِكَ وَ أَنْتَ مُسَدِّدٌ لِلصَّوَابِ بِمَنِّكَ

وَ أَيْقَنْتُ أَنَّكَ أَنْتَ أَرْحَمُ الرَّاحِمِينَ فِي مَوْضِعِ الْعَفْوِ وَ الرَّحْمَةْ

وَ أَشَدُّ الْمُعَاقِبِينَ فِي مَوْضِعِ النَّكَالِ وَ النَّقِمَهْ وَ أَعْظَمُ الْمُتَجَبِّرِينَ فِي مَوْضِعِ الْكِبْرِيَاءِ وَ الْعَظَمَهْ

اللَّهُمَّ أَذِنْتَ لِي فِي دُعَائِكَ وَ مَسْأَلَتِكَ فَاسْمَعْ يَا سَمِيعُ مِدْحَتِي

وَ أَجِبْ يَا رَحِيمُ دَعْوَتِي وَ أَقِلْ يَا غَفُورُ عَثْرَتِي

فَكَمْ يَا إِلَهِي مِنْ كُرْبَهْ قَدْ فَرَّجْتَهَا وَ هُمُومٍ (غُمُومٍ) قَدْ كَشَفْتَهَا

وَ عَثْرَهْ قَدْ أَقَلْتَهَا وَ رَحْمَهْ قَدْ نَشَرْتَهَا وَ حَلْقَهْ بَلَاءٍ قَدْ فَكَكْتَهَا
الْحَمْدُ لِلَّهِ الَّذِي لَمْ يَتَّخِذْ صَاحِبَهْ وَ لَا وَلَداً وَ لَمْ يَكُنْ لَهُ شَرِيكٌ فِي الْمُلْكِ

وَ لَمْ يَكُنْ لَهُ وَلِيٌّ مِنَ الذُّلِّ وَ كَبِّرْهُ تَكْبِيراً الْحَمْدُ لِلَّهِ بِجَمِيعِ مَحَامِدِهِ كُلِّهَا عَلَى جَمِيعِ نِعَمِهِ كُلِّهَا

الْحَمْدُ لِلَّهِ الَّذِي لاَ مُضَادَّ لَهُ فِي مُلْكِهِ وَلاَ مُنَازِعَ لَهُ فِي أَمْرِهِ

الْحَمْدُ لِلَّهِ الَّذِي لاَ شَرِيكَ لَهُ فِي خَلْقِهِ وَ لاَ شَبِيهَ (شِبْهَ) لَهُ فِي عَظَمَتِهِ

الْحَمْدُ لِلَّهِ الْفَاشِي فِي الْخَلْقِ أَمْرُهُ وَحَمْدُهُ الظَّاهِرِ بِالْكَرَمِ مَجْدُهُ

"O Allah, I begin the glorification with praise of Thee; Thou, from Thy bounties, gives out freely the truth and salvation; I know for certain that Thou art the most merciful in disposition of forgiveness and mercy, [but] very exacting at the time of giving exemplary punishment and chastisement to wrongdoers, the Omnipotent in the domain of absolute power and might.

O Allah, thou have given me permission to invoke Thee and beseech Thee, so listen, O Hearer, to my words of praise, and give a favourable reply to my supplication, and minimize my falling into misery, O the often-forgiving.

O my Allah, many a trouble Thou hath removed; many a sorrow hath Thou dispelled; many a misery hath Thou mitigated; and at all times Thou spread out mercy, and cut short the tightening circles of misfortunes.

All praise be to Allah, who has not taken unto Himself a wife, nor a son, and Who has no partner in sovereignty, nor any protecting friend through dependence. Magnify Him with all magnificence.

All praise be to Allah, with full gratitude for all his bounties.

All praise be to Allah, who has no opposition to His rule, nor any challenge to His commands.

All praise be to Allah, who has no counsel to meddle with His operation of creation, nor is there anything similar to Him in His greatness."[3]

Dr: This is very good. It clarifies that supplication has a highly regarded place for the Ahl al Bayt. It is a teaching and also a request for being thankful. For example, in the supplication of Kumeyl firstly, it introduced God so we would know whom we have come to. God's mercy, power, and forgiveness and ...then it introduces itself with how he has sinned and then asks for mercy from all the sins he has made and it seems that his sins were forgiven by the end of the supplication. God wished to place him close to the other men he has chosen beside himself.

Sh: It was very interesting. I had not paid attention to it in that way.

Sh: In my opinion, in this supplication, it teaches what you mentioned before. In the beginning, it starts thanking the Lord for the blessings he has given and then asks for the things he wants.

Dr: Almost all of the supplications are this way.

---

[3] - Abbas Qummi

Sh: The supplication for the Mujeer is also describing the Lord's beauty; however, mentioning them this way is very appealing.

بِسْمِ الرَّحْمَنِ الرَّحِيمِ

سُبْحَانَكَ يَا اللَّهُ تَعَالَيْتَ يَا رَحْمَانُ أَجِرْنَا مِنَ النَّارِ يَا مُجِيرُ

سُبْحَانَكَ يَا رَحِيمُ تَعَالَيْتَ يَا كَرِيمُ أَجِرْنَا مِنَ النَّارِ يَا مُجِيرُ

سُبْحَانَكَ يَا مَلِكُ تَعَالَيْتَ يَا مَالِكُ أَجِرْنَا مِنَ النَّارِ يَا مُجِيرُ

سُبْحَانَكَ يَا قُدُّوسُ تَعَالَيْتَ يَا سَلَامُ أَجِرْنَا مِنَ النَّارِ يَا مُجِيرُ

سُبْحَانَكَ يَا مُؤْمِنُ تَعَالَيْتَ يَا مُهَيْمِنُ أَجِرْنَا مِنَ النَّارِ يَا مُجِيرُ

سُبْحَانَكَ يَا عَزِيزُ تَعَالَيْتَ يَا جَبَّارُ أَجِرْنَا مِنَ النَّارِ يَا مُجِيرُ

سُبْحَانَكَ يَا مُتَكَبِّرُ تَعَالَيْتَ يَا مُتَجَبِّرُ أَجِرْنَا مِنَ النَّارِ يَا مُجِيرُ

سُبْحَانَكَ يَا خَالِقُ تَعَالَيْتَ يَا بَارِئُ أَجِرْنَا مِنَ النَّارِ يَا مُجِيرُ

"In the name of Allah, the Beneficent, The Merciful, Glory be to You. O' Allah! Exalted are You. O' beneficent! Keep us safe from the everlasting fire O' Lenient Supporter! Glory be to You. O' merciful! Exalted are You. O' generous! Keep us safe from the everlasting fire O' lenient Supporter!

Glory be to You. O' Sovereign! Exalted are You. O' Generous! Keep us safe from the everlasting fire O' Lenient Supporter. Glory be to You. O Holy! Exalted are You. O Peace! Keep us safe from the everlasting fire O Lenient Supporter! Glory be to You. O' Source of security! Exalted are You. O' Loving Protector! Keep us safe from the everlasting fire O' Lenient Supporter

Glory be to You O Glorious! Exalted are You. O' Omnipotent! Keep us safe from the everlasting fire O' Lenient Supporter! Glory be to You. O' Proud Exalted are You. O' Dominant Helper! Keep us safe from the everlasting fire O' Lenient Supporter! Glory be to You. O' Creator! Exalted are You. O' Maker! Keep us safe from the everlasting fire O' Lenient Supporter!"

Dr: Until the end of this supplication it is just the same. It is all regarding begging God and for him to save us from his fire.

The Doctor & Sheikh's Debate

Sh: These supplications are oceans of theology. It is perfect for the youth to read in this era of inappropriate, vulgar culture. They can get to know God better and to rely on a source that is never going away. However, if the Sunnis see these supplications, they would be amazed. They will be surprised by how you see your Lord's greatness, and the way you express him has no replacement for how you feel about your Imams.

Dr: The supplication for Jawshan Kabir is the same way.

Sh: Yes, I have bookmarked it, please look.

Dr: This supplication has an exciting beginning. Please have a look. It is from Hazrat Seyed Al Sajidin that has cited this from his great grandfather The Messenger of God (s.a.w.a). Gabriel brought this supplication to the Prophet (s.a.w.a) regarding a blister that was on the Prophet's body from carrying heavy loads. It was hurting him so Gabriel was sent to him telling him: God sends his blessing and says that you can open the blister and read this supplication and he will protect you and your Ummah. The initial part of the supplication goes like this:

اَللَّهُمَّ إِنِّي أَسْأَلُكَ بِاسْمِكَ يَا اَللَّهُ يَا رَحْمَانُ

يَا رَحِيمُ يَا كَرِيمُ يَا مُقِيمُ يَا عَظِيمُ يَا قَدِيمُ يَا عَلِيمُ يَا حَلِيمُ يَا حَكِيمُ

سُبْحَانَكَ يَا لَا إِلَهَ إِلَّا أَنْتَ الْغَوْثَ الْغَوْثَ خَلِّصْنَا مِنَ النَّارِ يَا رَبِّ

"O' Allah, verily I beseech Thee in Thy name:
O' Allah, O' Most Merciful,
O' Most Compassionate, O' Most Generous,
O' Self-Subsisting, O' Greatest,
O' Eternal, O' All-Knowing,
O' Forbearing, O' Wise.
Praise be to Thee, there is no god but Thee, The Granter of all Succour, Protect us from the Fire, O' Lord."

يَا سَيِّدَ السَّادَاتِ يَا مُجِيبَ الدَّعَوَاتِ يَا رَافِعَ الدَّرَجَاتِ يَا وَلِيَّ الْحَسَنَاتِ يَا غَافِرَ الْخَطِيئَاتِ

يَا مُعْطِيَ الْمَسْأَلَاتِ يَا قَابِلَ التَّوْبَاتِ يَا سَامِعَ الْأَصْوَاتِ يَا عَالِمَ الْخَفِيَّاتِ يَا دَافِعَ الْبَلِيَّاتِ

"O' Master of Masters, O' Acceptor of prayers,
O' Elevator of rank, O' Guardian of good deeds,

O' Forgiver of evil deeds, O' Granter of requests,
O' Acceptor of repentance, O' Hearer of voices,
O' Knower of attributes, O' Repeller of calamities.
Praise be to Thee, there is no god but Thee, The Granter of all Succour, Protect us from the Fire, O' Lord."

يَا خَيْرَ الْغَافِرِينَ يَا خَيْرَ الْفَاتِحِينَ يَا خَيْرَ النَّاصِرِينَ يَا خَيْرَ الْحَاكِمِينَ يَا خَيْرَ الرَّازِقِينَ

يَا خَيْرَ الْوَارِثِينَ يَا خَيْرَ الْحَامِدِينَ يَا خَيْرَ الذَّاكِرِينَ يَا خَيْرَ الْمُنْزِلِينَ يَا خَيْرَ الْمُحْسِنِينَ

"O' Best of forgivers, O' Best of deciders,
O' Best of helpers, O' Best of rulers,
O' Best of providers, O' Best of inheritors,
O' Best of praisers, O' Best of rememberers,
O' Best of Dischargers, O' Best of benefactors.
Praise be to Thee, there is no god but Thee, The Granter of all Succour, Protect us from the Fire, O' Lord."

يَا مَنْ لَهُ الْعِزَّةُ والْجَمَالُ يَا مَنْ لَهُ الْقُدْرَةُ وَ الْكَمَالُ يَا مَنْ لَهُ الْمُلْكُ وَ الْجَلَالُ

يَا مَنْ هُوَ الْكَبِيرُ الْمُتَعَالِ يَا مُنْشِئَ السَّحَابِ الثِّقَالِ يَا مَنْ هُوَ شَدِيدُ الْمِحَالِ

يَا مَنْ هُوَ سَرِيعُ الْحِسَابِ يَا مَنْ هُوَ شَدِيدُ الْعِقَابِ يَا مَنْ عِنْدَهُ حُسْنُ الثَّوَابِ يَا مَنْ عِنْدَهُ أَمُّ الْكِتَابِ

"O' He, to Whom is all glory and virtue,
O' He, to Whom is all might and perfection,
O' He, to Whom is all dominion and sublimity,
O' He, Who is great above all,
O' He, Who creates heavy clouds,
O' He, Who is the most powerful,
O' He, Who metes out the severest punishment,
O' He, Who is quick to reckon,
O' He, with Whom is the excellent reward,
O' He, with Whom is the Original Book.
Praise be to Thee, there is no god but Thee, The Granter of all Succour, Protect us from the Fire, O' Lord."

The Doctor & Sheikh's Debate

O' Allah, verily I beseech Thee in Thy name:
O' Charitable One, O' Benefactor,
O' Judge, O' Proof,
O' Sovereign, O' Approver,
O' Forgiver, O' Elevated One,
O' Helper, O' Holder of blessings and manifestation. "[4]

Sh: There is a part in the supplication of Jawshan where you repeat for one hundred times repeating: ", after every sentence. This part is so holy that it acquaints the soul of any person that reads this supplication and pays attention to its meaning in so many ways. It allows a person to see the face of the names and attributes of God and it enables the person to return to God, the one that is the greatest, so he can be protected from the destructing fires of this world and the fires of his sins in the next world.

Dr: Did you read the Jawshan?

Sh: I reviewed all of it.

Dr: What about the rest of the supplication?

Sh: I will be honest with you. I spent the whole night reading these supplications until it was dawn. I read the Morning Prayer, and then I slept until it was close to Zuhr prayer.

Dr: I wish I had given you these supplications sooner.

Sh: Actually, these supplications are very important in introducing real Shi'ism and the Ahl al Bayt.

Dr: I think that based on these supplications, you have a better understanding of where God, the Prophet, Ali, and the rest of the Ahl al Bayt are placed.

Sh: If I am honest, your God is much more of a God than ours is. This is because some things are mentioned in the Sihah al Sittah, but we have no feasibility in determining where it has come from but to say that we do not have a correct chain of transmission.

4- Abbas Qummi.

Dr: Yes, I have also seen that. For instance, compare the God that wrestles with Moses in Bukhari and Sahih Muslem with the same attributes of God that Jawshan or supplication of Mujeer describes.

Sh: That is correct; you are right. If you agree let's pray here for Asir so we would have more time to discuss the supplications.

Dr: I would be happy to be of any service.

Sh: Okay, let's have a look at the supplication of Khams Ashar, especially this part where it is the supplication of Moteein Lelah (people that obey God):

اللَّهُمَّ أَلْهِمْنَا طَاعَتَكَ وجَنِّبْنَا مَعْصِيَتَكَ و يَسِّرْ لَنَا بُلُوغَ مَا نَتَمَنَّى مِنِ ابْتِغَاءِ رِضْوَانِكَ

"O Allah, inspire our hearts with your service and obedience keep away any transgression from us and simplify the path to what we desire as we are delighted by your heaven"

وَ أَحْلِلْنَا بُحْبُوحَةَ جِنَانِكَ وَ اقْشَعْ عَنْ بَصَائِرِنَا سَحَابَ الِارْتِيَابِ وَ اكْشِفْ عَنْ قُلُوبِنَا أَغْشِيَةَ الْمِرْيَةِ وَ الْحِجَابِ

"Keep away any transgression from us and simplify the path to what we desire as we are delighted by your heaven and keep away darken clouds and evil doubtness from our eyes and inner belief."

وَ أَزْهِقِ الْبَاطِلَ عَنْ ضَمَائِرِنَا وَ أَثْبِتِ الْحَقَّ فِي سَرَائِرِنَا

"Keep us in your eternal heavenly home destroy any desire in invalidity and place us in situations where justice and conducting it would be in our path"

فَإِنَّ الشُّكُوكَ وَ الظُّنُونَ لَوَاقِحُ الْفِتَنِ وَ مُكَدِّرَةٌ لِصَفْوِ الْمَنَائِحِ وَ الْمِنَنِ

"As doubt and invalid thoughts is substance for corruption"

اللَّهُمَّ احْمِلْنَا فِي سُفُنِ نَجَاتِكَ وَ مَتِّعْنَا بِلَذِيذِ مُنَاجَاتِكَ وَ أَوْرِدْنَا حِيَاضَ حُبِّكَ

"O Lord place us in your survivor archs and fulfull us with the delight of praising you and run us through your rivers of affection"

وَ أَذِقْنَا حَلَاوَةَ وُدِّكَ وَ قُرْبِكَ وَ اجْعَلْ جِهَادَنَا فِيكَ وَ هَمَّنَا فِي طَاعَتِكَ

"Let us taste the sweetness of your kindness and give us the will to see k you and give us the strength to obey your desires"

وَ أَخْلِصْ نِيَّاتِنَا فِي مُعَامَلَتِكَ فَإِنَّا بِكَ وَ لَكَ وَ لاَ وَسِيلَةْ لَنَا إِلَيْكَ إِلاَّ أَنْتَ

"Give us the pure feeling of exchanging with you as whatever we are, we are from you and will return to you. We only have you to assist us to come to you"

إِلَهِي اجْعَلْنِي مِنَ الْمُصْطَفَيْنَ الْأَخْيَارِ وَ أَلْحِقْنِي بِالصَّالِحِينَ الْأَبْرَارِ

"O Lord appoint me as your distinguished and the good and join me with the other pure servants of yours"

السَّابِقِينَ إِلَى الْمَكْرُمَاتِ الْمُسَارِعِينَ إِلَى الْخَيْرَاتِ الْعَامِلِينَ لِلْبَاقِيَاتِ الصَّالِحَاتِ

السَّاعِينَ إِلَى رَفِيعِ الدَّرَجَاتِ إِنَّكَ عَلَى كُلِّ شَيْءٍ قَدِيرٌ وبِالْإِجَابَةْ جَدِيرٌ بِرَحْمَتِكَ يَا أَرْحَمَ الرَّاحِمِينَ

"As they are persistent in obtaining higher ranks as you are able with anything and grant prayers. I beg your thoughtfulness O kind-heart of all kinder spirits in the universe"

Sh: This was supplication of Raajin.

Dr: Yes, why did you pick this one?

Sh: I saw that it has really interesting concepts.

Dr: Please go ahead.

Sh: This is the supplication of Mohebbin.

Dr: Have a little break, and then we can talk about these supplications.

Sh: Please allow us to discuss them after I finish this supplication.

Dr: I haven't got anything to discuss if there is anything you wish to say about them, please do so.

Sh: To be honest, I have nothing to discuss them also. I am just so overwhelmed by them that I wish to applaud them by showing you some parts of them.

Dr: Very well. Could you show me the parts?

Sh: This is supplication of Mohebbin.

إِلَهِي مَنْ ذَا الَّذِي ذَاقَ حَلاَوَةَ مَحَبَّتِكَ فَرَامَ مِنْكَ بَدَلاً

"In the name of God O Most Compassionate, O Most Generous, O God who has tasted your generosity and asked for anyone but you?"

وَمَنْ ذَا الَّذِي أَنِسَ بِقُرْبِكَ فَابْتَغَى عَنْكَ حِوَلاً

"Who is the one that acquainted him with your presence and then turn away from you?"

إِلَهِي فَاجْعَلْنَا مِمَّنِ اصْطَفَيْتَهُ لِقُرْبِكَ وَوِلاَيَتِكَ وَ أَخْلَصْتَهُ لِوُدِّكَ وَ مَحَبَّتِكَ وَ شَوَّقْتَهُ إِلَى لِقَائِكَ

"O God place us with the ones that you have placed as your company and friend and purified for you love and eager to your presence"

وَرَضَّيْتَهُ بِقَضَائِكَ وَ مَنَحْتَهُ بِالنَّظَرِ إِلَى وَجْهِكَ وَ حَبَوْتَهُ بِرِضَاكَ وَ أَعَذْتَهُ مِنْ هَجْرِكَ وَ قِلاَكَ

"You have contented them with your judging and have blessed them with your expression and have chosen them as you desire and protected them from your absence or separation"

وَ بَوَّأْتَهُ مَقْعَدَ الصِّدْقِ فِي جِوَارِكَ وَ خَصَصْتَهُ بِمَعْرِفَتِكَ وَ أَهَّلْتَهُ لِعِبَادَتِكَ وَ هَيَّمْتَ قَلْبَهُ لِإِرَادَتِكَ

"You have placed them at your side next to the truth and knowledgable of the universe. You have appointed them to the rank of your loyalty and given them the worthyness of praising you and be smittened with your kindness"

وَاجْتَبَيْتَهُ لِمُشَاهَدَتِكَ وَأَخْلَيْتَ وَجْهَهُ لَكَ وَ فَرَّغْتَ فُؤَادَهُ لِحُبِّكَ وَ رَغَّبْتَهُ فِيمَا عِنْدَكَ

"You have chosen them to see you and have given them the privilege of seeing your ways. You have emptied their hearts from anything but loving you and have given them no desire but what you desire"

وَأَلْهَمْتَهُ ذِكْرَكَ وَأَوْزَعْتَهُ شُكْرَكَ وَ شَغَلْتَهُ بِطَاعَتِكَ

"You have given them the words to praise you and have taught them how to thank you and have occupied them with obeying you"

وَصَيَّرْتَهُ مِنْ صَالِحِي بَرِيَّتِكَ وَاخْتَرْتَهُ لِمُنَاجَاتِكَ وَ قَطَعْتَ عَنْهُ كُلَّ شَيْءٍ يَقْطَعُهُ عَنْكَ

"You have placed them as your righteous servants and chosen them to pray to you and have prevented anything that would come in the way of them to you"

The Doctor & Sheikh's Debate

اللَّهُمَّ اجْعَلْنَا مِمَّنْ دَأْبُهُمْ الِارْتِيَاحُ إِلَيْكَ وَ الْحَنِينُ وَ دَهْرُهُمْ الزَّفْرَةُ وَ الْأَنِينُ

جِبَاهُهُمْ سَاجِدَةٌ لِعَظَمَتِكَ وعُيُونُهُمْ سَاهِرَةٌ فِي خِدْمَتِكَ

"O Lord Place us like them as they are joyful as they are and are blissful from within and spend all their lives with your love"

وَدُمُوعُهُمْ سَائِلَةٌ مِنْ خَشْيَتِكَ وَ قُلُوبُهُمْ مُتَعَلِّقَةٌ بِمَحَبَّتِكَ وَ أَفْئِدَتُهُمْ مُنْخَلِعَةٌ مِنْ مَهَابَتِكَ

"They are your servant and their tears are from fear of your anger and their hearts are desired to your love and attention"

يَا مَنْ أَنْوَارُ قُدْسِهِ لِأَبْصَارِ مُحِبِّيهِ رَائِقَةٌ وسُبُحَاتُ وَجْهِهِ لِقُلُوبِ عَارِفِيهِ شَائِقَةٌ

"O God your greatness is fully apparent to the eyes of those who love you and the brightness of the hearts of your believers are from the excitement of your love"

يَا مُنَى قُلُوبِ الْمُشْتَاقِينَ ويَا غَايَةَ آمَالِ الْمُحِبِّينَ

أَسْأَلُكَ حُبَّكَ وَ حُبَّ مَنْ يُحِبُّكَ وَ حُبَّ كُلِّ عَمَلٍ يُوصِلُنِي إِلَى قُرْبِكَ وَ أَنْ تَجْعَلَكَ أَحَبَّ إِلَيَّ مِمَّا سِوَاكَ

وَ أَنْ تَجْعَلَ حُبِّي إِيَّاكَ قَائِداً إِلَى رِضْوَانِكَ وَ شَوْقِي إِلَيْكَ ذَائِداً عَنْ عِصْيَانِكَ

"O the wishes of the desired hearts O endless desire of loved ones

I seek your help, your friendship, your love and the ones that are your friends. Assist me in anything that will get me closer to you and keep me away from anything that will separate me from you"

وَ امْنُنْ بِالنَّظَرِ إِلَيْكَ عَلَيَّ وَ انْظُرْ بِعَيْنِ الْوُدِّ وَ الْعَطْفِ إِلَيَّ وَ لَا تَصْرِفْ عَنِّي وَجْهَكَ

وَ اجْعَلْنِي مِنْ أَهْلِ الْإِسْعَادِ وَ الْحِظْوَةِ (الْحُظْوَةِ) عِنْدَكَ يَا مُجِيبُ يَا أَرْحَمَ الرَّاحِمِينَ

"Allow me the honor of a glimpse of your beauty and bestow me your kind and generous nature and never look away from me O Most Merciful Most Generous"

Dr: Typically, supplications are like this. The morning supplication that we saw yesterday was the same. It first introduced God then mentions the blessings that God has given us.

يا من ارقدني في مها دامنه و اما نه... و كف اكف الاسوء عني بيده و سلطانه

Then it sends it greetings to the Prophet that showed us the way to him. Then again it introduces itself. What would happen if God was not around? What has my inner self brought on me?

الهي قرعت باب رحمتك بيد رجايي

"I am empty handed but I am hopeful"

Sh: I am astonished by the sequel these supplications have. I mean, it seems as though all of them follow a particular trend.

Dr: Yes, typically it is that way, and we evaluate the authenticity of the supplication.

Sh: Unfortunately, we are unaware of these supplications. The volumes of our supplications are, and most are the same ones that are mentioned in the Quran, and it starts with Dear Lord or My Lord.

Dr: Praise the Lord, regarding this matter, we are prosperous.

Sh: How many books do you have like this Mafatih?

Dr: We have many supplication books. This is because many of our old clerics cited authentic supplications from the Ahl al Bayt, in their papers.

Sh: Do you mean that you have more supplications other than this one?

Dr: We have so many supplications that if we had time and dedicated all of the hours of our Hajj to it, we still would not have enough time.

Sh: These daily supplications, just like I said: before, are very beautiful, especially Sunday and Tuesday.

Dr: You are right.

Sh: The supplications being read after the prayers are also very good. For every pray, there is a supplication afterward.

Combining the Zuhr, Asir and Maghrib, Isha Prayer

Sh: If you read the Zuhr and Asir pray together and read Maghrib and Isha together, then what do you do for the Taghibat (supplications after Prayer)?

The Doctor & Sheikh's Debate

Dr: Between the Zuhr and Asir pray we read the Taghibat for Zuhr pray after Zuhr pray and the Taghibat for the Asir pray after Asir pray.

Sh: In your opinion, do you not see any problem in reading the Zuhr, Asir, Maghrib, and Isha pray at the same time? When the rest of the Muslims are reading them separately.

Dr: I have to admit I think that our Sunni brothers are acting better than we are here. I mean that they read each Prayer at its own time.

Sh: Thank the Lord that you at least approve of one thing that we do.

Dr: Dear Sheikh, I did initially start to discuss the similarities between us and did tell you that we didn't have many differences in these grounds, and praying was one of them.

Sh: Yes, regarding the essential Prayer we agreed, but the fact that we read them separately was what I wanted to point out.

Dr: Reading the prayers together is allowed but it isn't necessarily better, and therefore many of our clerics will delay a bit between the Maghrib and Isha, Zuhr and Asir Prayer so that it could slowly be implicated.

Sh: Do you have a reason for reading the prayers together?

Dr: Yes, please look at the software on my mobile. On page 105 of Sunan, "Tarmazi" says from Ibn Abbas:

جمع رسول الله بين الظهر والعصر و بين المغرب و العشا بالمدينه من غير خوف ولا مطر قال فقيل لابن عباس ما اراد بذلك؟ قال اراد ان لا يحرج امته،

"The Prophet while staying in Medina delayed no time between the Zuhr and Asir, Maghrib and Isha prayer even though there was no rain or a scare of anything. They asked Ibn Abbas: What was the intention of the Prophet doing that? He replied: It was because he did not want to trouble his Ummah (meaning at times when if you delay between the prayers, it will cause any trouble it is okay to use this method).

"Sh: They are trying to find a Fatwa for the same thing in Egypt so they can read the Zuhr and Asir prayer together.

Dr: In any case, it is better to read them separately, but it is also allowed to be read together.

Sh: Let's go back to the supplications.

Dr: I agree, let's go back to the supplications.

Sh: By the way, the supplication of Jawshan Kabir and Mujeer strengthened my belief in what you were saying regarding the Fact that you don't consider God to be on the same level as the Prophet and Ali.

Dr: Yes, all of the supplications of Mujeer expressed the attributes of God, and we read, "O Shelterer, please shelter us."

Sh: The Jawshan Kabir supplication is the same.

Dr: That is correct, that supplication has one thousand names and attributes of the Lord that after every ten times, we mention God's name and his attributes again. Dear Lord, please save us from the fire of hell. I am not sure if you have seen Jawshan Saghir as well?

Sh: Yes, I did get to see it, but it had a significant difference.

Dr: What difference?

Sh: It appears that this particular supplication is used for succeeding in war.

Dr: You are correct. It was read in the thirty-three days of the war in Hezbullah Lebanon with Israel which succeeded in Lebanon. Hezbullah had asked the Jawshan Saghir to be ready for success.

Sh: Let's, please go back to Sahifa Sajjadiya.

Supplication for Repentance

اَللَّهُمَّ یَا مَنْ لاَ یَصِفُهُ نَعْتُ الْوَاصِفِینَ

وَ یَا مَنْ لاَ یُجَاوِزُهُ رَجَاءُ الرَّاجِینَ

وِیَا مَنْ لاَ یَضِیعُ لَدَیْهِ أَجْرُ الْمُحْسِنِینَ

وِیَا مَنْ هُوَ مُنْتَهَى خَوْفِ الْعَابِدِینَ

وِیَا مَنْ هُوَ غَایَةُ خَشْیَةِ الْمُتَّقِینَ

هَذَا مَقَامُ مَنْ تَدَاوَلَتْهُ أَیْدِي الذُّنُوبِ وَقَادَتْهُ أَزِمَّةُ الْخَطَایَا وَاسْتَحْوَذَ عَلَیْهِ الشَّیْطَانُ

فَقَصَّرَ عَمَّا أَمَرْتَ بِهِ تَفْرِیطاً وَ تَعَاطَى مَا نَهَیْتَ عَنْهُ تَغْرِیراً
کَالْجَاهِلِ بِقُدْرَتِكَ عَلَیْهِ أَوْ کَالْمُنْکِرِ فَضْلَ إِحْسَانِكَ إِلَیْهِ حَتَّى إِذَا انْفَتَحَ لَهُ بَصَرُ الْهُدَى وَ تَقَشَّعَتْ عَنْهُ سَحَائِبُ

The Doctor & Sheikh's Debate

الْعَمَى

أَحْصَى مَا ظَلَمَ بِهِ نَفْسَهُ وفَكَّرَ فِيمَا خَالَفَ بِهِ رَبَّهُ فَرَأَى كَبِيرَ عِصْيَانِهِ كَبِيراً وجَلِيلَ مُخَالَفَتِهِ جَلِيلاً

فَأَقْبَلَ نَحْوَكَ مُؤَمِّلاً لَكَ مُسْتَحْيِياً مِنْكَ وَ وَجَّهَ رَغْبَتَهُ إِلَيْكَ ثِقَةً بِكَ فَأَمَّكَ بِطَمَعِهِ يَقِيناً وَ قَصَدَكَ بِخَوْفِهِ إِخْلَاصاً

قَدْ خَلَا طَمَعُهُ مِنْ كُلِّ مَطْمُوعٍ فِيهِ غَيْرِكَ وأَفْرَخَ رَوْعُهُ مِنْ كُلِّ مَحْذُورٍ مِنْهُ سِوَاكَ

فَمَثَلَ بَيْنَ يَدَيْكَ مُتَضَرِّعاً وَ غَمَّضَ بَصَرَهُ إِلَى الْأَرْضِ مُتَخَشِّعاً وَ طَأْطَأَ رَأْسَهُ لِعِزَّتِكَ مُتَذَلِّلاً

"O God, O He whom the depiction of the describers fails to describe!

O He beyond whom passes not the hope of the hopers!

O He with whom is not lost the wage of the good-doers!

O He who is the ultimate object of the fear of the worshipers!

O He who is the utmost limit of the dread of the God fearing!

This is the station of him whom sins have passed from hand to hand

Offenses reins have led him on

And Satan has gained mastery over him

He fell short of what Thou hast commanded through neglect

And he pursued what Thou hast prohibited in delusion

Like one ignorant of Thy power over him

Or one who denies the bounty of Thy beneficence toward him

Until, when the eye of guidance was opened for him

And the clouds of blindness were dispelled

He reckoned that through which he has wronged himself

And reflected upon that in which he had opposed his Lord

He saw his vast disobedience as vast and his great opposition as great

So, turned to Thee, hoping in Thee and ashamed before Thee

And he directed his beseeching toward Thee, having trust in Thee

He repaired to Thee in his longing with certitude and he went straight to Thee in fear with sincerity

His longing was devoid of every object of longing but Thee

And his fright departed from every object of fear but Thee

So, he stood before Thee pleading

His eyes turned toward the ground in humbleness

His head bowed before Thy might in lowliness"

Dr: Would you like us to read the whole supplication?

Sh: No, I wish to show you these parts, you have read them before.

Sh: I have a problem with this supplication of Taubat because contrary to the supplication of Mujeer or Jawshan Kabir, it implores to the Prophet and the Imams instead of God.

Dr: We discussed the imploring before. In this supplication, it seeks intercession just like the ones that the Sunni clerics in Smarghand implored to Bukhari's grave, and now we urge to the Prophet and his Ahl al Bayt.

Sh: I accept, I acknowledge, however, the month of Shaban had less supplication and instead Ramadan had more.

Dr: That is because we do not know just supplication independently. There must be an order from the Imams to read a specific supplication. I do agree, however, that the month of Shaban has fewer supplications.

Sh: The month of Ramadan also has very interesting supplications. The important point there was that in most of the supplications it was requesting God to permit them to go to Hajj.

The Doctor & Sheikh's Debate

Dr: That is correct. Some believe that the allowance of Pilgrimaging the Prophet and Hajj is decided in the month of Ramadan.

Sh: But the supplication for Abu Hamza Thumali is also for the month of Ramadan.

Dr: Yes, it has been recommended for the dawns of the month of Ramadan.

Sh: Then you would have to stay up all night to read that supplication.

Dr: Yes, it is a very long supplication. Even though it is possible that some read the whole supplication every night but typically one or two pages of the supplication is read every night.

Sh: The important fact about this supplication is that it explains many of the punishments. For instance, we see in the supplication of Abu Hamza Thumali:

لعلك فقد فقدتني من مجالس العلماء فخذ لتي

او لعلك رأيتني في الغافلين فمن رحمتك آيستني...

Dr: As I said: our supplications are all thanking, learning and seeking. In this part it is teaching many things for instance in the supplication of Ramadan:

اللهم ادخل على اهل القبور السرور

supplication starts for the people in the graveyard and those that are dead and then follows up to the deprived, poor, sick, travellers and ...This teaches us not to just think about ourselves.

Sh: Yes, you are correct, that was a very interesting fact that you mentioned. What is the supplication of Ahd?

Dr: That is one those discussions that I would like to have with you on a separate matter.

Sh: These separate discussions are increasing.

Dr: It is because I have studied mathematics and can deal with discussions one by one, 1,2,3, and so on.

Pilgrimaging in Shia'sm and the license Permission for Sunni to Pilgrimage

Sh: I agree however there were many supplications in this book.

Dr: Our supplications are very different to yours.

Sh: In our supplications we say:

السلام عليك يا نبي‌الله و رحمةُ الله و بركاته

"Peace be upon you, O' Prophet and the mercy and blessings of God"

Dr: Well your supplications are a bit longer than that, however, because they are based on a chain of incorrect transmissions of Hadith, they are very short.

Sh: I say not as long are your supplications and not as short as ours. Some of your supplications are either one page or ten pages long even though I have not read them. What is the story behind them?

Dr: For the Ahl al Bayt, pilgrimage and supplications are different from pilgrimage for our Sunni brothers.

Sh: Why do you class yourself as followers of Ahl al Bayt? Are we not followers of Ahl al Bayt?

Dr: No, you are not supporters of Ahl al Bayt. You respect Ahl al Bayt, and you like them, but you don't follow them. We look at them as leaders that had the responsibility of guiding a society. However, you look at them as the Prophet's children and like them accordingly. I have to add that, this is the case with you guys, or else the Wahabis only view them as normal Muslims. Have a look at the books of Ibn Taymiyyah. It has gotten so bad that recently tens of books have been written against him.

Sh: We are talking about us, let's leave Ibn Taymiyyah alone.

Dr: Very well.

Sh: Pilgrimaging your way is certainly not allowed.

Dr: Let's have a look at the software on my mobile. Let's see what it says regarding pilgrimaging the graves.

Sh: We are permitted to pilgrimage them; we do not need the software.

Dr: That is true, but you said: first that pilgrimaging the graves was forbidden then was freed.

The Doctor & Sheikh's Debate

Sh: We have many Hadith's, very many.

Dr: There are many Hadith's in your books saying that the Prophet forbids three things and one of them was pilgrimaging the graves. That was allowed later on and was said that it teaches remembrance of the next world and prudence and piety in this world.

Sh: Yes, there are many mentions of this Hadith in Sihah al Sittah.

Dr: Yes, the majority of the context from Sihah al Sittah is regarding this and more than 150 more books talk about this in my software.

اني كنت نهيتكم عن زيارةً القبور فزوروها فان فيها عبره

Only the end is different for instance:

تزهد في الدنيا و تذكر الاخره

Sh: That is correct. This context is available in most books.

Dr: I am no Hadith expert but based on my knowledge from religion, Quran, God and the Prophet, I can say that this Hadith is wrong and fraud.

Sh: Why is it wrong? Why is it fraud?

Dr: I believe that based on Quran the Prophet is:

ما ينطق عن الهوى ان هوالا وحي يوحي

Therefore, the Prophet cannot say something from his own belief and then that gets corrected especially not one thing but three things.

Sh: Why can that not happen?

Dr: Have a look at this Hadith so one case of a certain mistake can be clarified. In the chain of transmissions below you will see proof of the Prophet pilgrimaging his mother's grave:

Zak al Masir Ibn Jazi, volume 3, page 237, Aldar al Mansour, volume 5, page 177; Tafsire Ghartabi, volume 9, page 159; Tafsir Khazan, volime 3, page 350 and Al Tazakor Ghartabi, volume 1, page 12, Al Sayarah Al Habiya, volume 2.

ان النبي مر بقبر امه آمنه، فتوضا، صلي ركعتين ثم بكي فبكي الناس لبكائه ثم انصرف عليهم فقالو ما الذي بكاك ـ فقال مررت بقبر امي فصلت ركعتين ثم استاذت ربي ان استغفرلها

"The Prophet went to his mother's grave, Aminah. He then did ablution and read two Sermon Salat (Pray). He then cried and everyone cried with him. He then went towards the people they asked him: who was this that you cried for? He replied: It was my mother's grave, I read two Sermon Salat and then requested God's permission for forgiveness for her."

Sh: Yes, this is also correct.

Dr: This Hadith also discusses praying in the graveyard that you guys loathe so much and question.

Sh: Yes, slowly, everything about us is questioned.

Dr: I am bringing proof from your books.

Sh: What happened to the answer regarding the Hadith that forbid pilgrimaging and then allowed it?

Dr: We agreed that firstly the Quran would be our criteria and then Hadith.

Sh: Correct, but which part of this Hadith is contrary to what the Quran says?

Dr: What more than it being 100% contradicting what the Quran says? The Prophet has never changed what he has said: in his entire lifetime. There might be times when the ordinances have been tighter and harder (for example, drinking alcohol), but it has never wholly changed. I mean that something Lawful has never become unlawful. Even the ordinances that have become harder or like the ones that have become easier have verses of the Quran to back them up. In other words, the Quran abrogates an ordinance by another verse of its own.

Sh: Well, do you have any other Hadith that is contradicting this one?

Dr: We have plenty in our books, but since our deal is to bring proof from your books we can have a look at these: Hadith volume 5, page 44, Sunan Ibn Majah number 1599. Aisha says: a look at these ones: Hadith volume 5, page 44, Sunan Ibn Majah number 1599. Aisha says:

رخص في زيارةْ القبور فان تزهد في الدنيا وتذكرةْ الاخره

This Hadith is without the prohibition of the first Hadith.

Sh: Maybe it is permission given after something that has been forbidden?

Dr: But I think once Aisha saw that people are discussing forbiddance from pilgrimaging, she then decided to mention the Prophet's Hadith.

Sh: Well, that could also be a possibility.

Dr: But this cancels the doubt of the Prophet changing his decision.

Sh: If we class that as a problem then yes, we can use it to cancel the doubt.

Dr: Do you mean to say that it is okay for the Prophet to change the ordinance that Quran has had no opinion on?

Sh: If I say no then you will bring the Quran and:" ما ينطق عن الهوى " up again.

Dr: Do you not see this as reasonable?

Sh: Of course, it is reasonable.

Dr: Please look at Madarik Al Tanzil Al Beyhaghi, volume 2, page 84, that I have referred to it before as well:

لقد بكى رسول الله على ابراهيم و قال القلب يحزن و العين تدمع و لا نقول ما اسخط الرب و انا عليك يا ابراهيم لمحزونون

"The Prophet cried for Ibrahim and he told him that the hearts are mournful and the eyes tear but we do not say anything to anger God. We are mournful for you O Ibrahim."

Sh: Yes, that is correct.

Dr: The other false belief is another Hadith saying that the women are forbidden to pilgrimage the graveyards.

Sh: There are many Hadith's confirming this that cannot be denied.

Dr: The majority of the Hadith come from Abu Huraira citing in various books of Sihah al Sittah that the Prophet said:

لعن زوارات القبور

"Curse the women whom are pilgrimaging the graves"

Sh: Is it only Abu Huraira citing regarding this?

Dr: Others have cited it too, but most of the Hadith's that are in the same content come from Abu Huraira.

Sh: Others have still cited regarding this in Sihah al Sittah.

Dr: Yes, Vali Tarmazi in Sunan, volume 4, page 94, believes that it would not be logical. He says that some of the cleric's opinions are that this Hadith was before the permission of pilgrimaging any grave and when the permission was given, it was also given for women as well.

Sh: But you said that condemning a Hadith that is forbidden cannot be allowed afterward.

Dr: Precisely, that is the reason why I say that accepting some of the scholars Hadith's, for example, Tarmazi is a mistake. This is just like how they are trying to find an excuse for this Hadith as well.

Sh: I don't recall any Hadith permitting a woman to pilgrimage the graves.

Dr: I have them in the program on my mobile. Please have a look at these chains of transmissions: Musnad Abi Yaali, volume 10, page 131, Ibn Abi Malika says:

اقبلت ذات اليوم من المقابر فقلت لها من اين اقبلت يا ام‌المؤمنين(عايشه)، قالت:

من قبر اخي عبد الرحمن. فقلت لها ام‌المؤمنين،

اكان رسول ينهي عن زيارةَ القبور، قالت نعم كان نهي عن زيارتها فاجازه...

"I saw Aisha walking back from the graveyard one day and I said: O Umul Momenin, where are you coming from? She said: I come from my brother's grave, Abdul Rahman. I said: to her: Hasn't the Prophet forbidden pilgrimaging the graves? She said: Yes, the forbidding was before and then he allowed it..."

Sh: This Hadith proves the previous one.

Dr: But it contradicts the forbiddance of woman pilgrimaging. It means that it validates what Tarmazi said.

Sh: Yes, that permits them.

Dr: Then if that is the case, it can be said that this Hadith did not exist just like the first one.

The Doctor & Sheikh's Debate

Sh: But you said this based from the Quran. You said that his Hadith is incorrect based on the Quran. Therefore, we can use the same analysis regarding forbidding woman pilgrimaging the graves using the Quran. Aisha and Tarmazi's Hadith confirmed it.

Dr: It is good that eventually, you agreed to believe the truth over incorrect Hadith's.

Sh: What advantage could the companions have from making up Hadith's such as this?

Dr: I am not quite sure. However, I think that because the Calipha felt that the presence of people especially woman would not be wise to witness crimes such as when Muawiyah's mother ate martyr Hamza's heart out or the Karbala's martyr's and Hura. It would jeopardize their intentions and so therefore, they had to do something to prevent people from pilgrimaging the dead, keeping their crimes un-seen.

Sh: That was an interesting possibility.

Dr: Let's discuss now what to say when pilgrimaging. In the Baqi graveyard there is a sign saying that we are only allowed to say the following:

السلام عليكم و نحن انشاءلله بكم لاحقون

Sh: That is true although it is different in various countries and religions.

Dr: That is correct. I have read some of the pilgrimage books of Muslim countries such as Pakistan, Indonesia and Malaysia. It is very detailed. However, in Saudi Arabia and amongst Wahabis the above verse is the only thing that is said and publicized in Baqi.

Sh: We don't have any more than these sayings.

Dr: Yes, you do. You have in Mu'jam al-Tabarani, volume 4, page 58. Wahb Zydbn says: When Ali would return from Siffin he would pilgrimage the graves and say:

السلام عليكم يا اهل الديار من المؤمنين أنتم لنا سلف فارط و نحن لكم تبع عما قليل لاحق. اللهم اغفرلنا و لهم و تجاوز بعفوك عنا و عنهم. طوبي لمن ذكر المعاد وعمل الحساب و قنع بالكفاف و رضي عن الله

"Salam Alaikum (Hello) to you O' from the land of the believers. You are before the time of us and we will join you soon. O' God forgive and pardon us and them. I envy the person that reflects on his actions on judgment day and acts accordingly and is content with sufficient and is fulfilled with God."

Sh: I have not seen it but it is possible.

Dr: Here you go. Have a look at my mobile.

Sh: Yes, but I said that the supplications for pilgrimaging the graveyards are not the only ones that are written in Baqi.

Dr: And I brought up an example of one. For instance, please have a look at this sample too:

Sh: Which sample?

Pilgrimaging and Its Ritual's Based on Alazhar

Dr: In Fatwa Alazhar, Chapter Hajj, Volume 1, page 198, supplication of Medina:

"If this Haji was not able to initial a travel to pilgrimage the Prophet (peace be upon him) then it would be tradition for him to pilgrimage the Prophet after he is done with Hajj. This is because it is one the biggest sectors and highest approached. There are many Hadith regarding the advantages of undertaking this. You have to instead, pray in the shrine of the Prophet in order to obtain reward. In the Hadith of Sharif, from the Prophet (peace be upon him): "Praying in my shrine is 1000 times more rewarding other than Masjid Al Haram" Ahmad says in his Musnad from Abdullah that: The pilgrim should conduct ablution and wear his best clothes and smell well. If he was not able to conduct ablution he can Wudu. Then head towards the Shrine of the Prophet with humility and humbleness. Once he enters the shrine head towards the Rawda Sharif (Prophet's shrine, garden of heaven) that is between the honourable grave and the Prophet's tribune and read two sermon prayers named Tahiyat in the Mosque and call God and pray to him because he is in the presence of one of the gardens of the heavenly gardens. He is in the place where mercy is given and prayers are answered to. Once the pilgrim is done with salution of the Mosque he then turns towards the grave of the Prophet (peace be upon him) and stands by the side of the Prophet's blessed head and salutes the Prophet (peace be upon him) with a lowered voice and send his regards from himself and the people that have asked him to salute on their behalf."

Sh: This is just like how your pilgrimage.

Dr: This is Fatwa from Alazhar. Although this exact saying is also mentioned in the collected Fatwa's of Egypt.

Sh: You are right. This is exactly believed in Egypt.

Dr: Then you just wished for me to explain it all.

The Doctor & Sheikh's Debate

Sh: I have seen these in Egypt, but the truth is that I have not even had the chance to read these chains of transmissions. Moreover, it is fascinating to me that you have sat down and have done it.

Sh: You initially mentioned in our discussion that regarding Pilgrimaging, there had been many sayings.

Dr: Yes, that is because usually, the Imams of Shia and the children of the Ahl al Bayt are under scrutiny and accusations from the Umayyad and Abbasid's. To prevent the allegations from becoming a belief and to also continue their direction towards protesting through their believers, they include their great sayings via these supplications. That is why the contents of these supplications are lovely.

Sh: Yes, I saw this in some of the supplications, such as the supplication of Ashura; however, I was not able to dismantle the educational concepts.

Dr: Supplications normally start with a salute. It is normally a remembrance of the beginning, meaning the start of Adam, until it reaches the Imam in question. This is because it wants to show that we have one righteous path and that the path only starts from Adam and finishes with the Prophet Muhammad and that you are on that same path.

Sh: It is a delicate point.

Dr: The second point is martyrdom in Islam and believing in the actions that they do especially this one:

اشهدانك اقمت الصلوةْ واتيت الزكوةْ وأمرت بالمعروف و نَهَيْتَ عن المنكر...

This part is only there because the Umayyad and Abbasid's would accuse the Imams of rebelling against religion.

Sh: Yes, you are right, but all of them accept Ali.

Dr: Muawiyah has insisted on cursing Ali and most of the people of Shaam abided by it.

Sh: That was done for a short, and it was then obviated.

Dr: When Ali was killed, and it was announced that he was killed in the Mosque, the people from Shaam asked: How could Ali be killed in a Mosque when he wouldn't pray?

Sh: Yes, these were only happening in Muawiyah's time.

Dr: Didn't these actions continue until Umar Ibn Abdul Aziz's time?

Sh: Yes, it did continue until then.

Dr: Didn't Yazid say that Hussain Ibn Ali had revolted against Islam and the people of Koofeh have to kill him and to hold his family captive? Did Yazid not accuse them of being outcasts?

Sh: Yes, that is correct.

Dr: Things were no better within Abbasi's either. Even though they do not kill the Imams in broad daylight, that is why we have kept these martyrdoms for the history of martyrdom.

Sh: Martyrdom is not appointed to die at all.

Dr: Of course, it isn't. We only appoint them to Imams and their children. We read the verses of the Quran and Surat Al Fatihah for the people who are familiar and have passed away.

Sh: But these supplications are more extended than these discussions.

Dr: Yes, in some of these supplications, it has been mentioned how they tortured the Ahl al Bayt and even in some of them how they were martyred. For instance, in the supplication of Ashura, many of the comments are mentioned.

Sh: There are also many curses.

Dr: Yes, I did explain those. That is because the curses itself teach you something. It shows you not to go killing the Prophet's children.

Sh: Your analysis is correct.

When the discussion got to this point, Mr. Karbalayi came over with some tea and Persian sweets and snacks. As usual, my friends were quite the whole duration for the discussion and were listening. The ones that were unable to speak Arabic would quietly leave the room.

At this moment, the Spiritual guide of the trip which was familiar with Arabic entered the room. Due to his young age and inexperience, I was scared that he would say something to offend the Sheikh, but thankfully, after I introduced the Sheikh and noted that he was one of the scholars from Alazhar, he only asked some minor questions, and I translated some of it. He said: Why is Shi'asm not taught in Alazhar? Among other items that were a representative of his lack of experience in publications and external relations. Shia'sm does get shown in Alazhar.

The Confessions of Mohammad Ibn Abudl Wahab

Dr: By the way dear Sheikh, have you seen the book called "مفاهيم يجب أن تصحح" "Concepts that are in need of correction"?

Sh: I have heard about it but not read it.

Dr: That book is written by Seyed Mohammad Alavi al-Maliki al-Hassani from Mecca.

Sh: Yes, I have heard about it, its content must be interesting. The concepts that need correction are intriguing to know.

Dr: I have it. Please have a look at it. It rejects most of the Sunni beliefs and it says that it needs correcting. It quotes from Muhammad Ibn Abdulwahab and that the Wahabis on watch for Baqi are acting against what it is supposed to be.

Sh: Which Fatwa?

Dr: On page 310, in this book, mentions the Al-Dor Al Sonniya book, volume 1, page 52.

Muhammad Ibn Abdul Wahab has declared 12 things to be false and an accusation. They are as followed:

1- I voided the books of Mazaheb.

2- People had nothing for 600 years ago.

3- I claimed my Ijtihad.

4- I am against imitating.

5- It is a catastrophe to socialize with scholars.

6- I class anyone that invokes towards the righteous, to be infidels.

7- If I had the power to demolish the Prophet's shrine, then I would do so.

8- I deny supplicating the Prophet's grave.

9- I refuse to supplicate the parent's grave.

10- I class anyone that bows to anyone but God to be an infidel.

Moreover, ...

Dr: On my program, via my mobile, I have the book of Sheikh Muhammad Ibn Abdul Wahab, volume 1, page 15 saying:

Sheikh Muhammad forbids imitating for the people that can identify guidance and evidence. People that do not have the aptitude of identifying all cases they are allowed and in need of mirroring. Therefore, Sheikh Muhammad Bataan has formally denied imitating when people that are present in Baqi talk as if Muhammad Ibn Abdul Wahab has forbidden it.

The Dynamics of Authority and Imitating in Shia'sm

Sh: You are right. This is because this subject has been discussed in some of the books, but no one has, in particular, has pointed it out to be against imitating.

Dr: Then how come when it comes to discussing Shia' so they question why we imitate? Are we not to imitate at all?

Sh: Yes, some ordinary people say this but our scholars spend less time regarding it.

Dr: Actually, I believe that scholars influence the mind of the familiar people in the wrong way even though they think in imitating.

Sh: It appears to me that you only follow the ordinances from people that are alive. While we act on the laws that the four scholars have appointed out and have no Fatwa for them unless of course something serious happens.

Dr: In fact, imitating in Shia'sm is not for the principles of Din (religion), but it is for the branches of Din. What I mean is that no one can rely its recognition and belief on God, its Prophet, Quran, and resurrection by relying on imitating. That would be wholly reprobated. Imitating should only be on the branches of Din.

Sh: You mean Salat (praying), fasting, and...

Dr: Yes, however, this imitating has two conditions. Firstly, the person should not be a researcher in religion and or be religious Jurist in any shape or form, which would be prohibited. Secondly, the person can only imitate someone that has is well aware of the science of Din and has particular circumstances.

The Doctor & Sheikh's Debate

Sh: We have the first condition that you mentioned as well. We do not have the other one condition, though. What I mean is that typically, the Scholars that are being imitated are the scholars running the government.

Dr: You are right, in your school if the person is a scholar or researcher, then he does not imitate someone else. There is one difference, though, and that is, some of the sayings of your four Imams are required to be complied with, and it cannot be altered. However, in Shia'sm the scholar that is being imitated on can research on his own accord regarding all subjects and can claim Ijtihad and innovate a new idea.

Sh: Do you mean to say that he would say something over Imam Jafar?

Dr: If there is a certainty that what he is about to say is not going against what they have said then yes. However, there is no restriction for them to claim Ijtihad and to interpret what the imams have said.

Sh: What do you mean? This is a little complicated for me now.

Dr: It isn't complicated. A researcher of religion that is familiar with the required various sciences of Din can quickly, by using the verses of the Quran, authentic Hadith, and his logic, appoint necessary ordinances for the secondary principles of the Din that is needed.

Sh: This would provide too many alterations to the matters that are considered to be branches of religion. People could pray in different styles.

Dr: That is not the case because 99% of the structures of the branches are uniform and steady. They do not have many differences, either. There is, however, the difference in matters of Ijtihad and some excellent subjects.

Sh: Regarding Salat (Pray), Fasting, Hajj, and Zakat (Alms), there are no differences between our schools.

Dr: You do have differences, but they are minor. For instance, some read the initial part of the verses where it says: "الرحيم الرحمن الله بسم" loudly, some read it with a whisper. Some keep their arms open while praying, and some close them.

Sh: Yes, these cases are not that important.

Dr: In Shia'sm the differences between our Religious Jurist's is not even as much as yours. All of our practices and recitals regarding praying are the same. It might be possible for some of the chains of transmissions while prostrating is different, very rarely of course or else their opinions in praying are all the same.

Sh: If they are so similar, then why did you open up a discussion regarding imitating?

Dr: There is a difference between choosing to imitate and to not having any gaps in imitating. Jurists, Scholars that you can refer to cannot work based on their taste. They have to be very reasonable once they are trying to extract an ordinance from the Quran. What I mean is, they must have, a thorough dominance on the Arabic language and Sciences such as the contextual, study of Hadith, biographies of the narrators of traditions and ordinances that have been previously extracted, so they can be able to implement a new directive.

Sh: We only implement new Fatwa's (provisions) based on contemporary issues, and for the old problems we pursue what the Four Imams in their books have said.

Dr: Based on the beliefs and Fatwa's that our scholars have given, one cannot imitate someone dead. However, if a person was previously imitating someone that has recently passed away then based on the thing he is imitating on, he can follow the ordinances of the old one.

However, for a person that has not had any previous imitates and is now of time to do so, he cannot choose someone that has passed away and is under no circumstances allowed to follow them.

Sh: So, everyone is imitating a person that is alive?

Dr: Precisely, this is because, in reality, a religious Jurist that is being imitated is acting as an Imam. It is not possible to imitate an Imam that is dead, or if a question arises, it is not possible to ask them anything.

Sh: We can answer questions, but we are not allowed to change any practices and recitals in praying.

Dr: The problem is that our issues are not always just for praying. For instance, for Hajj, there are consistency changes in place of Safa and Marwah, where to Sacrificial slaughter, Remy Jamrat (Pebbles Remy) and similar to these situations. These new issues need to be answered to.

Sh: These things are not changed until the people in charge question them.

Dr: It appears as if though that the people in charge act based on needs, and it is highly unlikely to question the Jurists.

Sh: Would they at least ask for their approval?

Dr: Yes, they ask for their approval, but if you pay attention, these approvals are consistently being changed, and the order of the government has been more influential.

Sh: The government's order is more influential, that is correct; however, the opinions of the highly honored scholars are also considered.

Dr: Has there ever been any questioning from the University of Alazhar saying that they wish to change a specific thing regarding the current situation of one of the practices, for instance, Remy Jamrat (that is consistently being changed)?

Sh: No, they ask the Sheikhs and highly honored scholars of Saudi Arabia.

Dr: Do they imitate other Sheikhs and Jurists of other countries too?

Sh: They have no choice because these changes have been already done.

Dr: Well, our scholars call for opinions when they want to change anything.

Sh: Give me an example.

Dr: For instance, if the slaughterhouse is outside of the Valley of Mena, then the sacrificial is not accepted. Some of the slaughterhouses are currently out of Mena. Sh: Then, what do you guys do?

Dr: The Iranian associations of Hajj have chosen slaughterhouses that are inside of Mena.

Sh: This complicates things.

Dr: This is an example. Not all of the Imams that are being imitated on having the same opinions on this matter but I just wanted to give you an example that in this case, Ijtihad and imitating, dynamics and activation are happening. The livelihood of the Mufti in this situation is not under any pressure to follow whatever change that has occurred.

Sh: But Islam is permissive.

Dr: There is a difference between being permissive and being active.

Sh: But being active will complicate things more.

Dr: Allow me to give you an example. Thirty years ago, when I came to Hajj, your scholars did not allow any toilets to be installed in Arafa. This matter inconvenienced so many pilgrimages. Every year many people would suffocate in barrels of contaminated water. Now after many efforts there is not only toilets but also, they allowed tree planting, and now the pilgrimages are in relative calmness.

Sh: Yes, those days were terrible.

Dr: When we talk about livelihood we mean that proportional to the circumstances the Imams and Jurists should set ordinances. The main reason for our Imams setting any Fatwa's is all because they wish to simplify the practices of Hajj.

Sh: Yes, you are right; the Fatwas are meant to facilitate people's needs.

Dr: We don't concentrate on simplifying or making strict ordinances. We say the laws are there. In essence, the directives are already simplified. We would never change any ordinances just because some feel that it is hard to do.

Sh: Yes, you are correct, but the Prophet has said be permissive.

Dr: Our religion is simplified in the practices, but there is wisdom necessary for managing it. For instance, do you remember they were burying two million slaughtered sheep when several Islamic countries were suffering poverty and lack of protein?

Sh: These issues have been resolved now.

Dr: Yes, but it was due to the many follow-ups of the advanced Islamic countries in specific Iran and the Fatwa's of its Jurist regarding this matter that induced them to currently package the meats and send them off to poor Islamic countries.

Sh: Praise be to Allah, it is much better.

Dr: There are still many problems. Every year when it comes to Hajj, we still are losing life due to different causes such as fire or bridge falls.

Sh: These accidents are unpredictable.

Dr: It can be predicted that it just needs stronger management.

Sh: For instance, flooding has nothing to do with management, or if a bridge falls, there is nothing administration can do about that.

Dr: You can prevent flooding by gathering all the waste regularly. That reduces the risk of flooding, and unfortunately, that is not happening. For instance, on the way to Remi Jamarat, there are many empty bottles, slippers, shoes, wasted food, and worse, people are sleeping in the corners of the street. There are two reasons why bridges fall. Firstly, the amount of weight it can carry has been calculated by mistake. Secondly, the ordinances that are not compulsory have been deemed mandatory therefore everyone wishes to conduct it in its specific time causing chaos, for instance, the Remi Jamarat or circling the Kaaba. If the Jurists announced a change of opinion that it is not necessary for Hajj for pilgrims to conduct non-compulsory ordinances, this would not happen.

Sh: Of course, that would work better. Most of the scholars don't even conduct on ordinances that are non-compulsory at these times, but the familiar people still insist on performing them.

Dr: But surely you can understand our debate on livelihood. This clarifies what the point is that I am trying to make.

Sh: If it is okay with you. Let's hold on with our debate for now today. I have a problem with meeting you tomorrow for Zuhr because an old friend has invited me from the University of Medina.

Dr: That is not a problem. My roommates have asked me to have a chat with them tomorrow lunchtime when they have more free time. At night times they go out shopping with their women.

Sh: Then if it is okay, let's continue our debate the day after tomorrow as I am a guest somewhere.

Dr: I am at your disposal. Anytime you wish, I can be available to meet with you.

Sh: Then goodbye until the day after tomorrow.

We said goodbye, and he left. At night we went shopping for souvenirs with my friends and my wife. Not to compete with the other pilgrims of Hajj before us but to obey our duty as unfortunately after pilgrimaging and to pray, buying souvenirs is one of the most essential responsibilities of pilgrimage.

Unfortunately, these shopping questions the dignity of the Iranian pilgrims. When people from other countries see how the Iranian pilgrims raid the bazaars buying goods from China or non-Chinese products, they are amazed.

We went to buy a brief souvenir enough to say that you were in our thoughts. We purchased mostly for family and close friend and enough to at least commence on out non-compulsory duties.

The women would choose, and we would try to get involved and then end up paying for it. We returned to the hotel and continued doing what I always used to do which was to go to Al Masjid an Nabawi for the morning prayer, then to Baqi, then back to the hotel to have breakfast and to sleep until it was Zuhr and to get ready for the Zuhr prayer.

Day Twenty Fourth of Zyqadeh

I met the Sheikh when I went to the Mosque for the Zuhr prayer. I realised that he is accompanied with the friend that he was with the day before. I said hello and Sheikh introduced me as a professor of the University in Iran. He introduced his guest to be Sheikh Hamid Al Najdi a professor from the University of Medina.

Getting Acquainted with Sheikh Hamid Al Najdi

Dr: Dear Sheikh, you are from the same city as Sheikh Muhammad Ibn Abdul Wahab.

Sh Hamid: Yes, how did you know that Najd is the city where Sheikh Muhammad Ibn Abdul Wahab is born?

Dr: All of the books that have mentioned his life refer to that city.

I showed him my business card.

Sh Hamid: Are you involved in the automotive industry?

Dr: Yes.

Sh: He isn't just involved in the automotive industry he is a Sheikh as well.

Dr: No, I have worked in the automotive industry.

Sh Hamid: Where have you done your education?

Dr: I studied my bachelors in Iran, my Master's and Doctorate in England.

Sh Hamid: How did you learn Arabic?

Dr: I had much interest and to be able to understand the sources of religion better, I learned it.

Sh Hamid: I have met many Iranian scholars, but they are not able to speak Arabic this way.

Dr: Firstly, that is because I am not a scholar. Secondly, they were from the old ages, nowadays most of our scholars, especially our young students, are familiar with Arabic and can speak very well.

The call for the first prayer was sung, and then the request for the second prayer was made. The prayer started. Afterward...

Sh Hamid: Sheikh Ibrahim and I are alone; you can also be my guest.

Dr: No, thank you very much. I would not wish to be of any bother.

Sh: If you don't have to be anywhere else, please join us. It will be good. Just think of it as being our usual daily debate time. We could even discuss some things in the presence of Sheikh Hamid.

Sh Hamid: Please don't consider yourself to be of any bother. My family is not at home, and it is only Sheikh Ibrahim and me. Please allow a technical discipline amongst your group.

Dr: I will come with you, but I hope that I am of no inconvenience.

Sh Hamid: No, you are not an inconvenience.

Dr: All right then, I will come under one condition, and that is for us to stop at my hotel so I can bring the mobile that contains the program with me.

Sh Hamid: That won't be a problem.

We went to my hotel, driving Sheikh Hamid's car, and I took some Persian sweets and snacks with me. I told my friends where I was going and that I was having lunch with Sheikh Ibrahim and Sheikh Hamid, at his place. We drove until it was close to the Quba Mosque. Sheikh owned a charming villa there. I was a guest for lunch at his home. The outside design of his house was structured in a traditional Arabic way, and inside it was designed with beautiful traditional Arabic sofa and furniture. There was tea, coffee, juice, and lunch ready.

A Debate in Sheikh Hamid's House

There was only one male maid in Sheikh Hamid's house, and he appeared to be there for hospitality. Sheikh Hamid's family had gone to visit their family so that this gathering would have been without much ceremony.

They prepared lunch. Food was brought from the chained restaurant in Saudi Arabia called Al Baik. Sheikh Hamid started to explain what each meal was. Sheikh Ibrahim was familiar with the food too, and I also said that I knew most of the foods and that I even knew the owner of Al Baik, a pure Palestine. They were amazed once I told them that.

Sh Hamid: It is good that you are familiar with the food. How many times have you traveled to Saudi Arabia?

The Doctor & Sheikh's Debate

Dr: My 15th time.

Sh Hamid: 15th time? (he said with astonishment). Were they all Tamattu?

Dr: No, Seven times for Tamattu Hajj and 8 times for Umrah.

Sh Hamid: It appears that you are fond of traveling.

Dr: I am fond of traveling but mostly to the Holy shrines, Mecca, Medina. That is because the history of Islam was structured here.

Sh Hamid: History in Saudi Arabia is gradually being destructed because most of the historical sites have been demolished.

Dr: What is your opinion on this matter?

Sh Hamid: I am completely against it. In other countries, they preserve their cultural remains even though it might not have any ethical effect or also be against ethnicity and humanity. They also savor it for tourists to come and see, but here they destroy what they have without any hesitation.

Dr: Dear Sheikh, I came here thirty years ago. Most of the historical sites were around Al-Masjid an Nabawi, Bani Hashm's street, Quba Mosque, Mea Mosque (hundred), some of the most essential Islamic figures were still there. Now they have destroyed it all so that they can expand the Mosque.

Sh Hamid: They could have expanded the Mosque in other directions.

Dr: Dear Sheikh Hamid, may I ask you something?

Sh Hamid: Sure, please go ahead.

Dr: How can you be a professor of Medina University, and be against the actions of the government?

Sh: Does anyone who is a professor at Medina University has to agree with the actions of the government, especially the non-cultural aspects of it.

Dr: I was under the impression that you were allowed.

Sh Hamid: Well if we do have any objections, we do not state it publicly, but we do talk about it in our friendly gatherings inside or outside the university.

Dr: Allow me to ask you a more pressing question. Are you a Wahabi?

Sh: There are two kinds of Wahabis. One group is the ones that follow Sheikh Muhammad Ibn Abdul Wahab but are against the actions of the government regarding the religious sections. The reason behind that is because it has had a negative influence on the Muslims of other schools. The second group is the extremists that are working for the government, and mostly the religious works are under their supervision.

Dr: Do you see any difference between these two kinds?

Sh Hamid: Yes, the first kind recognizes Sheikh Muhammad Ibn Abdul Wahab to be a religious scholar just like other scholars and acknowledge that he has had some opinions that accompany with Ibn Teymiyah seven hundred years ago. Many were against Ibn Teymiyah, and he died in jail. However, Sheikh Muhammad Ibn Abdul Wahab was lucky because at his time there was a specified political era where it not only did not go against his opinions, but it even assisted in its distribution.

Dr: What is your opinion, Sheikh Ibrahim?

Sh: We had the same opinion as Sheikh Hamid before. The people outside of Saudi Arabia were more restricted; for instance, Sheikh Hamid is Saudi Arabian, and I am Syrian. Maybe that's why my immigration to Egypt and Alazhar was permitted.

Dr: Sheikh Ibrahim, you were defending the Wahabis beliefs.

Sh: Yes, I was favorable towards them and even promoted them, but after I went to Egypt, my opinions changed. Especially my beliefs were weakened.

Sh Hamid: How long have you two been meeting with each other?

Sh: A couple of days ago, accidentally we met in Al-Masjid an Nabawi and have been meeting up with each other. I have not been able to answer back any of the analysis the Doctor has been debating with me because as usual, he either cites the Quran or the books of Sunni faith. I have to be frank that there is not much I can debate with him anymore.

Sh Hamid: We are blessed, dear Sheikh Ibrahim. How come you have had nothing to respond against the analysis of a Doctor that specialized in the automotive industry?

Sh: [With laughter] I have not managed to respond to him accordingly if you can why you don't try.

Dr: No, he is a very honorable man, we talk to each other as two teachers, only he is an expert, and I am a student.

The Doctor & Sheikh's Debate

Sh Hamid: In which fields have you been debating?

Dr: Many, if you agree, let's have lunch and then I can ask you some questions. That is if you all decided to read the Asir prayer at your house.

Sh Hamid: We shall read the Asir pray at my house. So, let's have lunch first.

Lunch was finished and they cleared the table. Someone brought the snacks over with Arabian coffee. While we were having lunch, Sheikh Hamid talked a bit about Iran and its political situation, which were all excellent. The time for Asir prayer arrived.

Sh Hamid: Let us Wudu and pray. Will you be following leadership in prayer with us, or will you be praying again at another time?

Dr: Some believe that they should pray again after the congregational prayer finishes. That is because not all of the etiquette of the prayer is identical. However, most of the Authority of initiation does not see a problem with congregational prayer in Mosques, and therefore, there is no need for re-reading the prayer.

Sh Hamid: How about yourself?

Dr: The person I imitate from does not see the necessity for re-reading the prayer.

Sh Hamid: So, you can be following leadership in prayer with us?

Dr: Yes, I did read my Asir prayer after I finished reading my Zuhr in the Mosque, however; because of the congregation here I will learn again but intention it for a compensatory prayer (missed). I read the Asir prayer with Sheikh Hamid leading the congregational prayer. After the prayer:

Sh: Dear Doctor, what is the supplication after the Asir pray. Let us read it.

Dr: It is not the place.

Sh: Yes, it is, Sheikh Hamid, they have supplications after their prayers. It would be fascinating for you to hear. Please ask the Doctor to read them.

Sh Hamid: It would be nice if you read it, Doctor.

Dr: There is no necessity.

Sh Hamid: supplication after prayer is excellent. Please read on.

Dr: I will do as you wish.

اللهم اني اعوذبك من نفس لا تشبع و من قلب لا يخشع و من علم لا ينفع و من صلاةٍ لا ترفع و من دعا لا يسمع اللهم اني اسألك اليسر بعد العسر و الفرج بعد الكرب و الرخاء بعد الشدةٍ اللهم ما بنا من نعمه فمنك لا اله الا انت استغفرك و اتوب اليك

"O Allah, I surely seek your protection against a self that never has enough, a heart that does not feel apprehension, knowledge that does not avail, a prayer that is not accepted, and a supplication that is not responded, O Allah, I surely beseech You for easiness after difficulty, relief after misfortune and comfort after hardship. O Allah, you are certainly the source of each and every favor that covers us. There is no God save You. I pray Your forgiveness and repent before You."

Sh Hamid: That was interesting.

Sh: I said the same thing.

Sh Hamid: Well please go ahead. What was your question?

Dr: I have question regarding several cases.

Sh Hamid: What cases?

Dr: I have questions regarding Wudu, a chain of transmissions, standing, prostrating, and confession.

Sh: Dear Sheikh Hamid, please answer the Doctors questions. I will remain quiet and will listen.

Dr: Please still be active in this debate.

Sh: I have been in enough debates with you. Please allow Sheikh Hamid to be involved this time.

Dr: In any case, I will ask the question and anyone of your honorable people who wish to answer it, would be great.

Sh Hamid, there are no problems regarding Wudu and Salat between the Muslims. There is no difference between Wahabis or non-Wahabis.

Dr: In fact, that is why I asked the question. However, now that you mentioned Wahabis allow me to ask another question.

Sh Hamid: Please ask away.

Dr: Do you agree with assembling a congregational prayer by force?

Sh Hamid: There is no such thing as a forced congregational prayer.

The Doctor & Sheikh's Debate

Dr: I met with a Sudanese teacher a couple of years ago in Mecca, and he told me that half of the Saudis that participate in the prayers have not even commenced ablution. They might, later on, pray in their own time but they come, so they are in the congregational prayers of the Saudis.

Sh Hamid: Not all, but yes, some might do this.

Dr: He spoke of corruption too, and the pressure that the Government Wahabis have put on the people has not affected.

Sh Hamid: There might be corruption but not in the public eye. It is hidden.

Dr: Corruption is hidden in all cities.

Sh Hamid: Of course, there is much less corruption around the honorable Shrines in Mecca and Medina, but in other cities, there might be a bit more as there are possibilities that non-Muslims live there.

Dr: From what I have heard, there is very much corruption in between families. For instance, in of the European toll results, statistically, the Saudi woman is the most users exploited of websites that are morally corrupted in the world.

Sh Hamid: Do Saudi woman use the internet that much?

Dr: Yes, in fact, they have first place in the world.

Sh Hamid: First place in using the internet?

Dr: In Europe and industrial countries, women and men work therefore have less time to go on the internet. In African counties and most Asian countries, there is less opportunity of using the internet due to financial reasons. In Saudi Arabia, there is money, mobile (computers) and unemployment creating many opportunities for women that are unemployed and has no hobbies. Therefore, they use computers to access the net.

Sh Hamid: Seeking refuge in God, can you see how the westerners are bringing corruption into our homes.

Dr: One of the most critical institutions in the west and the Islamic countries has always been family. The imperialists and communists' hand in hand succeeded to corrupt the families in Europe and industrial countries. Because when people do not have a grounding institution such as functional family, they can easily be used and can be easily brainwashed culturally.

Sh Hamid: How can you say that the imperialists and the communists, hand in hand did this when they were against each other and were always at cold war with each other.

Dr: I believe that they had one thing in common, and that was to destroy the grounds of families. The Communists insisted on getting the people to become non-believers of God so they could destroy the spiritual values of the family. The imperialism disseminated corruption and chaos in families to obliterate them.

Sh Hamid: You studied in Europe. How did you see it there?

Dr: Europeans appeared to be lonely people. They seemed to focus on how to manage their own lives and the tourbillion around them.

Sh Hamid: How did you see the family structures?

Dr: There is a low percentage of people committed to their family and very few who do have a family.

Sh Hamid: They talk about how Jesus has given them happiness then how come there is no happiness between their families?

Dr: But the people who are running the shows have also stopped talking about family and love. Today in Europe, the women and their husbands that are from one family live apart. I mean to say they have separate bank accounts and have their income and spend on that and therefore after a while, they separate as they have no dependency on each other. A European man, on top of having different girlfriends before getting married, gets to also marry three to five times. The woman on top of their several boyfriends gets married five to eight times. Does a woman who gets married eight times have any emotion left?

Sh Hamid: So, they also have several marriages with a difference that it is not all in one time.

Dr: In fact, they do almost all of the things that they despise of us Muslims.

Sh Hamid: I hope to God that these problems do not get to Islamic countries.

Dr: If we are not careful, it will even now, some Islamic countries have already begun to start having the same problems.

Sh Hamid: Where for instance?

Dr: Towards the west, Al Jazeera and the Islamic countries in central Asia.

Sh Hamid: It is not as bad in Saudi Arabia. Families are still structured.

Dr: But it appears to me that these families in specifically the ones outside of Mecca and Medina are like bricks with no mortar built on top of each other and can be destroyed with just the smallest touch.

Sh Hamid: The government has started to concentrate on families, and most of the religious speeches and sermon prayers on the Friday pray are regarding family.

Dr: The problem is more than what you think though. Unfortunately, the faith of the woman in Islam has deteriorated in most of the Islamic countries, due to more restrictions, especially in Saudi Arabia; and therefore, they start creating questions for women, and then they destruct the grounds of the family. You have seen the western movies made and shown in cinema and television. Most of them come from families that have been destructed. They say that a woman does not have to have a sexual relationship with a man, and they advertise it in their films. They advertise sexual relationship between families and therefore, all of the scientists around the Islamic world have to put hand in hand to confront this western souvenir that is consuming the Islamic countries and the third world.

Ablution in Islam

Sh Hamid: Let's go back to the questions.

Dr: Yes, I firstly wish to ask regarding ablution.

Sh: What is your question? Please ask.

Dr: The question I have regarding ablution is this: Regarding anointing, why do you wash your feet instead of just stroking it with water?

Sh Hamid: The answer to this question is very clear and easy. Regarding washing our heads or feet we refer back to the verse in Quran.

Dr: But apparently the verse regarding ablution says nothing about that. The verse in Surat Al-Maidah says:

يَٰٓأَيُّهَا ٱلَّذِينَ ءَامَنُوٓا۟ إِذَا قُمْتُمْ إِلَى ٱلصَّلَوٰةِ فَٱغْسِلُوا۟ وُجُوهَكُمْ وَأَيْدِيَكُمْ إِلَى ٱلْمَرَافِقِ وَٱمْسَحُوا۟ بِرُءُوسِكُمْ وَأَرْجُلَكُمْ إِلَى ٱلْكَعْبَيْنِ ۚ وَإِن كُنتُمْ جُنُبًا فَٱطَّهَّرُوا۟ ۚ وَإِن كُنتُم مَّرْضَىٰٓ أَوْ عَلَىٰ سَفَرٍ أَوْ جَآءَ أَحَدٌ مِّنكُم مِّنَ ٱلْغَآئِطِ أَوْ لَٰمَسْتُمُ ٱلنِّسَآءَ فَلَمْ تَجِدُوا۟ مَآءً فَتَيَمَّمُوا۟ صَعِيدًا طَيِّبًا فَٱمْسَحُوا۟ بِوُجُوهِكُمْ وَأَيْدِيكُم مِّنْهُ ۚ مَا يُرِيدُ ٱللَّهُ لِيَجْعَلَ عَلَيْكُم مِّنْ حَرَجٍ وَلَٰكِن يُرِيدُ لِيُطَهِّرَكُمْ وَلِيُتِمَّ نِعْمَتَهُۥ عَلَيْكُمْ لَعَلَّكُمْ تَشْكُرُونَ ﴿٦﴾

"O you who have believed, when you rise to [perform] prayer, wash your faces and your forearms to the elbows and wipe over your heads and wash your feet to the ankles. And if you are in a state of janabah, then purify yourselves. But if you are ill or on a journey or one of you comes from the place of relieving himself or you have contacted women and do not find water, then seek clean earth and wipe over your faces and hands with it. Allah does not intend to make difficulty for you, but He intends to purify you and complete His favor upon you that you may be grateful."

Sh Hamid: This discussion has been mentioned in the Quran and also the Sunnat (tradition)

Dr: How can you translate such a clear verse of the Quran this way wrong? The Sunnat says otherwise too.

Sh Hamid: How can the Quran be mistranslated?

Dr: It is obvious. It firstly says face and hands, and then it says to anoint your heads and feet.

Sh: The way you read it changes its meaning. Dr: Allow me to continue this debate using your own books.

Sh Hamid: Please go ahead.

Dr: In your own books it explains the reason as to why you wash your feet this way: In the above verse the word "ارجلکم" goes back to the word "اغسلو" meaning wash your feet as well.

The Doctor & Sheikh's Debate

Sh Hamid: Yes, that is correct.

Dr: But in the verse 6 Surat Al-Maidah, based on the way you pronounce the word "ارجلكم" the word can be read in three conditions, you can act three different ways. If the letter "ل" in "ارجلكم" is lifted then it means that the whole feet have to be washed. If the letter is read lowered then it means that the feet should be anointed and if the letter has an accusative then it should be washed.

Sh Hamid: You are right. However, the way most of the people recite the Quran is in this way, and therefore, it has to be washed.

Dr: Well if the reader decided to read the letter with a Khafz, then you must anoint.

Sh Hamid: Yes, you are right, but no one reads it this way.

Dr: Well Nafie Ibn Amr and Hafs have read this letter using Khafz, even though the main reason for doing this is unscholarly and unreasonable.

Sh Hamid: Well, the rest of them have read the letter accusative way. Why did you say unscholarly and unreasonable?

Dr: Because the inflection on the "ل" word, read in this verse is beside the point.

Sh Hamid: All of the scholars are acting and saying this way.

Dr: All of the scholars are not saying this.

Sh Hamid: How come?

Dr: The source of this debate is regarding the two verbs that have been used close to each other.

Sh Hamid: Yes, that is correct.

Dr: Well, the source of the debate due to the verbs being close to each other is not the point because the first verb and the second have complete independencies. The part where it says anointing the feet is after when it means anointing the head. What does that have to do with the verbs being close to each other?

Sh Hamid: But everyone has accepted this.

Dr: Who do you mean by everyone?

Sh Hamid: All of the different religious Scholars.

Dr: Then let's see what your scholars think regarding this matter in your own books.

Sh Hamid: Please go ahead.

Dr: In Tafsir Ghorbati and also in Aldoor al Mansour, chapter 6, volume 3, page 331, Ibn Abbas says:

حجاج خطب بالاهواز: اغسلو ارجلكم وقال انس: صدق الله وكذب الحجاج

"Hajaj was reading a sermon in Ahwaz saying that they should wash their feet for conducting ablution. They told Anas. Anas said that God is truthful (saying that we should be anointing our feet) and Hajaj is a liar."

Sh Hamid: This is one case.

Dr: Here you go. In Al Tahrir and Al Tanvir chapter Surat Al-Maidah, volume 5, page 52 it cites the same Malik story and then says:

نزل القران بالمسح و السنه بالغسل

"What is sent down by Quran is anointing the feet but Sunnat tells us to wash our feet.

Then it says that after the era the followers of Jurists concurred to absolute the feet, meaning until then washing the feet was not the only way people would be anointing the feet as well was washing the feet."

Sh Hamid: Very well, we accept that you can wash or anointing the feet even though anointing has a Quranic Base. These are the only cases available.

Dr: No, that is not the case. In Jame Al Bayan Tabari, Volume 10, page 58 and 59; and Tafsir Ibn Kasir, volume 3, page 52:

Hadith number 11476 "نزل القرآن بالمسح والسنه الغسل"

"Anointing originates from the Quran but Sunat says to wash"

Hadith number 1147, "صدق الله و كذب الحجاج"

"God is truthful and Hajaj is a liar"

Hadith number 11478, "ليس علي الرجلين غسل، انما نزل فيها المسح "

"What mentioned regarding feet is not to wash, it is to anointing"

Hadith number 11479, "جابر عن ابي جعفر قال: «امسح علي رأسك وقدمي» "

The Doctor & Sheikh's Debate

"Anointing your head and feet"

Hadith number 11480,

"نزل جبرئيل بالمسح ثم قال: «الم تر ان التيمم ان يمسح ما كان غسلاً ويلقي ما كان مسحاً»"

"Gabriel revealed anointing (for the feet), then said: Have you not noticed that in Tayamom (dry ablution) they anointing the same places they wash (in Wudu) and the places where you have to wash (in Wudu) is let go in Tayamom."

Shukani says in Fath Al Ghadir, volume 2, page 277 says: Both cases regarding ablution and anointing is allowed.

Alusi says in Al Maani, volume 4, page 396:

"فعل الخلفاء لا يدل على اكثر من الندب والاستحباب"

What the Caliphas did caused nothing more than to implicate things.

Tafsir Neishabouri, volume 3, page 133 says:

"اختلاف الناس في مسح الرجلين وفي غسلها"

People are having debates over whether to wash their feet's or just to anoint.

Ibn Abbas, Anas Ibn Malik, Ikrimah, Al Shaabi and Ibi Jafar Muhammad Bagher says: "انّ الواجب فيها المسح", Ibn Abbas, Anas Ibn Malik, Ikrimah, Al Shaabi and Ibi Jafar Muhammad Bagher says: "The only thing that is mandatory is to anointing the feet"

Hasan Basri and Jarir Tabari believe:

"المكلف مخير بين المسح والغسل"

"The person whom is obligated to pray has the freedom to anoint the feet or wash"

Sh Hamid: The amount of chain of transmissions got too much. Which one should I respond to?

Dr: Whichever one you feel that is more important.

Sh Hamid: Regarding scholars having debates over this matter is obvious due to this many different sources.

Dr: Let's start with agreeing that at least this debate has been since the beginning of Islam.

Sh Hamid: Concerning the parts where it says that Tayamom (performing dry ablution) is equal to the places where Wudu is. If that is the case, then why do we not Tayamom from our elbow to our fingers. Therefore, in my opinion, we should not compare Tayamom with Wudu in this case.

Dr: To not consider Tayamom to be relevant to Wudu is strange because Tayamom is there to replace Wudu in the time of need (no water). So, they are relevant and concerning not Tayamoming from elbow there are a few things I would like to say: Firstly, this case is taken from your books. Secondly, does the face gets fully covered when you Tamamom for the arms to do the same? Also, please pay attention to the fact that Tayamom is for the time and place where water is scarce, and it is to ease up the situation one is in. It does not mean that you should do the exact you were doing once you wanted to Wudu. There are many clear Hadith's stating how Wudu was to be done, and it is not necessary to explain or analyze it. The way Malik handled the pilgrims is a clear indication of that.

Sh Hamid: We are conducting Wudu the exact way the Prophet was doing.

Dr: Actually, the Prophet was not conducting it that way because if it were the case, there would have been no reason for all those Hadith's.

Sh Hamid: How has it been then?

Dr: The face was washed and the hands and then the head and feet were anointed.

Sh Hamid: In ablution, we do have to wash the feet.

Dr: We have too many contradictions in the Hadith's that state that we should wash our feet so much so that we have no way to prove anything.

Sh Hamid: All the Muslims besides the Shias are conducting Wudu this way.

Dr: All the Muslims until the time when Usman was Califah were conducting Wudu the same way as the Shias are now, washing face and hands and anointing the feet and head.

Sh Hamid: We have several Hadith stating that the Prophet washed his feet.

Dr: if you look at all the Hadith concerning Wudu from all the followers of the Prophet's time, only two or three people have spoken about it.

Sh Hamid: No, we have plenty; everyone has spoken about it.

Dr: Abubakr and Umar have no Hadith regarding Wudu.

Sh Hamid: Aisha and Ali have spoken about it, yes that is correct.

The Doctor & Sheikh's Debate

Dr: Actually, let's have a look at what Aisha has said. In Sharh Ibn Majeh, volume 1, page 624 (Muslem and Nesaei have also stated this). Sharih Ibn Hani says: I asked Aisha about anointing in Wudu, Aisha said: Go and ask Ali he is the best person to ask regarding this. Ali's opinion is distinct; he says, anointing the head and two feet.

Sh Hamid: Ali has a Hadith for washing feet.

Dr: Yes, if you were listening to what Aisha was saying and had followed what Ali was doing, you would have been conducting Wudu the same way the Prophet was. He has 10 Hadith's regarding anointing for the feet and one weak Hadith about washing it.

Sh Hamid: You, yourself said that based on the Quran, we could agree on both ways.

Dr: Let's not go back to what we have already discussed. We agreed that if the "ل" letter in "ارجلكـم" is accusative or was mutual, then it meant to wash and if it was lowered, then it meant to anoint. However, just as we agreed no interpreter that has a high knowledge of understanding of Quran would mean this way, even though this book is there for the ordinary people to understand. Due to our perceptive, we know the ordinances in Quran do not have multivalent verses because there are chances where the text of Quran clearly states that we should wash our face and arms until our elbow and to anoint our feet and head. What I mean is we could sentimentalize and then, on the other hand, say that it meant for us to anointing our head and wash our feet.

Sh Hamid: But all of our scholars wash their feet.

Dr: Mostly people follow the government scholars that are old and made up Hadith's and misrepresentations.

Sh Hamid: Do you mean to say that everyone is making a mistake?

Dr: Please decide that with all the facts I am giving you. Are they making a mistake? Anas Ibn Malik says that they are making a mistake. Ali is saying they are making a mistake, Shafeii says it is wrong. Ibn Abbas says they are making a mistake. Many others say that both ways can be done.

Sh Hamid: What difference does it make anyway for you to be so sensitive about it.

Dr: It makes such a big difference. I want to prove that we follow the tradition of the Prophet, meaning we are the real Sunnis and you follow the Caliphas. In the Tafsir of Ibn Kasir chapter 6, volume 3, page 52, the stories of pilgrims and Anas have clearly stated this way. So, agree that we are the real Sunnis.

Sh Hamid: If you are Sunni, then we do not have a problem with that.

Dr: Yes, we are Sunnis meaning we are the followers of the Prophet's Sunnat and you are Sunnis that follow the Caliphas Sunnat. Sh Hamid: The Caliphas are the Prophet's Caliphas so for that reason we are also following the Sunnat of the Prophet.

Dr: I would instead not get into that specifically yet. However, do you agree that anointing is correct and the verse is true?

Sh: Doctor, every time I have come to the debate over the Caliphas, you have said another time. Would it not be suitable to discuss that in the presence of Sheikh Hamid? Dear Sheikh Hamid, the doctor also has opinions on the Caliphas.

Dr: But we agreed to discuss Wudu and Salat in the presence of Sheikh Hamid.

Sh Hamid: This is good. If you have any more sources concerning anointing, please discuss.

Dr: Reason says that the best source is the Quran. Once the Quran states something, then there should no longer be any recantation.

Sh Hamid: That is correct, people should all know that when it comes to ordinances, they should follow the Quran and refer to Sunnat for minor cases.

Dr: Concerning Wudu, many minor cases have been mentioned. For instance, there is no mention of the Sermon's of Salat or how-to Sajdah, Ruku, and what to say in the Quran. On the topic of fasting, there is no minor detail seven about Hajj, there is nothing. However, regarding Wudu, we have complete information. The Quran clearly says in Surat Al-Maidah to wash the face and hands and to anoint the head and feet. It is interesting that there is this much difference between something that has been clearly stated in the Quran compared to other things that have no mention at all, such as fasting and Hajj, etc... In the Quran, Surat Ash Shuraa verse number 10 says:

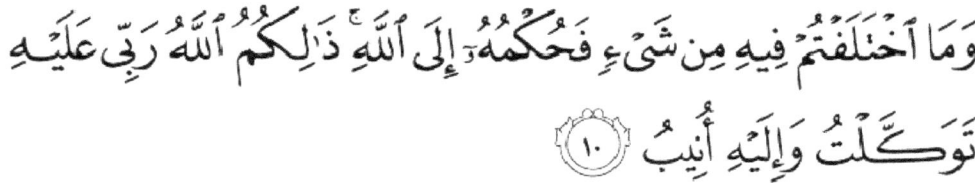

"And in anything over which you disagree - its ruling is [to be referred] to Allah. [Say], "That is Allah, my Lord; upon Him I have relied, and to Him I turn back."

Sh Hamid: We also have Sunnat regarding Wudu.

The Doctor & Sheikh's Debate

Dr: All of the Hadith's in the end are saying to anoint but you can just rely on what other Muslims are doing. For instance, in Sunan Kobra Beyhaghi, volume 1, page 44 it says:

عن رفاعةْبن رافع: جالساً عند رسول الله قال: لا تتم الصلوه احدكم حتى يسبع الوضوكما امره الله به، يغسل وجهه ويديه الي المرفقين ويمسح رأسه ورجليه الي الكعبين

"We were all sitting next to the Prophet and he said not one of your prayers are accepted unless you Wudu the way God as ordered. Wash your face and your hands up to your elbows and anointing your head and feet."

Sh Hamid: Sheikh Ibrahim do you have anything to say about this? What is your opinion?

Sh: Please continue. To be honest the truth is that our sayings concerning Wudu have no solid proof.

Dr: Dear Sheikh, please have a look at this Hadith from Bukhari, Hadith 5185, volume 17, page 332 says:

"Ali was in Kufeh and conducted Wudu this way. Ali read his Zuhr pray and then he addressed the needs of the people until it was time to pray the Asir prayer. He washed his face and arms and then he anointed his head and feet. Then got up and drank some water. He stood and said: People do not like to drink water as they stand but this is how the Prophet acted (He would drink whilst standing)."

This case shows that the Hadith's that Ali said about ablution are either wrong or we have to accept them because this has been taken from the time he was Calipha.

Sh Hamid: Yes, this can be considered another case too.

Dr: Now please have a look at the Hadith below. In Kanzol Amaal, Hadith 27659 and in Mukhtareh, volume 1, page 63 it says:

Hadith number 38042:

قال سعيد بن منصور حدثنا يعقوب بن عبد الرحمن عن أبي حازم: أنه رأى سهل بن سعد يتوضأ ومسح على الخفين فقلت ألا تنزع خفيك قال لا قد رأيت خيرا منى ومنك يمسح عليهما

"They saw Sahl Ibn Saad that was conducting anointing on his feet. I asked him: did you not wash your feet? He said: No, I have seen someone that was better than me and you and he was conducting anointing on his feet."

Sh Hamid: It is interesting that the Doctor has proof from the Quran and the Hadith's.

Dr: Then we agree that about Wudu, we have to anoint the feet. If that is the case, let's move onto the rest of the Salat.

Sh Hamid: One cannot put any faults on all of these analyses, especially the Quran. However, we can still say that it is up to their liberty, whether to wash or to anoint.

Dr: But that would be acting against what the Quran says. Denying all of these Hadith's that I mentioned with proof is unacceptable. We did agree to accept the Quran above anything else.

Sh: You are right; we did agree to this.

Dr: Dear Sheikh Hamid, what is your opinion after all of this?

Sh: I agreed to not go by any Sunnat or Hadith when the Quran clearly says something.

Sh Hamid: Of course, these notes are correct and I accept that even if it was acting on liberty we have stronger proof of Hadith to anoint for Wudu rather than wash the feet. Especially because the proof we have to wash are all after the time of the Prophet.

Dr: Then let's allow us to move on to the next topic "call for prayer" (Azan).

Call for Prayer in Islam

Sh Hamid: That is correct, by the way, why do you guys say:

" اشهد ان علياً ولي الله يا حجت الله "

When do you read your Azan or Iqama?

Dr: We do not categorize this component of the Azan to be the central part of it. We consider it to be a non-compulsory part (Mustahabat) and if a person classes that to be a necessary part of the Azan, we deem it invalid.

Sh Hamid: Then why do they read it?

Dr: All of the parts in Praying have sections where you can read non-compulsory things. It is sporadic to see any prayer to be done without any non-compulsory articles. Azan has some recommended meritorious action, and in our opinion one, it is this one.

Sh Hamid: Why is this non-compulsory saying is allowed to be said it is an innovation in Azan.

The Doctor & Sheikh's Debate

Dr: Mustahabat is no innovations because based on authentic Hadith's, the Prophet would also read extra mustahabat while in Sajdah and Ruku for obligatory prayers. The Prophet's companions also would read extra prayers while reading Salat.

Sh Hamid: This non-compulsory case was not allowed by the Prophet.

Dr: Just like the part when cursing Ali was allowed by Muawiyah, and the Prophet had not recognized that, but still, people of Shaam would insist on it with intensity.

Sh Hamid: But they do not do that now.

Dr: Actually, we added this part to the Azan so no one would ever dare to do that again. Dare to curse or insult Ali again as they did before. Once you have a brief look at the books of Ibn Teymiyah it shows that Muawiyah's nature in cursing Ali is broad as sunlight. His hatred is displayed even after roughly seven hundred years through Ibn Teymiyah's books.

Sh Hamid: Ibn Teymiyah is not the representative of all the Muslims. All of the Muslim's accept Ali to be the fourth Calipha and do not curse him.

Dr: You know very well that they didn't accept Ali as Calipha. It was only years after when they finally agreed that Ali was Calipha.

Sh Hamid: He is considered now, so there is no debate.

Dr: By the way, we class him as the first Calipha. However, these Muslims that you named in Ibn Teymiyah's time did not speak of it. They were busy destroying Ali and his children's grave by Wahabis and said nothing. So now we use prevention.

Sh Hamid: Of course, if once you say: "اشهد ان علياً ولي الله "

is not classed as part of the Azan and in the condition that Ali is not valued as equal to the Prophet, then reading it is permitted.

Dr: Now I have a question.

Sh Hamid: Please go ahead.

Dr: How come you guys say this: "الصلوةُ؟ خـير مـن الـنـوم"

Instead of this for the Morning Prayer: "العمـل خـير علـي حي"

Sh Hamid: They don't say it for all prayers. It is only for the Morning Prayer.

Dr: It doesn't make a difference.

Sh Hamid: This is the order of the second Calipha.

Dr: Can a Calipha change the Sunnat of the Prophet?

Sh Hamid: You have changed the Sunnat by saying "اشهد ان علياً ولي الله"

Dr: We have added this but noted that it is compulsory. We can remove it with another Mustahab saying, but you have eliminated the Prophet's meaning of

"العمل خير علي حي" and have added something else instead of it. You are saying that praying is better than sleeping.

Sh Hamid: I have to explain in this case that when the Calipha saw that people were not going to Jihad but they were going to pray and claiming that praying was more important and was not considering Jihad as of any importance; he said that I am changing it and for them to say that praying is better than sleeping but is not better than Jihad.

Dr: Dear Sheikh, this is not a correct justification. The Prophet was always saying that praying was the best action, even in war and Jihad. People were still going to Jihad and had many battles that were uneven, and they were again winning; therefore, this innovation is an entirely unacceptable one.

Sh Hamid: They must have considered sleeping to be better than praying, and that's why the second Calipha did this.

Dr: The conditions of war in the second Caliphas time were not so, you know. Iran and Rome were defeated then.

Sh Hamid: Yes, you are correct.

Dr: Then the problem is not very clear.

Sh Hamid: These reasons do not seem to be very convincing.

Dr: Even if it was convincing and for instance, they wanted to say that it was essential and insisted on mentioning it in one of their speeches; they could have just said that call to Jihad was not that important. They shouldn't have changed the whole Azan just because the second Calipha noted to improve the Sunnat of the Prophet.

Sh Hamid: This is mentioned in most of the Hadith's, and as I said, it is only read for the Morning Prayer.

Dr: It doesn't make a difference for which prayer it is for. If they had added for the other Azans that praying was better than dinner or praying was better than the morning breakfast, people would have just done it.

Sh Hamid: If we want to be realistic, we have to accept that this case was not at the time of the Prophet and therefore is not part of the Azan. Hence, saying what the Prophet used to say in his time meaning: "خير العمــل علــي حي" is even correct to be ready for the morning Azan.

Dr: Sheikh Ibrahim, what is your opinion?

Sh: I accepted this at the beginning of your debate. This is because what the Prophet said and did is absolute, and the actions and sayings of the Caliphas are only complete when they are not against what the Prophet's actions and sayings were.

Dr: Well, thank the Lord we managed to clarify that "خير العمــل علــي حي" is correct. Now I have another question.

Sh Hamid: Please ask away.

Amen and Taktuf (placing a hand on hand)

Dr: If we go back and have a look at the books of Hadith of Sahih al Sittah and Bukhari we can only find one Hadith from Abu Huraira mentioning the word Amen after Al Zaallin.

Bukhari Hadith number 40, volume 2, page 248, and Hadith 41/5, volume 13, page 318 and there is nothing else mentioned about this. This is when in other places we have cases where it says that the Surat Al Fatihah is not a supplication for us to say Amen after it. What is your opinion on this matter? Of course, Sheikh Ibrahim already knows what we think of the Hadith's that Abu Huraira has cited.

Sh Hamid: Whatever it is, it is Sunnat.

Dr: But it is not Sunnat. The teachings of Gabriel to the Prophet concerning praying has no Amen being said, which also has been mentioned in Bukhari's books. In the same education, Taktuf was not taught as well.

Sh Hamid: We do not have substantial proof over the Taktuf, and there are many debates over it. Many people do not obey that. However, regarding Amen, all of the Sunni schools agree on it.

Dr: If this is something that needs to be said while praying, then how come has it not been told In Zuhr and Asir prayer?

Sh Hamid: The congregational Imam who conducts the prayer, says it, and that is sufficient.

Dr: Would you know of any cases similar to this situation where there is a prayer done based on Sunnat and another prayer done based on something else.

Sh Hamid: If it is okay with you, let's move on from here because Amen and Taktuf are not that important.

Dr: So, you accept that it is not part of the prayer.

Sh Hamid: I said it is not essential. Let us pass it.

Dr: So Taktuf and Amen are not part of the prayer.

Sh Hamid: What is the next topic.

Dr: In my opinion, if you believe in innovation, this action that you do in prayer completely voids it. Amen is not even an Arabic word; it is a Hebrew word, and the Arabic language does not have such a word.

Sh Hamid: Before you void entirely the way we pray, let's move on to the next topic.

Loudly Reading "In the name of God the Beneficent, the Merciful (بسم الله الرحمن الرحيم)" While Praying

Dr: Why does the congregational Imam whispers "In the name of God the Beneficent the Merciful" or he does not even say that.

Sh Hamid: We have many Hadith's stating that the Prophet would say it with a low tone.

Dr: We do not have a correct Hadith saying that. What kind of a Hadith is this that states we read some part of it low pitched and some high?

Sh Hamid: In some of the Sunni schools reading "In the name of God the Beneficent the Merciful" loudly is normal.

Dr: We have a case where Muawiyah came to Medina and assembled a congregational prayer and read "In the name of God the Beneficent the Merciful" with a low pitch. He then was confronted

The Doctor & Sheikh's Debate

by many, and so for the next prayer, he read "In the name of God the Beneficent the Merciful," loudly.

Sh: That is interesting.

Dr: Therefore, if some people read out loudly and some not then it proves that there is no correct Hadith regarding "In the name of God the Beneficent the Merciful." Now if Sunnat was the base of proof, then some believe that it should be read loudly and some believe that it should be read with a lower tone. In such a debate if we look at the reason, then calling out God's name loudly while praying, which is the way to connect to God makes more sense.

Sh Hamid: Reading "In the name of God the Beneficent the Merciful" loudly while praying is not a crucial thing amongst us only the extremists believe and insist on reading it out with a low tone. Let's not continue this and move on to the next one.

Dr: We have proof that in Mukhtasar Tarikh Dameshgh Volume 7, page 33,

"عن ابن عباس ان النبي (ص) جهر بسم الله الرحمن الرحيم"

"From Ibn Abbas: Indeed, the Prophet would read "In the name of God the Beneficent the Merciful" loudly"

This topic was mentioned in Tabaghat Al Mohadesin: Chapter Abu Jafar Mansour volume 1, page 240, and in the history of Islam Zahabi: volume 10, page 435, it has been mentioned.

In Tafsir Saalabi volume 1, page 10 and in the Sunan Kobra Beyhaghi volume 2 page 49 and in Mastark Al Sahihin volume 1 page 357 and in Masnad Shafii, volume 1, page 36 and volume 9 page 48 and in Fath Al Bari, volume 3 page 361 and in Alkashf va Albayan, volume 1, page 105 from Abubakr Ibn Hafz Ibn Asem says that Muawiyah was in the Medina Mosque and was praying. He read the "In the name of God the Merciful" part of the Surat Al Fatihah loudly and then did not do the same for the next Surat. Anas Ibn Malik complained to him after wards and said:

اسرقت الصلاه ام نسيت

"Did you steal from the pray or you forgot?"

This proves that not only do they read "In the name of God the Beneficent the Merciful" loudly but they also read the full Surat as well.

Sh Hamid: These are significant cases. I will read "In the name of God the Beneficent the Merciful" loudly from now on.

Reading a Full Surat in Salat

Dr: My next question is about reading a full Surat while praying instead of reading some verses of the Quran after the Surat Al Fatihah. In my opinion, this action is wrong.

Sh Hamid: But no one has questioned this action, and everyone has been okay with the situation.

Dr: That is right, but if we look at it rationally a complete message is derived from an entire verse of a Surat. One verse on its own cannot bring a perfect word, therefore, reading a complete Surat is better as it brings about a message accurately.

Sh Hamid: One or several verses of the Quran can deliver a message.

Dr: Then how come they read two full Surats for the Friday prayer? This proves that learning an entire Surat is more accurate than a couple of verses. Another example is when they read two full Surats for the Morning Prayer on Fridays.

Sh Hamid: Yes, I also agree with you that a complete Surat is better.

Dr: It is not better; it is necessary to read a full Surat because the message that each Sermon brings should be complete.

Sh Hamid: We do have a proof for reading just several verses while praying.

Dr: Yes, for instance, in Tafsir Ibn Kasir, volume 1, page 118 it says:

"ما تيسر من القرآن"

This means that it is okay if we don't read the Surat Al Fatihah because it has not specified what exact Surat to read but everyone else has debated that the Prophet has said that if a prayer has no Surat Al Fatihah then it is incomplete.

In the book of Fatway Alazhar, volume 1, page 82 it has been quoted that Ibn Majah said:

"لاصلوةَ لمن لم يقراء في كل ركعه بالحمد و سورةَ في فريضةَ او غير ها"

It is not accepted a prayer if anyone does not read Surat Al Fatihah and Al Tawhid in any compulsory or non-compulsory prayer.

Sh Hamid: The truth is that it is not possible to determine exactly which action is correctly.

The Doctor & Sheikh's Debate

Dr: The problem is that unfortunately between the Sunni brothers they equalise the word of the Prophet's companion with the Prophet himself. When for a Muslim the main things should be the Prophet's action and words.

Sh Hamid: We say that the words and actions of the companions are equal as they act just like the Prophet.

Dr: Please have a look at this chain of transmission from Sunan Ibn Majah, volume 9, page 200, Hadith number 3065 we have:

حَدَّثَنَا هِشَامُ بْنُ عَمَّارٍ حَدَّثَنَا حَاتِمُ بْنُ إِسْمَعِيلَ حَدَّثَنَا جَعْفَرُ بْنُ مُحَمَّدٍ عَنْ أَبِيهِ قَالَ دَخَلْنَا عَلَى جَابِرِ بْنِ عَبْدِ اللَّهِ فَلَمَّا انْتَهَيْنَا إِلَيْهِ سَأَلَ عَنِ الْقَوْمِ حَتَّى انْتَهَى إِلَيَّ فَقُلْتُ أَنَا مُحَمَّدُ بْنُ عَلِيِّ بْنِ الْحُسَيْنِ... أَنَّ رَسُولَ اللَّهِ صَلَّى اللَّهُ عَلَيْهِ وَسَلَّمَ ثُمَّ قَامَ إِلَى مَقَامِ إِبْرَاهِيمَ فَقَالَ { وَاتَّخِذُوا مِنْ مَقَامِ إِبْرَاهِيمَ مُصَلًّى } فَجَعَلَ الْمَقَامَ بَيْنَهُ وَبَيْنَ الْبَيْتِ فَكَانَ أَبِي يَقُولُ وَلاَ أَعْلَمُهُ إِلاَّ ذَكَرَهُ عَنِ النَّبِيِّ صَلَّى اللَّهُ عَلَيْهِ وَسَلَّمَ إِنَّهُ كَانَ يَقْرَأُ فِي الرَّكْعَتَيْنِ قُلْ يَا أَيُّهَا الْكَافِرُونَ وَقُلْ هُوَ اللَّهُ أَحَدٌ

"It quotes from Jaber that we were with the Prophet for Hajj. As soon as we got to pray in Masjid Al Haram the Prophet said that we should pray for the honor of Ibrahim. He then placed the status of Ibrahim between himself and the Kabaa. My Father said that we didn't know anything unless the Prophet taught us. Therefore, the Prophet read the Surat Al Kafirun and Surat Al Tawhid for the two Sermon prayers."

So, you can see here that the Prophet read a full Surat for each Sermon. We have Hadith for the Friday prayer as well saying that the Prophet would read the complete Surat for the Two Sermon prayers.

Sh Hamid: Is there a Hadith from our books that says the Prophet would read one Surat for each Sermon besides the ones you mentoined?

Dr: Yes, here you go. Hadith number 9654 from Musnad Ahmad, volume 20, page 29:

حَدَّثَنَا مُحَمَّدُ بْنُ جَعْفَرٍ وَبَهْزٌ الْمَعْنَى قَالاَ حَدَّثَنَا شُعْبَةُ عَنِ الْحَكَمِ قَالَ بَهْزٌ فِي حَدِيثِهِ أَخْبَرَنِي الْحَكَمُ عَنْ مُحَمَّدِ بْنِ عَلِيٍّ أَنَّ رَجُلاً يَقْرَأُ فِي يَوْمِ الْجُمُعَةِ بِسُورَةِ الْجُمُعَةِ وَإِذَا جَاءَكَ الْمُنَافِقُونَ فَقَالَ أَبُو هُرَيْرَةَ كَانَ قَالَ لأَبِي هُرَيْرَةَ إِنَّ عَلِيًّا رَسُولُ اللَّهِ صَلَّى اللَّهُ عَلَيْهِ وَسَلَّمَ يَقْرَأُ بِهِمَا

Someone asked Abu Huraira that Ali read the Surat Al Jumuah and Munafiqun for the Friday prayer. Abu Huraira said that the Prophet would the same Surat's.

Sh: Doctor you agree on a Hadith from Abu Huraira?

Dr: First of all, I brought up a Hadith for Sheikh Hamid, who believes in Abu Huraira's Hadith's. Secondly, if the Hadith from Abu Huraira is as much as the thirty that we agreed to be the truth, then this one is one of them. We do have a similar Hadith to this one but not quoted from Abu Huraira.

Sh: But Sheikh Hamid this is the actions and words of the Prophet himself.

Sh Hamid: The unity of procedures between the Muslims is from the words and the actions of the Prophet.

Dr: If that is the case, then how come regarding Wudu or reading "In the name of God the Merciful" out loud while praying there are debates. Alternatively, for instance, Usman explains how everyone should Wudu. Had the companions around Usman not seen the way the Prophet would Wudu and pray?

Sh Hamid: Well, somewhere young and were born after the Prophet had passed away.

Dr: In that case, this young person could have asked their father or other companions how to Wudu or whether to read the "In the name of God the Merciful" loudly or not.

Sh Hamid: Well, Usman is like a father or a companion.

Dr: But I believe that the route of this Hadith is not correct. I mean to say that Usman has not answered this thing. This is because there is another place where they say that Ali said the same thing, and that is wrong too. Considering the disagreements between the companions and Usman, he has wanted to solidify his position as Calipha, and that's why he has said such a thing. Just like Umar who said that he brought two useful innovations to Din.

Sh Hamid: Well, people did not complain.

Dr: How do you know that? Maybe the complaints were not recorded. I mean in the Muawiyah case when he read the "In the name of God the Merciful" in Medina with a low tone people did complain, and he did read it loudly for the next prayer. This fact was recorded because Muawiyah did not have as much power as Usman did in Medina.

Sh Hamid: Well praise the Lord, the basis of the prayer is accepted between us and yours.

Dr: We have to pray the way the Prophet did. I believe that we do pray the way the Prophet did. For instance, we do have "Qunoot" in prayer, whereas you don't. You close your arms when your prayer but the Prophet would keep his arms open.

Sh Hamid: There is no clear indication between the debates which one was closer to the Sunnat of the Prophet.

Dr: Yes, there is.

Sh Hamid: How?

Dr: For instance, is it possible to class anything that the Caliphas have classed as non-existing in the time of the Prophet, not as part of Sunant?

Sh Hamid: The Prophet has said that if you follow whichever of my companions, they will guide you. They are just like the stars in the sky.

Dr: Please allow me not to debate over this matter again as we have already covered this with Sheikh Ibrahim and we received to an agreement. Therefore, the actions and sayings of the companions cannot be the basis, and if we put them aside when the real Sunant of the Prophet shows itself.

Sh Hamid: Sheikh Ibrahim is this faith that you have agreed that this Hadith is false?

Sh: Yes, the explanations that the Doctor brought were sufficient.

Sh Hamid: What should we put aside so we could see the real Sunnat of the Prophet.

Dr: We should put the things that we just mentioned.

Sh Hamid: Which ones?

Dr: The actions and saying of the companions in anointing the feet in Wudu or reading the "In the name of God the Merciful" in a low tone while praying or not reading a complete Surat, not conducting Qunoot and reading Tashahod.

Sh Hamid: Doctor, what is the problem with Tashahod!?

Dr: If you accept that the Surat needs to be read in complete while praying, then we can go forward and talk about Tashahod.

Sh Hamid: I do not have any discussion over this as it was not that important to me in the first place

Dr: Important or not necessary, do you accept it or not?

Sh Hamid: Yes, I accept.

Tashahod (Confession of Faith) in Praying

Dr: Let's discuss Tashahod now.

Sh Hamid: What is the discussion?

Dr: You have in your writings that the prayer should start with "Takbir" and finish with "Salam", is that correct?

Sh Hamid: Yes, that is correct.

Dr: We have proof of this.

Sh Hamid: Yes, we do.

Dr: Now let's look at the writings of your Tashahod.

التحيات لله و الصلوات الطيبات السلام عليك ايها النبي و رحمةُ الله و بركاته السلام علينا و علي عبادلله الصالحين، اشهدان لا الهاالاالله وحده لا شريك له واشهد ان محمداً عبده و رسوله»

«اللهم صل علي محمد وآل محمد كما صليت علي ابراهيم وآل ابراهيم

Sh Hamid: Yes, that is correct.

Dr: So here you finish the prayer with "Salam" (blessing) before Tashahod that is part of the prayer.

Sh Hamid: Which "Salam"?

Dr: Here before Tashahod to the Prophet, you say "Salam" and this "Salam" finishes the prayer.

التحيات لله و الصلوات الطيبات

السلام عليك ايها النبي و رحمةُ الله و بركاته

السلام علينا وعلي عبادلله الصالحين

And then after these "Salams" you say:

و اشهد ان محمد عبده و رسوله

Sh Hamid: The prayer finishes with

"السلام عليكم و رحمةُ الله".

The Doctor & Sheikh's Debate

Dr: "Salam", is "Salam". It makes no difference if it's meant for the Prophet or the people.

Sh Hamid: Are you saying this as your own opinion or do you have a Hadith for it?

Dr: I have Hadith from the Prophet.

Sh Hamid: Where does this Hadith come from?

Dr: In Sunan Beyhaghi, volume 2, page 140 we have a chapter entitled: "Priority of saying Tashahod to Salam". In there, we have many quotes from the companions such as Aisha, that the Tashahods should be said first, then "Salam" (blessing) to the Prophet and his Righteous followers and then finish the prayer with "السلام عليكم".

Sh Hamid: We say two "Salams" at first then we say the final "Salam" in the end.

Dr: That is clear because based on many Hadith's that are gathered and mentioned in the Sunan Beyhaghi, volume 2, page 140- 150 it quotes from the Prophet and Aisha that:

مفتاح الصلوه الطهور، احرامها بالتكبير واحلالها بالتسليم

"You enter the prayer with "Taharat" (Wudu) your "Ihram" (Start) with "Takbir" and for "Ahalal" (coming out of Ihram) you "Salam""

Regarding the same matter Ibn Hanifah quotes from Ali and in the end, he says:

وانقضائها التسليم

"The end of it you say "Salam"

Therefore, the way you pray finishes without Tashahod and blessing to the Prophet. Shafii has also mentioned this, which the Prophet has said: A praying that does not have a blessing to me is not a prayer. This means that you say the "Salam" after the praying as ended, which invalidates the prayer.

Sh Hamid: Doctor, you have invalidated everything we believe in today. Everything is void.

Dr: I am questioning it. The Prophet's Hadith that are cited in your books are saying this. If I had cited from the Shia books, then what you say would have been right.

Sh Hamid: The problem is here that in the books of Hadith there are many Hadith's contradicting each other and therefore to distinguish between the correct and incorrect, right and wrong, is not an easy job especially when it is regarding worship.

Dr: In fact, I say the same thing. In worship, the Sunnat of the Prophet exists and therefore, must not be followed by the companions or followers. The actions and words of the Prophet himself should be above all and should be trusted.

Sh Hamid: If the Hadith were from the number one companions and closest to the Prophet and the Hadith's following it was the same, then it would be considered correct.

Dr: To verify some of these Hadith, there is no need to refer to any severe strings of Hadith's. This is because reason can easily distinguish between two Hadith that says Salat is voided with Takbir and accepted with "Salam". There is a chapter in Fiqh (jurisprudential) entitled "Priority of Tashahod in salam". Well these two complete the way we should conduct.

Sh Hamid: Yes, you are right. But unfortunately, our scholars did not sit and gather all of these and then inform people to conduct in one way.

Dr: Well it has to be said that the government officials did this during different Era's of time. What I mean to say is that they announced their opinion in every case between the people and distributed it.

Sh Hamid: Yes, the governments.

Dr: Al Bahr Al Muhit, volume 1, page 37 and in Al Muharar Al Vajiz, volume 1, volume 1, page 1 there is proof that regarding Surat Al Fatihah there are many Hadiths that are very weird. For instance, where it says: "غیرالمغضوب علیهم" and "صراط من انعمت" or for instance "انعمت علیهمو، علیهمی" "and "غیر الضالین", it is questionable. These cases indicate that a person should also refer to their own mind and use it as well. For example, Ibn Davoud says that the book of Akramah has said: "غیر الضالین". So what Akramah said such a thing? Were the other companion's dead for us to just rely on what he said?

Sh Hamid: Praise to God that no one followed such jibberish.

Dr: But these people have still said it even if it is jibberish.

Sh Hamid: Unfortunately, there are plenty of debates such as, and it is filled in the books of Hadith's to confuse people's minds and to make our youth doubt.

Dr: If you refer to the School of Ahl al Bayt, there is one case that prevents you from deviation.

Sh Hamid: What case?

Dr: Having a living religious authority and dynamic Ijtihad.

Sh Hamid: Well, we have that as well.

Dr: Yes, you do, but you are not able to review a Hadith. Our scholars can void any Hadith even if it is essential and seem correct if it contradicts what the Quran says, especially if it is regarding ordinances. Therefore, for us, regardless of what era we are in, we have religious authorities that come in the place that can even disregard anything the previous person has said.

Sh Hamid: So, they abide by what the previous religious authority says?

Dr: They act on what their duty is, and the next ones do the same.
Sh Hamid: How is that possible?

Dr: For example: regarding Eid al-Fitr in your country it gets announced that Eid al-Fitr is on a Saturday. Then in several other countries, they say that it is on a Sunday, even in some parts of your own country some say that it is on a Sunday. Everyone acts on the proof that they have seen the moon. The ordinance is the same everywhere. The ordinances say that if two righteous people announce that they have seen the lunar phase. Then it is accepted that it is Eid.

Sh: Dear Sheikh Hamid I believe that you have now concluded what I said in the first place that this Doctor is not a Doctor in Engineering but a Doctor in religious sciences.

Sh Hamid: I think that his not even an Engineer but he is specialized in religious fields.

Dr: If you have internet in this house you could search me up on the University website, and you can see my picture with my students at work.

Sh Hamid: We are teasing you, we believe in what you say.

Dr: What I have done is not that hard. I haven't done anything unusual either. I just spent the same amount of time researching technical issues and interventions in the world on researching about the righteous path for the next world.

Sh Hamid: Well typically, Engineers and Medical people spend less time doing such a thing.

Dr: In Iran, there are many Engineers, and Medical people start studying religion and become a spiritual guide after they finish their primary education in Engineering. Alternatively, they major in both fields from the start or they start studying Hauza first and then sway towards Engineering and Medicine.

Sh Hamid: This trend does not happen in Arabian countries.

Dr: Well, in an Islamic country, a Muslim person that his opinion has a universal claim has to be able to defend its religion. You haven't even debated with our religious scholars yet, or else you would understand that I have no spiritual knowledge.

Sh Hamid: Do you mean to say that they know more than you?

Dr: Compared to what they know, I know nothing. If you wish I can take you to Iran and introduce you to some of them, and you can see for yourself that I have quoted things that I knew would defend what I believe in and nothing more.
Sh Hamid: No, thank you. I have no preference to do such a thing. Today you have questioned every essential ordinance such as praying that I believed in and brought doubt into my mind. If I were to go there, they would probably convert us to Shia'sm.

Sh: I have to say that I know about the people that Doctor is talking about. Even though there are some Engineers and medical people in Egypt that are aware of religion, but I do not think that they know as much as our Doctor does.

Dr: I have seen Egyptian Medical and Engineering people that have substantial religious knowledge. The problem though is that they have a vast experience of everything and not in dept sight.

Sh: We didn't make it for the Asir prayer but let's visit the Mosque for the Maghrib prayer and then head towards the hotel afterwards.

Sh Hamid: I will accompany you.

All three of us headed towards Masjid an Nabawi and because I was accompanied by two Sheikhs they allowed us to sit close to the chamber of the Prophet.

Sijdah (Prostration) On Soil

I had a thin mat 30 x 20 centimeter squared to prostrate, and frequently there was no objection to it. However, close to the Prophet's shrine, they objected, and one of the Officers came over and took it off me with severity.

Sh Hamid: Why do you use this mat? Is it for sanitary reasons or because of your Fiqh?

Dr: It is due to Fiqh. We believe that we should prostrate on specific things such as soil, natural rock. It cannot be related to food, clothes, or anything synthetic.

Sh Hamid: Prostrating on anything is allowed.

Dr: Have a look at the software on my Mobile. In Sahih Tarmazi volume 1, page 354; Sunan Beyhaghi, volume 3, page 167; Bukhari, chapter Tayamom, volume 1, page 91 and Musnad Ahmad volume 1, page 301 we have this:

The Doctor & Sheikh's Debate

جعلت لي الارض مسجداً وطهورا

"For me earth is the place to prostrate and is the purifier."

In history, we have a chain of transmissions that in the time of the Prophet, people would carry stones with them so the rocks would not heat up at war, meaning they would prostrate on rocks.

Sh Hamid: The Islamic Din is an easy-going religion. I believe that one can Sujdah on anything they want.

Dr: What do you think the philosophy of prostrating is?

Sh Hamid: Placing the head on the ground. It means that the best part of the human body that is the brain touches them, which is a kind of humility.

Dr: So, it isn't on rugs?

Sh Hamid: It is not clear if there is a difference between a rug or the ground.

Dr: Now instead of cloth and regular rugs if they replaced the surface with expensive carpets and cloths then the philosophy of prostrating should be demolished as it wouldn't be signifying humility anymore, would it?

Sh Hamid: But no one has done that.

Dr: Because the philosophy of Sujdah has been clear and that's why no one has done that. The Prophet has prevented anyone who would even think of trying such a thing by saying that one cannot Sujdah on anything they wish.

Sh Hamid: Sheikh Ibrahim what is your opinion on this matter?

Sh: The truth is that for when someone wishes to pray due to it being a connection between God and human then using anything as natural as possible is better. Especially if it is not expensive or else some might use Gold to pray on.

Dr: God bless the dead. We say the exact thing. Islam says the correct something too.

Sh Hamid: For sanitary purposes, it is best that we use the rug for prostrating.

Dr: I believe we shouldn't mix being sanitary with this. Let's firstly agree that soul and natural things that are not edible (spelling check) and non-related to clothes; in other words, non-expensive things are best to be used. Now if it is clean for the better. This is because we believe that the place where we Sujdah should be completely Taher (immaculate).

Due to many repetitive questions I get asked in Mosques regarding Turbat (soil) and Sujdah, I have these two parts of Hadith's ready. One is from Shahih Bukhari, volume 3, page 215, Hadith number 771 and 792 on the software of my mobile. Please have a look: Hadith 771:

حَدَّثَنَا مُوسَى قَالَ حَدَّثَنَا هَمَّامٌ عَنْ يَحْيَى عَنْ أَبِي سَلَمَةَ ۞ قَالَ انْطَلَقْتُ إِلَى أَبِي سَعِيدٍ الْخُدْرِيِّ فَقُلْتُ أَلَا تَخْرُجُ بِنَا إِلَى النَّخْلِ نَتَحَدَّثُ فَخَرَجَ فَقَالَ قُلْتُ حَدِّثْنِي مَا سَمِعْتَ مِنَ النَّبِيِّ صَلَّى اللَّهُ عَلَيْهِ وَسَلَّمَ فِي لَيْلَةِ ۞ الْقَدْرِ قَالَ اعْتَكَفَ رَسُولُ اللَّهِ صَلَّى اللَّهُ عَلَيْهِ وَسَلَّمَ عَشْرَ الْأَوَّلَ مِنْ رَمَضَانَ وَاعْتَكَفْنَا مَعَهُ فَأَتَاهُ جِبْرِيلُ فَقَالَ إِنَّ الَّذِي تَطْلُبُ أَمَامَكَ فَاعْتَكَفَ الْعَشْرَ الْأَوْسَطَ فَاعْتَكَفْنَا مَعَهُ فَأَتَاهُ جِبْرِيلُ فَقَالَ إِنَّ الَّذِي تَطْلُبُ أَمَامَكَ فَقَامَ النَّبِيُّ صَلَّى اللَّهُ عَلَيْهِ وَسَلَّمَ خَطِيبًا صَبِيحَةَ ۞ عِشْرِينَ مِنْ رَمَضَانَ فَقَالَ مَنْ كَانَ اعْتَكَفَ مَعَ النَّبِيِّ صَلَّى اللَّهُ عَلَيْهِ وَسَلَّمَ فَلْيَرْجِعْ فَإِنِّي رَأَيْتُ لَيْلَةَ ۞ الْقَدْرِ وَإِنِّي نُسِّيتُهَا وَإِنَّهَا فِي الْعَشْرِ الْأَوَاخِرِ فِي وِتْرٍ وَإِنِّي رَأَيْتُ كَأَنِّي أَسْجُدُ فِي طِينٍ وَمَاءٍ وَكَانَ سَقْفُ الْمَسْجِدِ جَرِيدَ النَّخْلِ وَمَا نَرَى فِي السَّمَاءِ شَيْئًا فَجَاءَتْ قَزْعَةٌ ۞ فَأُمْطِرْنَا فَصَلَّى بِنَا النَّبِيُّ صَلَّى اللَّهُ عَلَيْهِ وَسَلَّمَ حَتَّى رَأَيْتُ أَثَرَ الطِّينِ وَالْمَاءِ عَلَى جَبْهَةِ ۞ رَسُولِ اللَّهِ صَلَّى اللَّهُ عَلَيْهِ وَسَلَّمَ وَأَرْنَبَتِهِ تَصْدِيقَ رُؤْيَاهُ

The translation of the part where the Hadith ends is this:

> "In one of the secretions of month of Ramadan we were prostrating whilst praying on soil and mud and the Prophet did the same and I saw the residue of mud and soil on the Prophet's forehead."

Hadith 792:

حَدَّثَنَا مُسْلِمُ بْنُ إِبْرَاهِيمَ قَالَ حَدَّثَنَا هِشَامٌ عَنْ يَحْيَى عَنْ أَبِي سَلَمَةَ ۞ قَالَ سَأَلْتُ أَبَا سَعِيدٍ الْخُدْرِيَّ فَقَالَ: «رَأَيْتُ رَسُولَ اللَّهِ صَلَّى اللَّهُ عَلَيْهِ وَسَلَّمَ يَسْجُدُ فِي الْمَاءِ وَالطِّينِ حَتَّى رَأَيْتُ أَثَرَ الطِّينِ فِي جَبْهَتِهِ

Or this Hadith which is a summary of the Hadith above:

> "Abu Saeid cites: I saw the Prophet prostrating on mud (water and soil) in such a way that I could see the residue of the soul was on his face and forehead."

So, Sheikh Hamid, please explain how does the Prophet pray on soil even if it is rainy and muddy and then prays on a rug when the conditions are normal.

Sh Hamid: In my opinion this is also correct. Unfortunately, I have not seen any proof that the Prophet prostrated on anything else but soil. Especially when some rugs are very expensive and as the Doctor says it demolishes the philosophy of Sujdah if prayed on. Therefore, I accept.

Dr: Thank you for accepting.

After praying the Maghrib prayer we sat a little. Some were supplicating and some were facing the chamber and the Officers were repeatedly saying:

لاترفعوا صوتكم فوق صوت نبي

The Doctor & Sheikh's Debate

Do not raise your voice louder than the voice of the Prophet

I got up and asked the Sheikh Officer by the chamber: I am sorry, is the Prophet dead or alive? He said: He is dead, "انك ميت و انهم ميتــون" "you will die, and so will they." I then asked: Then what is this written above someone dead and quiet, and that you repeatedly read it?

Sheikh Hamid started laughing, and he was waiting to see what the Officer guarding the chamber was going to respond. In return, the Officer just stared back at me with a blank face and said: Iranian go away.

I replied: I asked you a question you should respond, what do you care if I am Iranian or not?

He said: You are not asking to seek guidance you are requesting to create a problem.

Sheikh Hamid entered the debate and said: If you have an answer, please give it. The Officer replied: You are a higher honored Sheikh, please answer the question.

Sheikh Hamid said: I am friends with this gentleman and because he asked this question from you then it is best for you to answer it. His problem is this: If the Prophet is dead or alive, because if he is alive then what you say is correct, that we shouldn't raise our voice over his but if he is dead then what you say is meaningless.

Sheikh Officer said: You know that the verse of the Quran states that the Prophet is dead. Sheikh Hamid said: Please answer this gentleman and not me because I am on your side. Sheikh faced me and said: Do you not accept that the Prophet is dead? I replied: excuse me what is your name? So, I call you by your name. He said: My name is Faroogh.

Dr: Sheikh Faroogh, is it possible to be alive after death?

Sheikh Faroogh: No, someone whom dies, is dead because even God tells the Prophet that "انك ميت"

Dr: Then why do you say that we shouldn't read out loudly? The Prophet is dead and as you said a dead Prophet cannot hear anything.

Sheikh Faroogh: Are you saying that the Prophet is dead or alive?

Dr: Have you read this verse before?

وَ لا تَحْسَبَنَّ الَّذينَ قُتِلُوا في سَبيلِ اللَّهِ أَمْواتاً بَلْ أَحْياءٌ عِنْدَ رَبِّهِمْ يُرْزَقُونَ

"And never think of those who have been killed in the cause of Allah as dead. Rather, they are alive with their Lord, receiving ordinance"

Sheikh Faroogh: This is regarding life in "Barzakh" (limbo) it does not mean real life, and in any case, what does it have to do with the Prophet?

Dr: Is there any ordinances in Barzakh?

Sh Faroogh: Yes.

Dr: Isn't the Prophet more important than the Martyrs?

Sheikh Faroogh: He is more important, but he lives in Barzakh.

Dr: So, you mean to say that the Martyrs that are receiving ordinances from God are alive in Barzakh?

Sheikh Faroogh: Go away; I don't have time for you. Allow for others to not gather around and cause chaos here. Ask this Sheikh (referring to Sheikh Hamid), he will answer you. I don't have time.

We came to aside, and Sheikh Hamid laughed and said: These people are not in any position to know any better or to answer such questions. Their religious knowledge is deficient.

Dr: Then, whom should we be asking this question from?

Sh Hamid: You already know the answer to this question. We have to accept these things, or we have to admit that the Prophet is dead and take off what we have written above the chamber. Moreover, if he is alive, then we should all of the debates we had regarding Tawasol (implore) and the rest.

Sh: Dear Sheikh Hamid, if you accept, please accompany us these last two days that we are in Medina and participate in our discussions.

Sh Hamid: I won't participate because when I am around, you go all quiet. You discuss things with the Doctor by yourself.

Sh: I always start the debate, but I end up giving in to the things the Doctors say. There have been several cases that this has happened.

Sh Hamid: Well I don't have much to say against what the Doctor says either so its best you continue the debates yourself.

Dr: Well, even though if we continue this way, it will be a debate between two to one but I would be more than happy to resume this debate with both of your honorable people.

The Doctor & Sheikh's Debate

Sh Hamid: I apologize, even though I would love to, but I have a prior engagement.

We said goodbye and then headed towards our ways. Sheikh said: I think that Sheikh Hamid is scared of the government officials because the government officials warn them not to debate with Iranian scholars.

Dr: But I am not a very knowledgeable person, and I am not wearing an Imam outfit.

Sh: It doesn't matter. They are only allowed to talk to people that are willing and are ready to accept the Sunni way and especially the Wahabis.

Dr: Well, this is unfortunate for scholars do not speak with people that are just normal and have no previous religious knowledge and to avoid those that do.

Sh: By the way, we should slowly start packing to leave for Mecca. I have to go the day after tomorrow, and I still have questions left.

Dr: I am also leaving for Mecca in three days. If God willing, we could still meet up there.

Sh: It is not very clear where I would be staying, so it would good if we were to meet at Masjid Al Haram.

Dr: We also have mobiles. We will eventually find each other even though I do have the address of the hotel I am staying in when I am in Mecca. I will give it to you, so if we lose each other, you can come to my hotel.

Sh: That would be great. Do you have it with you now?

Dr: No, it is at the hotel. I will give it to you, God willing when I see you tomorrow.

Twenty Fifth of Zyqadeh

Issue Regarding Ahl al Bayt

I saw Sheikh again in the Mosque, and we sat where the As-hab Sofhe (companions of the ledge) were.

Dr: The As-hab Sofhe were people that did not even have a place to sleep. They would come here to rest also thought there was no roof. They were in a way in which you would see immigrants, but now, you see people come here and lean back, possessing two or more houses.

Sh: I don't think that the people you see around the chamber and the house of the Prophet, or even the Officers working here have many mundane things in their possessions. Most of them lead to ordinary and straightforward lives. They act more on belief and morality than for money.

Dr: It appears to be what you say. I once went downstairs for discussion in the basement of Baqi, and they didn't even have fresh water to drink from.

Sh: That is precisely so. If you visit their homes, you will see that they do not live very well. They are very different from politicians or religious leaders.

Dr: They are religious soldiers.

Sh: That is so. They are brainwashed from the beginning and even more so during secondary school. They are told that from seventy sects of Islam, there is only one righteous path, and the rest is polytheism, and the only right way is the way they are taught.

Dr: Normally, some soldiers carry weapons and only take orders from their commanders and act on what they have been told. They do not have much education, and therefore, they never question what rules they are determined to abide by.

Sh: Yes, last night, you were witness to one of those cases. The poor man was not able to handle a simple explanation of the verse that was written above the Prophet's shrine. The same verse they read 100 times daily for people.

Dr: It seems that we are slowly getting on the same page as each other.

Sh: Well, it was eventually going to happen. One of the characteristics of Hajj is that Moumenin (the faithful) get to exchange their thoughts. In my opinion, if there were a way to exceed this connection between us, then Hajj would be one of the most significant investments of the Islamic World. That is because the people that come to Hajj are unable to speak with each other using one language, so they are not able to connect. If you did not know how to talk to Arabic, then we would have just been praying and praying. However, many of the cases and beliefs that were considered under a precise debate were clarified and spoken about.

Dr: Unfortunately, people that come to Hajj are so focused on just praying that they lose sight of the primary source of importance. Even the people that come from countries such as Iran, Palestine, Lebanon, Syria, and Egypt; that have a higher patriotic attitude and are generally against American's and Israeli's, spend more time just praying and reading supplications or spending time in the Bazaars buying things. Most of their conversations are at the Mosque where they pray, and they only talk to the person next to them, asking with their fingers and hands, where are you from? They reply to Malaysia and Indonesia. There isn't much more conversation than that.

Sh: That is precisely so. Not knowing many languages is a great agony. Unfortunately, I only know Arabic. If I knew one other language, I could have spoken to one non-Arab at least.

Dr: The British have a saying that one person with two languages is better than two people knowing one language.

Sh: That is very right. Therefore, in Alazhar, we practice languages such as Urdu, Persian, Chinese, Turkish, and African.

Dr: This practice has also started in many Shia Centres of Scholarship. They even teach the Russian, Spanish, French, and German languages.

Sh: We had Russian from the start, but it wasn't as spread. If you notice we were the ones that started spreading Islam to the new Islamic countries, the Muslims of Russia based in central Asia were from us. We have good translations and good books.

Who are the Ahl Al Bayt?

Dr: Sheikh Ibrahim, the house of Hazrat Fatimah Zahra, the Prophet's daughter, appears to be in front of my hotel.

Sh: It is the house of the Prophet. What is not clear is how much of it used to be Fatimah's house.

Dr: I am confident because there are floor plans at the Mosque and we have a chain of transmissions in the books of Seerah (biography) and history stating that all of the doors to the

The Doctor & Sheikh's Debate

Mosque were closed at the time of the Prophet. There was only one that was kept open, and that was the door of the Prophet's house and Ali (Which Fatimah lived in).

Sh: Yes, what you are saying is correct the door of Ali's house was not closed; however, it is not clear if this was the actual door.

Dr: There is no other house, and nothing has been demolished that would be attached to the interior of the Mosque, therefore if where the Prophet is buried is Aisha's house then this house would be the house of Fatimah and Ali.

Sh: It is a possibility.

Dr: Look above. Do you see green colored writing that has now been covered up with green paint? Do you know what they are?

Sh: It is hard to read.

Dr: I was here thirty years ago, and the writing was not painted over then. The writing is from Ayat-ol-Tathir verse, and it says:

$$\text{إنما يُرِيدُ اللَّهُ لِيُذْهِبَ عَنكُمُ الرِّجْسَ أَهْلَ الْبَيْتِ ويُطَهِّرَكُمْ تَطْهِيرًا}$$

Sh: But the verse regarding Tathir was associated with the Prophet's wives.

Dr: It cannot be regarding all of the Prophet's wives, and in fact, it has been written above the house of Ali and Fatimah.

Sh: What does this prove?

Dr: It proves that Ahl al Bayt is the family of Ali.

Sh: Whom do you mean?

Dr: Meaning the Prophet, Ali, Fatimah, Hasan, and Hussein.

Sh: How can you come up with such a conclusion from this writing? There are several more verses written around the Mosque and the chamber.

Dr: Apparently, this was the same place the Prophet would come every morning and say:

$$\text{السلام عليكم يا اهل بيت النبوهْ و رحمهْ الله و بركاته}$$

Sh: Well, all of the wives were at home.

Dr: This house was only that of only Fatimah and her children and her husband.

Sh: Do you mean to say that these five people were the only Ahl al Bayt?

Dr: Yes, correctly, the other people are not classed as Ahl al Bayt. Of course, Ahl al Bayt does not conclude on these five people alone. These five people were the center and axis; the rest were associated because of them.

Sh: The verse for Tathir is regarded as the ones about the Prophet's wives and it discusses them.

Dr: Okay, let's read the verse.

Sh:

$$\text{إِنَّمَا يُرِيدُ اللَّهُ لِيُذْهِبَ عَنْكُمُ الرِّجْسَ أَهْلَ الْبَيْتِ وَ يُطَهِّرَكُمْ تَطْهِيراً}$$

Dr: Where it says "إِنَّما" it means limitations, restrictions. Allah intends only to remove from you the impurity [of sin], O people of the [Prophet's] household, and to purify you with [extensive] purification.

Sh: That is the correct translation, but where does it say these five people?

Dr: In Arabic, "عنکم" is used for Masculine plural pronoun. This means that at least, there were more males than females there. If this verse were about the Prophet's wives, then it would be ten women and one male being the Prophet. That wouldn't make sense.

Sh: You have to include the close companions as well.

Dr: No, we cannot include them.

Sh: Why not?

Dr: Because the debate is over the people of the household. If your case was genuine, then it should be saying the people that are around the house of the Prophet.

Sh: Are saying that Usman, the Prophet's son in law is not part of the Ahl al Bayt?

The Doctor & Sheikh's Debate

Dr: Usman is not the son in law of the Prophet, and even if we agreed that he was, there is absolutely no book stating that he was part of the Ahl al Bayt.

Sh: Why is Usman not the Prophet's son in law? They name him "النــورينذي," this means that he had two of the Prophet's daughters, Roqayah and Zainab.

Dr: Yes, they grew up in the house of the Prophet with Khadijah, but they were the "ربائــب" (stepdaughters) of the Prophet, and in reality, they were the daughters of Khadijah's sisters.

Sh: Where do you bring such information from? No one has ever made such an accusation.

Dr: Look at the book of Ansab Al Shiraf, volume 1, page 98, and Shazrat Al Zahab, volume 1, and page 14. It says that Khadijah was 28 years old and married the Prophet. She had not been married before, and Ghasem is their first son. There is no mention of these girls.

Sh: This is what Shias believe in. We do not accept this to be true.

Dr: Okay, there is a Lebanese researcher named Seyed Jafar Murteza. He wrote a book about this called "Rabaeb Al Nabi," and it has a proper chain of transmissions in it. Having said this, other books are saying the same thing such as Bala Zari in the book of Ansab Al Sahiraf and Abul Ghasem Kuni in the book of Al Istea'neh.

Sh: So Usman is not the Prophet's son in law?

Dr: No, he isn't. He is the husband of his stepdaughter.

Sh: Is there anyone in the Sunni faith saying such a thing?

Dr: The book of Khasais Ali written by Nesaei Shafia says that I have mentioned features of Ali that none of the other companions had and one of the highlights is that Ali was the Prophet's only son in law. Now if Usman were also the Prophet's son in law, then Nesaei would not have said such a thing.

Sh: Then no one is classed as Ahl al Bayt besides these five people?

Dr: No one else.

Sh: Maybe no one came forward to claim such a title due to its unimportance.

Dr: Actually, this is a fundamental matter.

Sh: What is the importance of a person being part of the Ahl al Bayt or not?

Dr: Any impurity would be nowhere near them.

Sh: Well, all of the companions were like this.

Dr: Have you forgotten our deal? We agreed that not all of the companions were considered good people, and not all were guiding towards the righteous path.

Sh: I accept this, but the ones around the Prophet and close to him were.

Dr: Have you forgotten us talking about the same people close to the Prophet that had gone to war against each other?

Sh: Yes, you are right. Well at last then we can say that the Prophet's wives and these five people were considered Ahl al Bayt. Dr: Actually no, only the five people were Ahl al Bayt. The Prophet's wives were not part of it.

Sh: Why not?

Dr: For the same reasons I just talked to you about.

Sh: Please tell me. Tell me again.

Dr: First reason is that the Quran says:

$$\text{لِيُذْهِبَ عَنْكُمُ}$$

Now "كم" is only used for the Masculine plural pronoun. This means that the majority were men, which makes sense as the Ahl al Bayt being Muhammad, Ali, Hasan, and Hussein are all men. There is only one woman, Fatimah so, therefore, the pronoun "كم" has been mentioned here. If there were nine women and one Prophet then it would add to be 10 people then the pronoun "كم" is for whom? In addition to everything I said we have Hadith that Uma Salama asked the Prophet. Am I part of your Bayt? The Prophet responds: You are, but you are not my Ahl al Bayt.

Sh: I have to say that "كم" is also used in Arabic for when the number of men is small.

Dr: Yes, but only if the number of women is not more than men. Here you have one man and nine women. The man is the Prophet, which there is no reason to emphasize him as Ahl al Bayt because of who he is. Therefore, the women should be Ahl al Bayt, and that contradicts the pronoun "كم" being used.

The Doctor & Sheikh's Debate

Sh: You are right, especially considering the Language of Quran which uses such eloquent language.

Dr: The second reason is Surat Ali Imran, verse 61 regarding Mubahila. Quran says:

$$\text{فَمَنْ حَاجَّكَ فِيهِ مِنْ بَعْدِ مَا جَاءَكَ مِنَ الْعِلْمِ فَقُلْ تَعَالَوْا نَدْعُ أَبْنَاءَنَا وَأَبْنَاءَكُمْ وَنِسَاءَنَا وَنِسَاءَكُمْ وَأَنْفُسَنَا وَأَنْفُسَكُمْ ثُمَّ نَبْتَهِلْ فَنَجْعَلْ لَعْنَتَ اللَّهِ عَلَى الْكَاذِبِينَ ﴿٦١﴾}$$

"Then whoever argues with you about it after [this] knowledge has come to you - say, "Come, let us call our sons and your sons, our women and your women, ourselves and yourselves, then supplicate earnestly [together] and invoke the curse of Allah upon the liars [among us]."

Now let's see who accompanied the Prophet in Mubahila? In all of the books it mentions that Hasan, Hussein, Fatimah and Ali went along with the Prophet.

Sh: Do you have proof in the books of Sunni faith too?

Dr: Yes, I do. This has been mentioned in many of the books. For instance, in Tafsir Aldar Mansour, volume 2, page 534 it says:

خرج معه على والحسن والحسين وفاطمه فابو ان يلاعنوه وصالحوه على الجزيه

With the Prophet, Ali and Hasan and Hussein and Fatimah went. So, they held back from cursing and by accepting the tributary tax.

In Tafsir Ibn Kasir, volume 2, page 54 it says:

"Ali and Hasan and Hussein were along his side and Fatimah was behind him as they headed to curse"

In Tafsir Qurtabi, volume 4, page 103, and Tafsir Tabari, volume 6, page 481, Hadith number 7183 and Jalalin, volume 1, page 361 in Zeyl the verse starting with "فمــن حاجك"... this subject has been mentioned.

Sh: This is very interesting.

Dr: Now if you pay attention, you will see that the sons of the Prophet mentioned here as "ابناء" are Hasan and Hussein. Where it says "نساء" you can see that Fatimah's name is mentioned from all of the women and Prophet's wives. Where it says "انفسنا" it means Ali was like the Prophet himself. Therefore, this verse interprets the Ayatol Tathir as well. It means that these people were the closest to the Prophet, and they are the Prophet's household.

Sh: You do know that once the leader of Nesara met with them, he gave up on Mubahila.

Dr: Yes, I know, you must already know the reason, right? He told everyone else that the Prophet must be telling the truth as he would never bring his closest family to a place where there was a chance that they would be killed. In other words, even the leader of Nesara realized that these five people were the Ahl al Bayt. However, some people don't want to pay attention to these things.

Sh: This Verse that these people are the closest to the Prophet.

Dr: And that they are the Prophet's household. Therefore, they are Ahl al Bayt.

Sh: There is no question that they are Ahl al Bayt; the problem only remains if these people are the only ones.

Dr: There is no question left as the Prophet didn't take anyone else with him to disregard any doubt of who are the Ahl al Bayt.

Sh: So, can we say that the people that were not in Mubihla are not Ahl al Bayt, even the Prophet's wives?

Dr: Was Uma Salama not in the house of Prophet? She is not considered as Ahl al Bayt. She wasn't in Mubahila either, so she wasn't mentioned in the verse of Tathir either.

Sh: Yes, you are right because no impurity or contamination ever rose from any of these people.

Dr: Other people in the Prophet's house did not conduct any evil or filth, but God did not class them as Ahl al Bayt because they had to be pure from birth. Just like Ali has other children from other wives, but they are not considered as Ahl al Bayt. They were also followers and servants of Ahl al Bayt.

Sh: We have exceptional and high regard towards this family too.

Dr: Yes, you do have high respect for them, but it seems Ibn Teymiyah did not and was at war with Ahl al Bayt. Dr. Sabih mentions in the book of Alazhar regarding Ibn Teymiyah and him opposing the Prophet's Ahl al Bayt.

The Doctor & Sheikh's Debate

Sh: Yes, Dr. Sabih is not a Sunni and is from the Azmiye Group of Egypt that are not Shias, but he likes the Ahl al Bayt a lot.

Dr: Yes, he also has a weblog and is consistently responding to questions regarding Ibn Teymiyah and the Wahabis deviating Islam.

Dr: We do have books from your school regarding Ayatol Tathir stating that it is regarding these five people.

Sh: You mean to say that it clearly states that the Ahl al Bayt are these five people?

Dr: Here you go. There are many proofs in your books, and this Hadith in specific has been mentioned many times.

Sh: Which Hadith?

Dr: In Khasais Nesaei this Hadith has been mentioned several times that Muawiyah asked Saad Ibn Qas why do you not class Ali as your enemy. He cited three reasons, and one of them was because he was the Prophet's Ahl al Bayt.

Sh: I have not heard of this Hadith.

Dr: Third chapter, Hadith number 15:

> 3/15/2 ـــ (أخبرنا) قتيبةُ بن سعيد البلخي، وهشام بن عمار الدمشقي قالا: حدثنا حاتم عن بكير بن مسمار عن عامر بن سعد بن ابي وقاص قال: أمر معاويةُ سعدا فقال: ما يمنعك ان تسب أبا تراب؟ فقال: أنا ذكرت ثلاثا قالهن رسول الله صلي الله عليه وسلم فلن أسبه لئن يكون لي واحدةُ منها احب إلي من حمر النعم، سمعت رسول الله صلي الله عليه وسلم يقول له وخلفه في بعض مغازيه، فقال له علي: يا رسول الله أتخلفني مع النساء والصبيان؟ فقال رسول الله صلي الله عليه وسلم: أما ترضى ان تكون مني بمنزلةُ هارون من موسى إلا انه لا نبوةُ بعدي.
> وسمعته يقول يوم خيبر: لاعطين الرايةُ غدا رجلا يحب الله ورسوله ويحبه الله ورسوله فتطاولنا إليها، فقال ادعوا علي، فأتي به أرمد، فبصق في عينيه ودفع الرايةُ إليه.
> ولما نزلت: «إنَّما يُريدُ اللَّهُ لِيُذهِبَ عَنكُمُ الرِّجسَ أَهلَ البَيتِ و يُطَهِّرَكُم تَطهيراً» دعا رسول الله صلي الله عليه وسلم عليا وفاطمةُ وحسنا وحسينا فقال: اللهم هؤلاء اهل بيتي.

"...Amer Ibn Saad Ibn Abi Vaqqas said: Muawiyah ordered Saaed Ibn Vaqas and said: What prevents you from calling Abu Torab (Ali) as your enemy? He replied: I remember three things that the Prophet said: About Ali and that is why I do not class him as enemy because if I had any one of those reasons I could be happier than the bests blessings. I heard the Prophet say to him: He was a successor for the Prophet in some wars (In Medina). Ali said: O,

Messenger of God, are you leaving me with the women and children? The Prophet said: Are you not happy to be replacing my presence just like Haroon was to Moses? As there is no Prophet assigned after me."

I heard that on the day of Kheybar he said: Tomorrow I shall give the flag to a man that loves his God and his Messenger and his God and his Messenger love him back. So we all started to wish that we were that man. Then he said: Bring Ali. As my eyes were hurting he rubbed his fingers on his lips and onto my eyes and then gave the flag to Ali.

When the verse "إِنَّمَا يُرِيدُ اللَّهُ لِيُذْهِبَ عَنْكُمُ الرِّجْسَ أَهْلَ الْبَيْتِ وَ يُطَهِّرَكُمْ تَطْهِيراً" was revealed the Prophet named Ali, Fatimah, Hasan, Hussein and he said: God these are my Ahl al Bayt.

Sh: Dear Doctor we spent debating in the Mosque today. If you agree with us meeting again in Mecca, then we could continue our debate there as I am leaving tomorrow and I only have this afternoon to spend time reading supplications. I have to go as I have some shopping to do as well.

Dr: That is not a problem. Allow me to write down my contact details and give them to you. You could write yours too and God willing after conducting the ordinances, please keep your phone on.

Sh: This is my number, please write your details on my book too.

Dr: Please consider me in your prayers.

Sh: I definitely will have you in my prayers.

Dr: Praise be to Allah, praise be to Allah, praise be to Allah.

Sh: You said it three times. Was there a philosophy behind that?

Dr: Yes.

Sh: What was the philosophy?

Dr: That you agreed to pray whilst reading your supplication for me. Because you used to say that the way you pray is different. That you say Salam and that is it.

Sh: Well when I read the book of Mafatih my opinions regarding supplications changed and therefore, I will definitely consider you in my prayers.

Why is Passing In front of Worshipers Prevented? Where does it originate from?

The Sheikh and I were sitting on the platform of As-hab Sofhe between a population, and we were waiting for the call for the prayer. An elderly Arab Sheikh that had a long beard was busy praying next to us. Someone came to pass in front of him; he suddenly hit the bypasser hard on his chest. The bypasser fell on the other people sitting, and everyone got disorganized over the chaos. The people surrounding gave the Sheikh a rude stare. When the Sheikh's praying was over, I said to him: Dear Sheikh, what you did was wrong. Why did you strike another person while you were talking to God? The Sheikh said: If I had killed him, it would have still been okay. I asked: Why? He said: Because he wanted to create separation between my God and me.

I said: How far away are you from Mecca, Masjid Al Haram, and Kabaa? He asked: What does that have to do with anything? I said: If you are talking about the distance between you and Qibla meaning Kabaa, then there are thousands of spaces separating you. Therefore, if someone bypasses you, then it is still okay. He said: But we have Hadith from the Prophet saying that if someone tried to avoid you while praying, then stop him and if he persisted you can even kill him.

I said: The Hadith you mentioned has no credit. He got angry was just about to hit me too. I left him and went back to Sheikh Ibrahim.

Dr: By the way, this case of passing through people that are praying or bypassing in front of them seems to be taken very seriously by some.

Sh: Yes, we have Hadith that we should not bypass someone that is praying.

Dr: Yes, that is right. However, this is another one of those discredited Hadith's.

Sh: No, that is not the case. Many believe in it and abide by it, especially in Saudi Arabia.

Dr: There are many people in countries such as Pakistan and Afghanistan that are like this too.

Sh: Well, it is the religious belief and faith of the person, and there is no harm in it as it prevents the person from praying not to get distracted.

Dr: But these unnecessary prejudice behaviors are the cause of the worshipers to be pessimistic against each other.

Sh: It isn't prejudiced there are some that believe in this and we should respect that.

Dr: What about the Officers and police and shrine officials who walk by and between people that are praying all the time?

Sh: They are making a mistake too because once someone is praying, no one should pass in front of them unless a barrier or obstacle is preventing them from moving behind the person.

Dr: Which credited Hadith do you have regarding this?

Sh: There are many.

Dr: If there is plenty then why do only a few Islamic Sects follow it?

Sh: Maybe they are not convincing enough to follow.

Dr: I don't have time to show you all of the Hadith's but here are some from your books stating that it is okay to pass in front of someone that is worshiping.

Sh: Let's see from which books you find such Hadith from.

Dr: God willing, let's see.

It was time to pray. Afterward:

Dr: Here you go, this is Bukhari, volume 12, page 134, Hadith 369 in Sunan Nisani and Musnad Ahmad, volume 51, page 150; volume 52, page 254 and Muslem volume 2, page 90 and 329 stating that Aisha said: When the Prophet was praying my feet was in front of him. When he wanted to prostrate, I would bend my legs, and then I would stretch them again.

This has been mentioned in ten other places too.

Sh: What else do you have?

Dr: Do you mean that was not enough?

Sh: You mentioned a couple of Hadith's.

Dr: But the same Hadith has been mentioned by several credited people such as Musnaf Abd ul Razaq, volume 2, page 22, Hadith 2373:

Abd ul Razaq says that Urur Ibn Zabir quotes from Aisha:

"The Prophet was praying, and I was between him and Qibla sitting on the mattress. Did I mention: Was the Mosque wall between you? Aisha said: No because the Prophet was in the house within his own four walls.

In the same book Hadith number 2374, it says: I was between him and the Qibla just like a dead person."

The Doctor & Sheikh's Debate

Sh: There appears to be more.

Dr: Yes, in the book of Sunan Kobra Beyhaghi, volume 2, page 276, it mentioned that Muslem and Bukhari said:

"Ibn Abbas says: On the day of Arafa the Prophet was conducting congregational prayer and people were praying with him. I and Fazl Ibn Abbas entered Arafa with our horse and donkey. We passed the lines and no one complained."

Afterwards it quotes from Bukhari and Muslem:

"We let go of the donkey and the donkey passed by the lines and no one complained either."

So, you can see that not only a person but a donkey can pass by between people that are praying and no one has complained. The Prophet said nothing too.

Sh: Please allow me to see this because I think that these sayings have real credited proof. Sheikh had a look at the chain of transmissions and repeatedly said: Forgive me, God, Forgive me, God.

Sh: I think that we should go over our chain of transmissions and read them with precision again.

Dr: a couple of years ago, we had a little get together with Doctor Hamdan Al-Ghamdi, the head of the Theology School of the University of Umm Al Qura University. After debating for about two hours, Doctor Hamdan said: I am inviting you to accompany two other University officials to come to Mecca as my guest next year for the month of Ramadan. I said: I asked him in return, but he insisted that we go first.

Sh: I have heard of Dr. Hamdan, and he is into debating with different kinds of people.

Dr: He has a Mosque that spends most of the time, answering questions and problems regarding Wahabis.

Sh: So, what happened in the end.

Dr: What I am trying to say is that after debating for two hours I told myself that if there were any questions or doubts regarding books of Ahl al Bayt, then by studying Arabic and many chains of transmissions and other historical novels I came to understand better and believe my school and the School of Ahl al Bayt. As I read through your books, I came to understand my faith because you have many chains of transmissions that strengthen the belief of the Shias.

Sh: I do agree that many of our scholars have not spent time reading our chain of transitions. I only have one question, and that is how did you get to study these?

Dr: I came over to Hajj for Umrah, and when I would see something happening between you guys I would go further investigate to see if what you were doing had any backup proof or if it is made up from superstitions.

Sh: This is precisely how one should be perusing their faith. If you allow me to leave for now and God willing, I will see you in Mecca.

In My Room with My Roommates

I spent the rest of the two days after the Sheikh left in Medina debating with my own friends. Every night after the Isha prayer we would sit in our room, and someone would mention a topic, and we would talk about it. When debates such as these start it then becomes very clear how much, even the ones that have come for Hajj, have problems with their theological discussions. There were so many unanswered questions, and some of them were so simple and some that did not a very straight forward simple answer. Maybe it would better if our television would spend more time in answering and debating theological debated discussions rather than all the soap opera series. Moreover, they should care who that person is because there are fundamental questions out there that this sympathetic momenin of the Islamic Republic have and once answered to it would prevent them from getting influenced by any doubt coming across their way as the answers were given hundred years ago.

Anyone of our dear friends that were too scared or shy to bring up a question would say: Let's imagine, or a friend of a friend asked me this question what I should say? However, it is evident that the problem was from their doubts.

Questions mentioned can be from principles of beliefs or entirely outside of it, or it could be about history and similar to that. With the hope that this problem is dealt with by our Islamic broadcasting countries so that our youth and older would be less scared. Moreover, most importantly if someone questioned something, we wouldn't be judgmental and accuse him of being an infidel.

Attention in Conducting Ordinances, Obsession and or Creating Concerns

Today was the last day. I read the farewell supplication in Baqi and the Shrine of the Prophet and started to get ready to Muhrem (Pilgrim clothes) and go to the Mosque of Shajarah. People that were doing this at the time were anxious and stressed out, and I managed to calm them, and thankfully, the problem was somehow sorted.

The Doctor & Sheikh's Debate

I have to add that the honored, religious clerks of the tour group do add extra stress to everything. They would say things that were not necessarily needed to be done. Alternatively, ideas would be discussed that the possibility of it happening would be close to nothing.

Being careful and making sure you conduct the ordinances correctly is a separate issue than creating concerns. The ordinances of Hajj are much more comfortable than some of the religious clerks of tour groups make them out to be. However, unfortunately, there is less attention made to the presence of the heart or the feelings they should have once they are conducting Ihram and Tawaf (walking around the Kabba) and say (Running ritual of the pilgrimage) and voghof (Hault at Arafat). There is mostly talk about the philosophy of Rami Jamrat so these stones get to hit Satan or how to hit the stones. However, focusing on just one thing disrupts the other. Once you look at the pilgrimages to Hajj, you realize that they are more focused on hitting Satan with stones than to understand the ordinances and rami-ing their inner soul. When the great Prophet returned from visiting Hajj the second time around he did Tawaf on his camel at once noticing how much attention should be paid in keeping your left shoulder aligned with the Kabba and how important it is to make sure that is done correctly. Yes, it all should be paid attention to, but some of the Grand Ayatollahs' that have come to Hajj and have realized the situation or their representatives that have happened over and reported back to them have made things a little easier. For instance, the Tawaf that needs to be done between the Maqam (Station of Ibrahim) and the Kabba which is not a necessity anymore and there are very few that ask for it to be done.

The same applies to Ihram too. For instance, when you conduct Ihram, there is a saying that when you want to start praying you enters it by saying: "الاحرامتكبيرةٌ" which is the same as saying "الله اكبر" for entering and by saying "Salam" you finish the Ihram of praying. Now for Ihram in Hajj by saying:

"لبيــك اللهـم لبيــك" and it ends with Taghsir and eventually with the Tawaf of Nisa. Now while you are in Ihram for Hajj if you accidentally conduct something that is forbidden it will not create a problem, but if you do it with full knowledge, then there are punishments which the most expensive of them all is a camel. Now a Hajji who has spent a couple of million Tomans just to come over, for any reason conducts something that is not allowed with full knowledge he should not disregard its contents within.

Eventually, all the rest of my friends entered Ihram in the Mosque of Shajarah. I wished that they would design Umrah to be much more comfortable than what is there now. Usually, the tour groups arrive at 1 am in Mecca.

Due to the weather being perfect most of the tour leaders insist on taking the pilgrim's the same night so they can finish their ordinances for Umrah. There are a couple of problems doing it this way. Firstly, most of the pilgrim's are tired and do not have enough strength to conduct the ordinances with their hearts thoroughly into it. Secondly, most of the Iranians and Shias arrive at the same time, creating a hectic atmosphere. Thirdly, most of the religious clerks despite the orders of the Ayatollahs', still recommend that the pilgrims conduct the non-compulsory ordinance of doing Tawaf between the Maqam and the Kabba. Fourthly, if the ordinances of some of the pilgrims especially the Tawaf are carried out at the same as the floor of Masjid Al Haram being washed, which happens early mornings, then the Tawaf of many pilgrims would come across as a problem. Moreover, last but not least, in Umra, the timing where Iranian pilgrims are carrying out the Tawaf of Nisa collides with the Morning Prayer. Lines are being made everywhere in the Mosque an hour before the Morning Prayer starts, and this causes a problem for them. Hopefully, these issues will be resolved in the future.

In any case, I went and carried out the ordinances for Ihram and exited it. I waited around to go to Arafah and to start another Ihram.

Day Third of Zihijjah

First Meeting with Sheikh Ibrahim in Mecca

I finished the ordinances that were required to be done for Umrah and headed towards the Mosque. The distance between my hotel and Masjid Al Haram was a lot, so I had to either use a taxi or a bus to get to the hotel. The quality of the service in this hotel, however, was much better than the one in Medina even though the rooms were a little smaller. I had Sheikh Ibrahim in my thoughts. I did try to contact him but was unable to reach him until eventually on the 3rd of Zihijjah in Masjid Al Haram, after praying my Asir prayer I gave him a call. He picked up and said that he was in Masjid Al Haram, so we agreed to meet in front of Bab Al-Umrah.

Going to Bab Al-Umrah is very difficult after the Zuhr and Asir prayer as it is jam-packed. I struggled to walk past all of the worshippers. On the way, I saw one of my friends that lived in the same city as me. I stopped to speak to him for a few minutes. I gave him the address to my hotel and asked him to visit me later as I didn't have time to speak to him any further and had to meet up with my Arab friend. I think that he got a little upset with me, but I had no choice.

I met the Sheikh as soon as I got to Bab Al Umrat. We met and greeted each other, and I started asking about a couple of days that we were apart. We sat close by until it got less crowded.

Sh: I got sick after conducting the Umrah ordinances but praise to the Lord I feel much better. Today is the first day that I came to the Mosque and its good that I got to see you on the first day.

Dr: I am glad to see you too. I did try contacting you a couple of times, but no one answered, or maybe it was out of service or even turned off. I thought to myself that you ran away from me and were not willing to meet up again.

Sh: No, May God forgive me, my mobile was off most of the time. It is because I hardly use my phone, therefore, don't pay much attention to it. I always take it with me when I am out, so if I needed to make a call I could. I am not only in no desire of running away from you, but I was looking for you. I was waiting to feel a little better and thank the Lord that I get to see you now.

Dr: Thanks, and praise to God as I enjoy talking to you too.

Sh: I have never managed to have a discussion and debate so thoroughly about things, and I think that out of all of my visits to Hajj, this one has been the most blessing. To be able to debate in such a clear way has been a treasure.

The Situation with Human Sciences in Iran

Dr: There is an exciting debate related to being re-compensated over debating humanity associated issues or other non-compulsory subjects in the School of Ahl al Bayt.

Sh: Scientific debates are highly regarded. There are so many mentions of the importance of talking about science.

Dr: Unfortunately, the Islamic Ummah is behind in the science world. We not only are not ahead in the experimental sciences, but we also have not displayed an excellent portrayal in the humanity and religious sciences either.

Sh: We are definitely behind in the experimental sciences, but in the sciences of interpretation, education, and history, we are prosperous.

Dr: Yes, but not to the extent where we would be able to respond to today's questions. If you go to any of the Universities that are in the Islamic countries you see that they only concentrate on the humanities or the translated books of psychologists and western professors of education.

Sh: Yes, that is unfortunate even though we do have a lot to show for ourselves.

Dr: Do you intend to have our debate here?

Sh: Yes, because the path is busy. It will calm down in an hour, and the Taxies will be cheaper; therefore, let's continue our conversation here.

Dr: Unfortunately, most of the various Islamic Universities research in fields such as social applications for the current and future situations, which in reality have no substantial effect on our youth.

Sh: Yes, that is correct. How is the situation in Iran?

Dr: Many educational narrative books concerning topics from the Prophet and Ahl al Bayt have been widely researched since the revolution and the war with Iraq. Thousands of bachelors, postgraduate and doctorate projects in the field of humanities have been carried out. However, in Iran the economics of Islam, Islamic Psychology, Islamic science of education, Islam in family, children's rights, parents, citizenship, marriage, human rights in Islam, the laws of war in Islam

The Doctor & Sheikh's Debate

and many more discussions have been extracted from Islamic books and some are already being taught in Universities and the rest is to be prepared to be trained.

Sh: Yes, but I doubt that if any of the other countries, including Egypt, have done anything as so detailed. The reason is that in our book of Sihah Al Sittah, we have no such thorough information to make books out of for every field.

Dr: There are thousands of Hadith's in the School of Ahl al Bayt that one could approach it from any corner and would be able to find Hadith's in the fields of humanity, life and mind.

Sh: We are unaware of many of the books of Hadith's that you have and we do not use.

Dr: But we do use your books even though they are not rich enough to be contented with by themselves.

Sh: Do you mean to say that we have that many books that are unrelated to worshiping?

Dr: Yes, for instance, we have a book called Bahar ul Anvar, which is 110 volumes.

Sh: One hundred and ten volumes?

Dr: Yes, One hundred and ten volumes.

Sh: Do you mean to say that you have this many Hadith's?

Dr: Yes, we have this many Hadith's.

Sh: Are all of these Hadith's originated from the Prophet's Ahl al Bayt?

Dr: They are all stated to be from the Ahl al Bayt but the writer or in better words the one that has gathered all the Hadith's together has said that not all of them are correct and the specialists have to sit and distinguish between the right and the wrong.

Sh: It still is a lot, even if half of them are correct.

Dr: We have many sources of research, and unfortunately, our Sunni brothers are derived from them.

Sh: They have not been computerized.

Dr: Most of them are now computerized.

Sh: On which programs?

Dr: For instance, the book is Nahj ul-Balagha, Bahar ul Anvar and let me make it easier for you; most of our authentic books of Hadith are now on software.

Sh: They say that the book of Nahj ul-Balagha is from Ali Karram Allah Vajha.

Dr: Yes, most of the sources used for research regarding humanity studies are from Nahj ul-Balagha, which contains his speeches, letters, and governs.

Sh: I have seen in Egypt that Sheikh Muhammad Abduh has written an interpretation about it.

Dr: Yes, and it is very famous.

Sh: Most consider him as Shia.

Dr: The content of the book shows that he is not a Shia, but he is a pious believer and a very fair Sunni.

Sh: If you have this software, please give them to me.

Dr: I have some that I can put on a temporary hard drive and will give it to you.

Sh: Thank you. Would it be possible to access the books too?

Dr: Yes, I have a friend in Lebanon that has all of these books. He participates in the Egyptian book fair. He will come to Egypt in two months. If you want, you can give me your number in Egypt, and I can ask him to contact you, and you can request any book from him. It will be my treat.

Sh: Thank you. Here is my telephone number in Egypt.

Dr: That is a very straightforward telephone number. Usually, the codes for Arabic countries are three numbers and not as straight forward.

Sh: To be honest, I am not familiar with the reason behind it.

Dr: I will tell him to contact you for sure.

Sh: By the way, what happened to the importance of having scientific discussions over other discussions?

Dr: Yes, you are right, in the nights of Qadr, there are many ordinances mentioned in our books. At the end of the ordinances, there is a saying written in Arabic (apparently, it's for any science.)

saying that the scholars have said above any ordinance there is a higher reward in having scientific discussions.

Sh: Wow, that is very interesting. Of course, this has also been recommended by the Quran. How many times have we read words like أفلا يتفكرون، أفلا تعقلون، أفلا يتدبرون in Quran?

Dr: Yes, they are mostly talking about the same thing. The values of our scientific discussions are possibly even higher than the Tamattu Hajj that is non-compulsory. That is because we are getting to understand many important scientific notes. Whereas someone who comes over for pilgrimage worships and carries out his Hajj and returns home. Not many changes in his life.

Sh: We have Hadith that the value of one hour of thinking is more than a lifetime of worship. Dr: This Hadith is completely correct. That is because the path of a person's life can change with an hour of thinking. A person can change his life where as if he spends a lifetime worshiping and not make a correct decision between right and wrong in an important moment of his life all of his worships can be wasted.

Sh: For instance, the arrangements and thoughts of the highly regarded companions throughout Islamic times were undoubtedly better than the non-obligatory prayers of others.

Dr: You must already know that the Prophet used Mecca as a place to preach Islam in his last years of life. Many of the people of Yasrib would come over from Medina, and the Prophet would sit and talk to them. The result of talking to them for two years in Hajj was the reason why the Prophet immigrated to Medina, and all the development of the world happened because of it.

Sh: Yes, that is correct. It was because of that. There were many people at the same time as the Prophet that had spoken with him and had come from Medina. Many of them came to Hajj but did not have a significant impact on the rest of the pilgrims of the world.

Dr: We have a phrase where we say it was an Ibrahimi Hajj meaning a Hajj that is enlightening and confirms the statement of facts.

Sh: By the way, where is your hotel situated? If you agree, let's go to my hotel while we are in Mecca because my hotel is closer.

Dr: I wouldn't want to impose.

Sh: Of course, your hotel would be much better, but it is further away. My hotel is less luxurious, but it is closer.

Dr: I do not have any objection but don't forget that in a couple of days I have to go to Arafa and Mena and the ordinances that come with it.

Sh: Actually, it would be nice to continue our discussions in Mena.

Dr: I believe based on what we discussed, then we would only have three days from now to have our discussions.

Sh: Do not forget the initial discussion, which is about the Caliphate. I am waiting for that debate.

Dr: Allow us to debate that after we have finished Arafa and Mena.

Sh: Okay, then come to my hotel after the Zuhr prayer. We shall meet in front of the door of Fath (Bab al Fath) in Masjid Al Haram.

Dr: It will be tough to get a driver from that door if you agree, let's use the exit from the entrance of Umrah (Bab al Umrah). That way, there are plenty of buses and taxis, and it would go smoother.

Sh: I agree but stand outside of the door of Umrah.

Dr: Very well. Goodbye.

Sh: Good to see you.

Day Fourth of Zihijjah

I finished my Zuhr Prayer in Masjid Al Haram and then headed towards the door of Umrah to meet with the Sheikh. I saw that Sheikh was with a couple of his friends. He introduced them to me and said that Doctor is our guest today. Sheikh's friends were from Egypt. One of his friends was Sheikh Abubakr Usman, a professor at the Alazhar that sold books and owned his own publishing company. The other was a medical doctor from Egypt who lived in England, Dr. Zohair. He had joined the tour group of Egyptians. Dr. Zohair had a friend name Dr. Amr Mosa, who was also an Egyptian from England working as a Medical doctor. I asked Amr Mosa if he had any relations with the famous Amr Mosa? He replied: Yes, we are both Egyptian, and we are both tall and named Amr Mosa (laughingly) what more relations would you need?

We came to pass the door of Umrah when we saw that the guidance office at the Masjid Al Haram was distributing books. Some people were gathered there looking for books too. I had heard that books of the Quran were distributed early mornings after the prayer and then for the rest of the day, there were only books preaching the Wahabi way. The friend of Sheikh that sold books said: I have seen these books. There are other ways the Wahabis advertise their faith, and frequently, most of them are discriminating the different religions. They forbid the reading of supplication for the graves; talking against cruelty and talking about politics are regarded as an innovation in Hajj.

I said: But they are spending much money on this and some people take these books and dump them further on all mostly take it to their hotel and leave them there.

Eventually, we got the Sheikh's hotel. The hotel was very much older than our hotel. People were sleeping on the floor in the hotel, and food was given to the rooms. The hotel almost looked like the hotels that the Iranian Pilgrims used to go to in the '80s.

A small plastic cloth was spread on the floor. Lunch was Arabic food made by the hotel. They were placing the food on plates for people and giving out plastic spoons and forks. It must be said that everything was in plastic, the forks, spoons, cups, and the cloth. The only thing that was not plastic was water and food.

Sheikh apologized if the food was terrible and said to me that my food was better than his. I started saying good things about the variety of Egyptian foods and Sheikh excused us and said that he wishes to leave me with as he wanted to continue our discussion. His friends objected and said that we should debate in his room together. Sheikh said that our conversations were specialized religious debates and tedious for them. The friend that sold book objected and said that he would like to be part of the debate. What is better than discussion religion on Hajj? Sheikh continued to, and the others continued to persist, and eventually, Sheikh gave in and accepted for the debate to stay in his room, accompanied by them. We had special Egyptian tea and coffee and sweets and plenty of other snacks. Of course, the Egyptian Medical Doctors from England enjoyed them more than I did, and they did end up offering some English sweets that they were carrying with them.

Sheikh said: Then allow us to continue our debate, and if you guys had any questions then you can ask away.

Doctor Zohair (Medical profession) said: But we are the debatable type and we cannot just sit and watch if we had any questions we will straight up ask away.

I said: I hope that our debate will not be tiresome for you and if there was anything you wished to ask, please ask away.

Islam and Politics

Sh: It would be good to talk about the interference of religion in politics? In Egypt, we get to be told many times how politics should not interfere with religion. It is best that I ask your opinion regarding this in the presence of my Egyptian friends as you come from a country that is the center of politics in the Islamic world, meaning Iran.

Dr: I am definitely in agreement to start such a discussion.

Sh: In most of the Islamic countries, religion is separated from politics, and the politicians are separate from the religious leaders, and in reality, they both are two independent governing bodies. Whereas in Iran, there is only governing religion and is famously known as the Shia government. Politics interfere with, and the politicians are the religious leaders, and this is a severe difference between the other Islamic countries.

Dr: It wouldn't be so bad to know the view of our other friends.

Dr. Zohair: I am a Medical Doctor and know nothing of politics. I have been living in England for a very long time, and I was born in Jamal Ab dul Naser time. I would not allow someone else to interfere with my profession, and a religious leader feels the exact way. For example, Sheikh Ibrahim, we would come to you if we had any moral questions, but we would never interfere with your profession. Why do we not respect the same thing for our politicians? Why do we interfere with their affairs? In my opinion, politics is also a specialized field.

The Doctor & Sheikh's Debate

Dr: Do any of our other friends have anything to say?

Jamal Ahmad (the bookseller): In some of the Arabian countries such as Egypt the religious leaders have their own governing body, and in a way, they are competing for power. Power is held on a two-way scale, but the range is holding up both of the weights.

Dr: How do the religious leaders get paid in Egypt? Where does the budget for securing the religious groups come from?

Jamal Ahmad: They have government funds, and they receive a yearly fund for different sections.

Dr: What is the role of these religious leaders in running the country?

Jamal Ahmad: They have no role in running the country they have rights in education the religious side of people and people follow them for their religious needs.

Dr: They must also get paid for not interfering in the political side of things every year.

Sh: That is not the case. The clerks themselves do not wish to interfere with politics. That is because they don't class it in their rank of being a religious leader or a scholar in religion. In politics, there are lies, deceits, accusations, backstabbing, murder, bribery, and changing justice to injustice, and therefore, it is better for the scholars not to have to deal with it.

Dr: Maybe then that is the reason why as soon as you talk to religious scholars they listen very carefully but as when you start talking about politics, like talk about Israel and America and they instantly say that it is Hajj season and that it is the season of God. Interfering in politics is not what we do.

Sh: This topic is, but I must add that some do like to interfere with politics but are scared and prefer a life of calmness compared to a hectic political life.

Dr: We, followers of the Ahl al Bayt's faith believe that if interfering in politics and guiding people's life and running the government is a mistake then this mistake (We seek refuge in God (بـــالله نعــوذ)) started from God and his Prophets.

Sh: Why do you say that it started with God and his Prophet?

Dr: I say this because God told Noah to go and guide the people. God told Ibrahim to go and free people from Namrud. God told Moses to go and free people from Pharaoh. God told Jesus to go and free people from the Jews.

Sh: But God didn't say govern the country. He said: guide the people.

Dr: If it was just guidance, then why did God kill all those that did not listen to what Noah was trying to tell them? He turned the people of Loot upside down. He drowned the people of Pharaoh so the people of Israel would listen to the words of wisdom of Moses. He saved Ibrahim from the fire so that people would listen to what was saying. They tortured Jesus so much because he was advising people in their lives. They kicked the Prophet out because of all the advice he was giving the people of Mecca.

Sh: The Quran says, "انذر," which means warn and advising is a warning.

Dr: Where did God ask Moses to warn? He said:

اذْهَبْ إِلَى فِرْعَوْنَ إِنَّهُ طَغَى

"Go to Pharaoh. Indeed, he has transgressed"

This means that God interferes with the government. He wanted to take away the government from the people of Pharaoh.

Sh: Well we say that there was no such thing in Islam. A good Mumen is one that guides its people. If they did not accept then the Quran says:

لا إِكْرَاهَ فِي الدِّينِ

"There shall be no compulsion in [acceptance of] the religion"

Dr: Based on this interpretation and assumption then the Prophet himself made a big mistake (We seek refuge in God (بـالله نعـوذ)) is going to the battle of Badr or sending people to the battle of Tabuk.

Sh: The battles that the Prophet was involved with were mostly out of, for example, Ohod or Ahzab.

Dr: Yes, you are right, but they all weren't out of defense, for instance, Tabuk, Badr, and Muatah.

Sh: Why did they go to Tabuk? Whose money were they to get back?

Sh: Yes, Tabuk was for invasion and was not defensive.

Dr: You must know that after the peacemaking of Hudibiyah the Prophet wrote to the three leaders of Iran, Rome, and Egypt that they must accept the Islamic religion or else whatever happens to you is not under my control.

Sh: Yes, these letters exist.

The Doctor & Sheikh's Debate

Dr: If the intention of the Prophet was not to rule then he could have just bought a Tasbih (bid beads) and sat in Masjid Al Haram and would cite "اللّسبحان" (Praise the Lord).

Dr. Amr Moosa: If he had done such a thing, then we would have been one of the most prominent rulers of the world. The Prophet doomed us and Iran and Rome by not sitting and citing "سبحان الله," and now we are the Arabs puppets.

Dr: You have become puppets of the west. That is because your Islam does not interfere with your politics or else at the time that Islam was interfering with the government, and politics was not separated from religion, Egypt was dominant in governing the world. If you look at England, the first person to build a metal bridge was an Egyptian.

Dr. Amr Moosa: Yes, you are right.

Dr: The British monarchy wrote a letter to the Egyptian rulers a few centuries ago so they would teach their children education. Now you go to England to educate yourself.

Dr. Zohair: I did not understand in the end whether it is suitable for Islam to interfere in the government or not.

Sh: We did not order anything strictly.

Dr: Then, where did this discussion start from. If every Muslim was to do its own business, then what were we doing in Spain? What were we doing in Iran, Egypt, and Sudan? They were not Arabs then.

Dr. Zohair: Dear Sheikh Ibrahim, it is better for you to answer Sheikh. I have nothing more to say.

Sh: We say that the times have changed. I mean to say that in the time of the Prophet, he and the Caliphas were ruling but now the world has changed in a way as though politics have been corrupted by everything that is immoral and it is best for the religious leaders to stay away from it.

Dr: Why do you think, in your opinion, the scholars and politicians of the Islamic countries agree with the leaders of the United States in saying that religion should be separated from politics? They don't care about the Mumenins or the immorality of politics.

Dr. Zohair: Due to the specialty of the field and the fact the there was no law and order before. There were no groups or parties or factions, and now politics is science, and the politicians cannot operate on the same level as a religious scholar.

Dr. Amr Moosa: No, they do sit with each other and are on the same level, however, the religious scholars and leaders of religion are just like the pope or the great Religious Jurists of other countries, they are mostly in agreement with the politicians and leaders of the government. In other words, the religious leaders are not commanders, but they take command.

Dr: God bless you. Then they interfere with politics but in the wrong part of it such as agreeing with cruelty, agreeing with corruption in the government and agreeing with killing and bloodshedding of Mujahid (worrier for the faith) people.

Sh: Of course, this does not apply to all religious scholars.

Dr: Of course, that is right. That is because religious scholars would abide by your suggestion and stay well away from politics and the ones that do, make a big mistake. I mean the part where they agree with the cruelty of the politicians.

Dr. Amr Moosa: When religion interferes with politics, it takes away that freedom and limits it. For example, The Egyptian brotherhood (Ikhvan Al Muslimin) wanted to devalue the role of the Jamal Abdul Naser's role and position, so they tortured him so much so that he was forced to kill their leader, Hasan Al Bana'.

Dr: In fact, this proves the debate we are having here. Politicians cannot tolerate religious leaders unless they agree with them. Jamal Abdul Naser was a great man, and great people make great mistakes. In my opinion, killing Hasan Al Bana' was a big mistake.

Dr. Amr Moosa: Yes, if he disagreed with him, then he should have just put him in jail.

Dr. Zohair: Well if he were jailed then his supporters would have caused a riot.

Sh: Their beliefs seem a little distant from the real Islam. It sounds like Marxism.

Dr: First of all, what they believed in is not close to Communism. Secondly, were their beliefs so different from some of the Jamal Abdul Naser's deputies from Islam? Did they not kill hundreds and thousands of Egyptian and Palestinian Muslims after him?

Sh: The people who worked with Jamal at the time were not like that and changed afterward.

Dr: That is a possibility, but one could also say that Jamal Abdul Naser did not even see the truth.

Dr. Zohair: At that time, we must not forget, there was no allowance of interference of religious scholars in politics and governing at all.

The Doctor & Sheikh's Debate

Dr: Do they accept such a thing now? Even now, most countries do not allow religious scholars to interfere with any discussions regarding the land.

Dr. Amr Moosa: It has gotten a bit better now. At least the leaders of the governments are a little scared of the religious leaders.

Dr: They are just scared, though and not from all of them but just the real scholars. They buy and set aside the one that only has the appearance of a religious leader.

Sh: Let's return to the question about whether religious leaders should interfere or not. If they interfere, then we say they have been bought if they don't we say they are apart from the real Islam.

Dr: Scholars should take the government into their own hands and not be the advisors of oppressed and oppressors. How was it when in the time of the Prophet? The Muslims did not have a separate governing leader or city leader besides the religious system the Prophet had?

Sh: The Prophet was different. He was a ruler in every aspect.

Dr: What about the Caliphas after him? Four Caliphas ruled after him.

Sh: Yes, they did.

Dr: Do you mean to say that besides them they had a separate system governing?

Sh: No, but they were different too. They were four of the closest companions to the Prophet.

Dr: So, you suggest that we not only do not follow the way the Prophet was, but we also do not follow the route of his Caliphas. So, whom do we listen to? Bani Umayyah and Bani Abbas said that the government should do its own thing and the companions, scholars, narrators, and reciters should follow their way.

Sh: No, that wouldn't be right.

Dr: If the Prophet was among us now, which governing system do you think he would accept in your opinion? Would you agree with the governing system that Iran has or the governing system of the Arabian countries? The Iranian government that is run by a Mujtahid and rules the country based on the rules of Islam or the Arabian government that have nothing to do with Islam and the religious leaders are sitting on the sidelines?

Dr. Zohair: I don't know about Iran, but he would not agree with the Arabian government.

Dr. Amr Moosa: This Iran has acted like Ali did at the time of his ruling as Calipha. It has created conflict between everyone.

Dr: What has Iran done? What was Ali doing?

Dr. Amr Moosa: At the time of Umar and Abubakr, the Islamic world was spreading, but at the time of Ali, there were mostly civil wars between the Muslims.

Dr: First of all, the problems within started from Usman, not Ali. At the time of Umar and Abubakr, the questions were mostly about Calipha and Ahl al Bayt, and no one else was disagreeing much. Therefore, they managed to conquest, but once that was done, and the estate of Kasra and Qeysar got mixed up with the Islamic Beytol Mal (treasury), the disagreements started.

Sh: How come the treasury that was around at the time of Umar did not cause any problem.

Dr: Yes, Umar was at least keeping up with the appearance of being fair, but the children of the first Calipha, Muhammad Ibn Abibakr and the old friends of the third Calipha that were companions were complaining about the third Calipha.

Sh: Some of the companions were also complaining about Ali too.

Dr: Yes, but they were complaining at Usman because he was splurging and complaining that Ali was being so precise on dividing the treasury and was not spending it or just giving it away.

Dr. Zohair: Sheikh Ibrahim, please agree that based on the explanations that were given Islam wishes to take over running the government and a leader and should run a country judge that is a scholar of Islam. In Arabian countries, the governing system that is being run is not based on Islam.

Dr. Amr Moosa: Yes, for instance, many of the countries do not ask the people's opinions on whom to be the king or Amir of the country. For example, we see that for many years, one family is governing the country as monarchy without their position being evaluated to see if they even have the highest priority to be where they are. Just because their father or grandfather was the king, they are given the rank of being king.

Sh: England is the same, so it is wrong.

Dr: We are talking about an Islamic country, not a Christian one in the west. Yes, it is right to say that the way England is running its government is wrong too even though the Prime Minister is chosen by the people and is the one running the show.

The Doctor & Sheikh's Debate

Dr. Amr Moosa: So, Sheikh Ibrahim do you agree that the Prophet and the Caliphas demonstrated that they wished to run the government and be in charge. So, we better not say that politics should be separated from Islam and that we shouldn't interfere with it and consider it as sin to do so.

Sh: In my opinion, the current situation is very different from when the Prophet and the Caliphas were around.

Dr: Tell me what difference does it have?

Sh: Well, all the equipment supporting social media such as the internet, satellite, mobiles, and computers have changed things.

Dr: These are types of equipment that instead of being useful for the governing systems that are non-religious and ruthless, they should be used for the religious governments.

Dr. Zohair: That is right. These are equipment that the modern world has made so they can strengthen their governments and be able to control people better or to train people's thoughts to their desires.

Dr: In fact, that is the exact reason why it is suitable for religious governments because they can use these specific devices to spread information to the world.

Dr. Amr Moosa: But there are so many sites and cables that are spreading immorality that even if anyone wished to use websites or cables to watch religious things they would stop on the way to see these other sites and will stay there instead.

Dr: Actually, people that are searching for religious sites and channels would not stop by these other channels. They would filter the ones that are useless to them.

Dr. Amr Moosa: I will not lie and say that every time I wish to look for news or something on the internet, I stumble on these other channels and websites and stay on them.

Dr. Zohair: Dr. Amr Moosa separated from his wife and children after twenty years. His wife left him for a British man that was disabled and married him instead; therefore; he does not have anyone and spends time on these websites.

Dr: So, the accomplishment of living in the west with one's family is to end up alone after 20 years of marriage.

Dr. Amr Moosa: We moved from Egypt to England to live a better life in the west. Unfortunately, my life, just like many others, got torn apart. Now it is me and my cigar and a triangle of repetitive places I go to, house, hospital, and park.

Dr: Really, that is what it comes to.

Dr. Amr Moosa: I wake up in the morning go to the hospital until 6 pm, then I go to the park and walk for half an hour and come home to have a simple dinner. I smoke some cigars, and then after a couple of hours, I get busy on the internet and cable. This is the result of all of the studying I did and spent all my youth to get a degree and make a family.

Dr: What if you had stayed in Egypt?

Dr. Amr Moosa: I would have had a family, kept my dignity and in other words had a highly regarded life. In England, we were seen as a lower, second, or third class even.

Dr: Does the thought of being second or third not bother you?

Dr. Amr Moosa: It upsets me, but I have gotten used to it now.

Dr: Used to hardship or being sad?

Dr. Amr Moosa: To both.

Sh: I studied in Saudi Arabia for a while, and they didn't consider me highly regarded either. Once you are looked at like this in an Islamic country, then it is obvious how you are viewed in England.

Dr: That is right. I have heard that there is racial discrimination in Saudi Arabia.

Sh: Where we are now is if a religious scholar, professor, or Imam is from Saudi Arabia, they are considered different to someone who is from Pakistan, Afghanistan, Syria, and even Egypt.

Dr: What differences, for instance?

Sh: He will have less of a chance in achieving a higher University or Hoaza (circle for religious studies). They even have them appear less on social media than the others.

Dr: Well it wouldn't be so far from reality because based on the religion of this country. The other Muslims are considered Infidels, and they are the only Muslims.

Sh: They mostly consider the Shias to be infidels as they do things that are against their beliefs. They also believe the Sunni's that follow the rules of Salafies to be infidels.

Dr: That is not true. I have seen that anyone that has a book in their hands is considered an infidel. Anyone reading a supplication is an infidel. Anyone that touches the chamber of the Prophet is considered an infidel.

The Doctor & Sheikh's Debate

Sh: Well, mostly Shias do these things.

Dr. Zohair: Dear Sheikh we go to Egypt to Zeynabiyah, Ra'asol Hussein, Seyedeh Nafisah and we touch, kiss the shrines and no one complains. However, here whenever I feel the pulpit of the Prophet, the Sheikh guarding it was close to chopping my hand off and then called me an infidel, this is a wood infidel. Therefore, they do class us who Shafeii and Egyptian as infidels too.

Dr: Do you see that the Shias are not the only ones that are considered as infidels. Shafeii, Maleki, Hanafi, and even Hanbalis' that are not Wahabis are all infidels.

Sh: Let's change the topic.

Dr: Does the way they think or the way they treat other Muslims upset you?

Sh: I am upset with both. It upsets me to see some consider their faith to be the only center of righteousness.

Dr: It is clear. In the Quran, we have a verse saying:

$$كُلُّ حِزْبٍ بِما لَدَيْهِمْ فَرِحُونَ$$

"And each group is content with what has been given to them"

Sh: It is wrong to name the people that declare their faith to be infidels.

Dr: Praise the Lord that's all I wanted.

Dr. Zohair: Let's go back to our discussion regarding government. Sheikh Ibrahim, do you now accept that Islam intends to rule?

Sh: Well, after the discussion, we had regarding the way the Prophet and the Caliphas where I do not have anything to say.

Dr: Until recently, any Muslim anywhere has been ruling.

Sh: Where have they ruled? What do you mean by saying recently?

Dr: This Government of Usmani, until Saudi Arabia was managed by it.

Sh: I accept that Islam is not separated from politics.

Dr: No, the point isn't for you to accept that Islam is not separated from politics. If you pay a little attention to the verses of the Quran, it becomes clear that there is way more than that. A political

Imam in Iran after seventy years being the leader of the parliament will also say that our politics are the same as our Islam and my religion is my politics.

Sh: Now that we accepted that Islam is not separate from the religion, he says that faith is in fact, politics.

Dr: I will not persist anymore if you accept this one thing. Leave this last part to myself then. I have to say though that if religion is not separated from politics, then they would be both impregnated.

Dr. Zohair: If you pay attention, you see that wherever a country is governed by having religion as its source, it is successful, for instance, compare Gaza to the Fat-h. The Fat-h did not have a religious reference. Fifty years have passed, and nothing has been done, but the Hamas and the Islamic Jihad or Lebanese Hezbullah that are Muslims managed to stand up against the unstoppable Israeli's in a brief period.

Dr: May God bless your deceased relatives. You saved me so much time.

Sh: I accept that Islam is not separated from politics and that if a country is governed based on religion, it would be better for the people as they would be guided in the right way. Doctor, politics are our religion, and religion is our politics.

Dr: Now, I wish to add two facts.

Sh: In what regard?

Dr: Regarding not supporting a country that is a government of oppression.

Sh: Please go ahead.

Dr: In Musnad Tayalasi, volume 1, page 143, Hadith 1064, we have:

حدثنا أبو داود قال حدثنا سليمان بن المغيرة قال حدثنا موسى الهلالي عن أبيه عن كعب قال: دخل علينا رسول الله صلي الله عليه وسلم المسجد فقال من هاهنا هل تسمعون انه يكون بعدي امراء يعملون بغير طاعة الله فمن شركهم في عملهم وايمانهم على ظلمهم فليس مني ولست منه ومن لم يشركهم في عملهم ولم يعنهم على ظلمهم فهو مني وانا منه

"The Prophet entered the Mosque and said: Have you heard that after me there will be leaders that will be acting against what God has said? So, anyone that supports the ones that oppress in their actions is not from me and I am not from them and anyone that does not support them is from me and I am from them."

Sh: Yes, this Hadith is correct.

The Doctor & Sheikh's Debate

Dr: Then based on this Hadith, half of the Saudi Arabian Scholars, Jordan, Egypt, and other Islamic countries are not from the Prophet.

Sh: What can I say? The truth is that scholars should not support the governments in oppressing people.

Dr: Now that the Islamic countries have started to act against the governments that are despotism, unfortunately, great scholars are not assisting as much. The dictatorship has even gone, but countries such as Egypt, Tunisia, Yaman, Bahrain, and Libya are still standing behind and are not getting involved in guiding people, and people have no religious role models.

Sh: Yes, this fact is apparent. Not having a religious leader is the main problem for all these countries.

Dr: Now I wish to say something new.

Sh: Is it still regarding the government? You managed to question not only all of the governments but the scholars by using these Hadith's, in which I agree with you.

Dr: But the Hadith said that any Scholar that does not support the government that is oppressing the people is from me.

Sh: What is the new thing you wish to say?

Dr: I think we are tired for today, allow us to talk about this new thing tomorrow.

Sh: I agree, so let's have a break and go to the Mosque.

Dr: If it is okay with you, please allow me to return to the hotel as my wife is waiting for me. God willing, I might get to see you again for the Maghrib prayer at the Mosque.

Sh: I agree. I hope you have a good day.

Day Sixth of Zihijjah

After finishing my Zuhr prayer we agreed to meet in front of the door of Umrah and to follow up our discussion at the Sheikh's hotel. We did that and ended up having lunch in the Sheikh's room and continued the conversation we were having yesterday.

Hazrat Mahdi in Ahl Sunnat's Books

Dr: Shall we start the new topic I wanted to talk about yesterday?

Dr. Amr Moosa: Doctor, do you not have anything else to talk about other than the government?

Dr: Do you agree that eventually in the future there will be one government in the world ruled by one person?

Dr. Zohair: There is one already. They call it a small village in the world. What I mean is that the world is considered as a village and is governed by America.

Dr: Have you heard of the name "Mahdi Al Muntazer" in your books?

Sh: We have heard something but not studied it well enough.

Dr: But it is familiar in any Islamic countries such as Turkey, Egypt, Sudan, Iraq, and other countries.

Sh: Apparently, he will also start a government.

Dr: He will appear at the apocalypse, and he will create a government that is solely based on religion in the world.

Dr. Zohair: Who is this Mahdi that is going to create a religious government?

Dr: He is one of the Prophet's grandsons.

Dr. Amr Moosa: Where is he? Where is he from? When is he born?

Dr: I don't wish to get involved with the details and this kind of discussion.

Sh: Then what did you want to talk about?

Dr: I wanted to say that the Mahdi that all of the Muslims are waiting for is also going to create a religious government in the world.

Sh: He isn't that well known.

Dr: This Mahdi is so well known that Hollywood has made a film about him named "Mahdi."

Dr. Amr Moosa: Mahdi?

Dr: Yes, Mahdi.

Dr. Zohair: What was it about?

Dr: It is about a man named Mahdi that appears in Sudan; he claims a worldwide government and conquers everywhere in Africa, Turkey, Iraq and some of the European countries and gets to Saudi Arabia. On his way, he comes across oil wells with western lasers and eventually fails and is killed.

Sh: But apparently, Mahdi does start a government and manages to conquer the world before he dies.

Dr: Yes, that is exactly right, but they wanted to say that we will also defeat the Mahdi that you all are waiting for.

Dr. Zohair: Now, why does Mahdi appear from Sudan?

Dr: That is because someone named Mahdi claimed to be him a couple of years ago. The famous Sadegh Al Mahdi in Sudan that managed to govern Sudan is his grandson. He also managed to be prime minister.

Dr. Zohair: Where does the real Mahdi appear from?

Dr: He will appear from Mecca.

Sh: Do you also believe in him?

Dr: The difference between you and the School of Ahl al Bayt is that in your books there is someone mentioned that is the exact match of Mahdi, but we say that he is born and is alive and will appear when the time is right, and you say that he is born close to the time.

Sh: Please tell us more so we can get to know him better.

Dr: I don't think it is necessary. What is essential is for us to know that there is such a leader coming and he will guide the human race in a way that there will no longer be any oppression and immorality.

Sh: Then, what is the story behind him alive?

Dr: Based on Hadith from the Prophet that has also been mentioned in your books, the world will not be lacking a Hujat (divine proof). Therefore, after the Prophet passing away, there must always be one Hujat and religious leader in the world.

Sh: Who were the people after the Prophet?

Dr: We agreed to discuss that at the end of our debate.

Sh: You are killing us with anticipation. Every time we come to the discussion regarding Calipha, you say later.

Dr: It is the same twelve people that you have in your Hadith's, but the people and their applicability's are others that you know of.

Sh: What number is this Mahdi?

Dr: He is the twelfth person.

Sh: Do you mean to say that he is alive and has been born and now has lived for 1400 years?

Dr: Yes.

Sh: There are many questions about this person, but please answer this one question, and then I will let go of the others.

The Age of Imam Mahdi

Dr: What question?

Sh: How is it possible for someone to live more than a thousand years?

Dr: I will bring two ways mentioned in the Quran and hope that God willing, it will convince you.

Sh: If it is from the Quran I will definitely be convinced.

Dr: Very well, first of all God regarding Noah in Surat Al Ankabut verse 14 says:

وَلَقَدْ أَرْسَلْنَا نُوحًا إِلَىٰ قَوْمِهِ فَلَبِثَ فِيهِمْ أَلْفَ سَنَةٍ إِلَّا خَمْسِينَ عَامًا فَأَخَذَهُمُ الطُّوفَانُ وَهُمْ ظَالِمُونَ ﴿١٤﴾

"And we certainly sent Noah to his people, and he remained among them a thousand years minus fifty years, and the flood seized them while they were wrongdoers."

This verse says that he lived for 950 years which means that it is possible to live that long is that right?

Sh: Yes, Noah lived for 950 years.

Dr: We do have many more Prophets that lived for long times.

Sh: That is right.

Dr: Now another proof from the Quran.

Sh: What is the other explanation from Quran?

Dr: Surat As Saffat, verse 139 - 144 it says:

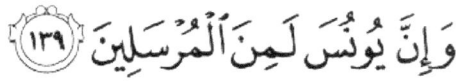

"And indeed, Jonah was among the messengers."

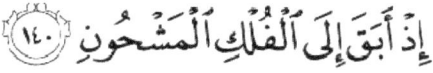

"[Mention] when he ran away to the laden ship."

The Doctor & Sheikh's Debate

"And he drew lots and was among the losers."

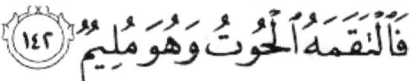

"Then the fish swallowed him, while he was blameworthy."

"And had he not been of those who exalt Allah,"

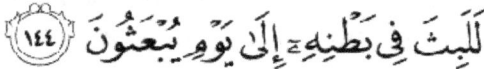

"He would have remained inside its belly until the Day they are resurrected."

That means that If God wishes, he can not only keep someone alive for 1400 years but for the end of time.

Sh: That was very interesting reasoning.

Dr: Now, please pay attention to another fact. Well, I have not seen this in the books of Tafsir.

Sh: What fact?

Dr: Quran says that Yunus was kept in the stomach of a whale; therefore, that means that the whale had also to stay alive and what if the whale lived forever too? At least if Yunus had to keep active, the whale has to live too.

Sh: Doctor I accept that it is possible to live for more than a thousand years.

Dr: Thank the Lord; let's go to the next discussion then.

Sh: Are there Hadith about Mahdi in our books too?

Dr: Yes, here you go In Jame ul Ahadis, volume 13, page 339:

سيكون بعدى خلفاء ومن بعد الخلفاء أمراء ومن بعد الأمراء ملوك ومن بعد الملوك جبابرةْ ثم يخرج رجل من اهل بيتى يملأ الأرض عدلاً كما ملئت جوراً... (ابن منده، والطبراني، وأبو نعيم في الحليةْ، وابن عساكر عن الأوزاعي، ورواه ابن لهيعةْ عن عبد الرحمن بن قيس بن جابر عن أبيه عن جده وهو الصحيح) أخرجه الطبرانى (22/374، رقم 937) قال الهيثمى (190/5) وابن عساكر (282/14).

"After me there will be Caliphas and then after them military commanders and then after them kings and after kings there will be wicked and oppressors so then a man will appear from my Ahl al Bayt that will fill the world with justice and righteousness just like it was with cruelty."

Sh: There are more topics than what you mentioned about Mahdi in our books.

Dr. Zohair: Sheikh Ibrahim the Doctor does not have much proof of Mahdi from our books.

Dr: I wanted to save them for later, but if you wish, here you go: In book Eshrat Al Sa'a, where it talks about the conditions of judgment day, volume 1 page 105 it says as below:

قال العلامةْ الشوكاني: «الأحاديث في تواتر ما جاء في المهدي المنتظر التي أمكن الوقوف عليها منها خمسون حديثا، فيها الصحيح والحسن والضعيف المنجبر، وهي متواترةْ بلاشك وشبهةْ، بل يصدق وصف التواتر على ما دونها في جميع الاصطلاحات المحررةْ في الأصول، وأما الآثار عن الصحابةْ المصرحةْ بالمهدي فهي كثيرةْ أيضا، إذ لا مجال للاجتهاد في مثل ذلك

"Allame Shukani says: The frequency of Hadith's regarding Mahdi Muntazar that requires reflection on is about 50 which in them there are correct, weak and good but without a doubt many frequent of them. There are many circumstances and the fact of its frequency that make them legit but there are many companions referring to him. Therefore, there is no other place to Ijtihad but in this case."

2. قال العلامةْ أبو عبدالله محمد بن جعفر بن إدريس الكتاني الحسني الفاسي، مؤرخ ومحدث: «والحاصل أن الأحاديث الواردةْ في المهدي المنتظر متواترةْ، وكذا الواردةْ في الدجال وفي نزول عيسى ابن مريم عليهما السلام

"Or in the same book there is this: Allame Muhammad Ibn Jafar Al Kitani says: The result regarding the Hadith's for Mahdi Muntazar is widely transmitted. There are many Hadith's regarding the Dajal (deceiver) and Isa Ibn Maryam"

3. يقول العلامةْ أبوالطيب شمس الحق العظيم آبادي: «واعلم أن المشهور بين الكافةْ من أهل الإسلام على ممر الأعصار أنه لا بد في آخر الزمان من ظهور رجل من أهل البيت يؤيد الدين ويظهر العدل ويتبعه المسلمون ويستولي على الممالك الإسلاميةْ ويسمى بالمهدي، ويكون خروج الدجال وما بعده من أشراط الساعةْ الثابتةْ في الصحيح على إثره، وأن عيسى عليه‌السلام ينزل من بعده فيقتل الدجال، أو ينزل معه فيساعده على قتله، ويأتم بالمهدي في صلاته

"Allame Abu Al Tayeb Shams Al Haq Al Azim Abadi says: I am aware that between all of the Ahl Islam it is known that at the end of the time where there is hardship a man from the Ahl al Bayt will appear whom will endorse religion, support justice and all the Muslims will follow him. He will be dominant on the rules of Islam and is named Mahdi. Whatever mentioned regarding the conditions of the judgement day is all correct and proved to be right. Christ will also appear shortly after him; he will kill Dajal or will appear at the same time and will assist in killing him. He will join Mahdi in prayer."

4. قد أحصى فضيلةْ شيخنا الشيخ عبدالمحسن بن حمد العباد البدر - حفظه الله - في كتابه القيم عقيدةْ أهل السنةْ والأثر في المهدي المنتظر عدد الصحابةْ الذين رووا أحاديث المهدي فبلغوا ستةْ وعشرين صحابيا، كما أحصى عدد الأئمةْ الذين خرجوا هذه الأحاديث والآثار في كتبهم فبلغوا ستةْ وثلاثين إماما، منهم أصحاب السنن الأربعةْ والإمام أحمد في مسنده وابن حبان في صحيحه والحاكم في المستدرك وغيرهم، كما ذكر بعض من ألف في شأن المهدي، والذين حكموا على أحاديث المهدي بالتواتر، كما ذكر بعض العلماء المحققين الذين احتجوا بأحاديث المهدي واعتقدوا موجبها وهم جمع كبير

"Sheikh Abdul Muhsen Ibn Hamd Al Ebad Al Badr in his book has strongly and strictly mentioned his opinion regarding Ahl Sunnat and has cited a couple of Hadith about Mahdi Muntazar and his phenomenon. It all count's to be 26 companions in addition to the Imams that have mentioned these Hadith's in their books that adds up to thirty-six Imams. From them in addition, the four companions of the Sunan (Nisani, Tarmazi, Ibn Majah and Abu Davood) and Imam Ahmad in his book of Musnad and Ibn Hayan in his book of Sahih and Hakim in his book of Al Mustarak have all mentioned Mahdi or have mentioned Hadith mentioning something regarding him. There are also scholars that have analysed the Hadith's regarding Mahdi and believe that they are true."

Dr Zohair: I accept.

Dr: There is more, for instance this same book mentions Bukhari in Mukhtasar Al Bukhari, page 324 Hadith numbers 1440 says:

كيف كنتم إذا نزل ابن مريم فيكم وإمامكم منكم

"How would you be if the son of Maryam would appear amongst you and you have your Imam amongst yourselves?"

It wouldn't be so bad to have a look at his signs and miracles too.

Sh: Which books mention his signs?

Dr: In the same book from Abu Naeem, book of Al Sa'a Le Esharat Al Sa'a, page 85 it mentions Ali Ibn Abitaleb citing the signs and miracles of Mahdi:

6. «في كتفهٔ علامةٌ النبي صلى الله عليه وسلم، وأنه يجتمع بعيسى عليه السلام ويصلي عيسى خلفه، وأن الأرض تخرج أفلاذ كبدها مثل الأسطوانات من الذهب ـ ومن علاماته عليه السلام غنى قلوب الناس وكثرةٔ بركات الأرض، ومنها ان يخرج كنز الكعبةٔ المدفون فيقسمه في سبيل الله، ومنها أن يغرس قضيباً في أرض اليابسةٔ فيخضر ويورق، وكذلك يطلب منه آيةٔ فيومئ إلى الطير في السماء فيسقط في يده

"The sign of the Prophet (s.a.w.a) is on his shoulder. He will be with Jesus and the Christ will stand to pray behind him. The earth will stand like golden columns and the people's hearts will be needless and blessing on earth will exceed. One of his signs is that he will bring out the treasures hidden in Kabaa and he will divide it among the people. A sign from him will be that the date tree will never die and it stay green and grow leaves. They will ask of him to show a miracle sign and he will point to a bird in the sky and the bird will come straight down on his hand."

Tarmazi in volume 1, page 174 in the section that says "ماجاء في المهدي" cites that:

2156 - «حَدَّثَنَا عُبَيْدُ بْنُ أَسْبَاطِ بْنِ مُحَمَّدٍ الْقُرَشِيُّ الْكُوفِيُّ قَالَ حَدَّثَنِي أَبِي حَدَّثَنَا سُفْيَانُ الثَّوْرِيُّ عَنْ عَاصِمِ بْنِ بَهْدَلَهٔ عَنْ زِرٍّ عَنْ عَبْدِ اللَّهِ قَالَ
قَالَ رَسُولُ اللَّهِ صَلَّى اللَّهُ عَلَيْهِ وَسَلَّمَ لَا تَذْهَبُ الدُّنْيَا حَتَّى يَمْلِكَ الْعَرَبَ رَجُلٌ مِنْ أَهْلِ بَيْتِي يُوَاطِئُ اسْمُهُ اسْمِي.

"The Prophet (s.a.w.a) said: The world will not end unless a man from my Ahl al Bayt rules amongst the Arabs and his name will be same as mine."

Dr. Zohair: Based on this Hadith, his name should be Muhammad, not Mahdi.

Dr: His actual name is that, but because they didn't want anyone to know who he is and to stay safe from the hand of the governments, therefore, he is famous for the other name.

Sh: I am not aware of the reason, but I do know that this Hadith is authentic and the name Mahdi has been mentioned a lot.

Dr: In Kanzol Amaal, volume 14, page 264, there is the following Hadith's:

38661- «يلي رجل من أهل بيتي يواطئ اسمه اسمي، لو لم يبق من الدنيا إلا يوم لطول الله ذلك اليوم حتى يلي

"A Man will rise from my Ahl al Bayt that will carry my name and if there was only one day before the end of the time God will stretch that day until he rises."

The Doctor & Sheikh's Debate

38662- «المهدي من عترتي من ولد فاطمةَ»

"Mahdi is from my descendants and he is from Fatimah's descendants"

38665- «المهدي أجلى الجبهةْ، أقنى الأنف، يملأ الأرض قسطا وعدلا كما ملئت جورا وظلما، يملك سبع سنين

"Mahdi has a blinding forehead, long shaped nose. He will spread justice and righteousness just like it is spread of injustice and impurity. He will rule for 7 years."

38666- «المهدي رجل من ولدي، وجهه كالكوكب الدري»

"Mahdi is a Man from my descendants, his forehead is shinning like the stars."

Sh: We accept Doctor, I did say that there are many chains of transmissions about him.

Dr: I mentioned them for Dr. Zohair.

Dr. Zohair: Doctor I accept, you have many chains of transmissions for Mahdi too.

Dr: The ones I mentioned are only from the books of Hadith, but there are plenty more in the writings of Tafsir.

Sh: I had seen them in the books but not in Tafsir.

Dr: Your interpreters know some verses of the Quran about Mahdi and have mentioned it in their Tafsirs.

Sh: Which verses?

Dr: Here you go:

Qurtabi in the book of Al Jamaah Al Ahkam Al Quran, volume 8, page III, for the interpretation of Surat at Tawbah verse 33:

هُوَ ٱلَّذِىٓ أَرْسَلَ رَسُولَهُۥ بِٱلْهُدَىٰ وَدِينِ ٱلْحَقِّ لِيُظْهِرَهُۥ عَلَى ٱلدِّينِ كُلِّهِۦ وَلَوْ كَرِهَ ٱلْمُشْرِكُونَ ﴿٣٣﴾

"It is He who has sent His Messenger with guidance and the religion of truth to manifest it over all religion, although they who associate others with Allah dislike it."

The only time that Islam actually wins over all of the other religions is when Mahdi rises. Until then men will either have to convert to Islam or they have to pay ransom. And it has been said that Mahdi is Jesus. That is wrong as we have Hadith stating that Mahdi will be from the Prophet's descendants.

Siyoti has mentioned in Al Dor ul Mansour, volume 1, page 264 for the interpretation of the verse 114 of the Quran from Surat Al Baqarah:

$$\text{وَمَنْ أَظْلَمُ مِمَّن مَّنَعَ مَسَٰجِدَ ٱللَّهِ أَن يُذْكَرَ فِيهَا ٱسْمُهُۥ وَسَعَىٰ فِى خَرَابِهَآ ۚ أُو۟لَٰٓئِكَ مَا كَانَ لَهُمْ أَن يَدْخُلُوهَآ إِلَّا خَآئِفِينَ ۚ لَهُمْ فِى ٱلدُّنْيَا خِزْىٌ وَلَهُمْ فِى ٱلْءَاخِرَةِ عَذَابٌ عَظِيمٌ ﴿١١٤﴾}$$

"And who are more unjust than those who prevent the name of Allah from being mentioned in his Mosques and strive toward their destruction. It is not for them to enter them except in fear. For them in this world is disgrace and they will have in the Hereafter a great punishment?"

It has been written: Abasement and humiliation will rise when Mahdi rises, and he will conquer Constantinople and kill them all. The same things have been mentioned in Tafsir Tabari and Tafsir Kashf ul Asrar.

Hafiz Qondozi in Yana bi' Al Moa'da page 514 mentions the following for the interpretation of verse number 17 Surat Al Hadid:

$$\text{ٱعْلَمُوٓا۟ أَنَّ ٱللَّهَ يُحْىِ ٱلْأَرْضَ بَعْدَ مَوْتِهَا ۚ قَدْ بَيَّنَّا لَكُمُ ٱلْءَايَٰتِ لَعَلَّكُمْ تَعْقِلُونَ ﴿١٧﴾}$$

The Doctor & Sheikh's Debate

> "Know that Allah gives life to the earth after its lifelessness. We have made clear to you the signs; perhaps you will understand."

He believes that: The Lord will keep him alive by keeping him existing and so he could do justice and to revive the earth from the judgment he possesses after his death because of the injustice spread on land.

It is also mentioned in the same book page 515 for the interpretation of verse number 24 Surat Al Jinn:

$$\text{حَتَّىٰ إِذَا رَأَوْا مَا يُوعَدُونَ فَسَيَعْلَمُونَ مَنْ أَضْعَفُ نَاصِرًا وَأَقَلُّ عَدَدًا ﴿٢٤﴾}$$

> "[The disbelievers continue] until, when they see that which they are promised, then they will know who is weaker in helpers and less in number."

It has been mentioned in this way that where it says "ما يوعدون" (What has been promised) in this verse, "قائم" is referred to Mahdi and his companions and when "قائم" raises his enemies will be weaker and their numbers will be small.

On page 506 in the interpretation of verse number 200 Surat Ali Imran:

$$\text{يَا أَيُّهَا الَّذِينَ آمَنُوا اصْبِرُوا وَصَابِرُوا وَرَابِطُوا وَاتَّقُوا اللَّهَ لَعَلَّكُمْ تُفْلِحُونَ ﴿٢٠٠﴾}$$

> "O you, who have believed, persevere and endure and remain stationed and fear Allah that you may be successful"

Muhammad Ali Al Baqir has cited regarding this verse: Be patient for spending time on the compulsory ordinances and persistent on confronting the harassments of the enemies and keep connected with your Imam, Mahdi.

Mumin Al Shablanji has mentioned in his book Noor Al Absar page 349 regarding the interpretation of verse number 86 for Surat Al Hud:

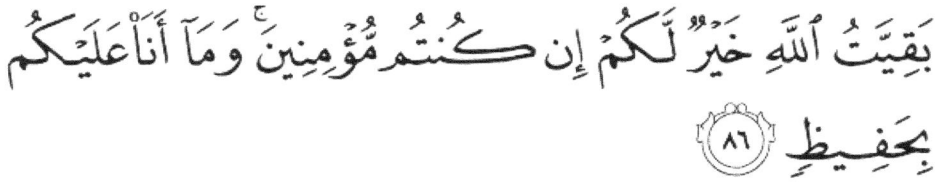

"What remains [lawful] from Allah is best for you, if you would be believers. But I am not a guardian over you."

He writes: When Mahdi rises he will have Kabaa as his base and 313 of his companions will join him and then for the first time he will cite this verse of the Quran: "What remains [lawful] from Allah is best for you, if you would be believers. But I am not a guardian over you" so he will say: "I am Baqiyatallah and the God's vicegerent and his Hujat for you".

Allamah Qabisi mentions in Maza Fi Al Tarikh, volume 3, page 145- 147 for the interpretation of verse number 8 Surat Taqhabun:

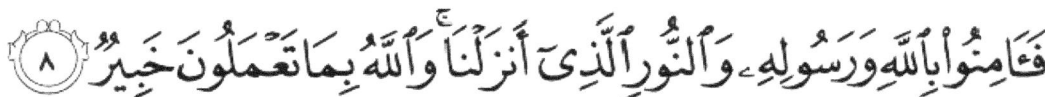

So, believe in Allah and His Messenger and the Qur'an which we have sent down. And Allah is acquainted with what you do.

He writes: Hafiz Abu Jafar Muhem Ibn Jarir Tabari said: At Hajj the Prophet (s.a.w.a) said: "Oh People," "آمِنُوا بِاللَّهِ وَ رَسُولِهِ وَ النُّورِ الَّذِى أَنْزَلْنَا" and then he said: Light is in me and then in Ali and then in his descendants until Qaem Mahdi rises.

Sh: God willing this worldwide ruler rises soon and with his ruling he amends this world.

Dr: People can be guided by ruling their government and can be swayed towards God that way. As how famously the Arabs say: "الناس علي دين ملوكهم " if the ruler is a politician and a non-believer then the people will then be and act the same as he is because he considered a role model.

Sh: That is correct.

The Doctor & Sheikh's Debate

Dr: compare this all with Lebanon. There was a time when it was the center of pleasure for the wealthy Arabs in the world. Now when you look at it, it is the center of Jihad and resistant.

Dr. Amr Moosa: It wasn't just a place of pleasure for the wealthy Arabs but also for the European Tourists too.

Dr: But now it is now a symbol of resistance against Israel.

Sh: Praise the Lord, praise the Lord. We got to know Mahdi much better.

Dr: It is time for Asir prayer. Please allow me to leave.

Sh: Have a good day, and we will see you tomorrow.

Day Seventh of Zihijjah (Friday)

We agreed to meet again at the Sheikh's hotel after the Zuhr's prayer and then after having lunch; we started talking still.

Dr: Before we start I wanted to ask your opinion on the Friday Sermon (Khutbah) that the Masjid Al Haram Imam was talking about.

Sh: What was your opinion?

Dr: I think that they have realized the attention people are now paying to the Ahl al Bayt and so, therefore, they too have started to talk about them.

Sh: Just the fact that they have come to realize the Ahl al Bayt by itself has its gratitude because no other country shows this much hatred towards the Ahl al Bayt. I have seen the love the people have for the Ahl al Bayt in Egypt.

Dr: It is the same everywhere. It's only when you come to Saudi Arabia and Pakistan that people are slightly less inclined to the Ahl al Bayt. Moreover, that is as because of the Wahabis. It has spread to Pakistan too.

Sh: Let's pass this part of the conversation. What happened to the continuation of the discussion? Let's not waste any time.

Dr: Time is never wasted at your side.

Sh: I am just scared that we run out of time and don't get to talk about the Caliphas.

Dr: Would you like to talk about the Caliphas today?

Sh: Praise the Lord for finally agreeing to talk about this topic now. Let's start.

The Debate over Caliphate

Dr: In the name of God. Let's start.

Sh: So, if you could tell me your opinion regarding the ruling of the Caliphas. Do you accept them or not?

Dr: It is perfect timing as we are in the hotel and primarily because besides you there are your friends and Sheikh Usman Abubakr is also a scholar from Egypt and Alazhar, so it's good that we are talking about this now.

Sh: Thank the Lord.

Dr: So, allow me first to bring up a couple of points regarding this topic independently and then we can summarize.

Sh: Would you mind giving me a list of them?

Dr: Yes, I can, but at the end of the discussion, we summarize not after every topic.

Sh: Please give me the list. I don't think it would be so crucial if we ended up summarizing it after every topic. Maybe it would be best to conclude after each item, so please give us the list.

Dr:

1. The difference between the Prophet and the Caliphas
2. The disagreement in the way the Caliphas were chosen
3. The number of Caliphas after the Prophet
4. The companion's objection over Ali not being selected as Calipha
5. Ali's superiority over the other Caliphas
6. The result of the actions over eliminating Ali from being chosen as Calipha after the Prophet
7. The Prophet's testimonial over Ali being Calipha after him
8. Ghadir Khumm

Sh: Very well, please start.

Dr: I will keep it short, but each one will take a day.

Sh: That is okay. Please start.

1- The Difference between the Prophet and the Caliphas

Dr: First of all, let me ask you a question. Would that be okay?

Sh: Yes, please.

The Doctor & Sheikh's Debate

Dr: Did the Prophet name a successor after him?

Sh: He did not choose a Calipha.

Sh Usman Abubakr: Well when the Prophet was sick Abubakr went to the Mosque and conducted the prayer instead of him, and because the Prophet did not object to this then it was clear that he was happy for him to be his successor.

Sh: Of course, this is not any proof of choosing a successor.

Dr: Can we come with an answer from you both honorable Sheikhs? Did he choose a Calipha after him or not?

Sh: He did not.

Dr: Very well. I have an extraordinary thing to state that might amaze you.

Sh: What thing?

Dr: This isn't my opinion, in reality, it is yours, but for me to analyze your opinion I would need to state it this way and then it will sound weird.

Sh: Is it eventually our opinion or yours? We agreed for you to state your opinion.

Dr: An opinion is an opinion. It doesn't matter whether it is from you or me or anyone else, but it is your belief.

Sh: What is this thing?

Dr: In my opinion, you believe that the Caliphas were wiser than the Prophet and cared more for the Ummah than he did.

Sh: We seek refuge in God (بــالله نعــوذ). When have we believed in such a thing? Where would you have seen such a statement? You have never stated such an item from us from the day we have started this discussion. Where is the source of this opinion? We do not consider the Caliphas to be even in the same rank as the Prophet never mind think them to be wiser or more compassionate.

Dr: Why did this offend you? Do you remember in the beginnings of our meetings I told you that I hear many times that us; Shias believe in Khan Al Amin, meaning Gabriel betrayed us and instead of sending God's words to Ali he sent it to the Prophet. I never got angry. I proved that such a thing doesn't exist. Please don't get upset. If I am wrong, then bring me proof that what I am saying is incorrect, but I proved that this belief is true then, as usual, please accept it.

Sh: Very well please tell me why do we consider the Caliphas to be wiser than the Prophet?

Dr: The reason why I say this is based on your books, Abubakr and Umar thought that an Islamic Ummah cannot be without a leader and that it needs one and therefore they acted wisely and passionately. After the passing of the Prophet to prevent people from being dispersed and scattered, they appointed a successor.

Sh: Well, how is that proof of them wiser than the Prophet?

Dr: You are stating that the Prophet did not do such a thing; he did not appoint a successor.

Sh: So, it is clear to me that you wish to start an attack. We agreed for you to state your opinion regarding the Caliphas. This is an attack on the Caliphas.

Dr: This is not an attack. I started with asking what your opinions are; do you consider the Caliphas to be wiser than the Prophet himself?

Sh: Just like Sheikh Usman said: The Prophet did assign a successor, however, not in a very straight forward way.

Dr: When did he do such a thing? You, just now stated that he did not.

Sh: Not in a straight forward way, but he did imply.

Dr: Just now stating that the Prophet did not explicitly choose a successor, but Abubakr and Umar did say that they were wiser than him.

Sh: We seek refuge in God (بـــالله نعــوذ). Please stop repeating such a thing. This is not true.

Dr: You are acting on it, and then you're asking me not to say it.

Sh: But we are saying that the Prophet didn't get a chance to announce a successor actively so. Therefore, Abubakr and Umar saw that he is about to pass away. Therefore, they published an heir. Umar didn't choose one either the council that he decided picked one.

Dr: Do you mean to say that the Prophet was not aware that he is passing away, but Abubakr knew and therefore picked an heir?

Sh: He was ill, and he knew he is passing away, and therefore, he chose Umar to be Calipha after him.

Dr: So, the thing that crossed Abubakr's mind did not pass to the Prophets?

The Doctor & Sheikh's Debate

Sh: From the experience, he had obtained from being Calipha after the Prophet passing and the problems he had encountered, Abubakr decided to choose the one after him so there wouldn't be any trouble.

Dr: I will say we seek refuge in God (بــالله نعـوذ) firstly so you wouldn't need to say it. So, we seek refuge in God (بــالله نعـوذ) the Prophet acted wrongly for not choosing a Calipha and caused dispute amongst the companions and Abubakr wanted this mistake not to be repeated and chose Umar as Calipha after him.

Sh: That is right; where is the problem?

Dr: The problem lays here. That the Prophet whom the Quran calls him: "ما يَنْطِقُ عَنِ الْهَوى" makes a mistake and does not choose an heir but Abubakr that is a companion, does not make such a mistake. This means that "نُؤْمِنُ بِبَعْضٍ وَ نَكْفُرُ بِبَعْضٍ." Meaning in this part, Abubakr is higher ranked than the Prophet.

Sh: Why did you start the debate from this angle?

Dr: Because I disagree with this way of thinking. I believe the Prophet not only is wiser than the Caliphas, but he acted based on what God told him, and therefore he did choose a Calipha.

Sh: Where did he choose a Calipha? We do not have any explicit announcement for choosing a Calipha.

Dr: We have an explicit announcement.

Sh: [With Laughter] I did think that you were going to bring up Ghadir Khumm but there the Prophet announced to like Ali he didn't say, have him as your Calipha.

Dr: This is a critical discussion. Thankfully we have my program and proof with me. I will explain this issue using your books as I have interesting points to make there.

Sh: God willing we shall see. I will wait for them. However, I do accept that the lack of choosing a Calipha by the Prophet is an interesting point.

2- The Disagreement over the way the Caliphas were Chosen

Dr: I wish to ask another question, and that is if we assume that the choosing of a successor was supposed to be by the Prophet, and he did not do so. How do you think the Caliphas acted?

Sh: Where is the problem?

Dr: The problem is that based on the credible history of our Sunni brothers, there are four ways to choose a Calipha.

1. The choosing of Abubakr: He got selected by the Saqifah council that had been assigned.

2. The choosing of Umar: Abubakr chose him, and there was no committee involved.

3. The choosing of Usman: The council did this. The same board that Umar had assigned. The board had agreed that if the votes were equal then whomever Abdul Rahman Ibn Ouf had voted to, will be designated as the Calipha. Usman was chosen.

4. The choosing of Ali: He was selected by the people and by their request.

I want you to tell me which of the ways I mentioned is the correct way? First was by committee. One person chose the second. The third was chosen by conditional committee, and fourth was by the people.

Sh: That is right. There are different methods, but all of them could be right because they were the decisions of the companions, and they were based on the situations they were under.

Dr: Did the companions base theses methods on the religious studies they had previously done or based on their taste?

Sh: They have been mostly based on personal taste.

Dr: Do you think for such an important task such as choosing a Calipha, can one go by their taste or by order of God and the Prophet's Sunnat.

Sh: There wasn't a way chosen by the Prophet for them to follow.

Dr: There was a way introduced, but they did not go.

Sh: Do you mean Ghadir?

Dr: Yes, what better way than that?

Sh: How do you mean by Ghadir?

Dr: Every Calipha could have chosen the next one. However, the problem was that they already knew that what they are doing is a mistake. That is because it did not comply with the other Hadith's. The Prophet had already chosen a Calipha.

Sh: What Hadith's do we have regarding this topic?

Dr: The Hadith's regarding the Caliphas.

Sh: Which Hadith?

3- The Number of Caliphas after the Prophet

Dr: We have Hadith from the Prophet saying that there will be twelve Caliphas after me and they are all from Quraysh.

Sh: I have seen and heard many times that there are to be twelve.

Dr: Please see how much proof we have. First Hadith is Sahih Bukhari number 6683 and Muslem Hadith number 3396:

لايزال هذا الامر عزيزاً ينصرون على من ناواهم، عليه اثني عشر خليفةً كلهم من قريش

"Be assured that Islam will be glorious with... for twelve Caliphas that are all from Quraysh."

Please have a look at my programme and you will see that there are 30 different books stating the same thing. The most important ones are Muslem and Bukhari that discuss the same topic. Muslem does have another Hadith, number 3393, 3394 and 3395:

لايزال امر امتي قائماً حتى يمضي اثنى عشر خليفه كلهم من قريش

"The lifeline of my Ummah will stay strong for the entire of the twelve Caliphas that are all from Quraysh."

In some of the Hadith's such as Musnad Ahmad Hanbal, Hadith number 3665, the number "Chiefs of Bani Israel" has also been mentioned.

Sh: That is correct.

Dr: The same is mentioned in Bukhari and Muslem but Fat-h Al Bari explains in the interpretation of Sahih Bukhari, volume 3, page 183 about government and choosing Amir's and then in the end there is an adverbial that is important.

يكون من بعدي اثني عشر اميراً كلهم من قريش، كلهم يعمل بالهدي ودين الحق

"After me there will be 12 Caliphas. All of them will be of Quraysh and all of them will act in accordance with guiding and a religion based on justice (God)"

Sh: That is very interesting that you have gathered all of this.

Dr: In Savaeq Muhraqah, volume 1, page 56, in Al Mataleb Al Aaliyah Ibn Hajar, volume 12, page 490, Hadith number 4608, in Umdat Al Qari correct interpretation of Bukhari, volume 35, page 328, in Fat-h Al Bari Fi correct interpretation of Sahih Bukhari, volume 13, page 213, Feyz Al Qadir, volume 2, page 583, in Dalayel Al Nobowah Beyhaqi, volume 7, page 473, Hadith number 2894 and you can see them all until the end. There are 16 cases and all of them say the following:

لا يهلك هذه الامه حتى يكون منها اثناعشر خليفه كلهم يعمل بالهدى ودين الحق

"My Ummah will not perish when they have twelve Caliphas that all act on guiding and conducting justice based on religion."

Sh: I accept. I had already accepted the twelve Imams from start.

Dr: Very well. You agree that the Prophet has named twelve Caliphas.

Sh: Yes.

Dr: Do you accept that these twelve have to be the real Caliphas and they should not make any mistake or at least a minimal number of errors?

Sh: Yes, of course, they couldn't be like the Prophet. They must have had small mistakes.

Dr: Well, not like the Prophet, but at least they should not be conducting sins.

Sh: You are right, yes, that is right.

Dr: Very well, let's have a look and see that who does our brother Sunni's accept as the twelve Caliphas.

Sh: Yes, let's have a look.

1. Abubakr
2. Umar
3. Usman
4. Ali
5. Hasan
6. Muawiyah Ibn Abusofiyan
7. Yazid Ibn Muawiyah

8. Muawiyah Sani (Yazid's son)

9. Marwan Hakam

10. Abd Al Melk Marwan

11. Walid Ibn Abdol Malek

12. Soleyman Ibn Abdol Malek

Sh: That is right. The twelve are these.

Dr: Now please elaborate could Muawiyah, Yazid, Marwan Ibn Hakam and the rest until at least Umar Ibn Abdul Aziz be chosen as the Prophet's Caliphas? Especially considering the last Hadith, I stated "الحق دين و بالهدي يعمل".

Sh: They did make mistakes, but the companions had chosen them.

Dr: Do we base the choosing of Calipha on what the companions think or having the competence and qualifications for being the Prophet's Calipha?

Sh: No, their competence and ability are much more critical.

Dr: All right then. Please tell me can Yazid that conducted all of those crimes or Muawiyah that fought with the Calipha that was chosen by the people or Marwan who was in war with Ali, could all possibly be the Prophet's Calipha? Even though some of the Sunni brothers consider them as kings, who agree with the last Hadith Muslem and Bukhari said.

Sh: They had problems.

Dr: It is past problems. A Calipha goes to war against another Calipha like Muawiyah going to war with Ali. What kind of Calipha is that? Dear Sheikh, come and see who Muawiyah is. His father Abu Sofyan was in combat with the Prophet which Muawiyah himself was in those wars too. His mother is Hend who cut out Hamza's (Prophet's uncle) heart out in the battle of Ohod.

Sh: He eventually claimed repentance and came to Islam.

Dr: He claimed repentance and came to Islam that is fine. He can be a Muslim, but he can also be the Prophet's Calipha?

Sh: Unfortunately, what you are saying is right.

Dr: Dear Sheikh, you are aware of this famous Hadith regarding Ammar and Yasir has been mentioned in all of your books, especially in Bukhari, Hadith number 428 and 2601; Sahih Muslem, Hadith number 5192 and 5193 and Musnad Ahmad 6211 volume 13, page 249 all say:

ويح عماراً تقتله الفئه الباغيه يدعوهم الي الله و يدعونه الي النار

"Ammar is considered to be part of the group that has exited religion. He invites them to God and they invite him to the fire."

Sh: Yes, this Hadith is in most of our books.

Dr: Then please let's not fool ourselves and be honest with ones' self. How can Muawiyah that as the Prophet has stated to be out of religion be chosen as his Calipha?

Sh: Unfortunately, that is right. He cannot.

Dr: Dear Sheikh, have a look at the program on my mobile. There are one hundred and seventy cases where this Hadith has been mentioned. Abdullah Ibn Amareb nel Aas discussed the killing of Ammar by Fe-a Baaqiyah and Muawiyah said Ali sent him to be killed. Also, you must have heard that Ali in response said Then Hamza must have been killed by the Prophet too and not the warriors of Abu Sofyan because the Prophet took him to the war.

Sh: We only accept the first four Caliphas, meaning the Rashedin Caliphas to be the rightful ones.

Dr: Then what happens to the twelve Prophet Caliphas?

Sh Usman: I have been a witness to the discussion between the Alazhar's scholars regarding the twelve Caliphas and no one has ever managed to give a proper answer about it.

Dr: They have no answer to give. How can Yazid be the Prophet's Calipha?

Sh: We don't pay much attention to the twelve people.

Dr: The twelve have to be identified. That is the Prophet's Hadith.

Sh: I confess that amongst these Caliphas there wasn't even one competent or more deserving to be the Prophet's Calipha.

Dr: Then we have to look for the twelve others than the ones you said.

Sh: Where are they?

Dr: The twelve Imams of the Shias which I will discuss them later.

The Doctor & Sheikh's Debate

Sh: I will wait for that.

Dr: Have a look at my mobile. Siyoti mentions in the book of Tarikh Caliphate, page 8 - 12 says something different as he knew that the twelve couldn't be the ones mentioned. He says:

ان المراد وجود اثني عشر خليفه في جميع مدةً الاسلام منظور

"The existence of the twelve Calipha is for all of the duration of the Islamic era"

Then he adds that the Rashedin Caliphas are the four people and Muawiyah and his two son's Zobair and Umar Iban Abdul Aziz is also included making eight people, and four people will be added in the future.

Sh: To summarize one thing at least and to end this debate based on all of the Hadith's mentions we agree that the twelve Caliphas that the Prophet mentioned could not have been the ones that did become Calipha. Yazid could not have been considered as the Prophet's Calipha.

Sh Usman: I even am doubtful over his father too.

Dr: I too am doubtful over both of them.

Sh: But you are debating all twelve of them.

Dr: I am debating ten of them because I agree with Ali and Hasan.

Sh: We too accept this. Even if we wanted to stretch it we could say 5.

Sh Usman: I think deep inside Sheikh only accepts the two.

Dr: Well If you all agree let's finish this and continue it on Arafa night in Arafa.

Sh: That is good. I agree.

Day Eighth of Zihijjah

We went to Arafa after sunset, eventually I managed to find Sheikh and his friends and after the normal meet and greets of Arafa we walked around the place and then...

Sh: Let's have a small amount of debate tonight as it is Arafa and scientific discussions are rewarding.

Dr: If you wish we could go and sit close to the tent here and continue our discussion. We can leave the rest of the rituals for later.

Sh: That is a good idea.

Dr: I agree as well.

Sh: In the name of God the merciful.

4- The Companions Objection over Ali Not Being Chosen as Calipha

We came and sat in a corner at Arafa and continued our discussion.

Dr: Very well, we had a look at the different ways that Caliphas were chosen and noticed that they were not done correctly.

Sh: Yes, we agreed that they were done badly.

Dr: The next debate is over some of the companions objecting over Ali not being chosen as the first Calipha. Now let's examine why they were opposing.

Sh: It was natural for some of them to object.

Dr: Well if the objections were from reasonable companions we could not see it as a problem, but what if they were the main companions?

Sh: I accept that.

Sh: Yes, some of these companions were of the Prophet's relatives.

Dr: These people were not just close to him. They were from the most prominent of them all.

Sh: Why prominent?

Dr: I will name them all, and you are already aware of their virtues and then realize why they are classed prominent.

Sh: Please continue.

Dr: Based on the chain of transmissions in your books, the following people did not claim their allegiance with Abubakr. Their names are mentioned in the book of Tarikh Belazari, Ibn Hajar Asqalani, and Yaqubi. Some are also mentioned in the Sihah Sittah which we will have a look at and they are all mostly unanimous.

1. Ali Ibn Abi Taleb
2. Fatimah
3. Salman Farsi
4. Abuzar Qafari
5. Zobair Ibn Awam
6. Meqdad Ibn Aswad
7. Talha
8. Abbas Ibn Abdul Mutaleb
9. Fazl Ibn Abbas
10. Saad Ibn Abbas
11. Baride Aslami
12. Abdullah Ibn Abbas
13. Qeys Ibn Saad
14. Khaled Ibn Saeed
15. Sahl Ibn Hanif Ansari
16. Usman Ibn Hanif Ansari

17. Jaber Ibn Abdullah Ansari

18. Bara Ibn Azeb

19. Khazima Ibn Saabet

20. Ibu Ayub Ansari

Sh: They are all prominent names, and maybe they objected because they were not involved in the choosing. However, to class them as the people who opposed, you are right.

Dr: They didn't object for not being able to interfere with the choosing of Calipha. They objected to the Calipha themselves as they were better suited than him. For instance, have a look at this Hadith in Musnad Ahmad.

Musnad Ahmad, Musnad Umar Ibn Khattab, volume 1, pahe 372, Hadith number 362 says:

حَدَّثَنَا إِسْحَاقُ بْنُ عِيسَى الطَّبَّاعُ حَدَّثَنَا مَالِكُ بْنُ أَنَسٍ حَدَّثَنِي ابْنُ شِهَابٍ عَنْ عُبَيْدِ اللَّهِ بْنِ عَبْدِ اللَّهِ بْنِ عُتْبَةَ بْنِ مَسْعُودٍ أَنَّ ابْنَ عَبَّاسٍ [عَلَى الْمِنْبَرِ فَلَمَّا سَكَتَ] أَخْبَرَهُ أَنَّ عَبْدَ الرَّحْمَنِ بْنَ عَوْفٍ رَجَعَ إِلَى رَحْلِهِ قَالَ ابْنُ عَبَّاسٍ وَكُنْتُ أُقْرِئُ عَبْدَ... فَجَلَسَ عُمَرُ الْمُؤَذِّنُ قَامَ فَأَثْنَى عَلَى اللَّهِ بِمَا هُوَ أَهْلُهُ ثُمَّ قَالَ أَمَّا بَعْدُ أَيُّهَا النَّاسُ فَإِنِّي قَائِلٌ مَقَالَةً [قَدْ قُدِّرَ لِي أَنْ أَقُولَهَا... أَلَا وَإِنَّ رَسُولَ اللَّهِ صَلَّى اللَّهُ عَلَيْهِ وَسَلَّمَ قَالَ لَا تُطْرُونِي كَمَا أُطْرِيَ عِيسَى ابْنُ مَرْيَمَ عَلَيْهِ السَّلَامُ فَإِنَّمَا أَنَا عَبْدُ اللَّهِ فَقُولُوا عَبْدُ اللَّهِ وَرَسُولُهُ وَقَدْ كَانَتْ فَلْتَةً] أَلَا وَإِنَّهَا [بَايَعْتُ فُلَانًا فَلَا يَغْتَرَّنَّ امْرُؤٌ أَنْ يَقُولَ إِنَّ بَيْعَةَ] أَبِي بَكْرٍ بَلَغَنِي أَنَّ قَائِلًا مِنْكُمْ يَقُولُ لَوْ قَدْ مَاتَ عُمَرُ أَلَا وَإِنَّهُ كَانَ مِنْ خَبَرِنَا حِينَ [كَانَتْ كَذَلِكَ أَلَا وَإِنَّ اللَّهَ عَزَّ وَجَلَّ وَقَى شَرَّهَا وَلَيْسَ فِيكُمْ مَنْ تُقْطَعُ إِلَيْهِ الْأَعْنَاقُ مِثْلُ أَبِي بَكْرٍ بِنْتِ رَسُولِ اللَّهِ صَلَّى اللَّهُ] تُوُفِّيَ رَسُولُ اللَّهِ صَلَّى اللَّهُ عَلَيْهِ وَسَلَّمَ أَنَّ عَلِيًّا وَالزُّبَيْرَ وَمَنْ كَانَ مَعَهُمَا تَخَلَّفُوا فِي بَيْتِ فَاطِمَةَ عَلَيْهِ وَسَلَّمَ وَتَخَلَّفَتْ عَنَّا الْأَنْصَارُ بِأَجْمَعِهَا فِي سَقِيفَةِ بَنِي سَاعِدَةَ وَاجْتَمَعَ الْمُهَاجِرُونَ إِلَى أَبِي بَكْرٍ رَضِيَ اللَّهُ

> "Ibn Abbas says that we were at Hajj with Umar and ...Umar said: If I was alive when I return to Medina there are some things I would like to tell people in Friday prayer. So, when he returned to Medina, on the Friday after the call of prayer he started to talk. Umar said: conducting our allegiance with Abubakr was a slip up and God saved us from its evil. Today, amongst us, there is no one like Abubakr that can assassinate people. And I had heard that Ali and Zobair and others that were with them objected and gathered at Fatimah's house, (The Prophets daughter). Ansar (Helpers of the Prophets) objected also and gathered in Saqifah Bani Saaidah. And the Muhajerin (immigrants) gathered around Abubakr."

This proves that it was not just some of the immigrants and or Ahl Al Bayt that were objecting to Abubakr being chosen, but many of the Ansar were there too.

Sh: Yes, Umar's speech has also been mentioned in many other places besides Musnad Ahmad too, but I cannot recall their names to state them. However, eventually, they all claimed their allegiance in the end.

Sh: Yes, they claimed their allegiance after pressure, scrutiny, threat's and causing scenes or else they all gathered in Fatimah's house, and it is not clear precisely whom claimed allegiance in the end but Ansar, immigrants and some of the Ansar from Saqifah Bani Saaidah were also there.

Sh: Well, in the end, some of the companions agreed with this and most claimed allegiance. Some did object, but they were the minority.

Dr: Were the people that gathered in Fatimah's house and the ones in Saqifah better or not? Let's go back and have a look at the companions that were classed as good by the Prophet.

Musnad Ahmad, volume 46, page 442, Hadith 21890:

حَدَّثَنَا ابْنُ نُمَيْرٍ عَنْ شَرِيكٍ حَدَّثَنَا أَبُو رَبِيعَةَ عَنِ ابْنِ بُرَيْدَةَ عَنْ أَبِيهِ قَالَ: قَالَ رَسُولُ اللَّهِ صَلَّى اللَّهُ عَلَيْهِ وَسَلَّمَ إِنَّ اللَّهَ عَزَّوَجَلَّ يُحِبُّ مِنْ أَصْحَابِي أَرْبَعَةً أَخْبَرَنِي أَنَّهُ يُحِبُّهُمْ وَأَمَرَنِي أَنْ أُحِبَّهُمْ قَالُوا مَنْ هُمْ يَا رَسُولَ اللَّهِ قَالَ إِنَّ عَلِيًّا مِنْهُمْ وَأَبُوذَرٍّ الْغِفَارِيُّ وَسَلْمَانُ الْفَارِسِيُّ وَالْمِقْدَادُ بْنُ الْأَسْوَدِ الْكِنْدِيُّ

"The Prophet (s.a.w.a) said: Indeed, the almighty God is fond of 4 of my companions and told me to like them too. They asked O' Messenger of God who are these people? He replied: Ali is amongst them and Abu Zarr Gheffari, Salman Farsi and Miqdad Ibn Asvad Kendi."

Do you agree that these people were higher ranked than the people in Saqifah?

Sh: Just as I said before, these were the quarrels of companions based on Ijtihad, and I accepted your analysis that our justification was wrong. We cannot have several right paths, and we cannot agree that wherever the companions decide to Ijtihad, then that is the right way to go.

Dr: The reason behind the discussion we had was because not all of the companions had the capability of conducting justice. The reason why they should not all be followed explicitly was because of what you just said exactly.

Sh: You cut the routes, and now you are cutting the stems and leaves.

Dr: If you cut the root, then water will not get to the stems and leaves, and if the stems and leaves get cut, then the whole thing will dry out.

Sh: Then let's continue this discussion.

Dr: If you agree that the First, second, and third Calipha was chosen by mistake, then we have nothing to discuss further.

Sh: The thing that I agree on is that the people who objected were better than others. However, I do not invalidate Abubakr, Umar, and Usman being Calipha.

Dr: Then let's continue.

Sh: Yes.

Dr: So, you agree that the people who objected to showing their allegiance with Abubakr were not just average people.

Sh: Yes, I agree they were not average, and the Prophet's speeches regarding these people of his companions are undeniable.

Dr: Then you can accept that there was a problem in the way they chose the Calipha and the objection of these people clarifies that the methodology of selecting the Calipha had a big question mark.

Sh: Yes, even then it was a question mark.

Dr: But this is a huge question mark.

Sh: What do you mean by significant?

Dr: What I mean is that some of the principal companions and Ahl Al Bayt were in a way that they were entirely against the Calipha and Caliphas and they undermined the whole thing.

Sh: What are you trying to get at?

Dr: What would you say to me if I showed you that some of these people that did not show their allegiance remained against the first Calipha until they passed away and the Prophet has said Hadith's about these disagreements.

Sh: Please speak more clearly.

Dr: Dear Sheikh, one of the people that were against Abubakr and remained that way and did not show her allegiance until the end of her life was Fatimah, the Prophet's daughter.

Sh: She didn't show her allegiance until the end?

Dr: She was alive two or three months after the Prophet and Abubakr being Calipha, and she did not show her allegiance to him, and this has been accepted everywhere.

Sh: Now, where is the problem?

Dr: Please pay attention to this Hadith in Sahih Bukhari, volume 5, page 82, Aisha says:

عن عائشةَ أن فاطمةَ بنت النبى صلى الله عليه وسلم أرسلت إلى أبى بكر تسأله ميراثها من رسول الله صلى الله عليه وسلم مما أفاء الله عليه بالمدينةَ وفدك ومابقى من خمس خيبر، فقال أبو بكر: إن رسول الله صلى الله عليه وسلم قال لا نورثما تركنا صدقةَ، إنما يأكل آل محمد في هذا المال، وإني والله لا أغير شيئا من صدقةَ رسول الله صلى الله عليه وسلم عن حالها التى كان عليها في عهد رسول الله صلى الله عليه وسلم ولاعملن فيها بما عمل به رسول الله صلى الله عليه وسلم.»
فأبى أبوبكر أن يدفع إلى فاطمةَ منها شيئا، فوجدت فاطمةَ على أبي بكر في ذلك فهجرته، فلم تكلمه حتى توفيت !!

"Aisha says: Fatimah, the Prophet's daughter sent someone to Abubakr and requested what was left from the Prophet's inheritance in Medina and Fadak and whatever that was left from Khams Kheybar. Abubakr said: The Prophet told me that there will be nothing inherited by me and whatever that was left is considered Alms. All of the Prophet's Ahl al Bayt can have these Alms as well. I will not change anything that was current at the time of the Prophet and will act in a way that the Prophet would have acted.

So Abubakr denied giving Fatimah her rights and for that reason Fatimah kept her distance from Abubakr and did not speak to him until she died."

Sh: This is correct information.

Dr: Now please read this regarding Fatimah (In Sahih Muslem, volume 12, page 201, Hadith number 4483 says:

حَدَّثَنِي أَبُو مَعْمَرٍ إِسْمَعِيلُ بْنُ إِبْرَاهِيمَ الْهُذَلِيُّ حَدَّثَنَا سُفْيَانُ عَنْ عَمْرٍو عَنْ ابْنِ أَبِي مُلَيْكَةَ عَنْ الْمِسْوَرِ بْنِ مَخْرَمَةَ قَالَ: قَالَ رَسُولُ اللَّهِ صَلَّى اللَّهُ عَلَيْهِ وَسَلَّمَ إِنَّمَا فَاطِمَةُ بَضْعَةٌ مِنِّي يُؤْذِينِي مَا آذَاهَا

"Fatimah is part of my body. Anyone whom hurts her has hurt me."

Sh: I am aware of the importance of Fatimah in the eye of the Prophet.

Dr: There are Hadith's in Khasais Nesaei regarding Hasaneyn and Fatimah. I have translated and bookmarked it. The following numbers are as below:

For instance, number 2/3/28, chapter 28, has three Hadith this is number two. Now let's see what we have in Khasais Nesaei regarding Fatimah:

3/3/27: (اخبرنا) «اسحاق بن ابراهيم بن مخلد بن راهويه، قال: اخبرنا جرير، عن يزيد بن زياد، عن عبد الرحمان بن ابي نعيم، عن ابي سعيد قال: قال رسول الله صلى الله عليه وسلم: الحسن والحسين سيدا شباب اهل الجنةْ وفاطمةْ سيدةْ نساء اهل الجنةْ إلا ما كان من مريم بنت عمران.»

"Ibn Saeed said: The Messenger of God said: Hasan and Hussein are the Masters of youth group in heaven and Fatimah is the Master of all women in heaven except Maryam daughter of Umran."

3/3/28: (أخبرنا) «محمد بن معمر البحراني، قال: حدثنا، أبو داود، حدثنا أبو عوانةْ، عن فراس، عن الشعبي، عن مسروق قال: اخبرتني عائشةْ قالت: كنا عند رسول الله صلى الله عليه وسلم جميعا لم تغادر منا واحدةْ، فجائت فاطمةْ تمشي ولا والله ان تخطى مشيتها من مشيةْ رسول الله صلى الله عليه وسلم حتى انتهت إليه فقال: مرحبا بابنتي، فأقعدها عن يمينه أو يساره، ثم سارها بشئ فبكت بكاء شديدا، ثم سارها بشئ فضحكت، فلما قام رسول الله صلى الله عليه وسلم قلت لها: اخصك رسول الله صلى الله عليه وآله من بيننا بالسراء وانت تبكين، اخبريني ما قال لك؟ قالت: ما كنت لافشي رسول الله صلى الله عليه وسلم سره، فلما توفي رسول الله صلى الله عليه وسلم قلت لها: اسألك بالذي عليك من الحق ما ارك به رسول الله صلى الله عليه وسلم؟ فقالت: اما الآن فنعم، سارني المرةْ الاولى فقال: ان جبريل عليه السلام كان يعارضني بالقرآن في كل سنةْ مرةْ وانه عارضني العام مرتين، ولا ادري الاجل إلا قد اقترب فاتقي الله واصبري، ثم قال لي: يا فاطمةْ أما ترضين انك تكوني سيدةْ نساء هذه الامةْ وسيدةْ نساء العالمين فضحكت»

"Aisha told me: We were all in the presence of the Prophet. No one was missing. Fatimah came walking towards us and I swear to God her way of walking was no different to the Prophet. As soon as she reached where the Prophet was the Prophet said: Welcome my daughter. Fatimah sat at his right- or left-hand side and the Prophet told her something in her ear that made her cry immensely. Then he told her something and Fatimah laughed. When the Prophet got up and left I asked Fatimah: The Prophet chose you out of all of us to share with you his secret. Tell us what it was. Fatimah said: I cannot tell his secret. Once the Prophet died I said: to her: I will ask you once again, I swear on the person that has right on you, what did you hear? Fatimah said: The first time he spoke to me he said: Gabriel gives me the Quran once a year but this year he gave me twice and this wouldn't have happened unless the end of my life would be near. So, prepare and put your trust in God and be patient. The second time he told me: O Fatimah do you not wish to be the Master of the women in this Ummah and the next world?"

: 1/5/29

(أخبرنا) «محمد بن شعيب، قال: أخبرنا قتيبةَُ، قال: حدثنا الليث، عن ابن ابي مليكةْ، عن المسور بن مخرمةْ قال: سمعت رسول الله صلى الله عليه وسلم وهو على المنبر يقول: ... فانما هي بضعةْ مني يريبنى ما رابها ويؤذيني ما آذاها، ومن آذى رسول الله فقد حبط عمله:

"Masroor Ibn Mukharamah said: I heard the Prophet said: Fatimah is part of my body. Whoever scares her has scared me and whoever hurts her has hurt me and whoever hurts the Prophet his actions are all void."

3/5/29: (أخبرنا) «احمد بن شعيب، قال: حدثنا الحرث بن مسكين قرأته عليه وانا اسمع، عن سفيان عن عمرو، عن ابن ابي مليكةْ، عن المسور بن مخرمةْ: ان النبي صلى الله عليه وسلم قال: ان فاطمةْ بضعةْ مني من أغضبها أغضبني

"Masoor Ibn Mukharamah informed us: The Prophet said: Fatimah is part of my body and whoever makes her angry has angered me."

4/5/29: (أخبرنا) «محمد بن خالد، قال: حدثنا بشر بن شعيب، عن ابيه عن الزهري قال: اخبرني علي بن الحسين خبر ان المسور بن مخرمةْ اخبره ان رسول الله صلى الله عليه وسلم قال: ان فاطمةْ لمضغةْ أو بضعةْ مني.»

"Masoor Ibn Mukharamah: informed us: The Prophet said: Fatimah is my flesh and or part of my body."

5/5/29: (أخبرنا) «عبدالله بن سعد بن ابراهيم بن سعد، قال: اخبرنا ابي، عن الوليد بن كثير، عن محمد بن عمرو بن طلحةْ، انه حدثه ان ابن شهاب حدثه ان علي بن الحسين حدثه ان المسور بن مخرمةْ قال: سمعت رسول الله صلى الله عليه وسلم يخطب على منبره هذا وأنا يومئذ محتلم فقال: ان فاطمةْ بضعةْ مني.»

"Masoor Ibn Mukharamah said: I heard from The Messenger of God that he was giving a speech on his chamber and I was young then. He said: Fatimah is part of my body."

Sh: I have seen some of these Hadith's, but some of them were new.

Dr: Like which one?

Sh: Whoever hurts Fatimah has hurt The Messenger of God, and whoever hurts The Messenger of God, his actions are all void.

Dr: Dear Sheikh I think by citing the Hadith that Aisha said and this Hadith, it voids all actions…

Sh Usman: Dear Doctor, we accept that the people that were against the Calipha were essential people.

The Doctor & Sheikh's Debate

Dr: But you do not accept that the actions of the person whom Fatimah was against and hurt her are considered void.

Sh: If we accept, then there will be nothing else to talk about.

Sh Usman: If we do not accept it, then we have gone against the deal you and Doctor made before.

Sh: I don't know why before we just trusted what everyone else told us, and we rarely reviewed our books.

Sh Usman: I accept, I don't know about Sheikh Ibrahim.

Dr. Zohair: I don't know much about these discussions or books and Hadith's but based on my sense of mind, I believe that what the Doctor is saying has no come back. I think that if I continue this discussion, I will return as a Shia to England.

Dr: Declare yourself as a true Muslim returning to England. That is because the School of Ahl al Bayt is the real Islam.

Sh: Doctor, let's go to the next discussion.

Sh Usman: I think it's better to continue our discussion for Arafa and Mena.

Sh: That is good. I also agree with this.

Dr: I am always happy to be at your service, but if you are tired we could meet with each other in Mena.

Sh Usman: I am not tired. I am scared that I will doubt believing in my conducts while I am applying my ordinances for Mena and Arafa.

Sh: By the way, if there is any difference between the ordinances of conducting Hajj, especially Mena and Arafa of Shia and Sunni, please tell us.

Dr: There aren't many essential things except a few minor details.

I told them a few details and agreed to meet again by calling each other on our mobiles and then to arrange the rest of the meetings. I had a walk about and talked about the opinion on Shia' sm regarding Mahdi in Hajj especially in Arafa, and then I invited them for the next day evening in the embassy of Iran (Baese) for the Arafa supplication.

Sh Usman: Sheikh Ibrahim it feels good to know that one's Imam currently exists on this earth.

Dr. Zohair: With the explanations that the Doctor mentioned regarding the Ahl Al Bayt's Hajj, Sheikh did not go to Mena and brought us all straight to Arafa. He wants to meet with Imam Mahdi.

Sh: No matter what I think, I see that the Doctor's words are very close to the heart. Even when I disagree, it's because I want him to tell me more.

Dr: Dear Sheikh, I am no scholar; it's just words of an Engineer that wishes to defend his religion. If you have time we could go to one of the tents of our scholars and start having a scholarly debate there, then you will realize that my knowledge is limited.

Sh Usman: Thank you very much. It is late, and I can't even handle you never mind your scholars.

Sh: I think that they might know more than you, but the way you discuss it in a very Engineering way. You take us right into a corner and leave us with nowhere to run. Therefore, I enjoy it more rather than a scholarly discussion.

Dr: By the way, how is Doctor Amr Mosa doing?

Dr. Zohair: He went with the others to Mena. He will come back to Arafa later.

Sh: To be honest, Dr. Zohair is more interested in the discussions we have and is no longer allowing me to see you alone.

Sh Usman: Be fair. I never thought that I would come to Hajj from Egypt and have such a scientific debate. Of course, I wouldn't miss it for anything. I told Sheikh not to meet up alone with you and to have me with him for it.

Dr: I found this meeting to be very helpful. God willing it will continue in Mena and Mecca.

They said goodbye and left. I also went after finishing my ordinances for the night of Arafa. The anticipating of seeing our Imam and leader has its merit. You continuously search between the people hoping that you might see Imam Mahdi and to know it is him. However, my soul is not yet ready to have the honor to see him, nonetheless. Maybe on the next trip and another Arafa, I will see him. That is considering our sinful eyes and God's blessing and attention and permission of Imam Mahdi himself. Dear God, Help us.

Day Ninth of Zihajjah (Arafa Day)

The Arafa Supplication

The next day all three of them showed up. We went to the place where they were reading the supplication of Arafa. They start with citing the Quran. The Iranian Qari (Quran reader) started with a nice voice. Surat Al Yusuf:

فَلَمَّا دَخَلُوا۟ عَلَيْهِ قَالُوا۟ يَـٰٓأَيُّهَا ٱلْعَزِيزُ مَسَّنَا وَأَهْلَنَا ٱلضُّرُّ وَجِئْنَا بِبِضَـٰعَةٍ مُّزْجَىٰةٍ فَأَوْفِ لَنَا ٱلْكَيْلَ وَتَصَدَّقْ عَلَيْنَآ ۖ إِنَّ ٱللَّهَ يَجْزِى ٱلْمُتَصَدِّقِينَ ﴿٨٨﴾

"So, when they entered upon Joseph, they said, "O Azeez, adversity has touched us and our family, and we have come with goods poor in quality, but give us full measure and be charitable to us. Indeed, Allah rewards the charitable."

The sound of mourning rose, as they understood the meaning of the verse.

Sh: Why are they crying? The verse is from the Quran.

Dr: Did you know that Joseph's brothers read this verse. They said that we have come empty-handed. He is saying to God that we are also empty-handed. Nevertheless, please give us your attention just as Joseph, the king did to his brothers.

Sh Usman: What a beautiful interpretation of the verse.

Dr: It has another interpretation too.

Sh: Please tell us what other interpretation is there of it?

Dr: As they are sure that Hazrat Mahdi is amongst them in Arafa and is hidden and in reality, lost in their eyes, and they are aware that he is Hazrat Fatimah's grandson they call him Fatimah's

Joseph. Therefore, this verse of the Quran is addressing him as well and saying that if we are empty-handed at least have us have his attention to us.

Sh: Wow, that was beautiful.

The supplication started. I gave them each a copy of the supplication so they could read it. As the supplication was being recited, I saw tears running down Sheikh Ibrahim and Sheikh Usman's face. Dr. Zohair was sometimes falling behind or would stop at a particular page and

would explain that he could not easily surpass them as easily. He said, now I understand why that night Sheikh Ibrahim came back with the Mafatih and was up until the Morning Prayer reading it.

The supplication took a while, and they unwillingly had to leave in the middle of it, as they had to go to mashaar with their tour group. That is another problem with the Iranian programs running for the supplications of Arafa. They take until sunset to read it and then be confronted with high congestion with other busy tour groups as they have to go back to their tents to read the Maghrib and Isha Prayer. Then they all have to go to mashaar (sacred monument). For that reason, many of the scholars of the religion that have experience with traveling to Hajj read the supplication of Arafa on their own in their tents. Even though reading the supplication of Arafa with a group is much more rewarding, and this event has been better organized compared to previous years.

At night, we went to mashaar and Voqoof (hault) and stayed until dawn. Then we went to Mena and then Rami Jumrah Aqbah. I informed them on the phone, that I had finished the provisions of Rami and that I had our five names for scarification. Our sacrification took until the evening to complete. After conducting Taghsir (hair cut), I exited Ihram. Unfortunately, some had come out of Ihram on the eleventh of Zihajjah.

At nighttime, we headed towards Mecca and Masjid Al Haram for Tawaf and Saay (running ritual of the pilgrimage) and Nisa Tawaf (women circumambulation). After the ordinances, I met with Sheikh and his friends. We planned for them to come to our tent on the eleventh in Mena. That was because I did not know where their tent was. I returned to the hotel in Mecca and had a rest. Later I made my way through the pavement to Mena in the evening. I read a prayer with the congregational Imam, had lunch, and rested again as I waited for the Sheikh and his friends.

Day Eleventh of Zihajjah

In the tents of the tour group, I was waiting for the Sheikh and his companions. No matter how long I expected, they didn't show up. The mobiles weren't working. I just had the Sheikh's number and trying anything else in the rush and traffic of Mena was pointless. I thought maybe the Sheikh has not managed to find my tent, so I headed outside my tent and stood outside close to the street for a whole hour. No news came from the Sheikh and his companions. After a while, I saw Dr. Zohair and Dr. Amr Moosa heading towards my tent.

Dr: Salam Alaikum, where have you been? Where is Sheikh?

Dr. Zohair: We have bad news. We were out with the Sheikh at Rami Jamrat, and unfortunately, due to the pressure of the population gathered, he fell and twisted his ankle so severely that it is tough for him to walk.

Dr: How is he now?

Dr. Amr Moosa: He is okay and resting in his tent.

Dr: Did his ankle gets twisted before or after Rami Jamrat?

Dr. Zohair: Thankfully, his Rami was finished, and we were returning backward close to the Jamrat. We were also taking care of him.

Dr. Amr Moosa: No, we weren't taking care of him. We were throwing stones from a long distance away from him. We weren't even sure if we hit anyone's head doing so, but the Sheikh didn't want the stones to hit anyone by mistake and so headed to go a little closer and …

Dr: I think that Sheikh wanted the stones to hit the pillar and walls of Jamrat instead of the people.

Dr. Zohair: You are right. Sheikh went closer so the stones wouldn't hit the peoples head and instead for it to hit Satan.

Dr: Well, please come into the tent and have a seat and meet with my friends.

Dr. Zohair: Sheikh has said that he is ready to speak but, in his tent, so that is why we have come to take you there.

Dr: Please allow the Sheikh to rest.

Dr. Zohair: Sheikh has rested. He slept right after we got him back via the ambulance. He is ready to get to see you.

Dr: Very well, it would be right to call upon the unwell.

Dr. Amr Moosa: I believe this ill person is more anticipating to debate with you rather than to be called upon.

Dr: Thank you, please allow me to go to my tent and wear something better and bring my mobile program with me.

Dr. Amr Moosa: Come and let's go what you are wearing is fine.

Dr: Let's go but having said that if I don't bring my mobile program with me, it's as if I have not brought a couple of thousands of books with me.

Dr. Zohair: You do not have to bring the program with you. You only need it when you wish to bring proof and for today don't show any evidence.

Dr: That is okay we might not debate at all today and get to see him instead.

Dr. Amr Moosa: I don't think Sheikh would leave you to that.

Dr: I hope that it is not the case. At least allow me to bring moisturizing oil for his feet from my tent and of course this way I can pick up the program as well.

Dr. Zohair: Sheikh has warmed up to you. He says that since he has met with you, issues have been clarified to him that he had never paid any attention to.

Dr. Amr Moosa: His beliefs are all over the place right now. I think the reason why he went closer to throw stones was that he said that Doctor has said that the stones have to hit the wall and just to throw them is not enough.

Dr: I like Sheikh as well. He is an astonishing, truth-seeking person. If he has heard something questioning, he is the kind of person that would admit to it. He does not say: I am a Sheikh. I am a professor of Alazhar. I am a religiously educated person. I shouldn't listen to this Engineer.

Dr. Zohair: I believe most of the professors in Alazhar have the same kind of personality. They are typically scholars and less fanatical. I think that is why Alazhar is so proudly known for not being ossified.

Dr: It is a crucial thing to be proud of.

The Doctor & Sheikh's Debate

Dr. Amr Moses: While we are heading towards there, let's stop talking about these things and have some fun. When we get to the Sheikh, we can start these kinds of conversations again.

Dr. Zohair: After thirty years of talking gibberish in England, what did you gain? Allow us to at least in this trip to Hajj hear some religious conversations, especially with the presence of the Doctor and Sheikh.

Dr. Amr Moosa: All right then, I will talk religiously. One person had gone to Rami Jamrat, and once he returned, his head was injured and bleeding. I asked him why did this happen? He said that he decided to get close to the pillar wall as close as possible to kiss it, but there were so many stones that he got injured.

Dr. Zohair: Well, that wasn't so bad.

Dr: It was good.

Dr. Amr Moosa: One person from the city of …comes to Mecca and once he arrives at Meeqat (place of meeting) he hesitates and thinks for a bit. Does he start wondering how do I Ihram? What do I say? They ask him: What is the problem? Why do you not Ihram? Don't you have your white towel? He replies: yes, I do. They responded: Then what are you waiting for? He answers because I am a Christian, and I just realized that I shouldn't have even come here.

Dr. Zohair: That was nice too.

Dr: It was good I just wished you hadn't mentioned the name of the city.

Dr. Amr Moosa: These were from what I knew. If you guys know any jokes, please share.

Dr: One person participated in the congregational prayer. The congregational Imam began to start citing Surat Nuh he read:

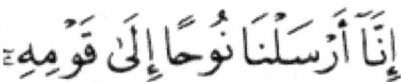

"Indeed, we sent Noah to his people, [saying]"

He forgot the rest of the verse and started to repeat the only thing he could remember. One of the impatient Officers that got tired of the Imam repeating the same part complained and said: Hey Mr if Noah isn't going to do it send someone else.

Dr. Zohair: That was good.

Dr. Amr Moosa: See, where is the fault with these kinds of conversations? I find it very relaxing.

Dr: Okay, well, the next one is about praying too. A person goes to congregational prayer he sees that the congregational Imam cites a verse loudly while praying. Once the pray finishes, he asks what verse was this? The Imam responds: It was Surat Annaml (Ant). At the next pray, he notices that the congregational Imam cites the Al-Fil (Elephant). So, he says: If that was Naml then I am not going to wait to see what Fil is going to be like. He leaves the prayer and goes.

Dr. Amr Moosa: Even your jokes are religiously related.

Dr: It is better than telling prosaic jokes.

Dr. Amru Moses: That was good. Tell us another one. We are getting close to Sheikh's tent.

Dr. Zohair: No, it isn't necessary, but I have realized in the past couple of our meetings that we are in dire need of exceeding our knowledge concerning our Islamic education. We just relied on the fact that our parents were Muslims and abided by that, whereas it shouldn't be that way.

Dr. Amru Moses: We are arrived at Sheikh's tent now let's go inside to see the Sheikh.

Dr: Salam Alaikum Dear Sheikh, what happened?

Sh: Alaikum Salam Doctor. I waited a while, so I thought that you are not coming.

Dr: Well, to be honest, I didn't want to come so that you would rest.

Sh: No, it isn't that important. I am much better now. I can't walk a lot.

Dr: Well it seems that you got to close to Satan and he got scared and knew any closer you're going to hurt him. So, he attacked you.

Sh: Well, he is always trying to hurt me so it wouldn't be so bad once in a while to attack him back and hit him with a stone. Of course, he is going to get upset.

Dr: I brought you moisturizing oil which is a combination of Mecca's Mummy, almond oil, olive oil, and sheep oil so you could rub it on your feet and get better soon.

Sh: Thank you, I will do it later.

Dr. Amr Moosa: I am a doctor. Allow me to massage it on your feet right now so it will affect as you are sitting. I won't take too long.

Sh: No, do it after the Doctor has left.

Dr: No, it is better for me to be here so I can tell Dr. Amr Moosa how the oil is more effective.

Sh: All right then, Dr. Amr Moosa starts your magic.

He started to massage the Sheikh's foot, and it slowly felt better.

Sh: Okay, so what happened to today's debate.

Dr: If you agree to allow me to visit you as someone visiting the ill.

Sh: No, the debate is right for me. We are sitting, and instead of talking about various things in Mena, we can have a religious discussion.

Dr: Alright then, we can continue the previous debate.

5- Ali's Superiority over the Other Caliphas

Dr: Let us go to the next section, and that is the superiority of Ali over the other Caliphas.

Sh: Why is this topic being chosen?

Dr: We debate now, and then you will see why.

Sh: Please start.

Dr: Very well. Today we will focus on Ali's position amongst the other companions.

Sh: Ali, without a doubt, should have an important position amongst the companions.

Dr: Yes, but they didn't choose him as Calipha.

Sh: Yes, they did. He was the fourth Calipha.

Dr: If he had such a prominent place, then how come he didn't become the first Calipha?

Sh: The reason why they didn't choose him as first Calipha was because he was too young.

Dr: Some people are chosen for times that decisions have to be made at the moment such as war and are not classed too young then, but for decisions made at a time of peace they are too young.

Sh: The fact that he was too young was mentioned, but in the end, it was a decision made by the Calipha.

Dr: Who has the authority to make that decision do you think?

Sh: By the companions, at the beginning of Islam, that made the decision.

Dr: If they did it against what the Prophet has said, would it still be acceptable? Moreover, of course, you saw that the choosing of Calipha was in three ways, and the first way was not repeated. It shows that the way they went about it was wrong.

Sh: If the Prophet had chosen a Calipha then no, the actions of the companions were wrong.

Dr: It wouldn't be so bad to see the position of Ali at the time of the Prophet. Did this person indeed not have the right to being Calipha, Imam, and have trusteeship.

Sh: Please tell us.

Dr: Very well. We will cite from your books.

Sh: We have many Hadith regarding the companions, especially for Ali in our books. Dr: That is right. One of the most important of the books that are also the most reliable and authentic is called the Khasais Amir Almumenin Ali Ibn Abi Taleb, written by Sheikh Ahmad Nesaei Shafia.

He begins on saying that the characteristics mentioned by the Prophet for Ali are just told about him and no other companion. Therefore, similar to these Hadith said about Ali, there are none identical to them for anyone else.

Sh: Ali's characteristics are undeniable.

Dr: You are aware that when Nesaei entered Shaam and saw that the people are cursing Ali at prayers, alters and chambers he wrote this book and names it the Khasais Amir Almumenin Ali Ibn Abi Taleb. I will only cite some of the specifications from the book.

Sh: Yes, this book that is extraordinarily written about him is very famous.

Dr: Yes, but this book was the reason why they killed him.

Sh: How come?

Dr: You do know that once he started to teach this book in the Mosque of Amavi in Damascus, they hit so many times that he got ill from it and died. Why? He was saying not to curse Ali.

Sh: Yes, Unfortunately, that is true.

Dr: I have translated this book to Persian, and it has Arabic and Persian writing. I have brought it with me. It has been published. I have bookmarked the pages and chapters and picked out the Hadith from it. For example, 8/17/11 from chapter 8 from the book says this. Hadith number seventeen and eleven. Now let's see what Nesaei says about the Prophet and what Hadith's do we have for Ali. To not repeat the same Hadith, I will cite a portion of them.

The Doctor & Sheikh's Debate

(All of the Hadith's discussed with the Sheikh are stated in Appendix one of this book, and it is written in Arabic, and the translations are all taken from the book of Khasais Nesaei.)

After reading the content of the Hadith's from the book of Khasais Nesaei Sheikh said.

Sh: Yes, these expressive definitions of Ali are accurate.

Dr: Please be fair, do we anyone amongst the companions of the Prophet with such characteristics?

Sh: Well, every single one of the companions has some definitions from the Prophet but not with this importance and the characteristics that are mentioned here.

Dr: So, we can agree that Ali was the best companion.

Sh: It has to be accepted as these Hadith's are almost unanimous.

I ended up having a small friendly chat with Sheikh and his friends and as usual Sheikh and his friends, especially Sheikh Usman expressed their remorse on taking a simple look at their religion as scholars. We said Goodbye and eventually set another time for the mid-Zihajjah to meet up as there would be less crowded.

I returned to my tent. I decided with some of the friends to start up till midnight at Mena and Beytooteh (passing the night). We did it and returned the next day on midday at Rami Jamarat. We didn't do it from inside the Mena but from the hotel that is only fifteen minutes away from it. We came back to the hotel, and I didn't see the Sheikh until the fifteenth of Zihajjah.

Day Fifteenth of Zihajjah

I had a meeting scheduled at Masjid Al Haram after the Zuhr prayer with the Sheikh. The Sheikh had come with one of his friends (Dr. Zohair). We started to walk together. Even though we had agreed to go to my hotel after the provisions of Mena the Sheikh said that Sheikh Usman and Abubakr had insisted on being present for the continuation of the debate and therefore we headed towards the Sheikh's hotel. On the way to their hotel, we had a conversation.

Dr: Did you make the provisions after the Mena?

Sh: Yes, Thank the Lord, I made all of the provisions.

Dr. Zohair: Sheikh did the Nisa Tawaf instead of the Veda Tawaf (Farewell Circumbulation). Sheikh was saying that the Doctor said the Nisa Tawaf is the correct one to read and not the Veda Tawaf. It appears that Sheikh has accepted what the Doctor has been saying.

Sh: What is the difference? Tawaf is Tawaf. It can be named Nisa or Veda.

Dr. Zohair: There is one difference. The Nisa is as the Doctor is saying, from the Ahl al Bayt. Veda is said to be from us, the Caliphas.

Sh: I thought to myself it would be better as I would be listening to what the Ahl al Bayt has said. Also, I have been studying the actual Tawaf, which is the duty of every Muslim.

Dr: Sheikh is a researcher. He wouldn't act on anything, especially regarding prayer until it lands right in the depth of his heart.

Dr. Zohair: Doctor, when you are not around Sheikh, is always talking about you. He says that we do not have a strong come back in return of what the Doctor tells us. We have not read our books very well, or else we would have realized that many of the ways we pray and the religious provisions we act upon are not actually from us. I also am saying that we should go and read it.

Sh: We are short on many things. There wouldn't be a problem for us to go read all of these books and review them.

Dr. Zohair: Why have you not read them before?

Sh: I had read about the books, but they were extractions of Hadith's taken from the source. For example, regarding Salat, I would read books that were written about the Prophet praying, and it would cite Hadith's from the source, but we never went back to read the topic from its source.

Dr. Zohair: Well, the Doctor lessened your trouble. He has got them all ready for you and presented them.

Sh: Yes, Doctor has troubled himself, but it is embarrassing that an engineer has gone and done the research about this and people like me or I have to refer to our books, only to see that we, for instance, have a problem in a section of our prayer.

Dr: Dear Sheikh, you are modest. You must have seen these cases, but because you have been focused on the things that are generally common in society, you haven't noticed them.

Sh: Please don't find excuses for me. I should have paid more attention.

Dr. Zohair: You have pointed out our lack of attention to detail, and now Sheikh is continuously complaining about the situation with the circle for religious studies and the Sunni Universities after meeting with you.

Sh: Never mind, we are at the hotel now. Let's have lunch and then continue our debate concerning the Caliphas.

Now I was the known face at the Sheikh's hotel. The Sheikh's friends surrounded me and started having many laughs and talks as we had an Arabian lunch, and then we headed towards Sheikh's room. Due to not seeing Sheikh Usman and the rest of the group for a while, the majority of the discussion concerned the provisions of Hajj, and I almost thought that we would not get to talk about our debate until Sheikh insisted that we should do so.

6- Consequences over Eliminating Ali from Being Chosen as Calipha after the Prophet

Dr: Now let's have a look at what have been consequences over eliminating Ali from being chosen.

Sh: What consequences? Thanks to the Lord, Islam has many followers in this world. What was wrong with what happened?

Dr: Maybe if Ali were chosen, the whole world would have been Muslim.

Sh: But Ali did become Calipha and if he was to do anything he could have them.

Dr: Ali became Calipha after twenty-five years of deflection. He had to build a house on foundations were already destroyed.

Sh: He could have started a new one.

Dr: They didn't let him.

Sh: How did they not let him?

Dr: When he wanted to start ruling he made a speech that has been mentioned in Sharh Nahj ul-Balagha written by Muhammad Abduh, professor of Alazhar saying:

لتبلبلن بكبله و لتغر بلن غربله حتي يعود اسفلكم اعلاكم و اعلا كم اسفلكم

"I will turn you inside out and I will turn you over! In such a way that the people above you would come down and the people below you will come up (I will create order)."

Sh: I had not seen this before.

Dr: Yes, it is in the books, especially in Nahj ul-Balagha.

Sh: It is a beautiful sentence.

Dr: We agreed that I do not refer to any of the chains of transmissions from the Ahl al Bayt or else at least I could have shown you cases from Nahj ul-Balagha that would have represented an ocean of science and information to you.

Sh: But Nahj ul-Balagha is correct. The Shias have collected them, and I have referred to it in Alazhar. We call it the two great sects of Islam, as Sheikh Muhammad Abduh has interpreted it.

Dr: Well, all in all, I mentioned this once case so that you could see why Ali could not save all of the foundations of Islam from their destruction.

Sh: But the result wasn't all bad.

Dr: There were three wars forced upon Ali. All of them were due to their companions.

Sh: We discussed the differences between the companions.

Dr: I consider them reasons for Ali not being victorious in trying to correct the system.

Sh: Ali defeated all of them, even the Nahravans.

Dr: But the results of them are the deflections that you see now.

Sh: Which cases?

Dr: The ruling of Muawiyah, Yazid, Marwan, all in all, the Amavis and then the Abbasis and then the demolishing of the Islamic system in the world.

Sh: Do you mean to say that if Ali had been chosen from the beginning, none of this would have happened?

Dr: If they had listened to the Prophet and had chosen Ali as Calipha after the Prophet none of this would have happened for sure. The twelve Caliphas that the Prophet had chosen would have ruled, and the world would be in Islam's hands.

Sh: Thank the Lord, there are many Muslims now too.

Dr: But we have two Islam's right now.

Sh: How come do we have two Islams?

Dr: One Islam started with the Rashedin becoming Calipha and it got to Muawiyah and Yazid and now in today's age the Arabian countries, all of the kings and Sultans, and presidents are following the same line and the other Islam that started with Ali and got to Hasan and Hussein and now it has gotten to Imam Khumeini and Hasan Nasrulah in Lebanon.

Sh: Do you mean to say that it got divided?

Dr: Yes, the School of Ahl al Bayt and the School of Caliphas. Am I right or not? Do we not have two schools right now?

Sh: With this explanation. Yes.

Dr: Dear Sheikh, we cannot have two righteous paths, can we?

Sh: Yes, we cannot have two righteous paths.

Dr: Now be fair and tell me which path and school is closer to the righteous path.

Sh: With this reasoning, the path and School of Ahl al Bayt. The Iranian Islam and Seyed Hasan Nasrulah are not comparable to any Arabian king or President of the Islamic countries.

Dr: Thank you, therefore, if Ali had been Calipha from the start all of the countries would have been Islamic like Iran and the people would have had Muslims just like the people of Iran and Lebanon.

The Doctor & Sheikh's Debate

Dr Zohair: Then Sheikh would have been like Khomeini and we would have been like the Doctor.

Sh: Well maybe God would help me and now that I didn't become like Khomeini at least I could be his follower like Hasan Nasrulah in Lebanon.

Dr: I think that is enough for today. I will have to go to the hotel and rest until the Maghrib prayer.

Sh: Very well. We can continue the debate tomorrow.

Dr: We will have the debate in my hotel with Sheikh Usman and your friends who are more than welcome.

Sh Usman: I will be there.

Dr: And that will make me happy. Farewell then until tomorrow after the Zuhr prayer.

Sh: Farewell.

I went back to my hotel. Some of my friends had come from Masjid an Nabawi in Tehran (our local Mosque) to my hotel and my other friends were busy hosting them. Many different debates were being discussed. They had questions concerning provisions as well for instance a certain thing had happened while they were doing Tawaf and what was to be done or not and whether had it ruined all of his provisions or not. Just like the cases I had mentioned before. They have created so many obsessions over everything that people start having doubts even if they decided to drink water on the way to Sa'ay (running ritual of the pilgrimage). My friends left eventually and I went off to run my errands.

Day Sixteenth of Zihajjah

As usual, I had an arrangement made to meet the Sheikh, but this time it was in front of the door of Ijyad. We had agreed to go to my hotel. The two Sheikhs appeared with Dr. Zohair and we called a cab, so we could head towards my hotel for lunch and then go to my room. As soon as my friends saw Sheikh, they became delighted. They also greeted Dr. Zohair and Sheikh Usman. Just like the first day, the Sheikh had come over to my hotel. He was served food and everything else. This Iranian tradition truly has its own rewards.

Sh Usman: Sheikh Ibrahim why didn't you allow us to come over here from the start? They have excellent service here. Our hotel cannot compare to this.

Sh: I asked the Doctor to come to our hotel so you guys would be able to get involved in our debates. I knew that from the love you have in research and discussions you would be happy to meet with the Doctor or else I already knew that the service at his hotel was much better.

Dr: Please do not flatter us as much as you have. We do not have anything more than what you have in your hotels.

Sh: Let us not waste time as we have to return soon. Please allow us to continue our debate.

Ghargham: But this is not fair as you guys speak in Arabic and we do not know the language.

Karbalayi: What they wish to debate about is none of our business. It is most likely regarding religion. Let us go to the shrine and conduct some non-compulsory Tawafs while the shrine is not crowded.

Dr. Ahmadi: He is right. You better go to the shrine so I can have a good sleep without your snoring.

Karbalayi: How come you can sleep while Doctor is debating, but you cannot fall asleep with me snoring?

Dr. Ahmadi: Because you're snoring is as loud as a tractor passing by. Their noise debating in the corner of the room is no comparison to yours.

Haj Abbas: Whoever wants to do whatever please get on with it. I know a little Arabic and wish to listen to this debate.

Sh: What are they talking about?

Dr: It is a discussion about snoring and the noise comparison to us debating and some of our friends heading to Masjid Al Haram and conducting Tawaf.

Sh: Please tell your friends that if they know any Arabic they must stay and listen to our debate. Looking to us would be much more rewarding.

7- The Prophet's Testimonial over Ali Being Calipha After Him

Dr: then. Let us go to the next section of our discussion regarding the Caliphas. What I mean is the Prophet's testimonial and Ali being Calipha.

Sh: Many people do not accept this section. They are the same people that also do not take what happened in Ghadir.

Dr: No, Ghadir is not in this section. Ghadir is separate from this and will be mentioned at the end of our debate.

Sh: Please go ahead then.

Dr: The cases that are mentioned in your books and are indications that the Prophet recommended Ali for Calipha are as follows.

Sh: Please mention the cases that are genuine and precise.

Dr: As you wish. Let us have a look at your book of Khasais Nesaei.

The Prophets own saying: "Ali is of me and I am of Ali."

1/4/11: (حدثنا) »بشر بن هلال، عن

جعفر بن سليمان، عن يزيد الرشك، عن مطرف بن عبد الله، عن عمران بن حصين، قال: قال رسول الله صلي الله عليه وسلم: ان عليا مني وأنا منه وولي كل مؤمن بعدي

"Umran Ibn Haseen said: The messenger of God said: Ali is of me and I am of Ali and he is Master of all the faithful."

4/10/16: (أخبرنا) »أبو داود، قال: حدثنا أبو نعيم، قال: حدثنا عبد الملك بن ابي عيينه، قال: أخبرنا الحكم، عن سعيد بن جبير، عن ابن عباس، عن بريدةَ، قال: خرجت مع علي إلى اليمن فرأيت منه جفوةً، فقدمت علي النبي صلي الله عليه وسلم فذكرت عليا

فتنقصته، فجعل رسول الله صلى الله عليه وسلم يتغير وجهه، فقال: يا بريدةَ، ألست أولى بالمؤمنين من انفسهم؟ قلت: بلى يا رسول الله، قال: من كنت مولاه فعلي مولاه»

"Ibn Abbas says that Baridah said: we accompanied Ali to Yaman. I did not feel good about him. So, I came to the Prophet and complained about Ali to the Prophet. The Prophet's face changed and said: Do I not possess priority on all of the believers from themselves? I replied: Yes, O Messenger of God. He said: whoever I am his Master then Ali is his Master."

16/10/5: (اخبرنا) «زكريا بن يحيى، قال حدثنا نصر بن علي، قال: حدثنا عبد الله بن داود، عن عبدالواحدبن أيمن عن ابيه، ان سعداً قال: قال رسول الله صلى الله عليه وسلم: من كنت مولاه فعلي مولاه

"Sa'ad said: The Messenger of God said: whoever I am his Master then Ali is his Master."

17/1/1: (أخبرنا) «احمد بن شعيب، قال: اخبرنا قتيبةَ بن سعيد، قال: حدثنا جعفر يعني ابن سليمان، عن يزيد، عن مطرف بن عبدالله، عن عمران بن حصين قال: جهز رسول الله صلى الله عليه وسلم جيشا واستعمل عليهم علي بن أبي طالب، فمضي في السريةَ فأصاب جاريةَ فأنكروا عليه، وتعاقد اربعةَ من اصحاب رسول الله صلى الله عليه وسلم إذا بعثنا رسول الله صلى الله عليه وسلم أخبرناه ما صنع

وكان المسلمون إذا رجعوا من السفر بدؤا برسول الله صلى الله عليه وسلم فسلموا عليه فانصرفوا إلى رحالهم.

فلما قدمت السريةَ سلموا على النبي صلى الله عليه وسلم فقام احد الاربعةَ فقال: يا رسول الله، ألم تر ان علي بن أبي طالب صنع كذا وكذا.

فأعرض عنه رسول الله صلى الله عليه وسلم، ثم قام الثاني فقال: مثل ذلك، ثم الثالث فقال مقالته، ثم قام الرابع فقال: مثل ما قالوا.

فأقبل إليهم رسول الله صلى الله عليه وسلم والغضب يبصر في وجهه، فقال: ما تريدون من علي؟ ان عليا مني وانا منه، وهو ولي كل مؤمن بعدي

"Umar Ibn Haseen said: The Messenger of God prepared an army and appointed Ali to be its leader. We moved forward as a unit. He then captured a woman as a prisoner and that angered us. Four of the Prophet's companions decided to confront the Prophet once they got back regarding what Ali had done. Once the Muslims returned, they came towards the Prophet and sent their blessings (before they went to their residence). After the group sent their blessings one of the four stood and said: O Messenger of God have you seen what Ali Ibn Abitaleb has done?

The Prophet objected to the complaint that was made and so the second person stood and just like the first, and then the third, all mentioned their complaints. After the fourth person finished complaining the Prophet went towards them and as he had an angry face said: What

do you want from Ali? Ali is from me and I am from Ali and he is the Master of all believers after me."

Sh: Sheikh Usman what is your opinion on this book of Nesaei?

Sh Usman: I haven't heard of anyone saying anything against the book. Nesaei has gone through much trouble and has gathered all of these citations from credible books.

Sh: Then why we do not see this book in Alazhar very much?

Sh Usman: Because we say that Ali is one of the Rashedin Caliphas. So, any attribution regarding him is justified.

Sh: But the other companions do not share such attributes mentioned in these discussions.

Sh Usman: Yes, with these explanations that the Doctor is mentioning the situation changes.

Dr: Very well, do you not think that with this straightforwardness, sentences such as "Master of all believers after me"; "Master for all believers after me is Ali," are not an indication for choosing a successor?

Sh Usman: These last words have ruined everything for us. If it did not say "after me," then we could have just said what we would always say about our Shia brothers. We would say that it meant friends. Now we cannot say that it means "After me, Ali is your friend." It just wouldn't make sense.

Sh: Are you saying that you accept the Prophet chose Ali as his successor?

Sh Usman: If you don't accept this sentence then can you please translate this "بعــدي مؤمن كل ولــي" "what does it mean?

Dr: Accept that the Prophet did choose a Calipha then I will talk about Ghadir to complete this section.

Sh Usman: If there any objections, please say something now.

Sh: I have to add that accepting this does not disqualify the other Caliphas.

Dr: Please allow me to explain this further in our Ghadir Khumm discussion.

Sh: Very well.

The Doctor & Sheikh's Debate

Dr: Now let's focus on a collection of Hadith's that have been accumulated by Kanzal Amaal, which is one of your famous books and is being used as a credible source. We can see that in his book, the assets and virtues of some of the companions have been mentioned. There are cases regarding the qualities of Ali Ibn Abi Taleb mentioned in this book that it would cause any fair Muslim to contemplate. It would make one think if Ali was even comparable or if he was utterly exceptional so that the Prophet chose him for his continuation of the line as a successor and Caliphate. I have translated these virtues of Ali from this book and would like to present you with it.

The writer of the book has mentioned at the beginning that: "For this book, I have gathered all of the Hadith's by ignoring the surfaces, and I have concentrated on the source." I have ignored the first chain of transmissions and have only focused on citing the origin of the Hadith's. Even better than that, I have ignored the parts of the Hadith's that explain the initial part of the story and have only mentioned the regions where it was related and specified the root of the issue such as the virtues of Ali. The writer has prevented even indicating the sources of his chain of transmissions and has only pointed out one source by using abbreviations. The intent for this conduct is to simplify the use of the book for the religious clerks and readers.

The writer of the book of Kanzal Amaal Fi Seni Nel Aqval Val Afaal, Alaedin al Motaqi Ibn Hesam Al-Din Hendi (Passed away in 1616 A.D), has mentioned 46000 Hadith's (with repetition) regarding this. Some parts of the book are regarding the virtues of the four Caliphas that we don't need to discuss. However, please pay attention to the fact that Abubakr has 42 Hadith, Umar has 87 and Usman has 85 Hadith. Ali has 197 Hadith all narrated from the Prophet, and they all have different contents compared to the other three Caliphas which you can see for yourself.

The interesting facts about these Hadith's are that most of the ones regarding Abubakr and Umar are the same. For instance, where it says: Abubakr and Umar, in my perspective, are like Haroon was for Moses. Now please be the judge, how it is possible for two people to be like one person? I can prove with several chains of transmissions and unified credible sources that this Hadith was said for one person, and that was for Ali. The Hadith goes by like this: One specific person is as equal to the Prophet as Haroon was for Moses. Not two people, which shows that at the time of faking the Hadith there was not much attention paid to it. Of course, this isn't to say that the Caliphas were happy about pretending Hadith's as these Hadith's were faked and written after them.

Sh: There are several Hadith's in Kanzal Amaal which ones would you recommend?

Dr: I won't repeat Hadith's number 32883 and 32. Hadith number 898, 895, 890, 990, 983, 977, 959, 958, 953, 945, 942, 941, 935, 910, 902, 900, 33011, 994, 993, and 33047. These also have matters concerning the Prophet choosing a successor and the Caliphates.

Sh: With what patience did you gather all this?

Dr: You don't need to have patience. You need to have love. I have found these Hadith's one by one from between your books so that if a person like Sheikh Ibrahim or Sheikh Usman or Dr. Zohair came along and asked me why do you believe in Ali being the first Calipha? I would then be able to say that I was ready to go to such a realization from reading your books. I told the same thing to Sheikh Hamdaan Al Qamedi, a professor at the Umm al-Qura University.

Sh Usman: Sheikh Ibrahim, with all the explanations that the Doctor has given us I believe that we look at religious issues like a job. Therefore, we have never had love to inspire us in looking for this detailed information and to extract is from such Hadith's.

Dr. Zohair: If what I am about to say would not offend you, I would like to say something. Your job just like me being a Medical Doctor is teaching religious studies. If the information that people seek is sufficient, then you would not need to look for more answers. You would not go and research. It has been a long time since I read a Medical book. However, the Doctor's job is not related to religion. He is a professor at the University. He does not get paid from doing anything religious, but he spends time and money seeking it. This kind of work requires love.

Dr: Let us pray so that God gives us the trouble of searching for information about our religion.

Dr. Zohair: Do you mean to say seeking religion is troublesome?

Dr: No, but the real Islam has no problems. The issue arises when after 1400 years so many alterations have been done to religion that the real Islam is no longer visible. So many branches and leaves have been surrounded by it that it is even harder to see what the real Islam is. This, you see, especially in Arabian countries. Religion is viewed as several provisions that need undertaking without any connection to the soul.

Sh Usman: I pray for God to innovate love in our religion and for us to pay attention to it as much as we do to our jobs.

Dr: God Willing. Shall I continue, or shall we leave the rest for later?

Sh: I think it is enough for the day. By seeing such Hadith's, one gets embarrassed and accepting the mistake becomes troublesome enough. Please allow us to talk to your friends a little. They must be bored by now.

Haj Abbas: I am not tired at all.

Sh: I was humorous.

Dr: Very well. Please tell me what you wish to say, and I will translate for my friends.

It took an hour of pleasant social talking then afterward:

Sh: I have something planned for tomorrow evening would it be okay if we saw each other after Maghrib.

Dr: It wouldn't be wrong. That would be very well planned.

Sh: How come?

Dr: Because I will be going to Iran in three days and tomorrow would possibly be the last time we can talk.

Sh: Then please let's finish our discussion regarding Ghadir Khumm.

Dr: In fact, tomorrow night is the 18th of Zihajjah, and it is the same night that Ghadir Khumm happened.

Sh: Very well then, the discussion of Ghadir Khumm on the night of Ghadir Khumm is excellent. It has its rewards.

Dr: God Willing, but I have a request to ask from you.

Sh: Please ask away.

Dr: It is a little different from the rituals of our debates.

Sh: What difference?

Dr: I wish to ask of you to read a section from a credible source taken from the School of Ahl al Bayt just for additional information, so then no one could say that the Prophet gathered people for three days in Ghadir Khumm and just mentioned several short sentences. We can then have a much broader discussion tomorrow night.

Sh: What Hadith from what source are you referring to?

Dr: The Prophet's speech in Hajatal Veda that was read in Ghadir Khumm.

Sh: Very well. Let me have it, and I will read it for tomorrow.

Sh Usman: Doctor could you please also give us the sources for it.

Dr: The speech has been cited from someone acceptable to you, and his name is mentioned in several of your chains of transmissions.

Sh: Whom are we talking about?

Dr: Muhammad Ibn Ali Albaqer.

Sh Usman: Yes, yes, you are right. His name is mentioned many times in our credible Hadith's.

Sh: That is very good.

Dr: I have to add that we have the same Hadith from Zeyd Ibn Arqam and also someone else named Haziqahte ibn Yamaan.

I mean to say that there are three chains of transmissions that are all the same and have been mentioned in this book.

Sh: This is very interesting, please allow me also to have a look at its chain of transmissions.

Dr: Here you go. These are all of the chains of transmissions for it. Two of the chains of transmissions are related to Muhammad Ibn Ali, and two of the other chains of transmissions are associated with Zeyd Ibn Arqam and Namaan.

Imam Baqer's saying has two chains of transmissions:

قال الشيخ أحمد بن علي بن أبي منصور الطبرسي في كتاب *الإحتجاج*:

«حدثني السيد العالم العابد ابو جعفر مهدي بن أبي الحرث الحسيني المرعشي ' قال: أخبرنا الشيخ أبو علي الحسن بن الشيخ أبي جعفر محمد بن الحسن الطوسي ' ، قال: أخبرنا الشيخ السعيد الوالد أبو جعفر قدس الله روحه، قال: أخبرني جماعةٌ عن أبي محمد هارون بن موسى التلعكبري، قال أخبرني أبوعلي محمد بن همام، قال: أخبرنا علي السوري قال: أخبرنا أبو محمد العلوي من ولد الأفطس ـ و كان من عباد الله الصالحين ـ قال: حدثنا محمد بن موسى الهمداني، قال: حدثنا محمد بن خالد الطيالسي، قال: حدثنا سيف بن عميرةَ و صالح بن عقبةَ جميعاً عن قيس بن سمعان عن علقمةَ بن محمد الحضرمي عن أبي جعفر محمد بن علي(الباقر   )».

ـ قال السيد بن طاووس في كتاب *اليقين*:

«قال أحمد بن محمد الطبري المعروف بالخليلي في كتابه «أخبرني محمد بن أبي بكر بن عبد الرحمان، قال: حدثني الحسن بن علي أبو محمد الدينوري، قال: حدثنا محمد بن موسى الهمداني، قال: حدثنا محمد بن خالد الطيالسي، قال: حدثنا سيف بن عميرةَ عن عقبةَ عن قيس بن سمعان عن علقمةَ بن محمد الحضرمي عن أبي جعفر محمد بن علي(الباقر   )

Zeyd Ibn Arqam's saying is as follows:

The Doctor & Sheikh's Debate

قال السيد إبن طاووس في كتاب *التحصين*:

المفضل محمد بن عبد الله الشيباني، قال: بن أحمد الجاواني في كتابه *نور الهدى و المنجي من الردى* : عن أبي قال الحسن بن سكين البلدي، قالا: حدثنا حميد بن الربيع الخزاز، قال: حدثنا بن عيسىأخبرنا أبو جعفر محمد بن جرير الطبري و هارون بن مبشر، قال: حدثنا الوليد بن صالح عن إبن امرأةْ زيد بن أرقم و عن زيد بن أرقميزيد بن هارون، قال: حدثنا نوح

Haziqahte ibn Yamaan's saying is as follows:

قال السيد بن طاووس في كتاب *الإقبال*:

قال مؤلف كتاب *النشر والطي*: عنأحمد بن محمد بن علي المهلب: أخبرنا الشريف أبو القاسم علي بن محمد بن علي بن القاسم الشعراني عن أبيه: حدثنا سلمهْ بن الفضل الأنصاري، عن أبي مريم عن قيس بن حيان (حنان) عن عطيهْ السعدي عن حذيفهْ بن اليمان

They thanked me for giving them the speech, and then I said goodbye to them. They left, and my friends and I continued talking about other things.

Day Seventeenth of Zihajjah (Eid Ghadir Night)

After the Maghrib and Isha prayer, the Sheikh and Doctor Zohair and I returned to my hotel. Upon entering the hotel, we had dinner together. The tour group leader had arranged a celebrating ceremony for Eid Ghadir at the restaurant. They had placed many Persian sweets for all of the pilgrims on large trays, and you could hear clapping and loud voices coming from the restaurant.

Sh: Is there an event at the hotel?

Dr: Yes, it is the night of the Eid Ghadir celebration.

Sh: Then it is good that we came here.

Dr: Please come with me. Let us have dinner, and then we can celebrate.

Sh: We don't need dinner. These sweets and fruits are sufficient.

Dr. Zohair: I wish to have dinner. If Sheikh Ibrahim does not want to have any that is fine, he does not have to eat.

Sh Usman: How can one let go of these delicious foods.

Sh: All right, then I will eat too.

Dr: Then let us go and take the seats over there where dinner hasn't been served yet.

After we had dinner and participated in the ceremony we had some Persian sweets and fruits and then headed towards my room for the continuation of our discussion.

Sh: We saw many new Persian sweets tonight.

Dr: Yes, they are for the pilgrims and therefore have more variety.

Sh: It is late. Let's start the Ghadir discussion.

8- Ghadir Khumm

Sh: We have time. Please tell us. However, do remember that at the first of our discussion, you eliminated the companions, and then you invalidated Abu Huraira's truth in his chain of transmissions, and now it is the Caliphates turn. I now know why you would not discuss this issue and would always say let us leave it to the end.

Dr: Well inevitably, the debate between the School of Ahl al Bayt and our Sunni brothers is an important thing.

Sh: Well, I agreed to listen to what you had to say, and until now, everything you have said, has been right and logical. So, I have accepted it.

Dr: Thank you. This only shows your will to seek the truth and your greatness or else I am no one special. I have only extracted information from your books.

Dr: Very well, we now come to the point where we talk about our last chapter of our debate, Ghadir Khumm.

Sh: Are you going to cite the story of what happens, or are we going to exchange knowledge.

Dr: No, I believe we should mention the event at Ghadir with all of its sidelines so we can understand the intention of the Prophet for his speech at Ghadir Khumm.

Sh: Let us start.

Dr: In your books, many parts of the Ghadir has been eliminated. The speech at Ghadir has been, and it is only in a couple of sentences. I will talk about the sideline of what happened because it will not have any effect on our debate. I will bring the chain of transmissions from the School of Ahl al Bayt. We will use your books for discussing the main speech of Ghadir.

Sh: Doctor, I have read the speech and have questions about it.

Dr: Very well, but I wish to point out some things first.

Sh: Please go ahead.

Dr: You do know that the event of Ghadir happened at the Prophet's Hajat Al Veda (The Farewell Pilgrimage).

Sh: Yes, that is right.

Dr: You do know that Surat Al Maidah is the last Surat in the Quran.

Sh: Yes.

The Doctor & Sheikh's Debate

Dr: The verse of Ghadir is in Surat Al Maidah. Even though many interpreters state that this Surat came to the Prophet three times in Mena and once on the way to Mecca but, let's pretend it came to him earlier.

Sh: Which verse?

Dr: Verse number 67:

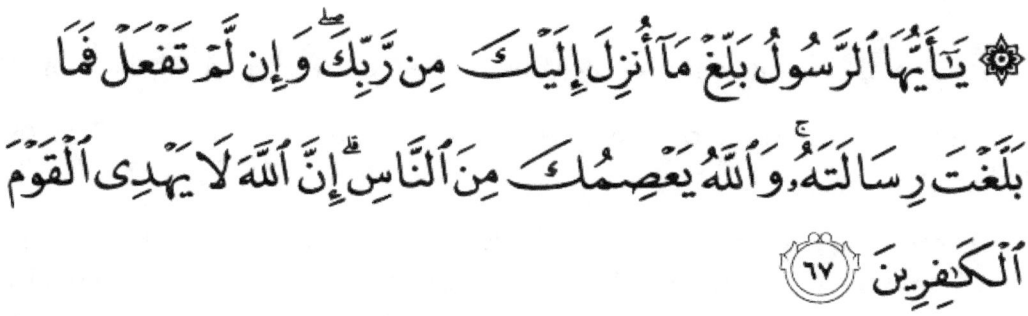

"O Messenger, Proclaim the message that has been sent down to you from your Creator and Nurturer! And if you do not do so then you would not have conveyed your duty as Allah's Messenger [know that] Allah will protect you from [The mischievous] people, Verily, Allah does not guide the disbelievers"

Sh: Yes, this was mentioned in Hajat Al Veda.

Dr: What do you think came to the Prophet and he was scared of telling them about it?

Sh: There are many debates in our books, but to be honest, the truth is that most say it had nothing to do with Ghadir.

Dr: Yes, I have seen them as well. Some say that this verse was not revealed to the Prophet in Ghadir, and some say that if it did explain to him, it only meant that the Prophet was asking us to like Ali.

Sh: That is correct. There are other things said as well, but it's been mostly about the same thing you mentioned.

Dr: Do you think that this event was so important that if the Prophet had not done so then, he had not accomplished his duty as a Messenger?

Sh: The history says such a thing, but to be honest, it is a little heavy.

Dr: I can make a logical analysis by just using your chain of transmissions.

Sh: Please do so, that would make us happy.

Dr: By looking at these Hadith's it can be quickly concluded how vital Ali was that if the Prophet had not put across the necessity of liking him to his Ummah, then his job as a Messenger would not have been completed.

Sh Usman: Do you accept the interpretation of the word, Vali (Master), to be being friends or liking someone?

Dr: Do you accept that the meaning of the verse in the Quran is regarding liking Ali?

Sh: Yes, many of our interpreters accept this, but they do not take the word Vali (Master) to be translated as Calipha.

Dr: I do not accept such an interpretation. However, I do say that this event is being made to tell us to like Ali and was so important to God that he asked the Prophet to do that or else his job was not completed as a Prophet. It just goes to show how important this person was for him to arrange such an event.

Sh: Yes, that is important. It must have been an essential piece of news.

Dr: Then such a person that God and his Prophet value him this much should have been Calipha after the Prophet, not someone else.

Sh: In the end, you will bring Ali as Calipha out of this Ghadir.

Dr: I won't do such a thing it is God and his Prophet. I am busy trying to dust away all of the uncertainty that history has brought upon this event.

Sh: Okay, let us return to the main case. Let us debate Ghadir from your perspective.

Dr: I believe that God and his Prophet intended to bring about a more important event than just telling us to like Ali. This important case, unfortunately, was eradicated by falsifications in your books of interpretations. Some books still state the intention of this event was for appointing a Calipha and a successor and that the Prophet had such an objective.

Sh: But there are no declarations in the Quran.

Dr: You are right, but we should examine what the Prophet did immediately after the Verse was given to him.

Sh: What did he do?

Dr: After Ghadir when he was a couple of kilometers away from Jahfe, the Prophet gathered all the pilgrims passing by and told them to stay, then asked the ones that had left to return also to wait as he had an important announcement to make.

Sh: This is stated in our books.

Dr: Yes, it is, and I have seen it too.

Sh: Very well, you may carry on.

Dr: At Ghadir, there was a lake named Khumm that had water. The Prophet had stopped the Caravan close to the lake of water and had stayed there for three days. He made a stand, out of the camel's apparatus positioned between two trees and under the shade. The Prophet prayed with the people and then made a full intensive speech which is written in the book I gave you to read last night.

Sh: I read that book. Do you wish to discuss it now or later?

Dr: No, we will discuss it later.

Sh: Very well.

Dr: Okay, let us agree entirely that Ghadir did happen and there were things that the Prophet talked about.

Sh Usman: We accept this.

Dr. Zohair: Let us be informed because I have never heard much of this information.

Sh: That is not a problem. Please tell us so Dr. Zohair can also know about them.

Dr: Whatever I will mention is from your books, and I will say the summary of it from Nesaei. You all know that the chains of transmission are unanimously agreed upon.

Sh: Nesaei is one of our famous transmitters of traditions.

Dr: Here you go. This is the book of Khasais Nesaei, and these Hadith's are just like before, numbered.

The Prophet's Remark: Whomever I am his Master, Ali is his Master

1/10/16: (أخبرنا) «احمد بن المثنى، قال: حدثنا يحيى بن معاذ، قال: اخبرنا أبو عوانةً، عن سليمان

قال: حدثنا حبيب بن ابي ثابت، عن ابي الطفيل، عن زيد بن ارقم قال: لما رجع النبي صلي الله عليه وسلم من حجةِ الوداع ونزل غديرخم أمر بدوحات فقممن ثم قال: كأني دعيت فأجبت واني تارك فيكم الثقلين احدهما اكبر من الآخر: كتاب الله وعترتي اهل‌بيتي، فانظروا كيف تخلفوني فيهما فانهما لن يفترقا حتي يردا علي الحوض.

ثم قال ان الله مولاي وأنا ولي كل مؤمن.

ثم انه اخذ بيد علي⦁ فقال: من كنت وليه فهذا وليه، اللهم وال من والاه وعاد من عاداه.

فقلت لزيد: سمعته من رسول الله صلي الله عليه وسلم؟ فقال: وانه ما كان في الدوحات أحد إلا رآه بعينه وسمعه بأذنيه.

"Abi Tofeyl says from Zeyd Ibn Arqam: When the Prophet was returning from Hajat Al Veda he stopped at Ghadir Khumm. The Prophet ordered for the luggage's to be put down and for the camels to be rested. They placed several big trees on the ground creating a stand and he stood over it and then said: It appears that God wishes for me to return to him and I have accepted (I am to die). I am leaving you two great sources amongst you and one of them is bigger than the other. One is the book of God and the other is my descendants and my Ahl al Bayt. So be careful with how you treat them after me because these two are inseparable until they return to me at Basin of Katthar.

He then said: Henceforth God is my Master and I am the master of all believers. He then held Ali's hand and said: Whoever accepts me as his master, Ali is his Master. O Allah, like whoever that like him and be the enemy of whomever that is his enemy.

I asked Zeyd: Did you hear this from the Prophet?

He replied: There was no one in the Caravan that did not hear him or to see this happen."

16/10/10: (اخبرنا): «أبو داود، قال: حدثنا عمران بن ابان، قال: حدثنا شريك، قال: حدثنا أبو اسحاق، عن زيد بن يثيغ قال: سمعت علي بن ابي طالب⦁ يقول علي منبر الكوفةِ: اني انشد الله رجلا ولا يشهد إلا اصحاب محمد سمع رسول الله صلي الله عليه وسلم يوم غديرخم يقول: من كنت مولاه فعلي مولاه، اللهم وال من والاه وعاد من عاداه.

فقام ستةٌ من جانب المنبر الآخر فشهدوا انهم سمعوا رسول الله صلي الله عليه وسلم يقول ذلك.

قال شريك: فقلت لابي اسحاق: هل سمعت البراء بن عازب يحدث بهذا عن رسول الله صلي الله عليه وسلم؟ قال: نعم.

"Zeyd Ibn Yasiq said: I heard Ali say on the Kufeh pulpit: I swear to God on one man's life and I would never vouch his word unless it was the Prophet's companion that I heard The Messenger of God said on the day of Ghadir: Whomever accepts me as his master, Ali is his Master. O Allah, like whoever that likes him, and be against those who are his enemies. Six

The Doctor & Sheikh's Debate

people rose from the other side of the pulpit and testified that they heard what the Prophet said.

Sharik said that he told Abi Eshaq: Did you hear what Bara Ibn Azeb said: about the Prophet's doing? He replied: Yes."

1/15/3: (أخبرنا) »هلال بن بشير البصري قال: حدثنا محمد بن خالد قال: حدثني موسى بن يعقوب قال: حدثنا مهاجر بن سمار بن سلمةَ عن عائشةَ بنت سعد قالت: سمعت أبي يقول: سمعت رسول الله صلى الله عليه وسلم يوم الجحفةَ فأخذ بيد علي، فخطب فحمد الله وأثنى عليه، ثم قال: أيها الناس اني وليكم، قالوا: صدقت يا رسول الله، ثم اخذ بيد علي فرفعها فقال: هذا وليي ويؤدي عني ديني، وأنا موالي من والاه ومعادي من عاداه

"Aisha Bint Sa'ad said that her father told her: I heard that the Prophet held Ali's hand on the day of Jahfeh and gave a speech and praised and worshiped. He then said: Oh people I am your Master. People responded: Yes, Oh Messenger of God you are. He then raised Ali's hand and said: This man is my successor and in charge of my debt and I like whoever that likes him and whoever is his enemy is my enemy."

1/4/20: (أخبرنا) »احمد بن شعيب قال: أخبرني هارون بن عبدالله البغدادي الحبال، قال: حدثنا مصعب بن المقدام، قال: حدثنا فطر بن خليفةَ، عن ابي الطفيل.

(وأخبرنا) أبو داود قال: حدثنا محمد بن سليمان، حدثنا فطر عن ابي الطفيل، عن عامر بن وائلةَ قال: جمع علي الناس في الرحبةَ فقال لهم: انشد بالله كل امرئ مسلم سمع رسول الله صلى الله عليه وسلم يقول: يوم غديرخم: ألستم تعلمون اني اولى المؤمنين من انفسهم وهوقائم ثم اخذ بيد علي فقال: من كنت مولاه فعلي مولاه، اللهم وال من والاه وعاد من عاداه.

قال أبو الطفيل: فخرجت وفي نفسي منه شيئ فلقيت زيد بن أرقم واخبرنا فقال: تشك أنا سمعته من رسول الله صلى الله عليه وسلم واللفظ لابي داود.«

"Amer Ibn Vaeleh said: Ali gathered people in Rahbeh and said: to them: I swear you people to God every Muslim Man has heard what the Prophet has said. Do you not know that I possess priority over any other believer than themselves? The Prophet was standing and held Ali's hand and then said: Whoever accepts me as his master, Ali is his Master. O Allah, please be favouring to those who are his friends, and be against those who are his enemies.

Abu Al Tofeyl said: So I left there and thought to myself that I saw Zeyd Ibn Arqam and he told me this and said: Don't you believe me? I heard this thing straight from the Prophet and Abu Davoud foresaw it."

2/4/20: (أخبرنا) »احمد بن شعيب، اخبرني أبو عبدالرحمان زكريا بن يحيى السجستاني، قال: حدثني محمد بن عبد الرحيم، قال: اخبرنا ابراهيم، قال: حدثنا معن، قال: حدثني موسى بن يعقوب، عن المهاجر بن مسمار، عن عائشةَ بنت سعد و عامر بن سعد، عن سعد: ان رسول الله صلى الله عليه وسلم خطب

فقال: أما بعد ايها الناس فاني وليكم.

قالوا: صدقت، ثم اخذ بيد علي فرفعها، ثم قال: هذا وليي والمؤدي عني، اللهم وال من والاه وعاد من عاداه.»

"Sa'ad says: The Prophet made a speech and said: O People, I am your Master. They replied: You are correct. So he held Ali's hand and raised it and said: This man is my friend and companion. O Allah, please be favouring to those who are his friends, and be against those who are his enemies."

20/4/3: (أخبرنا) «احمد بن عثمان البصري أبو الجوزاء، قال ابن عيينةَ بنت سعد، عن سعد قال: اخذ رسول‌الله صلى الله عليه وسلم بيد علي فخطب: فحمد الله واثنى عليه ثم قال: ألم تعلموا اني أولى بكم من انفسكم؟

قالوا: نعم، صدقت يا رسول الله.

ثم اخذ بيد علي فرفعها،

فقال: من كنت وليه فهذا وليه وان الله ليوالي من والاه ويعادي من عاداه.»

"Sa'ad said: The Messenger of God held Ali's hand and gave a speech and then he praised the Lord and then said: Do you not know that I possess more priority than yourself? They replied: You are right, O Messenger of God. He then held Ali's hand and raised it. He then said: Whoever accepts me as his master, Ali is his Master. Here forth Allah loves whoever loves him and is enemy to whoever classes him as an enemy."

20/4/4: (أخبرنا) «احمد بن شعيب، قال: أخبرنا زكريا بن يحيى، قال: حدثنا يعقوب بن جعفر بن ابي كثير، عن مهاجر بن مسمار، قال: اخبرتني عائشةَ بنت سعد، عن سعد قال: كنا مع رسول الله صلى الله عليه وسلم بطريق مكةَ وهو متوجه إليها، فلما بلغ غديرخم وقف للناس، ثم رد من تبعه ولحقه من تخلف، فلما اجتمع الناس إليه قال: ايها الناس من وليكم؟ قالوا: الله ورسوله، ثلاثا.

ثم اخذ بيد علي فأقامه، ثم قال:

من كان الله ورسوله وليه فهذا وليه، اللهم وال من والاه وعاد من عاداه.»

"Aisha Bint Asad told me that Saa'd told her: O Messenger of God we were on our way to Mecca and he was more concentrating on the path. When we got to Ghadir Khumm he told people to stop. He then returned the ones that had gone and the ones that were on their way coming. Whenever people gathered around him he said: O people, who is your master? They replied: God and his Messenger (They said this three times). So then he held Ali's hand and raised it and said: Then whoever God and his Messenger is his Master this Ali is his master. God loves whoever loves him and is enemy to whoever classes him as an enemy."

The Doctor & Sheikh's Debate

2/3/21: (أخبرنا) «احمد بن شعيب، قال: اخبرنا الحسين بن حريث المروزي، قال: اخبرنا الفضل بن موسى، عن الاعمش، عن ابي اسحاق عن سعيد بن وهب قال: قال علي كرم الله وجهه في الرحبةْ: أنشد بالله من سمع رسول الله صلى الله عليه وسلم يوم غديرخم يقول: ان الله ورسوله ولي المؤمنين، ومن كنت وليه فهذا وليه، اللهم وال من والاه وعاد من عاداه، وانصر من نصره.

قال: فقال سعيد: قام إلى جنبي ستةْ، وقال زيد بن يثيع: قام عندي ستةْ، وقال عمرو ذي مر: احب من أحبه وأبغض من أبغضه.»

"Abi Es-haq says that Saeid Ibn Wahab said: Ali said in Rahbah: I swear to God and ask anyone who heard what the Prophet said on the day of Ghadir Khumm to stand here as a witness. The Prophet said: Here forth God and his Messenger are the Masters of all believers and whoever I am his Master, Ali is his Master. God love whoever loves him and be the enemy of whoever that classes him as an enemy. And assist whoever that assists him. Saeid then said: six people rose from my side and Zeyd Ibn Yasiq said: six other people rose from another side. Amr Zi said: (The continuation of the Hadith was this): God love whoever loves him and be angry with whomever that has vengeance on him"

3/3/21: (أخبرنا) «احمد بن شعيب، قال: اخبرنا علي بن محمد بن علي، قال: حدثنا خلف بن تميم، قال: حدثنا اسرائيل، قال: حدثنا ابو اسحاق، عن عمرو ذي مر قال: شهدت عليا بالرحبةْ ينشد اصحاب محمد: أيكم سمع رسول الله صلى الله عليه وسلم يقول يوم غديرخم ما قال؟ فقام اناس فشهدوا انهم سمعوا رسول الله صلى الله عليه وسلم يقول: من كنت مولاه فعلي مولاه، اللهم وال من والاه، وعاد من عاداه، واحب من احبه، وابغض من ابغضه، وانصر من نصره.»

"Amr Zimar said: I witnessed that in Rahba Ali was swearing on the Prophets companions: Which one of you heard the Prophet on Ghadir Khumm? Therefore, people rose and claimed witness that they had heard it from the Messenger of God. Whoever has me as his Master, Ali is his Master. And be the enemy of consider whoever that is his enemy and love whoever that loves him and be angry to whoever that shows vengeance on him and assist whoever that assists him."

Dr: All of these chains of transmission that I brought up from Nesaei are uniformly accepted elsewhere, please take this.

Sh: That is right; I have seen this in other books.

Dr: Almost all of the other books have cited that the Prophet said:

«من كنت مولاه فهذا علي مولاه»
"Whoever has me as his Master here forth Ali is his Master"

Dr. Zohair: Doctor, do you only have a chain of transmissions from Nesaei?

Dr: No, here you go. You can view other chains of transmissions in this mobile program.

Sahih Muslem, 2408:

> «الصحيح ما أخرجه الإمام مسلم في صحيحه من حديث زيد بن أرقم أنه قال: قام رسول الله - صلى الله عليه وسلم - فينا خطيبًا بماء يدعى خُمًّا بين مكةَ والمدينةِ، فحمد الله وأثنى عليه، ووعظ وذكر ثم قال: «أما بعد، ألا أيها الناس فإنما أنا بشر يوشك أن يأتي رسول ربي فأجيب وأنا تارك فيكم ثقلين، أولهما كتاب الله فيه الهدى والنور، فخذوا بكتاب الله واستمسكوا به»، فحث على كتاب الله ورغّب فيه ثم قال: «وأهل بيتي أذكركم الله في اهل بيتي، أذكركم الله في اهل بيتي، أذكركم الله في اهل بيتي»»

"Muslem says in the Hadith of Sahih that Zeyd Ibn Arqam said: The Messenger of God stood up amongst us close to the Khumm waters and prepared himself for a speech. The water was between Mecca and Medina. After sending praise to God he began to preach and then said: So now people I am a human being. It is close to the time for the God's sender to come and I will give him my answer (My time has come). I am leaving you two very valuable things behind. One is the book of God that you can obtain guidance and light from. So, keep the book of God and clincher it. He emphasised on paying attention to it. He then said: And my Ahl al Bayt. In protecting my Ahl al Bayt I remind you to remember God."

Dr. Zohair: Do you mean to say that Muslem has spoken of Ghadir?

Dr: Yes, these were from Muslem, showing that the Prophet spoke in Ghadir. Zeyd Ibn Arqam says those chains of transmissions I mentioned above and the speech is all from him. In the next Hadith, it also shows that some parts of it have been taken out. Because it says "He did mention some other things and then this and that happened," and we still have it as below:

Musnad Ahmad, volume 39, page 297, Hadith 18497:

> «حَدَّثَنَا حُسَيْنُ بْنُ مُحَمَّدٍ وَأَبُو نُعَيْمٍ الْمَعْنَى قَالَا ثَنَا فِطْرٌ عَنْ أَبِي الطُّفَيْلِ قَالَ جَمَعَ عَلِيٌّ رَضِيَ اللَّهُ تَعَالَى عَنْهُ النَّاسَ فِي الرَّحَبَةِ ثُمَّ قَالَ لَهُمْ أَنْشُدُ اللَّهَ كُلَّ امْرِئٍ مُسْلِمٍ سَمِعَ رَسُولَ اللَّهِ صَلَّى اللَّهُ عَلَيْهِ وَسَلَّمَ يَقُولُ يَوْمَ غَدِيرِ خُمٍّ مَا سَمِعَ لَمَّا قَامَ فَقَامَ ثَلَاثُونَ مِنَ النَّاسِ وَقَالَ أَبُو نُعَيْمٍ فَقَامَ نَاسٌ كَثِيرٌ فَشَهِدُوا حِينَ أَخَذَهُ بِيَدِهِ فَقَالَ لِلنَّاسِ أَتَعْلَمُونَ أَنِّي أَوْلَى بِالْمُؤْمِنِينَ مِنْ أَنْفُسِهِمْ قَالُوا نَعَمْ يَا رَسُولَ اللَّهِ قَالَ مَنْ كُنْتُ مَوْلَاهُ فَهَذَا مَوْلَاهُ اللَّهُمَّ وَالِ مَنْ وَالَاهُ وَعَادِ مَنْ عَادَاهُ
> قَالَ فَخَرَجْتُ وَكَأَنَّ فِي نَفْسِي شَيْئًا فَلَقِيتُ زَيْدَ بْنَ أَرْقَمَ فَقُلْتُ لَهُ إِنِّي سَمِعْتُ عَلِيًّا رَضِيَ اللَّهُ تَعَالَى عَنْهُ يَقُولُ كَذَا وَكَذَا قَالَ فَمَا تُنْكِرُ قَدْ سَمِعْتُ رَسُولَ اللَّهِ صَلَّى اللَّهُ عَلَيْهِ وَسَلَّمَ يَقُولُ ذَلِكَ لَهُ»

"He said that Ali gathered people in Rahbah and said: to them: I swear to God on any Muslim man who ever heard The Messenger of God on Ghadir Khumm. Thirty people stood that day. Abu Naeem said that many people stood that day and testified that while the Prophet had held Ali's hand up he said: Do you not know that I possess priority over any other believer? They replied: Yes, O Messenger of God. He then said: Whoever has me as his Master then this Ali is his Master. O God like whoever that likes him and is the enemy of whoever that is his enemy."

Sh: This is another of the repetitive Hadith's that have been mentioned in many books.

Dr: That is right. Now this is in the book of Mosuah Hadith that is mentioned in the book of Musnad Al Tayalesi: Volume 1, page 23, Hadith 154:

»حدثنا أبو داود قال حدثنا الأشعث بن سعيد حدثنا عبد الله بن بسر عن أبي راشد الحبراني عن علي قال عممني رسول الله صلى الله عليه وسلم يوم غديرخم بعمامةٍ سدلها خلفي ثم قال إن الله عز وجل أمدني يوم بدر وحنين بملائكةٍ يعتمون هذه العمهْ فقال إن العمامهْ حاجزهْ بين الكفر والإيمان«

"Ali said: The Messenger of God placed a turban on me. It was the kind that fell on my shoulders. He then said: Henceforth the Almighty God assisted me on the day of Badr and Hunayn with angels that were wearing the same turban and then said: Turban is the gap separating between infidelity and belief."

Dr: In fact, this chain of transmission also talks about the Prophet's turban that he placed it on Ali's head.

Dr. Zohair: Did the Prophet give his turban to Ali?

Dr: Yes, This Hadith is from your own books. There are many more Hadith's. I have more here:

This Hadith is in the book of Kanzol Amaal. Volume 13, page 138, Hadith number 36437 and also in Jame ul Ahadis, volume 34, page 198, Hadith number 37124 and Mujam Kabir Tabarani, volume 2, page 379 with the number below all say:

2505: »حدثنا علي بن سعيد الرازي ثنا الحسن بن صالح بن زريق العطار حدثنا محمد بن عون أبو عون الزيادي ثنا حرب بن سريج عن بشر ابن حرب عن جرير: قال: شهدنا الموسم في حجةٍ مع رسول الله صلى الله عليه وسلم وهي حجةْ الوداع فبلغنا مكانا يقال له غديرخم فنادى الصلاةْ جامعةْ فاجتمعنا المهاجرون والأنصار فقام رسول الله صلى الله عليه وسلم وسطنا فقال: (أيها الناس بم تشهدون؟) قالوا: نشهد أن لا إله إلا الله قال: (ثم مه؟) قالوا: وأن محمدا عبده ورسوله قال: (فمن فأقامه فنزع عضده فأخذ بذراعيه فقال: [وليكم؟) قالوا: الله ورسوله مولانا قال: (من وليكم؟) ثم ضرب بيده على عضد علي (من يكن الله ورسوله مولياه فإن هذا مولاه اللهم وال من والاه وعاد من عاداه اللهم من أحبه من الناس فكن له حبيبا ومن أبغضه فكن له مبغضا«

"Jarir said: We were at the season of Hajj with The Messenger of God and that was in the Farewell Pilgrimage. As soon as we got to the place where it is called Ghadir Khumm he invited everyone for the Friday prayer. All the immigrants and supporters gathered up. The Prophet stood and said: O people what do you testify in? They replied: We testify that there is no God but God. He then said: What else do you testify in? They said that Muhammad is the servant and the Messenger of God. He then said: Who is your Master? They replied: God and his Messenger. He then asked: Who is your Master? He then placed his hand on Ali's shoulder and raised his hand as high as the length of an arm (Zar'e) and then said: Whoever God and his Prophet is his Master then this Ali is his Master. O God love whoever loves him and be enemy to whomever that is his enemy. O God whoever loves Ali, like him and whoever that has vengeance on Ali then have vengeance on him."

Dr: In the book of Jame ul Ahadis, volume 35, page 42:

37808: «عن ميمون أبي عبد الله قال: كنت عند زيد بن أرقم فجاء رجل فسأل عن علي قال: كنا مع رسول الله ـ صلى الله عليه وسلم ـ في سفر بين مكةَ والمدينةَ. فنزلنا مكانا يقال له غديرخم فأذن الصلاةَ جامعةَ، فاجتمع الناس فحمد الله وأثنى عليه ثم قال: يا أيها الناس ألست أولى بكل مؤمن من نفسه قلنا: بلى يا رسول نحن نشهد أنك أولى بكل مؤمن من نفسه، قال: فإن من كنت مولاه فهذا مولاه وأخذ بيد علي ولا أعلمه إلا قال: اللهم وال من والاه وعاد من عاداه.» (ابن‌جرير) [كنز العمال، 36342]

"Meemun Abi Abdullah said: I was with Zeyd Ibn Arqam. A man came and I spoke about Ali. He said: I was with the Prophet for Hajj and when we got to a place called Ghadir Khumm that was placed between Mecca and Medina. He then invited everyone for Friday Prayer. People gathered up. Afterwards, The Messenger of God sent praise to the Lord he then said: Do I not possess priority on any Believer to himself? We replied: Yes, O Messenger of God we vouch that you possess priority over any other Muslim. He then said: So, whoever I am his Master, this Ali is his Master. And I didn't know this until God told me that love whoever that loves him and be the enemy of whoever that is his enemy."

Dr: In the book of Sunan Kobra, Nesaei, volume 5, page 45:

8148: «أخبرنا محمد بن المثنى قال ثنا يحيى بن حماد قال ثنا أبو عوانةَ عن سليمان قال ثنا حبيب بن أبي ثابت عن أبي الطفيل عن زيد بن أرقم قال لما رجع رسول الله صلى الله عليه وسلم عن حجةِ الوداع ونزل غديرخم أمر بدوحات فقممن ثم قال كأني قد دعيت فأجبت إني قد تركت فيكم الثقلين أحدهما أكبر من الآخر كتاب الله وعترتي اهل‌بيتي فانظروا كيف تخلفوني فيهما فإنهما لن يتفرقا حتى يردا علي الحوض ثم قال إن الله مولاي وأنا ولي كل مؤمن ثم أخذ بيد علي فقال من كنت وليه فهذا وليه اللهم وال من والاه وعاد من عاداه»

The Doctor & Sheikh's Debate

"Abi Tofeyl says from Zeyd Ibn Arqam: When the Prophet was returning from Hajat Al Veda he stopped at Ghadir Khumm. The Prophet ordered for the luggage's to be put down and for the camels to be rested. They placed several big trees on the ground creating a stand and he stood over it and then said: It appears that God wishes for me to return to him and I have accepted (I am to die). I am leaving you two pure sources amongst you and one of them is bigger than the other. One is the book of God and the other is my descendants and my Ahl al Bayt. So be careful with how to treat them after me because these two are inseparable until they return to me at Basin of Kawthar. He then said: Here forth God is my Master and I am the master of all believers. He then held Ali's hand and said: Whoever accepts me as his master, Ali is his Master. O Allah, please be favouring to those who are his friends, and be against those who are his enemies."

Dr: This is another chain of transmission from Musnad Ahmad.

Sh: Please let us see it.

Dr: In Musnad Ahmad, volume 37, page 436 it says:

حَدَّثَنَا عَفَّانُ حَدَّثَنَا حَمَّادُ بْنُ سَلَمَةَ أَخْبَرَنَا عَلِيُّ بْنُ زَيْدٍ عَنْ عَدِيِّ بْنِ ثَابِتٍ عَنِ الْبَرَاءِ بْنِ عَازِبٍ قَالَ كُنَّا مَعَ رَسُولِ اللَّهِ صَلَّى اللَّهُ عَلَيْهِ وَسَلَّمَ فِي سَفَرٍ فَنَزَلْنَا بِغَدِيرِخم فَنُودِيَ فِينَا الصَّلَاةَ جَامِعَةً وَكُسِحَ لِرَسُولِ اللَّهِ صَلَّى اللَّهُ عَلَيْهِ وَسَلَّمَ تَحْتَ شَجَرَتَيْنِ فَصَلَّى الظُّهْرَ وَأَخَذَ بِيَدِ عَلِيٍّ رَضِيَ اللَّهُ تَعَالَى عَنْهُ فَقَالَ أَلَسْتُمْ تَعْلَمُونَ أَنِّي أَوْلَى بِالْمُؤْمِنِينَ مِنْ أَنْفُسِهِمْ قَالُوا بَلَى قَالَ أَلَسْتُمْ تَعْلَمُونَ أَنِّي أَوْلَى بِكُلِّ مُؤْمِنٍ مِنْ نَفْسِهِ قَالُوا بَلَى قَالَ فَأَخَذَ بِيَدِ عَلِيٍّ فَقَالَ مَنْ كُنْتُ مَوْلَاهُ فَعَلِيٌّ مَوْلَاهُ اللَّهُمَّ وَالِ مَنْ وَالَاهُ وَعَادِ مَنْ عَادَاهُ قَالَ فَلَقِيَهُ عُمَرُ بَعْدَ ذَلِكَ فَقَالَ هَنِيئًا يَا ابْنَ أَبِي طَالِبٍ أَصْبَحْتَ وَأَمْسَيْتَ مَوْلَى كُلِّ مُؤْمِنٍ وَمُؤْمِنَةٍ قَالَ أَبُو عَبْدِ الرَّحْمَنِ حَدَّثَنَا هُدْبَةُ بْنُ خَالِدٍ حَدَّثَنَا حَمَّادُ بْنُ سَلَمَةَ عَنْ عَلِيِّ بْنِ زَيْدٍ عَنْ عَدِيِّ بْنِ ثَابِتٍ عَنِ الْبَرَاءِ بْنِ عَازِبٍ عَنِ النَّبِيِّ صَلَّى اللَّهُ عَلَيْهِ وَسَلَّمَ نَحْوَهُ

"We were travelling with the Prophet. We stopped by at Ghadir Khumm. So the call for prayer started and we got ready for the congregational prayer. So we made a tent for The Messenger of God between the two trees. He then prayed the Zuhr prayer and rose Ali's hand and said: Do you not know that I possess priority over any believer to himself? They replied: Yes. He then said: Do you know that I am the Master of any man and woman believer? They replied: Yes. So he held Ali's hand and said: Whoever has me as his Master this Ali is his Master. O God love whoever likes him and be enemy to whoever is his enemy. So Umar afterwards came towards Ali and said: I congratulate you O son of Abitaleb you finished your day this way. You are

now the Master of any believer, man and woman."

Dr: Do you now accept that Ghadir did take place and the Prophet did say these things?

Sh Usman: We knew, but we had not read it like this detailed.

Dr. Zohair: I had never heard any of this. This is the first time as a Muslim I have listened to something called Ghadir Khumm.

Sh: Because the discussion is, so there was no reason for the public to know about it.

Dr. Zohair: What kind of a specialized discussion is this when a Mechanic Engineer knows this much about it and only you have heard about it, but I and the majority of Sunni Muslims have never heard about it?

Dr: Just like Sheikh said, there was no reason for you to know, if you found out, questions would have risen.

Sh Usman: Yes, but the Muslims should know what the Prophet was doing in his last years as a Prophet and what he said in his last Hajj.

Dr. Zohair: You should have told us about this. Now you say that they should have said something. Who is responsible expect you, religious scholars?

Sh: We have worked very little towards this; we are very behind.

Sh Usman: I think that our work is cut out for us after this Hajj.

Sh: If the Doctor leaves us with it.

Dr: We are debating to achieve the truth.

Sh: And we accepted every truth we got to.

Dr: Thank the Lord that you do not have any prejudice on things that are not scientific.

Sh Usman: Why would we have prejudice on non-scientific things. We can't be responsible for the actions we have done if we were like that on judgment day. God says:

$$\text{«إِنَّما يَخْشَى اللَّهَ مِنْ عِبادِهِ الْعُلَماءُ»}$$

"Only those fear Allah, from among His servants, who have knowledge."

Dr: This verse does have one important fact. It means that whoever is scared of God is wise.

The Doctor & Sheikh's Debate

Sh: This is also an important fact.

Dr. Zohair: Let us return to the Ghadir discussion. Please do not go into sidelines I am scared that we won't have enough time.

Dr: Yes, let us return to our discussion.

Sh: Yes, you are right.

Dr: Now that you all accept that Ghadir does exist and that the Prophet did speak about it. I have a question.

Sh: Please go ahead.

Dr: In your opinion, the Prophet stayed for three days at Ghadir Khumm gathering people to only then speak for ten minutes and mention just a few sentences?

Sh: There must have been more.

Dr: Then why is there no reference to it?

Sh: I do not know.

Dr: We have a Hadith from the Prophet in our books that work well with many things.

Sh Usman: What is that, Hadith?

Dr:

" «العقل ما عبد به الرحمان واكتسب به الجنان»

"The mind is what people use to praise God and to obtain heaven".

Dr. Zohair: This is very interesting.

Dr: Well, now let us use our brain as a judge. Please study the small book of Ghadir speech that I gave you. Can that book be closer to what happened and closer to the Prophet's speech or a couple of sentences that were mentioned in your books?

Sh Usman: The mind says that it would be justice to say that the long and loud and clear speech that looked more like a will and its substantial part primarily consisted on Ali and him being The Prophet's successor is closer to the truth. Because it is also mentioned in our books that the Prophet said: It's his last years. However, we accept this then we have to admit that the Ahl al Bayt School is closer to the true Islam.

Dr. Zohair: Have you not already accepted this? I already started to doubt my beliefs from day one, and it has been two or three days that I have come to a firm conclusion that the Doctor's words are the truth.

Sh Usman: I think that Sheikh Ibrahim was feeling the same and that is why he was telling us that it is bad for us that we do not have anything wise to respond in return to what the Doctor says in Medina.

Sh: To be honest with you once I read the Prophet's speech yesterday, I was ashamed as a religious scholar for not having read the book before. In regards to using my mind just like the Doctor is saying, I believe that the long speech is closer to what truthfully happened in Ghadir.

Sh Usman: There is one thing that we can conclude from, and that is the Hadith's that the Doctor brought forth from our books.

Dr: What conclusion?

Sh Usman: This conclusion: If we gather all of the Hadith's regarding Ghadir from all of our various books and take away the similar parts and add all the elements that our clerks have either removed (as the Doctor said) or remained quiet and never spoke of it; we end up with the same content the Doctor gave us which is the long speech of Zeyd Ibn Arqam.

Dr: You are right.

Sh: But my heart still has a little doubt over the word "Vali" Meaning "Master" or "protector" even though we have talked about this before.

Dr: Dear Sheikh, it is only because your Scholars have not managed to interpret the word very well.

Sh: Our language is Arabic. Even though we are not initially from Arab ethnic background, our countries such as Syria, Egypt, Iraq, Sudan and all of Africa were conquered, and Islam made them Arabs. "Moala" Means friend to us not Master.

Dr: Our Language isn't Arabic and even for us "Moala" is translated with many meanings, and one of them is "friends." In fact, in the book of words, "friends" is in the fourth or fifth possible translation for "Moala."

Sh: Yes, it does have other meanings too, but all of our scholars say that when the Prophet said: "Moala" he meant, be friends with Ali and not Ali is your Master.

The Doctor & Sheikh's Debate

Dr: Do you mean to say that the Prophet gathered people for three days, kept them under the heated sun so he would tell people to be friends with Ali?

Sh: Of course, what you say also makes sense.

Dr: We have many verses in the Quran that talk about the word: "Vali" and its meaning. The verse in Al Surat Al-Maida that I brought up so that this confusion would not arise says:

$$رَسُولُهُ وَ اللَّهُ وَلِيُّكُمْ إِنَّما$$

Do you think that this "Vali" means "friends"? So, it is saying God and his Prophet are your friends? Alternatively, does it mean God and his Prophet are your Master's?

Sh: Here, it means Masters.

Dr: How come in the Ghadir's speech, it means friends when it is such a vital affair so much so that if it was not done, then his duty as a Messenger was not completed.

Sh: Unfortunately, I have not seen even one book stating that the word "Vali" in Ghadir meaning Master. That is why in all of our books, it is mentioned this way or else you are right. It does not make sense for the Prophet to gather all those people to say be friends with Ali.

Dr: I did explain before. These books were written one hundred and fifty years after the Prophet died. It was natural for such a translation as the Caliphate had already happened and they had to defend it.

Sh: Defend what?

Dr: When Muawiyah, Yazid and Marwan end up being Caliphas and then all of the Amavis and then Abbasies after them, looking upon being Caliphate as a monarchy instead of being the Prophet's Caliphate. It is only just for them to interpret the meaning of the Hadith and the Prophet's speech in such a way. If they had allowed the truth to be out, they would have had to give the Caliphate to the Ahl al Bayt.

Sh: That is also correct. We do have in history that at the time of the debate over Caliphate, Abubakr and Ali told the companions that have you forgotten Ghadir? They replied: No.

Dr: We discussed before that because the Prophet said: "بعــدي مؤمن كل ولــي" then we cannot afterward define its meaning and say "Vali" means friend.

Sh: Of course, even if it did mean friends, we could also say what you were saying before. That it shows, Ali was such an important person that because of him the Prophet stopped at Ghadir. So, such a person should have been the Calipha.

Sh Usman: Dear Sheikh, it is not right to say that "بعدي مؤمن كل ولي" means friends of all believers after the Prophet. Ali was already the friend of believers before and after the Prophet.

Dr: God bless your parents. That is precisely what I'm trying to say.

Sh: Sheikh Usman, I am trying to respect your presence as you are older and wiser and I was trying to answer on your behalf or else it only makes sense to say "بعدي مؤمن كل ولي" means Master.

Dr: You made my job easier. I was beginning to doubt that we are back to square one.

Sh Usman: Doctor, did the Prophet not appoint Abubakr to pray for the last time and asked for him to be Imam and as a result, he became Calipha?

Dr: The Prophet's straightforward speech in front of one hundred and twenty thousand people, for three days under the sun means befriending Ali. However, the silence of the Prophet regarding Abubakr's praying is a clear indication for choosing his successor as Calipha after him.

Sh: I always thought that you had a hidden intention for not talking about this part of the debate earlier on.

Dr: This is the most important Islamic debate that, unfortunately, does not get much-paid attention.

Sh: But it is astonishing how people at the time of the Prophet did not listen to such things.

Dr: Some of the companions did listen, but no one else listened to them.

Sh: Had all the people not heard this?

Dr: Yes, they had, but there was still prejudice over tribal and ethnic immigrants and supporters of Ous and Khazraj.

Sh: Why did the closest companions not say anything?

Dr: Have you not heard of the Saqifah Bani Saida, which was the place where they were debating?

Sh: Please tell us.

Dr: In your history books it is a uniformly agreed thing that the following event happened: The day that the Prophet died Saeid Ibn Ibadeh, the leader of the tribe Khazraj Kabir, was ill. They wrapped a rug around him and brought him to Saqifah. Some of the supporters were also there. He said: O supporters if we were not here then there would have been no religion and no Prophet We prepared Medina.

We gave the Prophet the government he wanted. Now that he is dead, it is our time to be Calipha and Masters. He then started to prepare himself for becoming Calipha. His cousin, Saed Ibn Jobayr, leader of the Khazraj Saqir was jealous of Saeid Ibn Ibadeh becoming Calipha so he told someone to go to the Mosque so that he could tell the immigrants what was happening so that the supporters could be involved in choosing a Calipha. Abubakr and Umar came over, and the great discussion began to start from there. That Quraysh and the immigrants and supporters were to become ministers. Therefore, the choosing of the Calipha at the Saqifah was not a request God had made. They didn't want the supporters to get the power of running the government and let the government fall into the hands of Quraysh. As some of them were named like, Abu Sofyan, who had gone to war against the Prophet for many years.

Sh: Exactly who was in Saqifah at the time?

Dr: I don't see it necessary to mention all of the names that were there. I care more about the Calipha affair.

Sh Usman: Dear Sheikh, it is an essential thing, but it isn't necessary right now to talk about singling people out. The Doctor wishes to discuss the Caliphate, so let us not go after naming anyone.

Dr: I agree. I don't want us to focus on naming anyone. The source of the affair is essential. If you remember before I mentioned that after the Prophet, two things happen. One was regarding the School of Ahl al Bayt, and the other was the choosing of Calipha. My debate is proving this affair, that the real Islam is the Ahl al Bayts. Therefore, if you wish to have more reasoning, please ask me.

Sh: We are after the truth and not to preserve our own beliefs, especially if they are incorrect.

Dr: May God bless you.

Sh: Have you seen the word "Vali" (Master) used for Ali in our books?

Dr: Yes, there is.

Sh: May I see?

Dr: In the book of Munaqib Ali Ibn Abitaleb regarding Ibn Mardaviyah that passed away on 1031. A.D, page 102 says:

1. «عن انس بن مالك قال: قال رسول الله ان اخي ووزيري وخير من اخلف بعدي علي بن ابي طالب.»

"Ins Ibn Malek says that the Prophet said: the best brother and minister and best person that I have to leave after myself is Ali Ibn Abitaleb."

2. «قال رسول‌الله: ان خليلي ووزيري وخليفتي وخير من اترك بعدي يقضي ديني وينجز موعدي علي بن ابي طالب.»

"The Prophet said: My friend, minister and Calipha after me and the best person that I leave after myself and he is in charge of my debt and to practice my legacy is Ali Ibn Abitaleb."

3. «عن سلمان قال: قلت يا رسول الله عمن نأخذ بعدك وبمن نثق؟ فسكت عني حتى سألت عشراً ثم قال يا سلمان ان وصيي وخليفتي واخي ووزيري وخير من اخلف بعدي علي‌بن ابي‌طالب يؤدي عني و ينجز موعدي»

"Salman says: I asked the Prophet: Who can we trust and follow your religion after you are gone? He remained quiet but I repeated my question for ten times. He then replied: Henceforth my successor, Calipha, brother and minister and the best person I leave behind, Ali Ibn Abitaleb he is in charge of my debt and is to practice my legacy."

Sh: These are interesting Hadith's.

Dr: Here you are. In Jame Al Ahadis has also mentioned the other books chains of transmissions.

Jame Al Javamah, volume 1, page 5591:

112: «أما ترضى يا علي أن تكون مني بمنزلةْ هارون من موسى إلا أنك لست بنبي إنه لا ينبغي لي أن أذهب إلا وأنت خليفتي (أحمد عن ابن عباس بإسناد حسن)
أخرجه أحمد (1/330، رقم 3062). وأخرجه أيضًا: الطبراني (12/97، رقم 12593)، والحاكم (3/143، رقم 4652). قال الهيثمي (9/120): رواه أحمد، والطبراني في الكبير، والأوسط باختصار، و رجال أحمد رجال الصحيح غير أبي بلج الفزاري، وهو ثقةْ، وفيه لين.

"O Ali are you not happy to be like Haroon was to Moses for me? With the difference that you are not a Prophet and I cannot pass away unless you are my Calipha."

Sh: But this was regarding the war of Tabuk.

Dr: Yes, but you didn't say where this was said. Then you would see then the actual meaning of Calipha has been persisted. Of course, there are more samples.

In Kanzal Amaal regarding the virtues of Ali, volume 13, page 158:

36488: «عن علي أن النبي صلي الله عليه وسلم قال: خلفتك أن تكون خليفتي، قلت: أتخلف عنك يا رسول‌الله؟ قال: ألا ترض أن تكون مني بمنزلةْ هارون من موسى إلا أنه لا نبي بعدي.»

The Doctor & Sheikh's Debate

"Ali says the Prophet said: I leave you to be my Calipha after me. I asked him: You want me to be your Calipha O Messenger of God? He replied: Are you not happy to be like Haroon was to Moses for me? Unless, there is no Prophet after me."

Sh: This one is a little different even though it was regarding the Tabuk affair.

Dr: This one goes back to Ghadir but just like other issues; these Hadith's don't mention Ghadir. It is from the book of Al Marefah and Al Tarikh, volume 1, page 294:

296: «حدثنا عبيدالله قال: أخبرنا شريك عن الركين عن قاسم بن حسان عن زيد بن ثابت قال: قال رسول الله صلي الله عليه وسلم: إني تارك فيكم خليفتي، كتاب الله عزوجل وعترتي اهل‌بيتي وإنهما لن يتفرقا حتى يردا علي الحوض»

"Zeyd Ibn Sabet said that the Prophet said: I leave behind my Calipha and the Book of Almighty God, My descendants and my Ahl al Bayt. And these two are inseparable and at Basin of Kawthar they will return to me"

Sh: This was interesting as it says that the Calipha is his Ahl al Bayt.

Dr: These other Hadith's also speak about the word "Vali" meaning Master as well: In Sunan Tarmazi; Manaqib Hadith, number 3646; Musnad Ahmad and Musnad Al Kunin Hadith numbers 17749 and 18476 and 18497.

Sh: Please show us.

Dr: Here you are in my mobile programme, Sunan Tarmazi and the rest: That the Prophet at Ghadir Khumm after his speech said:

«يا ايها الناس ان الله مولاي و انا مولي المؤمنين و انا اولي بانفسهم. فمن كنت مولاه فهذا مولاه، اللّهمّ و ال من والاه، عاد من عاداه»

"O people, here forth God is my Master and I am the Master of all believers and I possess priority over them. So, whoever I am his Master, this is his Master- O God love whoever loves him and be the enemy of whoever is his enemy."

Dr: Please look here it says God is my Master. You cannot translate this as God is my friend, and I am the friend of believers. So, it shows that "Vali" here is meant as Master.

Sh: I accept.

Sh Usman: Sheikh Ibrahim accepted a long time ago he just has not wanted to admit it.

Dr: Hajj Sheikh Ibrahim, is Sheikh Usman.

Sh: الحمد لله الذي هدانا لهذا و ما كنا لنهتدي لو لا ان هدانا الله

Dr: A beautiful symmetry has happened.

Sh: What symmetry?

Dr: That the Ghadir speech was on the day of 18th of Zihajjah at Ghadir Khumm; and the day that Ali became Calipha, after Usman being killed, was also the 18th of Zihajjah.

Sh Usman: Doctor tonight also seems to be accidentally the 18th of Zihajjah.

Dr: It is a good accident.

Sh Usman: Yes, and the fact that we in such a night accepted that the Prophet chose Ali as his successor is also exciting.

Dr. Zohair: Sheikh Usman are you saying that you are done and you accept that Ali should have been the first Calipha?

Sh Usman: You were the one saying two days ago that the Doctor's discussions were right and the true Islam was the School of Ahl al Bayt.

Dr. Zohair: Yes, I said that. I, but for me, your acceptance was exciting.

Sh Usman: Dear Sheikh Ibrahim, what is your opinion?

Sh: To be honest from the first days, I realized that our information regarding the true Islam was minimal. Mostly the information we have been chosen for us in a way that it can confirm the current cultural state in the Sunni countries. If from the beginning our religious scholars had gone back and looked at our books, they would have realized some good things, especially our researchers.

Dr. Zohair: Are you saying that you also accept that the School of Ahl al Bayt is the real Islam?

Sh: If I say anything but this then I will have to admit to being doing wrong for sixty years. However, I will not do that. I could never ignore reaching to such an obvious truth in religion and then not accept it.

The Companions Remarks after Ali Started as Calipha

Dr: Now that you all accepted that Ali should have been the first successor after the Prophet it wouldn't be so bad if you saw in your own book of Tarikh Yaqubi, volume 1, page 178, how he governed as Calipha after twenty-five years of delay when people showed their allegiance to him. Some of the distinctive companions say these about him.

The Doctor & Sheikh's Debate

Sh: Let us see.

Dr: Here you are in my mobile programme:

> «وقام قوم من الأنصار فتكلموا، وكان أول من تكلم ثابت بن قيس بن شماس الأنصاري، وكان خطيب الأنصار، فقال: والله، يا أميرالمؤمنين، لئن كانوا تقدموك في الولايةْ فما تقدموك في الدين، ولئن كانوا سبقوك أمس فقد لحقتهم اليوم، ولقد كانوا وكنت لا يخفى موضعك، ولا يجهل مكانك، يحتاجون إليك فيما لا يعلمون، وما احتجت إلى أحد مع علمك.»

"And a group of the supporters stood up and began to talk. The first person to speak was Sabet Ibn Qeys Shamas Ansari. He was the spokesperson for the supporters. He said: I swear to God that O Commander of the Faithful, if they went ahead in ruling people they didn't fall ahead of you in religion and if they passed you yesterday you caught up to them today. As they were there you were also there and you never hid your agenda and never hid where you were. They didn't know that they needed you in the times that they didn't know and you never needed anyone because of you being so wise."

> «ثم قام خزيمةْ بن ثابت الأنصاري، وهو ذو الشهادتين، فقال: يا أميرالمؤمنين! ما أصبنا لأمرنا هذا غيرك، ولا كان المنقلب إلا إليك، ولئن صدقنا أنفسنا فيك، فلأنت أقدم الناس إيماناً، وأعلم الناس بالله، وأولى المؤمنين برسول الله، لك ما لهم، وليس لهم ما لك.»

"Then Khazima Ibn Sabet Ansari Zoo Shahadateyn rose and said: O Commander of the Faithful, we didn't want anyone else but you in this affair and there is no one more revolutionary than you and if we wanted to speak honestly about you we then have to say that you are above every person in belief and above everyone wiser to God and closer to the Prophet. Even though they (previous Caliphas) had what you have but what you have they don't"

> «وقام صعصعةْ بن صوحان فقال: والله، يا أميرالمؤمنين، لقد زينت الخلافةْ وما زانتك، ورفعتها وما رفعتك، ولهي إليك أحوج منك إليها.»

"Sa'sa'a Ibn Savahan stood and said: I swear to God O Commander of the Faithful, you have graced being a Calipha and it didn't grace you. You have raised it but it didn't raise you. And it is more dependent on you than you on it"

> «ثم قام مالكْ بن الحارث الأشتر فقال: أيها الناس، هذا وصي الأوصياء، ووارث علم الأنبياء، العظيم البلاء، الحسن الغناء، الذي شهد له كتاب الله بالإيمان، ورسوله بجنةْ الرضوان. من كملت فيه الفضائل، ولم يشك في سابقته وعلمه وفضله الأواخر، ولا الأوائل.»

"Then Malek Ibn Hares Ashtar rose and said: O people here is the trustee of the trustees and the heir of the Prophets wisdom and the greatest in passing all trials and is needlessly so beautiful that the book of God has testified to his faith and his Prophet has testified for him to heaven. He is someone that all of the virtues have completed in him and others from first to last cannot come close to his experience, wisdom and virtues."

«ثم قام عقبةْ بن عمرو فقال: من له يوم كيوم العقبةْ وبيعةْ كبيعةْ الرضوان، والإمام الهدى الذي لا يخاف جوره، والعالم الذي لا يخاف جهله»

"Then Iqba Ibn Amr rose and said: Who else do we have that can be better than the day of Aqabah or can show allegiance better than the Rezvan or be a guiding Imam that there is no fear in his injustice or so wise that no one is scared of his lack of knowledge (he knows everything.)"

Sh: These are incredible testimonials.

Dr. Zohair: We now understand what is Islam? Who is the Calipha? And who are the Ahl al Bayt.

Sh: Just like me.

Dr: I think that our debate is at its end.

Why Is the Imam not Mentioned as Calipha In the Quran?

Before I finish our discussion, I wanted to add something that most Wahabi's find troublesome. Do they say that if the Imam was there why has the Quran not mentioned anything about the Prophet's Calipha?

Sh: Yes, I had heard about it before.

Dr: The response is in the speech of Ghadir.

Sh: How come?

Dr: In the speech of Ghadir, we talk about "Velayat" (Guardianship) not "Imamat" (Supreme leadership).

Sh: What do you mean?

Dr: It means that God and his Prophet have Velayat over us; therefore, the successor of the Prophet has Velayat over the people. Imamat is the job of a rector, but Velayat has admissibility and guardianship. Even though we have Imamat in Quran regarding Ibrahim but that particular Imamat is even higher valued than some of the Prophets.

Sh: That is an interesting point.

Dr: Yes, in the culture of Quran and School of Ahl al Bayt we have something called the "Vali Amr," "Master of affairs" but it is not like an Imam. For people to not confuse Imam with Calipha in the Shia culture, this has been spread or else the original path is Velayat. Surat Al-Maida, verse 55, is one of the historical subjects for the Imamat affair. We have a Vali, that while prostrating would do "Zakat" (Legal Alms).

Sh: But you do not recognize the Prophet's Caliphas to be Vali.

Dr: We know the Caliphas to be the twelve Prophet's Shia Imams so for them not to get confused with the Caliphas that we were discussing we use the word Imams instead. Of course, it is also said to be like this in the Speech of Ghadir.

Sh: Some say that the Shia's consider the Imams to be higher valued than the Prophet because they say that Imamat was given to Ibrahim after he was assigned as the Prophet.

Dr: Just like I said before if the Imamat is in the same content as Velayat then it is considered in the same lines as the Prophet's Velayat and the God's Velayat, but it is not higher value than that. Ibrahim's Imamat was higher than his Prophecy.

Sh: The word Vali is used less than Imam in Shia' sm.

Dr: Imam has also meant someone that is a pioneer in going to war with deviation. However, we consider them as Vali Amr in action, and they are mostly called Imams amongst Shia people. The scholars debate that the Imam in response is more discussed and currently in Iran, we have Ruling Jurists (Vali Faqih), and we say he is Vali Amr. Imam can also be a slang term.

Sh: That is very interesting.

Dr: Thank the Lord for this blessing.

Sh: Thank the Lord it had a good outcome.

Sh Usman: Thank the Lord for giving us a good reward for this trip to Hajj.

Dr. Zohair: Our poor fathers thought that they were acting based on real Islam in the world.

Sh: But the Quran tells us not to follow our fathers and their fathers' religion if they are wrong.

Sh Usman: The Quran reproaches people that say we will not go against our fathers and their father's religion.

Dr: Yes, Quran says in Surat Al Maida, Verse 104 that the infidels said:

$$\text{وَإِذَا قِيلَ لَهُمْ تَعَالَوْا إِلَىٰ مَا أَنزَلَ اللَّهُ وَإِلَى الرَّسُولِ قَالُوا حَسْبُنَا مَا وَجَدْنَا عَلَيْهِ آبَاءَنَا ۚ أَوَلَوْ كَانَ آبَاؤُهُمْ لَا يَعْلَمُونَ شَيْئًا وَلَا يَهْتَدُونَ ﴿١٠٤﴾}$$

"And when it is said to them, "Come to what Allah has revealed and to the Messenger," they say, "Sufficient for us is that upon which we found our fathers." Even though their fathers knew nothing, nor were they guided?"

Or in Surat Ibrahim, verse number 10 says:

$$\text{وَالَّذِينَ كَفَرُوا وَكَذَّبُوا بِآيَاتِنَا أُولَٰئِكَ أَصْحَابُ الْجَحِيمِ ﴿١٠﴾}$$

"But those who disbelieve and deny our signs - those are the companions of Hellfire."

In Surat Az-Zukhruf, verse number 22 says:

$$\text{بَلْ قَالُوا إِنَّا وَجَدْنَا آبَاءَنَا عَلَىٰ أُمَّةٍ وَإِنَّا عَلَىٰ آثَارِهِم مُّهْتَدُونَ ﴿٢٢﴾}$$

"Rather, they say, "Indeed, we found our fathers upon a religion, and we are in their footsteps [rightly] guided.""

In Surat Luqman, verse number 21 says:

The Doctor & Sheikh's Debate

$$\text{وَإِذَا قِيلَ لَهُمُ ٱتَّبِعُوا۟ مَآ أَنزَلَ ٱللَّهُ قَالُوا۟ بَلْ نَتَّبِعُ مَا وَجَدْنَا عَلَيْهِ ءَابَآءَنَآ ۚ أَوَلَوْ كَانَ ٱلشَّيْطَٰنُ يَدْعُوهُمْ إِلَىٰ عَذَابِ ٱلسَّعِيرِ ﴿٢١﴾}$$

And when it is said to them, "Follow what Allah has revealed," they say, "Rather, we will follow that upon which we found our fathers." Even if Satan was inviting them to the punishment of the hellfire?"

Dr. Zohair: We are not saying that we wish to follow our fathers. There is no reason why should we follow the wrong ways.

Sh Usman: If we do such a thing, then just as these verses are telling us we are no more than infidels. The Quran is saying that only infidels say such a thing.

Dr. Zohair: Now, what shall we do with all the mistakes we made by following the School of Caliphas?

Dr: I know something that might help.

Sh: Please go ahead.

Dr: You are only moving from one sect to another like from Hanbali to Shafia.

Dr. Zohair: When we have not been acting as the Prophet has been telling us. What kind of Muslim are we? It is as if we have now become Muslim. I believe that the other religions are not in the path of Islam, and it is not as if we have moved from the Hanbali faith to the Shafia religion. We have moved from the distorted Islam to true Islam.

Dr: But from the order of the Quran, whoever says his Shahadateyn (Credo of the Islamic faith) then we know him as a Muslim.

Sh: He is just a Muslim it does not mean that he is a believer to all Islam.

$$\text{«نُؤْمِنُ بِبَعْضٍ وَ نَكْفُرُ بِبَعْضٍ»}$$

"We believe in some and disbelieve in others"

Dr. Zohair: In reality, we had problems with after the Prophet, and as the Doctor said, they were not part of Islam.

Dr: Of course, choosing the Calipha that the Prophet assigned for us is part of Islam but not accepting a Calipha that people have chosen is not part of Islam. If you remember Mufti Alazhar, Dr. Ahmad Tayeb says that agreeing with Abubakr and Umar is not part of Islam, for it to be a problem if someone was against it.

Dr. Zohair: How do you know Ahmad Tayeb?

Sh: Mufti Alazhar knows us as well.

Dr. Zohair: From where?

Dr: Yes, I know him. We have even spoken on the phone once.

Dr. Zohair: Where did Ahmad Tayeb say that agreeing or not agreeing with Abubakr and Umar is not part of religion?

Dr: It was being broadcasted once in one of the Egyptian programs on television that were being streamed on our satellite. Dr. Tayeb spoke for eight sessions regarding the differences between the Shia and Sunni.

Sh Usman: What was he saying?

Dr: He was saying that based on the Fitwa that was given fifty years ago by Sheikh Shaltut, the Mufti of the time in Alazhar: Shia' sm is one of the Islamic Schools just like the four other official schools. He said that all of the rumors regarding Shia' sm are a lie.

Dr. Zohair: Did he mention that accepting Abubakr and Umar is not part of Islam, in the same program?

Dr: Yes. The interviewer asked him many of the youth in Egypt have gone towards Shia' sm. Is their Islam correct? Dr. Tayeb responded: Yes, it is accurate. Then the interviewer asked: But the 'Shia's do not agree with Abubakr, Umar, and Usman. Dr. Tayeb said: Are accepting the Caliphas as part of our beliefs?

Dr. Zohair: This means that he agreed with Shia' sm.

Dr: Yes, he was saying that Shia' sm is part of the fifth School of Islam. The interviewer even asked: How is marrying one of them allowed? Dr. Tayeb said: It is as if you are marrying from another School of religion.

Dr. Zohair: Now that I have accepted the School of Ahl al Bayt. It is going to be difficult for me to learn their Fiqh. I need to marry a Shia.

The Doctor & Sheikh's Debate

Dr: Thankfully, the School of Ahl al Bayt has spread so much in the world that you can have all of its provisions available to you quickly.

Sh Usman: Where can we buy the books of Fiqh from?

Dr: As I said before it can be found in Egypt as well. You can also try accessing over a thousand Shia sites and information on the School of Ahl Al Bayt before even trying to find books. You can find all of the Fiqh provisions from there.

Dr. Zohair: But I prefer to get a Shia wife so she could teach me everything.

Sh: I would like to ask the Doctor to keep in touch with us so we could contact him with any questions we may have. This is because some of the contents may be in the Persian language.

Dr: In the past twenty years, the School of Ahl al Bayt has spread in the world. From the survey I have from the Muslim Scholars Council which is run by Doctor Qarzavi from Qatar; I heard that Muslim countries such as Indonesia or Nigeria that have had no Shia have now, thirty million and twenty million respectively. In other countries, the trend is also rising. This was confirmed by the Iranian representative that was in the council. Therefore, the jurisprudential books for them are available in their languages.

Sh: Is it growing that fast?

Dr: Yes, very much. Thank the Lord after the revolution of Islamic Iran a positive message spread, and after the war of 2006 between Lebanon and Israel, the School of Ahl al Bayt has been very eye-catching in Arabian countries especially Egypt, Saudi Arabia, Turkey, and African countries.

Dr. Zohair: They must have had a Doctor like you to guide them.

Dr: They don't have people like Sheikh Ibrahim or Sheikh Usman that know so much of the details of the School of Ahl al Bayt. I have seen people that have converted just by talking to them for a brief couple of sessions in my various trips of Mecca. Only by answering straightforward and logical questions they have started to follow the School of Ahl al Bayt.

Dr. Zohair: The Doctor is right. For instance, after observing some of your sessions and listening to what he had to say, I realized how logical and informative he was. That is why it has been a couple of days since I have understood that the School of Ahl al Bayt is the true Islam.

Sh: Dear Doctor Zohair is mustn't be that problematic to accept the truth so speedily. However, for people like Sheikh Usman and me it is not just acceptable to agree with it we have to answer back to people in Alazhar and tell them why we have chosen the Ahl al Bayt over the Caliphate. Alternatively, else, it is evident to me at the beginning of the days that the School of Ahl al Bayt was the right one. However, after asking many questions, I went into depth for it to be clear for me, and now I have all of my questions answered.

Sh Usman: Unfortunately, I was not there at the beginning of your discussion, and I have lost many of the information that was talked about.

Sh: In the session that we were at Sheikh Hamid Najdi, Doctor used our own Hadith's and showed us that our Wudu, call for prayer, Hamd, and Surah, Tashahod, etc... were all wrong. He questioned all of our ways that we pray and Sheikh Hamid had nothing to say and almost agreed to everything the Doctor said.

Sh Usman: A wise person would never object or disagree with anything that is analytically logical not only regarding religion but even in life.

Sh: Now, if we go back and look at the previous discussion and all of the cases that have been talked about there is not one question that the School of Ahl al Bayt cannot answer. Whereas in our School or better say, as the Doctor says, School of Caliphates, there are thousands of questions that we hear "No" as an answer to it. Even our greatest scholars cannot answer to them. Now in School of Ahl al Bayt, a person that is specialized as a Mechanical Engineer has this much information. That is, in my opinion, the reason because their information is so logical and straightforward.

Sh Usman: Yes, I agree. If you realized, Sheikh Ibrahim and I were weak at the parts where the debate was logical and straightforward.

Dr: I did also bring up Hadith's and citations from your books and the Quran.

Sh: But just like you had said, your discussions were much organized like one, two, and three.

Dr: I am not that knowledgeable regarding my religious affairs. I only know enough to defend my religion and beliefs. If you have accepted the School of Ahl al Bayt after a month of discussing it, with the truth-seeking personalities that you all have, I am sure that if you had come to a religious clerk, you would have accepted it in one or two days.

Sh Usman: But we do not have access to many books regarding the information on the Ahl al Bayt.

Dr: That is not a problem if you wish we could go to the Iranian cultural exchange of Hajj. There are plenty of books and CDs there that you could buy and have for now and then you can buy more from Egypt and Lebanon. God willing, you can purchase books for School of Ahl al Bayt there.

Sh: What about from Iran?

Dr: If the relationship between Egypt and Iran became better than I would love to send you books.

Sh: So, let us go at ten O'clock in the morning tomorrow to the Iranian cultural exchange book store.

Dr: God willing, ten in the morning tomorrow to this address...We shall go, and you can buy many books and CDs.

Sh: Inevitably our last expression is: "دعوانا الحمدلله رب العالمين"

This book was written and completed on the twentieth day

First of Ramadan,

The Anniversary of the Martyrdom of Imam Ali.

Appendix One: The Complete Speech of Ghadir in Arabic by The Messenger of God

بسم الله الرحمن الرحيم

اَلْحَمْدُ لِلَّهِ الَّذِي عَلا فِي تَوَحُّدِهِ وَ دَنا فِي تَفَرُّدِهِ وَجَلَّ فِي سُلْطانِهِ وَعَظُمَ فِي أَرْكانِهِ، وَأَحاطَ بِكُلِّ شَيْءٍ عِلْماً وَ هُوَ فِي مَكانِهِ وَ قَهَرَ جَمِيعَ الْخَلْقِ بِقُدْرَتِهِ وَ بُرْهانِهِ، حَمِيداً لَمْ يَزَلْ، مَحْمُوداً لايَزالُ (وَ مَجِيداً لايَزُولُ، وَمُبْدِئاً وَمُعِيداً وَ كُلُّ أَمْرٍ إِلَيْهِ يَعُودُ). بارِئُ الْمَسْمُوكاتِ وداحِي الْمَدْحُوَّاتِ وَجَبّارُ الْأَرَضِينَ وَ السَّماواتِ، قُدُّوسٌ سُبُّوحٌ، رَبُّ الْمَلائِكَةِ وَالرُّوحِ، مُتَفَضِّلٌ عَلى جَمِيعِ مَنْ بَرَأَهُ، مُتَطَوِّلٌ عَلى جَمِيعِ مَنْ أَنْشَأَهُ. يَلْحَظُ كُلَّ عَيْنٍ وَالْعُيُونُ لاتَراهُ. كَرِيمٌ حَلِيمٌ ذُوأَناةٍ، قَدْ وَسِعَ كُلَّ شَيْءٍ رَحْمَتُهُ وَ مَنَّ عَلَيهِمْ بِنِعْمَتِهِ. لا يَعْجَلُ بِانْتِقامِهِ، وَلايُبادِرُ إِلَيهِمْ بِمَا اسْتَحَقُّوا مِنْ عَذابِهِ. قَدْفَهِمَ السَّرائِرَ وَ عَلِمَ الضَّمائِرَ، وَلَمْ تَخْفَ عَلَيْهِ اَلْمَكْنُوناتُ ولا اشْتَبَهَتْ عَلَيهِ الْخَفِيّاتُ. لَهُ الْإِحاطَةُ بِكُلِّ شَيْءٍ، والْغَلَبَةُ عَلى كُلِّ شَيْءٍ والْقُوَّةُ فِي كُلِّ شَيْءٍ والْقُدْرَةُ عَلى كُلِّ شَيْءٍ وَلَيْسَ مِثْلَهُ شَيْءٌ. وَ هُوَ مُنْشِئُ الشَّيْءِ حِينَ لاشَيْءٌ دائِمٌ حَيٌّ وَقائِمٌ بِالْقِسْطِ، لاإِلهَ إِلاّ هُوَ الْعَزِيزُالْحَكِيمُ. جَلَّ عَنْ أَنْ تُدْرِكَهُ الْأَبْصارُ وَ هُوَ يُدْرِكُ الْأَبْصارَ وَ هُوَاللَّطِيفُ الْخَبِيرُ. لايَلْحَقُ أَحَدٌ وَصْفَهُ مِنْ مُعايَنَةٍ، وَلايَجِدُ أَحَدٌ كَيْفَ هُوَمِنْ سِرٍّ وَ عَلانِيَةٍ إِلاّ بِمادَلَّ عَزَّوَجَلَّ عَلى نَفْسِهِ. وَأَشْهَدُ أَنَّهُ اللهُ الَّذِي مَلَأَ الدَّهْرَ قُدْسُهُ، وَالَّذِي يَغْشَى الْأَبَدَ نُورُهُ، وَالَّذِي يُنْفِذُ أَمْرَهُ بِلامُشاوَرَةِ مُشِيرٍ وَلامَعَهُ شَرِيكٌ فِي تَقْدِيرِهِ وَلايعاوَنُ فِي تَدْبِيرِهِ. صَوَّرَ مَا ابْتَدَعَ عَلى غَيْرِ مِثالٍ، وَ خَلَقَ مَا خَلَقَ بِلامَعُونَةٍ مِنْ أَحَدٍ وَلا تَكَلُّفٍ وَلاَ احْتِيالٍ. أَنْشَأَها فَكانَتْ وَ بَرَأَها فَبانَتْ. فَهُوَاللهُ الَّذِي لا إِلهَ إِلاّ هُوَالْمُتْقِنُ الصَّنْعَةَ، اَلْحَسَنُ الصَّنِيعَةِ، الْعَدْلُ الَّذِي لايَجُورُ، وَالْأَكْرَمُ الَّذِي تَرْجِعُ إِلَيْهِ الْأُمُورُ. وَأَشْهَدُ أَنَّهُ اللهُ الَّذِي تَواضَعَ كُلُّ شَيْءٍ لِعَظَمَتِهِ، وَذَلَّ كُلُّ شَيْءٍ لِعِزَّتِهِ، وَاسْتَسْلَمَ كُلُّ شَيْءٍ لِقُدْرَتِهِ، وَخَضَعَ كُلُّ شَيْءٍ لِهَيْبَتِهِ. مَلِكُ الْأَمْلاكِ وَ مُفَلِّكُ الْأَفْلاكِ وَمُسَخِّرُ الشَّمْسِ وَالْقَمَرِ، كُلٌّ يَجْرِي لِأَجَلٍ مُسَمّىً. يُكَوِّرُاللَّيْلَ عَلَى النَّهارِ وَيُكَوِّرُالنَّهارَ عَلَى اللَّيلِ يَطْلُبُهُ حَثِيثاً. قاصِمُ كُلِّ جَبّارٍ عَنِيدٍ وَ مُهْلِكُ كُلِّ شَيْطانٍ مَرِيدٍ. لَمْ يَكُنْ لَهُ ضِدٌّ وَلا مَعَهُ نِدٌّ أَحَدٌ صَمَدٌ لَمْ يَلِدْ وَلَمْ يُولَدْ وَلَمْ يَكُنْ لَهُ كُفُواً أَحَدٌ. إِلهٌ واحِدٌ وَرَبٌّ ماجِدٌ يَشاءُ فَيُمْضِي، وَيُرِيدُ فَيَقْضِي، وَيَعْلَمُ فَيُحْصِي، وَيُمِيتُ وَيُحْيِي، وَيُفْقِرُ وَيُغْنِي، وَيُضْحِكُ وَيُبْكِي، (وَيُدْنِي وَ يُقْصِي) وَيَمْنَعُ وَ يُعْطِي، لَهُ الْمُلْكُ وَلَهُ الْحَمْدُ، بِيَدِهِ الْخَيْرُ وَ هُوَ عَلى كُلِّ شَيْءٍ قَدِيرٌ. يُولِجُ اللَّيْلَ فِي النَّهارِ وَيُولِجُ النَّهارَ فِي اللَّيْلِ، لاإِلهَ إِلاّهُوَالْعَزِيزُ الْغَفّارُ. مُسْتَجِيبُ الدُّعاءِ وَمُجْزِلُ الْعَطاءِ، مُحْصِي الْأَنْفاسِ وَ رَبُّ الْجِنَّةِ وَالنّاسِ، الَّذِي لايَشْكُلُ عَلَيْهِ شَيْءٌ، وَ لايَضْجِرُهُ صُراخُ الْمُسْتَصْرِخِينَ وَلايُبْرِمُهُ إِلْحاحُ الْمُلِحِّينَ. اَلْعاصِمُ لِلصّالِحِينَ، وَالْمُوَفِّقُ لِلْمُفْلِحِينَ، وَ مَوْلَى الْمُؤْمِنِينَ وَرَبُّ الْعالَمِينَ. الَّذِي اسْتَحَقَّ مِنْ كُلِّ مَنْ خَلَقَ أَنْ يَشْكُرَهُ وَيَحْمَدَهُ (عَلى كُلِّ حالٍ). أَحْمَدُهُ كَثِيراً وَأَشْكُرُهُ دائِماً عَلَى السَّرّاءِ والضَّرّاءِ والشِّدَّةِ وَالرَّخاءِ، وَأُومِنُ بِهِ وَ بِمَلائِكَتِهِ وكُتُبِهِ وَرُسُلِهِ. أَسْمَعُ لِأَمْرِهِ وَأُطِيعُ وَأُبادِرُ إِلى كُلِّ مايُرْضِيهِ وَأَسْتَسْلِمُ لِماقَضاهُ، رَغْبَةً فِي طاعَتِهِ وَ خَوْفاً مِنْ عُقُوبَتِهِ، لِأَنَّهُ اللهُ الَّذِي لايُؤْمَنُ مَكْرُهُ وَلايَخافُ جَوْرُهُ.

أمرٌ إلهيٌ في موضوع هامّ

وَأُقِرُّلَهُ عَلى نَفْسِي بِالْعُبُودِيَّةِ وَ أَشْهَدُ لَهُ بِالرُّبُوبِيَّةِ، وَأُؤَدِّي مَا أَوْحى بِهِ إِلَيَّ حَذَراً مِنْ أَنْ لا أَفْعَلَ فَتَحِلَّ بِي مِنْهُ قارِعَةٌ لايَدْفَعُها عَنِّي أَحَدٌ وَإِنْ عَظُمَتْ حِيلَتُهُ وَصَفَتْ خُلَّتُهُ ـ لاإِلهَ إِلاّهُوَ ـ لِأَنَّهُ قَدْأَعْلَمَنِي أَنِّي إِنْ لَمْ أُبَلِّغْ مَا أَنْزَلَ إِلَيَّ (فِي حَقِّ عَلِيٍّ) فَما بَلَّغْتُ رِسالَتَهُ، وَقَدْ ضَمِنَ لِي تَبارَكَ وَتَعالَى الْعِصْمَةَ (مِنَ النّاسِ) وَ هُوَاللهُ الْكافِي الْكَرِيمُ. فَأَوْحى إِلَيَّ: (بِسْمِ اللَّهِ الرَّحْمَنِ الرَّحِيمِ، يَا أَيُّهَا الرَّسُولُ بَلِّغْ مَا أُنْزِلَ إِلَيْكَ مِنْ رَبِّكَ ـ فِي عَلِيٍّ يَعْنِي فِي الْخِلافَةِ لِعَلِيِّ بْنِ أَبِي طالِبٍ ـ وَ إِنْ لَمْ تَفْعَلْ فَما بَلَّغْتَ رِسالَتَهُ وَ اللَّهُ يَعْصِمُكَ مِنَ النَّاسِ).

مَعاشِرَالنّاسِ، مَا قَصَّرْتُ فِي تَبْلِيغِ مَا أَنْزَلَ اللهُ تَعالى إِلَيَّ، وَ أَنَا أُبَيِّنُ لَكُمْ سَبَبَ هذِهِ الْآيَةِ: إِنَّ جَبْرَئِيلَ هَبَطَ إِلَيَّ مِراراً ثَلاثاً يَأْمُرُنِي عَنِ السَّلامِ رَبِّي ـ وَ هُوَالسَّلامُ ـ أَنْ أَقُومَ فِي هذَا الْمَشْهَدِ فَأُعْلِمَ كُلَّ أَبْيَضَ وَأَسْوَدَ: أَنَّ عَلِيَّ بْنَ أَبِي طالِبٍ أَخِي وَ وَصِيِّي وَ خَلِيفَتِي (عَلى أُمَّتِي) وَالْإِمامُ مِنْ بَعْدِي، الَّذِي مَحَلُّهُ مِنِّي مَحَلُّ هارُونَ مِنْ مُوسى إِلاّ أَنَّهُ لانَبِيَّ بَعْدِي وَهُوَ وَلِيُّكُمْ بَعْدَاللهِ وَ رَسُولِهِ.

The Doctor & Sheikh's Debate

وَقَدْ أَنْزَلَ الله تبارك و تعالي عَلَي ذَالِكَ آيَةً مِنْ كِتَابِهِ (هي): (إنَّمَا وَلِيُّكُمُ اللَّهُ وَ رَسُولُهُ وَ الَّذِينَ آمَنُوا الَّذِينَ يُقِيمُونَ الصَّلاةَ وَ يُؤْتُونَ الزَّكَاةَ وَ هُمْ رَاكِعُونَ)، وَ عَلِيُّ بْنُ أَبِي طَالِبٍ الَّذِي أَقَامَ الصَّلاةَ وَ آتَي الزَّكَاةَ وَهُوَ رَاكِعٌ وَهُوَ يُرِيدُالله عَزَّوَجَلَّ فِي كُلِّ حَالٍ.

وَسَأَلْتُ جَبْرَئِيلَ أَنْ يَسْتَعْفِي لِي (السَّلامَ) عَنْ تَبْلِيغِ ذَالِكَ إِلَيْكُمْ ـ أَيُّهَاالنَّاسُ ـ لِعِلْمِي بِقِلَّةِ الْمُتَّقِينَ وَكَثْرَةِ الْمُنَافِقِينَ وَإِدْغَالِ اللَّائِمِينَ وَ حِيَلِ الْمُسْتَهْزِئِينَ بِالْإِسْلامِ، الَّذِينَ وَصَفَهُمُ الله فِي كِتَابِهِ بِأَنَّهُمْ يَقُولُونَ بِأَلْسِنَتِهِمْ مَالَيْسَ فِي قُلُوبِهِمْ، وَيَحْسَبُونَهُ هَيِّناً وَ هُوَ عِنْدَالله عَظِيمٌ.

وَكَثْرَةَ أَذَاهُمْ لِي فِي غَيْرِ مَرَّةٍ حَتَّي سَمَّوْنِي أُذُناً وَ زَعَمُوا أَنِّي كَذَالِكَ لِكَثْرَةِ مُلازَمَتِهِ إِيَّي وَ إِقْبَالِي عَلَيْهِ (وَ هَوَاهُ وَ قَبُولِهِ مِنِّي) حَتَّي أَنْزَلَ الله عَزَّوَجَلَّ فِي ذَالِكَ (وَ مِنْهُمُ الَّذِينَ يُؤْذُونَ النَّبِيَّ وَ يَقُولُونَ هُوَ أُذُنٌ، قُلْ أُذُنُ ـ (عَلَي الَّذِينَ يَزْعُمُونَ أَنَّهُ أُذُنٌ) ـ خَيْرٍ لَكُمْ، يُؤْمِنُ بِاللهِ وَ يُؤْمِنُ لِلْمُؤْمِنِينَ) الآيَةَ.

وَلَوْشِئْتُ أَنْ أُسَمِّي الْقَائِلِينَ بِذَالِكَ بِأَسْمَائِهِمْ لَسَمَّيْتُ وَأَنْ أُومِئَ إِلَيْهِمْ لَأَوْمَأْتُ وَأَنْ أَدُلَّ عَلَيْهِمْ لَدَلَلْتُ، وَلَكِنِّي وَالله فِي أُمُورِهِمْ قَدْ تَكَرَّمْتُ. وَكُلُّ ذَالِكَ لايَرْضَي الله مِنِّي إِلاَّ أَنْ أُبَلِّغَ مَا أَنْزَلَ الله إِلَيَّ (فِي حَقِّ عَلِيٍّ)، ثُمَّ تَلا: (يَا أَيُّهَا الرَّسُولُ بَلِّغْ مَا أُنْزِلَ إِلَيْكَ مِنْ رَبِّكَ ـ فِي حَقِّ عَلِيٍّ ـ وَ إِنْ لَمْ تَفْعَلْ فَمَا بَلَّغْتَ رِسَالَتَهُ وَ اللَّهُ يَعْصِمُكَ مِنَ النَّاسِ).

الإعلان الرسمي بإمامةِ الأئمةِ الاثني عشر عليهم السلام و ولايتهم

فَاعْلَمُوا مَعَاشِرَ النَّاسِ (ذَالِكَ فِيهِ وَافْهَمُوهُ وَاعْلَمُوا) أَنَّ الله قَدْ نَصَبَهُ لَكُمْ وَلِيّاً وَإِمَاماً فَرَضَ طَاعَتَهُ عَلَي الْمُهَاجِرِينَ وَالْأَنْصَارِ وَ عَلَي التَّابِعِينَ لَهُمْ بِإِحْسَانٍ، وَ عَلَي الْبَادِي وَالْحَاضِرِ، وَ عَلَي الْعَجَمِي وَالْعَرَبِي، وَ عَلَي الْحُرِّ وَالْمَمْلُوكِ، وَالصَّغِيرِ وَالْكَبِيرِ، وَ عَلَي الْأَبْيَضِ وَالْأَسْوَدِ، وَ عَلَي كُلِّ مُوَحِّدٍ.

مَاضٍ حُكْمُهُ، جَازٍ قَوْلُهُ، نَافِذٌ أَمْرُهُ، مَلْعُونٌ مَنْ خَالَفَهُ، مَرْحُومٌ مَنْ تَبِعَهُ وَ صَدَّقَهُ، فَقَدْ غَفَرَالله لَهُ وَلِمَنْ سَمِعَ مِنْهُ وَ أَطَاعَ لَهُ.

مَعَاشِرَالنَّاسِ، إِنَّهُ آخِرُ مَقَامٍ أَقُومُهُ فِي هَذَا الْمَشْهَدِ، فَاسْمَعُوا وَ أَطِيعُوا وَانْقَادُوا لِأَمْرِ (الله) رَبِّكُمْ، فَإِنَّ الله عَزَّوَجَلَّ هُوَ مَوْلاكُمْ وَإِلَهُكُمْ، ثُمَّ مِنْ دُونِهِ رَسُولُهُ وَنَبِيُّهُ الْمُخَاطِبُ لَكُمْ، ثُمَّ مِنْ بَعْدِي عَلِيٌّ وَلِيُّكُمْ وَ إِمَامُكُمْ بِأَمْرِالله رَبِّكُمْ، ثُمَّ الْإِمَامَةُ فِي ذُرِّيَّتِي مِنْ وُلْدِهِ إِلَي يَوْمٍ تَلْقَوْنَ الله وَرَسُولَهُ.

لاحَلالَ إِلاَّ مَا أَحَلَّهُ الله وَ رَسُولُهُ وَهُمْ، وَلاحَرَامَ إِلاَّ مَا حَرَّمَهُ الله (عَلَيْكُمْ) وَ رَسُولُهُ وَ هُمْ، وَالله عَزَّوَجَلَّ عَرَّفَنِي الْحَلالَ وَالْحَرَامَ وَأَنَا أَفْضَيْتُ بِمَا عَلَّمَنِي رَبِّي مِنْ كِتَابِهِ وَحَلالِهِ وَ حَرَامِهِ إِلَيْهِ.

مَعَاشِرَالنَّاسِ، عَلِيٌّ (فَضِّلُوهُ). مَامِنْ عِلْمٍ إِلاَّ وَقَدْ أَحْصَاهُ الله فِيَّ، وَ كُلُّ عِلْمٍ عُلِّمْتُ فَقَدْ أَحْصَيْتُهُ فِي إِمَامِ الْمُتَّقِينَ، وَمَا مِنْ عِلْمٍ إِلاَّ وَقَدْ عَلَّمْتُهُ عَلِيّاً، وَ هُوَ الْإِمَامُ الْمُبِينُ (الَّذِي ذَكَرَهُ الله فِي سُورَةٍ يس: (وَ كُلَّ شَيْءٍ أَحْصَيْنَاهُ فِي إِمَامٍ مُبِينٍ).

مَعَاشِرَالنَّاسِ، لاتَضِلُّوا عَنْهُ وَلاتَنْفِرُوا مِنْهُ، وَلاتَسْتَنْكِفُوا عَنْ وِلايَتِهِ، فَهُوَالَّذِي يَهْدِي إِلَي الْحَقِّ وَيَعْمَلُ بِهِ، وَيُزْهِقُ الْبَاطِلَ وَيَنْهَي عَنْهُ، وَلاتَأْخُذُهُ فِي الله لَوْمَةُ لائِمٍ. أَوَّلُ مَنْ آمَنَ بِاللهِ وَ رَسُولِهِ (لَمْ يَسْبِقْهُ إِلَي الْإِيمَانِ بِي أَحَدٌ)، وَالَّذِي فَدَي رَسُولَ الله بِنَفْسِهِ، وَالَّذِي كَانَ مَعَ رَسُولِ الله وَلا أَحَدَ يَعْبُدُالله مَعَ رَسُولِهِ مِنَ الرِّجَالِ غَيْرُهُ.

(أَوَّلُ النَّاسِ صَلاةً وَ أَوَّلُ مَنْ عَبَدَالله مَعِي. أَمَرْتُهُ عَنِ الله أَنْ يَنَامَ فِي مَضْجَعِي، فَفَعَلَ فَادِياً لِي بِنَفْسِهِ).

مَعَاشِرَالنَّاسِ، فَضِّلُوهُ فَقَدْ فَضَّلَهُ الله، وَاقْبَلُوهُ فَقَدْ نَصَبَهُ الله.

مَعَاشِرَالنَّاسِ، إِنَّهُ إِمَامٌ مِنَ الله، وَلَنْ يَتُوبَ الله عَلَي أَحَدٍ أَنْكَرَ وِلايَتَهُ وَلَنْ يَغْفِرَ لَهُ، حَتْماً عَلَي الله أَنْ يَفْعَلَ ذَالِكَ بِمَنْ خَالَفَ أَمْرَهُ وَأَنْ يُعَذِّبَهُ عَذَاباً نُكْراً أَبَداً الْآبَادَ وَ دَهْرَ الدُّهُورِ. فَاحْذَرُوا أَنْ تُخَالِفُوهُ. فَتَصْلُوا نَاراً وَقُودُهَا النَّاسُ وَالْحِجَارَةُ أُعِدَّتْ لِلْكَافِرِينَ.

مَعاشِرَ النّاسِ، بي ـ وَاللهِ ـ بَشَّرَ الْأَوَّلُونَ مِنَ النَّبِيّينَ وَالْمُرْسَلينَ، وَأَنَا ـ (وَاللهِ) ـ خاتَمُ الْأَنْبِياءِ وَالْمُرْسَلينَ وَالْحُجَّةُ عَلى جَميعِ الْمَخلوقينَ مِنْ أَهْلِ السَّماواتِ وَالْأَرَضينَ. فَمَنْ شَكَّ في ذاِلكَ فَقَدْ كَفَرَ كُفْرَ الْجاهِلِيَّةِ الْأُولى وَمَنْ شَكَّ في شَيْءٍ مِنْ قَوْلي هذا فَقَدْ شَكَّ في كُلِّ ما أُنْزِلَ إِلَيَّ، وَمَنْ شَكَّ في واحِدٍ مِنَ الْأَئِمَّةِ فَقَدْ شَكَّ في الْكُلِّ مِنْهُمْ، وَالشّاكُّ فينا فِي النّارِ.

مَعاشِرَ النّاسِ، حَبانِي اللهُ عَزَّوَجَلَّ بِهذِهِ الْفَضيلَةِ مَنّاً مِنْهُ عَلَيَّ وَإِحْساناً مِنْهُ إِلَيَّ وَلا إِلاهَ إِلّاهُوَ، أَلا لَهُ الْحَمْدُ مِنّي أَبَدَ الْآبِدينَ وَدَهْرَ الدّاهِرينَ وَ عَلى كُلِّ حالٍ.

مَعاشِرَ النّاسِ، فَضِّلُوا عَلِيّاً فَإِنَّهُ أَفْضَلُ النّاسِ بَعْدي مِنْ ذَكَرٍ وَأُنْثى بِنا أَنْزَلَ اللهُ الرِّزْقَ وَبَقِيَ الْخَلْقُ. مَلْعُونٌ مَلْعُونٌ، مَغْضُوبٌ مَغْضُوبٌ مَنْ رَدَّ عَلَيَّ قَوْلي هذا وَلَمْ يُوافِقْهُ.

أَلا إِنَّ جَبْرَئيلَ خَبَّرَني عَنِ اللهِ تَعالى بِذالِكَ وَيَقُولُ: «مَنْ عادى عَلِيّاً وَلَمْ يَتَوَلَّهُ فَعَلَيْهِ لَعْنَتي وَغَضَبي»، (وَ لْتَنْظُرْ نَفْسٌ ما قَدَّمَتْ لِغَدٍ وَاتَّقُوا اللهَ ـ أَنْ تُخالِفُوهُ فَتَزِلَّ قَدَمٌ بَعْدَ ثُبُوتِها ـ إِنَّ اللهَ خَبيرٌ بِما تَعْمَلُونَ).

مَعاشِرَ النّاسِ، إِنَّهُ جَنْبُ اللهِ الَّذي ذَكَرَ اللهُ في كِتابِهِ الْعَزيزِ، فَقالَ تَعالى (مُخْبِراً عَمَّنْ يُخالِفُهُ): (أَنْ تَقُولَ نَفْسٌ يا حَسْرَتى عَلى ما فَرَّطْتُ في جَنْبِ اللهِ).

مَعاشِرَ النّاسِ، تَدَبَّرُوا الْقُرآنَ وَ افْهَمُوا آياتِهِ وَانْظُرُوا إِلى مُحْكَماتِهِ وَلاتَتَّبِعُوا مُتَشابِهَهُ، فَوَاللهِ لَنْ يُبَيِّنَ لَكُمْ زَواجِرَهُ وَلَنْ يوضِحَ لَكُمْ تَفْسيرَهُ إِلَّا الَّذي أَنَا آخِذٌ بِيَدِهِ وَمُصْعِدُهُ إِلَيَّ وَشائِلٌ بِعَضُدِهِ (وَ رافِعُهُ بِيَدي) وَ مُعْلِمُكُمْ: أَنَّ مَنْ كُنْتُ مَوْلاهُ فَهذا عَلِيٌّ مَوْلاهُ، وَ هُوَ عَلِيُّ بْنُ أَبي طالِبٍ أَخي وَ وَصِيّي، وَ مُوالاتُهُ مِنَ اللهِ عَزَّوَجَلَّ أَنْزَلَها عَلَيَّ.

مَعاشِرَ النّاسِ، إِنَّ عَلِيّاً وَالطَّيِّبينَ مِنْ وُلْدي (مِنْ صُلْبِهِ) هُمُ الثِّقْلُ الْأَصْغَرُ، وَالْقُرآنُ الثِّقْلُ الْأَكْبَرُ، فَكُلُّ واحِدٍ مِنْهُما مُنْبِئٌ عَنْ صاحِبِهِ وَ مُوافِقٌ لَهُ، لَنْ يَفْتَرِقا حَتّى يَرِدا عَلَيَّ الْحَوْضَ.

أَلا إِنَّهُمْ أُمَناءُ اللهِ في خَلْقِهِ وَ حُكّامُهُ في أَرْضِهِ. أَلا وَقَدْ أَدَّيْتُ. أَلا وَقَدْ بَلَّغْتُ. أَلا وَقَدْ أَسْمَعْتُ، أَلا وَقَدْ أَوْضَحْتُ، أَلا وَ إِنَّ اللهَ عَزَّوَجَلَّ قالَ وَ أَنَا قُلْتُ عَنِ اللهِ عَزَّوَجَلَّ، أَلا إِنَّهُ لا «أَميرَ الْمُؤْمِنينَ» غَيْرَ أَخي هذا، أَلا لاتَحِلُّ إِمْرَةُ الْمُؤْمِنينَ بَعْدي لِأَحَدٍ غَيْرِهِ.

ثُمَّ قالَ: «أَيُّهَا النّاسُ، مَنْ أَوْلى بِكُمْ مِنْ أَنْفُسِكُمْ؟ قالُوا: اللهُ وَ رَسُولُهُ. فَقالَ: أَلا مَنْ كُنْتُ مَوْلاهُ فَهذا عَلِيٌّ مَوْلاهُ، اللّهُمَّ والِ مَنْ والاهُ وَ عادِ مَنْ عاداهُ وَانْصُرْ مَنْ نَصَرَهُ وَاخْذُلْ مَنْ خَذَلَهُ.

مَعاشِرَ النّاسِ، هذا عَلِيٌّ أَخي وَ وَصِيّي وَ واعي عِلْمي، وَ خَليفَتي في أُمَّتي عَلى مَنْ آمَنَ بي وَ عَلى تَفْسيرِ كِتابِ اللهِ عَزَّوَجَلَّ وَالدّاعي إِلَيْهِ وَالْعامِلُ بِمايَرضاهُ وَالْمُحارِبُ لِأَعْدائِهِ وَالْمُوالي عَلى طاعَتِهِ وَالنّاهي عَنْ مَعْصِيَتِهِ. إِنَّهُ خَليفَةُ رَسُولِ اللهِ وَ أَميرُ الْمُؤْمِنينَ وَالْإِمامُ الْهادي مِنَ اللهِ، وَ قاتِلُ النّاكِثينَ وَالْقاسِطينَ وَالْمارِقينَ بِأَمْرِ اللهِ. يَقُولُ اللهُ: (ما يُبَدَّلُ الْقَوْلُ لَدَيَّ).

بِأَمْرِكَ يارَبِّ أَقُولُ: اللّهُمَّ والِ مَنْ والاهُ وَعادِ مَنْ عاداهُ (وَانْصُرْ مَنْ نَصَرَهُ وَاخْذُلْ مَنْ خَذَلَهُ) وَالْعَنْ مَنْ أَنْكَرَهُ وَاغْضِبْ عَلى مَنْ جَحَدَ حَقَّهُ.

اللّهُمَّ إِنَّكَ أَنْزَلْتَ الْآيَةَ في عَلِيٍّ وَلِيِّكَ عِنْدَ تَبْيينِكَ ذالِكَ وَنَصْبِكَ إِيّاهُ لِهذَا الْيَوْمِ: (الْيَوْمَ أَكْمَلْتُ لَكُمْ دينَكُمْ وَ أَتْمَمْتُ عَلَيْكُمْ نِعْمَتي وَ رَضيتُ لَكُمُ الْإِسْلامَ ديناً)، (وَ مَنْ يَبْتَغِ غَيْرَ الْإِسْلامِ ديناً فَلَنْ يُقْبَلَ مِنْهُ وَ هُوَ فِي الْآخِرَةِ مِنَ الْخاسِرينَ). اللّهُمَّ إِنّي أُشْهِدُكَ أَنّي قَدْ بَلَّغْتُ.

التأكيد على توجه الأمّة نحو مسألة الإمامة

مَعاشِرَ النّاسِ، إِنَّما أَكْمَلَ اللهُ عَزَّوَجَلَّ دينَكُمْ بِإِمامَتِهِ. فَمَنْ لَمْ يَأْتَمَّ بِهِ وَبِمَنْ يَقُومُ مَقامَهُ مِنْ وُلْدي مِنْ صُلْبِهِ إِلى يَوْمِ الْقِيامَةِ وَالْعَرْضِ عَلَى اللهِ عَزَّوَجَلَّ فَأُولئِكَ الَّذينَ حَبِطَتْ أَعْمالُهُمْ (فِي الدُّنْيا وَالْآخِرَةِ) وَ فِي النّارِ هُمْ خالِدُونَ، (لايُخَفَّفُ عَنْهُمُ الْعَذابُ وَلاهُمْ يُنْظَرُونَ).

مَعاشِرَ النَّاس، هذا عَلِيّ، أنصَرُكم لي وَأحَقُّكم إلَيّ وَأقرَبُكم إلَيّ وَأعَزُّكم عَلَيّ، وَالله عَزَّوَجَلّ وَأنَاعَنهُ راضِيان. ومَانَزَلَتْ آيَةُ رِضَاً (في القرآن) إلاّ فيهِ، وَلا خَاطَبَ الله الَّذِينَ آمَنُوا إلاّ بَدَأ بِهِ، وَلاَنَزَلَتْ آيَةُ مَدحٍ في القرآنِ إلاّ فيهِ، وَلاَشَهِدَ الله بِالجَنَّةُ في (هَلْ أتَى عَلَى الإنسانِ) إلاّ لَهُ، وَلا أنزَلَها في سِواهُ وَلامَدَحَ بِها غَيرَهُ.

مَعاشِرَ النَّاس، هُوَ ناصِرُ دِينِ الله وَالمُجادِلُ عَن رَسُولِ الله، وهُوَ التَّقِيُّ النَّقِيُّ الهادِي المَهدي. نَبِيُّكم خَيرُ نَبِي وَوَصِيُّكم خَيرُ وَصِيّ (وَبَنُوهُ خَيرُ الأوصِياءِ).

مَعاشِرَ النَّاس، ذُرِّيَّةُ كُلِّ نَبِي مِن صُلبِهِ، وَ ذُرِّيَتِي مِن صُلبِ (أميرِالمُؤمِنينَ) عَلِي.

مَعاشِرَ النَّاس، إنّ إبليسَ أخرَجَ آدَمَ مِن الجَنَّةُ بِالحَسَدِ، فَلاتَحسُدُوهُ فَتَحبَطَ أعمالُكم وتَزِلَّ أقدامُكم، فإنّ آدَمَ أهبِطَ إلَي الأرض بِخَطيئَةُ واحِدَةُ، وَهوَ صَفوَةُ الله عَزَّوَجَلّ، وَكيفَ بِكم وَأنتُم وَ مِنكُم أعداءُالله، ألا وَ إنَّهُ لايُبغِضُ عَلِياً إلاّ الأشقى، وَ لايوالي عَلِياً إلاّ تَقِي، وَ لايُؤمِنُ بِهِ إلاّ مُؤمِنٌ مُخلِصٍ.

وَ في عَلِيّ ـ وَالله ـ نَزَلَتْ سُورَةُ العَصرِ: (بِسمِ اللهِ الرَّحمنِ الرَّحيمِ، وَ العَصرِ، إنّ الإنسانَ لَفِي خُسرٍ) (إلاّ عَلِياً الَّذي آمَنَ وَ رَضِيَ بِالحَقّ وَ الصَّبرِ).

مَعاشِرَ النَّاس، قَدِ استَشهَدتُ الله وَبَلَّغتُكم رِسالَتي وَ ما عَلَي الرَّسُولِ إلاّ البَلاغُ المُبينُ. مَعاشِرَ النَّاس، (اتَّقوا الله حَقَّ تُقاتِهِ وَلاتَمُوتُنّ إلاّ وَأنتُم مُسلِمُونَ).

الإشارَةُ إلى مقاصد المنافقين

مَعاشِرَ النَّاس، (آمِنُوا بِالله وَ رَسُولِهِ وَالنّورِ الَّذي أنزَلَ مَعَهُ مِن قَبلِ أن نَطمِسَ وُجُوهاً فَنَرُدَّها عَلى أدبارِها أو نَلعَنَهُم كَما لَعَنّا أصحابَ السَّبتِ). (بِالله ما عني بِهَذِهِ الآيَةُ إلاّ قَوماً مِن أصحابي أعرِفُهُم بِأسمائِهِم وَأنسابِهِم، وَقَد أُمِرتُ بِالصَّفحِ عَنهُم فَليَعمَلْ كُلُّ امرِئٍ عَلَي ما يَجِدُ لِعَلِي في قَلبِهِ مِنَ الحُبِّ وَالبُغضِ).

مَعاشِرَ النَّاس، النّورُ مِنَ الله عَزَّوَجَلّ مَسلوكٌ فِيَّ ثُمَّ في عَلِي بنِ أبي طالِبٍ، ثُمَّ في النَّسلِ مِنهُ إلَي القائِمِ المَهدي الَّذي يَأخُذُ بِحَقِّ الله وَ بِكُلِّ حَقٍّ هُوَ لَنا، لِأنَّ الله عَزَّوَجَلّ قَد جَعَلَنا حُجَّةً عَلَي المُقَصِّرينَ وَالمُعانِدينَ وَالمُخالِفينَ وَالخائِنينَ وَالآثِمينَ وَالظالِمينَ وَالغاصِبينَ مِن جَميعِ العالَمينَ.

مَعاشِرَ النَّاس، أُنذِرُكم أنّي رَسُولُ الله قَدخَلَت مِن قَبلي الرُّسلُ، أفَإن مِتُّ أوقُتِلتُ انقَلَبتُم عَلَي أعقابِكم؟ وَمَن يَنقَلِبْ عَلى عَقِبَيهِ فَلَن يَضُرَّ الله شَيئاً وَسَيَجزي اللهُ الشَّاكِرينَ (الصَّابِرينَ). ألاوإنَّ عَلِياً هُوَ المَوصُوفُ بِالصَّبرِ وَالشُّكرِ، ثُمَّ مِن بَعدِهِ وُلدي مِن صُلبِهِ.

مَعاشِرَ النَّاس، لاتَمُنُّوا عَلَيَّ بِإسلامِكم، بَل لاتَمُنُّوا عَلَي الله فَيحبَطَ عَمَلَكُم وَيسخَطَ عَلَيكم وَيبتَلِيكم بِشَواظٍ مِن نارٍ وَنُحاسٍ، إنّ رَبَّكم لَبِالمِرصادِ.

مَعاشِرَ النَّاس، إنَّهُ سَيَكونُ مِن بَعدي أئِمَّةٌ يَدعُونَ إلَي النَّارِ وَيومَ القِيامَةُ لاينصَرونَ. مَعاشِرَ النَّاس، إنّ الله وَأنا بَرِيئانِ مِنهُم.

مَعاشِرَ النَّاس، إنَّهُم وَأنصارَهُم وَأتباعَهُم وَأشياعَهُم في الدَّركِ الأسفَلِ مِنَ النَّارِ وَلَبِئسَ مَثوَى المُتَكَبِّرينَ. ألا إنَّهُم أصحابُ الصَّحيفَةُ، فَليَنظُرْ أحَدُكم في صَحيفَتِهِ!!

مَعاشِرَ النَّاس، إنِّي أدَعُها إمامَةُ وَ وِراثَةُ (في عَقِبي إلَي يَومِ القِيامَةُ)، وَقَد بَلَّغتُ ما أُمِرتُ بِتَبليغِهِ وَإن حُجَّةُ عَلَي كُلِّ حاضِرٍ وَغائِبٍ وَ عَلى كُلِّ أحَدٍ مِمَّن شَهِدَ أولَم يَشهَد، وُلِدَ أولَم يُولَد، فَليُبَلِّغِ الحاضِرُ الغائِبَ وَالوالِدُ الوَلَدَ إلي يَومِ القِيامَةُ. وَسَيَجعَلُونَ الإمامَةُ بَعدي مُلكاً وَ اغتِصاباً، (ألا لَعَنَ الله الغاصِبينَ المُغتَصِبينَ)، وَعِندَها سَيَفرُغُ لَكُم أيُّها الثَّقَلانِ (مَن يَفرُغُ) وَيُرسِلُ عَلَيكما شُواظٌ مِن نارٍ وَنُحاسٌ فَلاتَنتَصِرانِ.

مَعاشِرَالنَّاس، إنَّ الله عَزَّوَجَلَّ لَمْ يَكُنْ لِيَذرَكُمْ عَلى ما أنْتُمْ عَلَيْهِ حَتَّى يَميزَ الْخَبيثَ مِنَ الطَّيِّبِ، و ما كانَ الله لِيُطْلِعَكُمْ عَلَى الْغَيْبِ.

مَعاشِرَالنَّاس، إنَّهُ ما مِنْ قَرْيَةٍ إلاّ وَالله مُهْلِكها بِتَكذيبِها قَبْلَ يَوْمِ الْقِيامَةِ و مُمَلِّكها الْإمامَ الْمَهْدي وَالله مُصَدِّقٌ وَعْدَهُ.

مَعاشِرَالنَّاس، قَدْ ضَلَّ قَبْلَكُمْ أكْثَرُالأوَّلينَ، وَالله لَقَدْ أهْلَكَ الْأوَّلينَ، وَهُوَ مُهْلِكُ الْآخِرينَ.

قالَ الله تَعالى: (أَ لَمْ نُهْلِكِ الْأَوَّلينَ، ثُمَّ نُتْبِعُهُمُ الْآخِرينَ، كَذلِكَ نَفْعَلُ بِالْمُجْرِمينَ، وَيْلٌ يَوْمَئِذٍ لِلْمُكَذِّبينَ). مَعاشِرَالنَّاس، إنَّ الله قَدْ أمَرَني وَنَهاني، وَقَدْ أمَرْتُ عَلِيّاً وَنَهَيتُهُ (بِأمْرِه). فَعِلْمُ الْأمْرِ وَالنَّهْيِ لَدَيْهِ، فَاسْمَعوا لِأَمْرِهِ تَسْلَموا وَأَطيعوهُ تَهْتَدوا وَانْتَهوا لِنَهْيِهِ تَرْشُدوا، (وَصيروا إلى مُرادِهِ) وَلا تَتَفَرَّقْ بِكُمُ السُّبُلُ عَنْ سَبيلِهِ.

أولياء أهل البيت عليهم‌السلام وأعداءهم

مَعاشِرَالنَّاس، أنَا صِراطُ الله الْمُسْتَقيمُ الَّذي أمَرَكُمْ بِاتِّباعِهِ، ثُمَّ عَليٌّ مِنْ بَعْدي. ثُمَّ وُلْدي مِنْ صُلْبِهِ أئِمَّةٌ (الْهُدى)، يَهْدونَ إلَى الْحَقِّ و بِهِ يَعْدِلونَ.

ثُمَّ قَرَأَ: «بِسْمِ اللَّهِ الرَّحْمنِ الرَّحيمِ الْحَمْدُ لِلَّهِ رَبِّ الْعالَمينَ...» إلى آخِرِها، وَقالَ: في نَزَلَتْ وَفيهِمْ (وَالله) نَزَلَتْ، وَلَهُمْ عَمَّتْ وَإيَّاهُمْ خَصَّتْ، أولئكَ أوْلِياءُالله الَّذينَ لاخَوفٌ عَلَيْهِمْ وَلاهُمْ يَحْزَنونَ، ألا إنَّ حِزْبَ الله هُمُ الْغالِبونَ. ألا إنَّ أعْداءَهُمْ هُمُ السُّفَهاءُالْغاوُونَ إخْوانُ الشَّياطينِ يوحي بَعْضُهُمْ إلى بَعْضٍ زُخْرُفَ الْقَوْلِ غُروراً. ألا إنَّ أوْلِياءَهُمُ الَّذينَ ذَكَرَهُمُ الله في كِتابِهِ، فَقالَ عَزَّوَجَلَّ: (لا تَجِدُ قَوْماً يُؤْمِنونَ بِاللَّهِ وَ الْيَوْمِ الْآخِرِ يُوادُّونَ مَنْ حَادَّ اللَّهَ وَ رَسولَهُ وَ لَوْ كانوا آباءَهُمْ أوْ أبْناءَهُمْ أوْ إخْوانَهُمْ أوْ عَشيرَتَهُمْ أولئكَ كَتَبَ في قُلوبِهِمُ الْإيمانَ) إلى آخِرِالآيَةِ.

ألا إنَّ أولِياءَهُمُ الْمُؤْمِنونَ الَّذينَ وَصَفَهُمُ الله عَزَّوَجَلَّ فَقالَ: (الَّذينَ آمَنوا وَ لَمْ يَلْبِسوا إيمانَهُمْ بِظُلْمٍ أولئكَ لَهُمُ الْأمْنُ وَ هُمْ مُهْتَدونَ).

(ألا إنَّ أوْلِياءَهُمُ الَّذينَ آمَنوا وَلَمْ يَرْتابوا).

ألا إنَّ أولِياءَهُمُ الَّذينَ يَدْخُلونَ الْجَنَّةَ بِسَلامٍ آمِنينَ، تَتَلَقَّاهُمُ الْمَلائكَةُ بِالتَّسْليمِ يَقولونَ: سَلامٌ عَلَيْكُمْ طِبْتُمْ فَادْخُلوها خالِدينَ.

ألا إنَّ أولِياءَهُمْ، لَهُمُ الْجَنَّةُ يُرْزَقونَ فيها بِغَيْرِ حِسابٍ. ألا إنَّ أعْداءَهُمُ الَّذينَ يَصْلَونَ سَعيراً.

ألا إنَّ أعْداءَهُمُ الَّذينَ يَسْمَعونَ لِجَهَنَّمَ شَهيقاً و هِيَ تَفورُ و يَرَوْنَ لَها زَفيراً. ألا إنَّ أعْداءَهُمُ الَّذينَ قالَ الله فيهِمْ: (كُلَّما دَخَلَتْ أُمَّةٌ لَعَنَتْ أُخْتَها) الْآيَةُ.

ألا إنَّ أعْداءَهُمُ الَّذينَ قالَ الله عَزَّوَجَلَّ: (كُلَّما أُلْقِيَ فيها فَوْجٌ سَأَلَهُمْ خَزَنَتُها أ لَمْ يَأْتِكُمْ نَذيرٌ، قالوا بَلى قَدْ جاءَنا نَذيرٌ فَكَذَّبْنا و قُلْنا ما نَزَّلَ اللَّهُ مِنْ شَيْءٍ إنْ أنْتُمْ إلاّ في ضَلالٍ كَبيرٍ) إلى قَوْلِهِ: (فَسُحْقاً لِأَصْحابِ السَّعيرِ). ألا إنَّ أولِياءَهُمُ الَّذينَ يَخْشَوْنَ رَبَّهُمْ بِالْغَيْبِ، لَهُمْ مَغْفِرَةٌ وَأجْرٌ كَبيرٌ.

مَعاشِرَالنَّاس، شَتَّانَ مابَيْنَ السَّعيرِ وَالْأجْرِ الْكَبيرِ.

(مَعاشِرَالنَّاس)، عَدُوُّنا مَنْ ذَمَّهُ الله وَلَعَنَهُ، و وَلِيُّنا (كُلُّ) مَنْ مَدَحَهُ الله و أحَبَّهُ.

مَعاشِرَ النَّاس، ألاوَإنّي (أنَا) النَّذيرُ و عَلِيٌّ الْبَشيرُ.

(مَعاشِرَالنَّاس)، ألا وَ إنّي مُنْذِرٌ وَ عَلِيٌّ هادٍ.

مَعاشِرَ النَّاس (ألا) وَ إنّي نَبيٌ وَ عَلِيٌّ وَصيّي.

(مَعاشِرَالنَّاس، ألاوَإنّي رَسولٌ وَ عَلِيٌّ الْإمامُ وَالْوَصِيُّ مِنْ بَعْدِهِ وُلْدُهُ. ألاوَإنّي وَالِدُهُمْ وَهُمْ يَخْرُجونَ مِنْ صُلْبِهِ).

الإمام المهدي

ألا إنَّ خاتَمَ الأئمَّةِ مِنّا القائِمَ المَهدِي.

ألا إنَّهُ الظّاهِرُ عَلَي الدِّينِ.

ألا إنَّهُ المُنتَقِمُ مِنَ الظّالِمينَ.

ألا إنَّهُ فاتِحُ الحُصُونِ وَهادِمُها.

ألا إنَّهُ غالِبُ كُلِّ قَبيلَةٍ مِن أَهلِ الشِّرْكِ وَهاديها.

ألا إنَّهُ المُدْرِكُ بِكُلِّ ثارٍ لأَولِياءِالله.

ألا إنَّهُ النّاصِرُ لِدينِ الله.

ألا إنَّهُ الغَرّافُ مِن بَحرٍ عَميقٍ.

ألا إنَّهُ يَسِمُ كُلَّ ذي فَضلٍ بِفَضْلِهِ وَ كُلَّ ذي جَهلٍ بِجَهلِهِ.

ألا إنَّهُ خِيَرَةُ اللهِ وَ مُختارُهُ.

ألا إنَّهُ وارِثُ كُلِّ عِلمٍ وَالمُحيطُ بِكُلِّ فَهمٍ.

ألا إنَّهُ المُخبِرُ عَن رَبِّهِ عَزَّوَجَلَّ وَ المُشيدُ لأَمرِ آياتِهِ.

ألا إنَّهُ الرَّشيدُ السَّديدُ.

ألا إنَّهُ المُفَوَّضُ إلَيهِ.

ألا إنَّهُ قَد بَشَّرَ بِهِ مَن سَلَفَ مِنَ القُرونِ بَينَ يَدَيهِ.

ألا إنَّهُ الباقي حُجَّةً وَلاحُجَّةَ بَعدَهُ وَلا حَقَّ إلّا مَعَهُ وَلا نُورَ إلّا عِندَهُ.

ألا إنَّهُ لا غالِبَ لَهُ وَلا مَنصُورَ عَلَيهِ.

ألا وَإنَّهُ وَلِيُّ اللهِ في أرضِهِ، وَحَكَمُهُ في خَلقِهِ، وَأمينُهُ في سِرِّهِ وَ عَلانِيَتِهِ.

التمهيد لأمر البيعة

مَعاشِرَ النّاسِ، إنِّي قَد بَيَّنتُ لَكُم وَأفهَمتُكُم، و هذا عَلِيٌّ يُفهِمُكُم بَعدي. ألا وَإنِّي عِندَ انقِضاءِ خُطبَتي أدعُوكُم إلي مُصافَقَتي عَلي بَيعَتِهِ وَ الإقرارِبِهِ، ثُمَّ مُصافَقَتِهِ بَعدي. ألا وَإنِّي قَد بايَعتُ اللهَ وَ عَلِيٌّ قَد بايَعَني. وَأنَا آخِذُكُم بِالبَيعَةِ لَهُ عَنِ اللهِ عَزَّوَجَلَّ. (إِنَّ الَّذِينَ يُبَايِعُونَكَ إِنَّمَا يُبَايِعُونَ اللَّهَ يَدُ اللَّهِ فَوْقَ أَيْدِيهِمْ فَمَن نَكَثَ فَإِنَّمَا يَنكُثُ عَلَى نَفْسِهِ وَ مَنْ أَوْفَى بِمَا عَاهَدَ عَلَيْهُ اللَّهَ فَسَيُؤْتِيهِ أَجْراً عَظِيماً).

مَعاشِرَ النّاسِ، إنَّ الحَجَّ وَالعُمرَةَ مِن شَعائِرِاللهِ، (فَمَنْ حَجَّ الْبَيْتَ أَوِ اعْتَمَرَ فَلَاجُنَاحَ عَلَيْهِ أَن يَطَّوَّفَ بِهِمَا) الآيَةَ.

الحلال و الحرام، الواجبات و المحرّمات

مَعاشِرَ النَّاس، حُجُّوا الْبَيت، فَمَا وَرَدَهُ اهلبيت إلاَّ اسْتَغْنَوْا وَ أُبْشِروا، وَلاتَخَلَّفوا عَنْهُ إلاَّ ابْتَرُّوا وَ افْتَقَروا. مَعاشِرَ النَّاس، ماوَقَفَ بِالْمَوْقِفِ مُؤْمِنٌ إلاَّغَفَرَ الله لَهُ ماسَلَفَ مِنْ ذَنْبِهِ إلي وَقْتِهِ ذالِكَ، فَإذَا انْقَضَتْ حَجَّتُهُ اسْتَأنَفَ عَمَلَهُ. مَعاشِرَ النَّاس، الْحُجّاجُ مُعانُونَ وَ نَفَقاتُهُمْ مُخَلَّفَةٌ عَلَيْهِمْ وَالله لايُضيعُ أجْرَالْ مُحْسِنينَ.

مَعاشِرَ الْبَيت، حُجُّوا الْبَيتَ بِكَمالِ الدّين وَالتَّفَقُّهِ، وَلاتَنْصَرِفوا عَنِ الْمَشاهِدِإلاّ بِتَوْبَةٍ وَ إقْلاع. مَعاشِرَ النَّاس، أقيموا الصَّلاةَ وَ آتوا الزَّكاةَ كَما أمَرَكُمُ الله عَزَّوَجَلَّ، فَإنْ طالَ عَلَيكُمُ الأمَدُ فَقَصَّرْتُمْ أو نَسيتُمْ فَعَلِيٌّ وَلِيُكُمْ وَمُبَيِّنٌ لَكُمْ، الَّذي نَصَبَهُ الله عَزَّوَجَلَّ لَكُمْ بَعْدي أمينَ خَلْقِهِ. إنَّهُ مِنّي وَ أنا مِنْهُ، وَ هُوَ وَ مَنْ تَخْلُفُ مِنْ ذُرّيّتي يُخْبِرونَكُمْ بِماتَسْألُونَ عَنْهُ وَيُبَيِّنونَ لَكُمْ ما لاتَعْلَمونَ.

ألا إنَّ الْحَلالَ وَالْحَرامَ أكْثَرُ مِنْ أنْ أحْصيهِما وَأعْرِفَهُما فَآمَرَ بِالْحَلالِ وَ أنْهي عَنِ الْحَرامِ في مَقامٍ واحِد، فَأُمِرْتُ أنْ آخُذَ الْبَيعَةَ مِنْكُمْ وَالصَّفْقَةَ لَكُمْ بِقَبولِ ماجِئتُ بِهِ عَنِ الله عَزَّوَجَلَّ في عَلِيٍّ أميرِ الْمُؤْمِنينَ وَالأوْصِياءِ مِنْ بَعْدِهِ الَّذينَ هُمْ مِنّي وَمِنْهُ إمامَةٌ فيهِمْ قائِمَةٌ، خاتِمُها الْمَهْدي إلي يَومٍ يَلْقي الله الَّذي يُقَدِّرُ وَ يَقْضي.

مَعاشِرَ النَّاس، وَ كُلُّ حَلالٍ دَلَلْتُكُمْ عَلَيهِ، وَ كُلُّ حَرامٍ نَهَيتُكُمْ عَنْهُ فَإنّي لَمْ أرْجِعْ عَنْ ذالِكَ وَ لَمْ أُبَدِّلْ. ألا فَاذْكُروا ذالِكَ وَاحْفَظوهُ وَ تَواصَوْابِهِ، وَلا تُبَدِّلوهُ وَلاتُغَيِّروهُ. ألا وَ إنّي أُجَدِّدُالْقَوْلَ: ألا فَأقيموا الصَّلاةَ وَ آتوا الزَّكاةَ وَأمُروا بِالْمَعْروفِ وَانْهَوْا عَنِ الْمُنكَر.

ألا وَإنَّ رَأسَ الأمْرِ بِالْمَعْروفِ أنْ تَنْتَهُوا إلي قَوْلي وَتُبَلِّغوهُ مَنْ لَمْ يَحْضُرْ وَ تَأمُروهُ بِقَبولِهِ عَنّي وَتَنْهَوْهُ عَنْ مُخالَفَتِهِ، فَإنَّهُ أمرٌ مِنَ الله عَزَّوَجَلَّ وَمِنّي. وَلا أمَرَ بِمَعْروفٍ وَلا نَهْي عَنْ مُنكَرٍ إلاّ مَعَ إمامٍ مَعْصومٍ.

مَعاشِرَ النَّاس، الْقُرآن يُعَرِّفُكُمْ أنَّ الأئِمَّةَ مِنْ بَعْدِهِ وُلْدُهُ، وَعَرَّفْتُكُمْ إنَّهُمْ مِنّي وَمِنْهُ، حَيثُ يَقولُ الله في كِتابِهِ: (وَ جَعَلَها كَلِمَةً باقِيَةً في عَقِبِهِ). وَقُلتُ: «لَنْ تَضِلُّوا ما إنْ تَمَسَّكْتُمْ بِهِما».

مَعاشِرَ النَّاس، التَّقْوي، التَّقْوي، وَاحْذَروا السَّاعَةَ كَما قالَ الله عَزَّوَجَلَّ: (إنَّ زَلْزَلَةَ السَّاعَةِ شَيءٌ عَظيمٌ). أذْكُروا الْمَماتِ (وَالْمَعادَ) وَالْحِسابَ وَالْمَوازينَ وَالْمُحاسَبَةَ بَينَ يَدَي رَبِّ الْعالَمينَ وَالثَّوابَ وَالْعِقابَ. فَمَنْ جاءَ بِالْحَسَنَةِ أُثيبَ عَلَيها وَ مَنْ جاءَ بِالسَّيِّئَةِ فَلَيسَ لَهُ فِي الْجِنانِ نَصيبٌ.

البيعةُ بِصورَةٍ رسميةٍ

مَعاشِرَ النَّاس، إنَّكُمْ أكْثَرُ مِنْ أنْ تُصافِقوني بِكَفٍّ واحِدٍ في وَقْتٍ واحِدٍ، وَقَدْ أمَرَني الله عَزَّوَجَلَّ أنْ آخُذَ مِنْ ألْسِنَتِكُمُ الإقْرارَ بِما عَقَّدْتُ لِعَلِي أميرِ الْمُؤْمِنينَ، وَلِمَنْ جاءَ بَعْدَهُ مِنَ الأئِمَّةِ مِنّي وَ مِنْهُ، علي ما أعْلَمْتُكُمْ أنَّ ذُرّيّتي مِنْ صُلْبِهِ.

فَقولوا بِأجْمَعِكُمْ: «إنّا سامِعونَ مُطيعونَ راضونَ مُنْقادونَ لِما بَلَّغْتَ عَنْ رَبِّنا وَرَبِّكَ في أمْرِ إمامِنا عَلِي أميرِ الْمُؤْمِنينَ وَ مَنْ وُلِدَ مِنْ صُلْبِهِ مِنَ الأئِمَّةِ. نُبايِعُكَ عَلي ذالِكَ بِقُلوبِنا وَأنْفُسِنا وَألْسِنَتِنا وَأيدينا. عَلي ذالِكَ نَحْيي وَ عَلَيهِ نَموتُ وَ عَلَيهِ نُبْعَثُ. وَلانُغَيِّرُ وَلانُبَدِّلُ، وَلا نَشُكُّ (وَلانَجْحَدُ) وَلانَرْتابُ، وَلا نَرْجِعُ عَنِ الْعَهْدِ وَلا نَنْقُضُ الْميثاقَ.

وَعَظْتَنا بِوَعظِ الله في عَلي أميرِ الْمُؤْمِنينَ وَالأئِمَّةِ الَّذينَ ذَكَرْتَ مِنْ ذُرِّيَّتِكَ مِنْ وُلْدِهِ بَعْدَهُ، الْحَسَنِ وَالْحُسَينِ وَ مَنْ نَصَبَهُ الله بَعْدَهُما. فَالْعَهْدُ وَالْميثاقُ لَهُمْ مَأخوذٌ مِنّا، مِنْ قُلوبِنا وَأنْفُسِنا وَألْسِنَتِنا وَضَمائِرِنا وَأيدينا. مَنْ أدْرَكَها بِيَدِهِ وَ إلاّ فَقَدْ أقَرَّ بِلِسانِهِ، وَلا نَبْتَغي بِذالِكَ بَدَلاً وَلايَري الله مِنْ أنْفُسِنا حِوَلاً. نَحْنُ نُؤَدّي ذالِكَ عَنْكَ الدّاني وَالْقاصي مِنْ أوْلادِنا وَأهالينا، وَ نُشْهِدُالله بِذالِكَ وَ كَفي بِالله شَهيداً وَأنْتَ عَلَينا بِهِ شَهيدٌ».

مَعاشِرَ النَّاس، ماتَقولونَ؟ فَإنَّ الله يَعْلَمُ كُلَّ صَوْتٍ وَ خافِيَةِ كُلِّ نَفْسٍ، (فَمَنِ اهْتَدي فَلِنَفْسِهِ وَ مَنْ ضَلَّ فَإنَّما يَضِلُّ عَلَيها)، وَمَنْ بايَعَ فَإنَّما يُبايِعُ الله، (يَدُالله فَوْقَ أيديهِمْ).

مَعاشِرَ النَّاس، فَبايِعُوا الله وَ بايِعُوني وَبايِعُوا عَلِيّاً أميرَالْمُؤْمِنينَ وَالْحَسَنَ وَالْحُسَينَ وَالأئِمَّةَ (مِنْهُمْ فِي الدُّنْيا وَالآخِرَةِ) كَلِمَةً باقِيَةً.

يُهْلِكُ الله مَنْ غَدَرَ وَ يَرْحَمُ مَنْ وَ في، (وَ مَنْ نَكَثَ فَإنَّما يَنْكُثُ علي نَفْسِهِ وَ مَنْ أوْفي بِما عاهَدَ عَلَيهُ الله فَسَيُؤتيهِ أجْراً عَظيماً).

The Doctor & Sheikh's Debate

مَعاشِرَ النَّاسِ، قُولُوا الَّذي قُلْتُ لَكُمْ وَسَلِّمُوا عَلى عَلِيٍّ بِإِمْرَةِ الْمُؤْمِنينَ، وَقُولُوا: (سَمِعْنا وَ أَطَعْنا غُفْرانَكَ رَبَّنا وَ إِلَيْكَ الْمَصيرُ)، وَ قُولُوا: (اَلْحَمْدُ لِلَّهِ الَّذي هَدانا لِهذا وَ ما كُنّا لِنَهْتَدِيَ لَوْلا أَنْ هَدانَا اللهُ) الآيَةَ.

مَعاشِرَ النَّاسِ، إِنَّ فَضائِلَ عَلِيِّ بْنِ أَبي طالِبٍ عِنْدَاللهِ عَزَّوَجَلَّ ـ وَ قَدْ أَنْزَلَها فِي الْقُرْآنِ ـ أَكْثَرُ مِنْ أَنْ أُحْصِيَها في مَقامٍ واحِدٍ، فَمَنْ أَنْبَأَكُمْ بِها وَ عَرَفَها فَصَدِّقُوهُ.

مَعاشِرَ النَّاسِ، مَنْ يُطِعِ اللهَ وَ رَسُولَهُ وَ عَلِيّاً وَ الْأَئِمَّةَ الَّذينَ ذَكَرْتُهُمْ فَقَدْ فازَ فَوْزاً عَظيماً. مَعاشِرَ النَّاسِ، السَّابِقُونَ إِلى مُبايَعَتِهِ وَ مُوالاتِهِ وَ التَّسْليمِ عَلَيْهِ بِإِمْرَةِ الْمُؤْمِنينَ أُولئِكَ هُمُ الْفائِزُونَ في جَنّاتِ النَّعيمِ. مَعاشِرَ النَّاسِ، قُولُوا ما يَرْضَي اللهُ بِهِ عَنْكُمْ مِنَ الْقَوْلِ، فَإِنْ تَكْفُرُوا أَنْتُمْ وَ مَنْ فِي الْأَرْضِ جَميعاً فَلَنْ يَضُرَّاللهَ شَيْئاً. اللهمَّ اغْفِرْ لِلْمُؤْمِنينَ (بِما أَدَّيْتُ وَأَمَرْتُ) وَاغْضِبْ عَلَي (الْجاحِدينَ) الْكافِرينَ، وَالْحَمْدُ لِلَّهِ رَبِّ الْعالَمينَ.

The Translation of the Speech in English

Bismillah al-Rahman al-Raheem

In the Name of Allah, the Beneficent, the Merciful[5]

Praise and Glorification of Almighty Allah

All praise belongs to Allah who has exalted in His oneness [above His creation], while He has drawn near [to His creation] in His uniqueness, [He is] Majestic in His dominance and Mighty in His power. He encompasses everything in [His] knowledge while He is in His position, and has overpowered all creation with His power and reason. [He is] continually praiseworthy, unceasingly praised, and forever glorified and perfect. He is the originator and the restorer, and every matter returns to Him.

He is the Creator of the seven-heavens, the un-folder of the planets, and the Compeller of the earths and the heavens; Holy and Glorified, the Lord of the Angels and the Spirit. He continually graces all whom He originated, bestows favours to all He created.

He observes all eyes while the eyes cannot see Him. He is Kind/Generous, Clement, of restraint and leniency. He has made His Mercy reach and encompass everything, and He confers upon them His Grace. He does not haste in His retribution, and He does not rush to them with what they deserve of His chastisement.

He is aware of the hearts and knows the minds; the concealed are not hidden from Him, nor are the unseen unclear to Him. His is the encompassing of everything, the overpowering of everything, the ability in [doing] everything, the strength and power over everything, and nothing is like His similitude. He is the creator of the thing when it is not a thing. He is eternal, living, and maintainer of justice; there is no deity but He, the Exalted in Power, the Wise.

He is glorified and exalted from being comprehended by visions, while He comprehends [all] visions, and He is All Subtle, All Aware. No one can apprehend His description through inspection or observation, and no one can find out how He is through covert or overt [means] except through that which He Almighty and Majestic guided onto Himself.

22- Researched by Muhammad Baqir Ansari

And I bear witness that He is Allah whose Holiness has filled the space of time, whose light has encompassed eternity, and who implements His command without consulting an adviser. He does not have with Him a partner in decision-making, nor is He assisted in planning and running His affairs.

He fashioned and formed that which He created without following a [pre-existing] example or model, and He created what He created without receiving any help from anyone, nor with any hardship, skill, or excellence.

He initiated them, and so they were, and He created them, and so they became evident. Thus, He is Allah whom there is no deity other than Him, He is perfect in His making, beautiful in His product, He is the Just One who never oppresses, and He is the most kind to Whom all matters return.

And I bear witness that He is Allah before whose Greatness everything is humbled, before whose Might everything is humiliated, before whose Power everything surrenders, and before whose Awe everything is lowly. [He is] the King of kings, the maker of the orbits, the harnesser of the sun and the moon, each flowing for an appointed time, He winds the night over the day, and winds the day over the night which it pursues swiftly. [He is the] destroyer of every obstinate tyrant, and annihilator of every mutinous devil.

He has no opponent and nor has He a peer along with Him, [but He is] One, the Absolute Authority, He never begets, nor is He begotten, and none can ever be His equal. [He is] the one deity and the Glorious Lord. [He] proceeds as He wishes, determines as He wills, He knows so He encompasses, He causes death and gives life,[16] impoverishes and enriches, makes laugh and makes weep, brings near and sends far, withholds and bestows, His is the kingdom and His is all the praise, in His hand is all goodness, and He is competent of everything.

He merges night into day and merges day into night, there is no deity except He, the All-Mighty the All-Forgiving, the answerer of prayers, the giver in abundance, the counter of the breaths, and the Lord of the jinn and man kind. He is the One, whom nothing confuses, nor do the cries of the help-seekers tire Him, nor does the insistence of the unrelenting ones exhaust Him. He is the protector of the virtuous, the facilitator to the successful, the *mawla* (Patron) of the faithful, and the Lord of the worlds, who deserves to be thanked by every one He created, and to be praised in every circumstance.

I praise Him greatly, and thank Him continuously for every happiness and suffering, and for every hardship and ease, and I believe in Him and His angels, and His books, and His messengers. I listen to His command and obey, and I hasten to everything that pleases Him, and submit and surrender to what He determines, [all out of my] desire/eagerness to be in His obedience, and out of fear of His chastisement, for He is Allah whose plot is not secured against, and whose injustice is not feared.

Divine Command of Ultimate Importance

I confirm my servitude to Him, and I testify to His Lordship, I carry out whatever He has revealed to me, out of fear if I do not do it of being subjected to a calamity from Him that no one can repel from me no matter how great his skill and excellence may be, and how elite and influential he might be; there is no god but He.

For indeed He has informed me that if I do not convey what He has revealed to me about the right of Ali, I would not have conveyed His Message, and indeed He, Blessed and Exalted He is, has guaranteed me protection from the people, for He is Allah the Sufficient/Protector, the Kind/Generous So He revealed to me, In the name of Allah the Beneficent the Merciful, O Messenger! Convey that that has been sent down to you from your Lord about Ali, meaning the succession for Ali Ibn Abitaleb and if you do not, then you would not have conveyed His Message, and Allah will protect you from the people

O companies of mankind! I have not been negligent in delivering what Allah has sent down unto me, and I shall explain to ye the reason behind the revelation of this ayah. Indeed Gabriel descended unto me three times ordering me on behalf of my Lord The Salam for He is The Salam [The Peace/The Faultless] that I stand up here in this site and let every white and black know that **indeed Ali Ibn Abitaleb, is my brother and my *wasiy* (trustee and executor of will and teaching), my successor over my Ummah (nation), the Imam after me, whose station to me is like that of Aaron to Moses save that there will be no Prophet after me and he is your *waliy* (patron/authority) after Allah and His messenger.**

In fact, Allah, Blessed and Exalted, has sent down upon me about this an ayah from His Book which is, indeed your *waliy* (patron/authority) is Allah and His Messenger, and those who believe who uphold the prayer and give the alms while they are bowing, and Ali Ibn Abitaleb is the one who upheld the prayer and gave the alms while he was bowing seeking Allah, Exalted and Majestic, in all circumstances.

I asked Gabriel to plead to The Salam to excuse me from having to convey this to ye – O people knowing how few are the pious, and how great are the masses of the hypocrites, the mischief and the plotting of the wicked, and the manoeuvrings of those who scorn Islam, those whom Allah describes in His Book as they say with their tongues what is not in their hearts, and they consider it a trifle but in the sight of Allah it is grave, and due to their hurting me excessively on more than one occasion, such that they labelled me "ears", and they claimed that I am so because of him (Ali) being with me for so much, for my welcoming him and paying attention to him, for him always being in line with me, and for accepting from me [all my words and commands], such that Allah, Exalted and Majestic, revealed about that Among them are those who torment the Prophet, and they say, 'He is an ear'. Say, 'An ear against those who claim he is an ear is good for ye'. He has faith in Allah and trusts the faithful, and is a mercy for those of ye who have faith. As for those who torment Allah's messenger, there is a painful punishment for them

Had I wished to name those who have said this, I would have called them by their names, and if I wished to point them out individually one by one I would have pointed them out, and if I wished to single them out, I would have singled them out, but by Allah I have been magnanimous about their affairs.

Yet despite all of that, Allah would not be pleased with me unless I convey what Allah has sent down upon me about the right of Ali, O Messenger! Convey that that has been sent down to you from your Lord_ *about the right of Ali* _and if you do not, then you would not have conveyed His Message, and Allah will protect you from the people.

Formal Announcement of the Leadership and Mastership of Ali and the 12 Imams

So comprehend what I have just said about him O companies of mankind and understand it, and know that Allah has indeed appointed him as your *waliy* (authority/patron) and *imam* (leader) whose obedience is obligatory upon the Muha jereen (the Immigrants), the Ansar (the Supporters), those who follow them (the Tabe'een) in good faith, and upon people of the deserts and the people of the towns, and upon the non-Arab and the Arab, the free and bonded, the young and the old, the white and the black, and upon every monotheist; [unquestionably] his judgement is upheld, his word is forgone and undisputable, his command is executed. Cursed [expelled and excluded from the mercy of Allah] is he who opposes him, blessed with mercy is he who follows him and confirms him; for Allah has indeed forgiven him as well as he who listens to him and obeys him.

O companies of mankind, this is the last stand I make in such a site, so listen to, obey, and follow the command of Allah your Lord, for Allah, Almighty and Majestic, is your *mawla* (master and authority) and your deity, and then after Him, His Messenger and His Prophet – who is addressing ye – is your *waliy* (authority/patron), then after me Ali is your *waliy* and your *imam* (leader) by the command of Allah your Lord, then the *imamah* (leadership) is in my progeny from amongst his offspring until the Day ye stand before Allah and His Messenger.

There is no halal except that which Allah has prescribed as halal, His messenger, and them, and there is no haram except that that Allah has prescribed as haram for ye, His messenger and them (i.e. the *Imams*). Indeed Allah, Almighty and Majestic, taught me the halal and the haram and I passed on what my Lord taught me from His Book and about His halal and His haram to him.

O companies of mankind! Prefer him [over all others]. There is no knowledge except that Allah has registered and gathered in me [and has made me encompass it], and every knowledge that I have been taught I have indeed registered in the Leader of the Pious (*Imam al-Muttaqeen*), and there is no knowledge except that I have taught to Ali, for he is The Manifest Leader (*al-Imam al-Mubeen*) whom Allah has mentioned in the surah of YaSeen and We have registered everything in a manifest leader (*Imam Mubeen*).

O companies of mankind! Do not deviate from him and do not disband from him, do not disdain or scorn his *wilayah* (authority/patronage), for he is the one who guides to the truth and acts upon it, and vanquishes falsehood and prohibits it, and in the cause of Allah he is not taken by the blame of any blamer.

He is the first to believe in Allah and His Messenger; no one preceded him to the belief in me. He is the one who offered himself as a sacrifice for Allah's Messenger, and he is the one who was with Allah's Messenger when there was no one who worshiped Allah with His Messenger from amongst the men other than him. He is the first of mankind to perform the prayers and the first who worshiped Allah with me. I commanded him, on Allah's behalf, to remain in my bed, and he did, offering himself as a sacrifice himself for me.

O companies of mankind! Prefer him over others for Allah has preferred him, and accept him for Allah has appointed him [as your *Imam*].

O companies of mankind! He is an *imam* from Allah, and Allah will never accept the repentance of anyone who denies his *wilayah* (authority), nor will He ever forgive him; it is a definite certainty for Allah to do that to whoever disobeys his command and that He will punish him a grave punishment perpetually forever, and throughout space and time. So, beware of disobeying him (Ali) for ye will burn in a Fire whose fuel is humans and stones, prepared for the disbelievers.

O companies of mankind! By Allah, all past Prophets and messengers gave the glad tidings of my advent, and I, by Allah, am the seal of the Prophets and of the messengers, and I am the proof (*hujjah*) upon all beings of the heavens and the earths. Whoever doubts this, he has indeed disbelieved like the disbelief of the early ignorance (*jahiliyyah*), and whoever doubts anything of this statement of mine, he has indeed doubted all that has descended upon me, and he who doubts any one of the Imams, he has indeed doubted all of them, and anyone who doubts us is in the Fire.

O companies of mankind! Allah, Almighty and Majestic, bestowed me with this grace out of His favour unto me, and out of His kindness to me, and there is no deity other than He. O to Him is all the praise from me eternally for ever and ever, as long as time exists and in all circumstances.

O companies of mankind! Give preference to Ali for he is the best of mankind after me male or female so long as Allah brings down the sustenance, and creation exists.

Cursed and again cursed, wrathed and again wrathed is he, who objects to this speech of mine and does not concur to it. Indeed, Gabriel has informed me of this, on behalf of Almighty Allah, saying, "he who opposes Ali and does not accept his authority, *wilayah*, then upon him is My curse and My wrath", so let every soul consider what it sends ahead for tomorrow, and be wary of Allah– in opposing him –when the feet would slip after being firm, indeed Allah is well aware of what ye do.

O companies of mankind! He is the "Side of Allah" (*janb-Allah*) whom He mentions in His Glorious Book; so, the Exalted says, informing of those who oppose him, lest anyone should say, Alas for my negligence in the side of Allah!

O companies of mankind! Reflect on the Qur'an and understand its verses, look into its definitive verses and do not follow its resembling/analogous verses, for by Allah no one can ever elucidate and reveal for ye its prohibitions, nor explain to ye its explanation and interpretation other than the one whose hand I am holding and elevating him to myself, lifting his arm, hoisting him with my hand. I [hereby] announce to ye that **whoever's *mawla* (authority/patron) I have been, then this, Ali, is his *mawla*, and he is Ali Ibn Abitaleb, my brother, my *wasiy* (trustee/executor), and the mandate of his authority and patronage is from Allah, Almighty and Majestic, which He sent it down upon me.**

O companies of mankind! Indeed, Ali and the pure ones from amongst my offspring – who are from his loins – are the Lesser Weight, and the Qur'an is the Greater Weight, and each one of them two informs about and leads to its companion, and agrees with it; those two will never part until they return to me at the Pool [of Kawthar on the Day of Judgement].

O Indeed they are the Trustees of Allah over His creation and His rulers on His earth. O Indeed I have fulfilled [my duty], O indeed I have conveyed [the message], O indeed I have made myself heard, O indeed I have elucidated. O Indeed Allah, Almighty and Exalted, has said, and I have said on behalf of Allah, Almighty and Exalted.

O Indeed there is no "Amir al-Mo'mineen" (Commander of the Faithful) other than this brother of mine. O Indeed the commandership of the believers is not permissible for anyone after me other than him.

Allah's Messenger Publicly Appoints His Successor

Then Allah's messenger grabbed Ali on the arm lifting him up. Since the time when Allah's messenger went up the stand Amir al-Mo'mineen was a step lower than his level on his right, they looked as if they were on the same level. Allah's messenger lifted him with his hand, and [Ali's hands] spread towards the sky; he raised Ali until his leg was along the knees of Allah's messenger. Allah's messenger then said: **O people! Who has more authority over ye than ye have over yourselves?**

They said: "Allah and His Messenger". So, Allah's messenger said:

So, whoever's authority and patron *(mawla)* I have been, then this, Ali, is his authority and patron. O Allah be the patron of whoever takes him as the patron, and be hostile to whoever is hostile to him, succour whoever succours him and desert whoever deserts him.

O companies of mankind! This Ali is my brother, my *wasiy*, and the one who knows and comprehends [all] my knowledge. He is my successor over my Ummah; over everyone who believes in me, and [he is my successor] for the interpretation of the Book of Allah, Almighty and Majestic, [he is] the Caller to Him; the one who works that which pleases Him, the combater of His enemies, the devotee of His obedience, and the forbidder of His disobedience.

Indeed, he is the Successor (*caliph*) of Allah's Messenger, the Commander of the Faithful (*Amir al-Mo'mineen*), and the Guiding Imam (*Imam al-Hadi*) assigned by Allah. [He is] the killer of the Perfidious (*al-nakitheen*), the Fanatics (*al-qasiteen*), and the Renegades (*almariqeen*) by the command of Allah.

Allah says: _The Word is unalterable with Me. By Your command O Lord, I say, **O Allah be the patron of whoever takes him as the patron, and be hostile to whoever is hostile to him; succour whoever succours him, and desert whoever deserts him; curse whoever rejects him, and be wrathful to whoever obstinately denies his right.**

O Allah You brought down the ayah about Ali Your *waliy* (authority) when illustrating that and appointing him on this day, Today I have perfected your religion for ye, and I have completed my blessing upon ye, and I have approved Islam for ye as a religion, and You said, indeed the religion with Allah is Islam, and You said, Should anyone seek a religion other than Islam, it shall never be accepted from him, and he will be among the losers in the Hereafter. O Allah I take you as a witness that I have indeed conveyed [Your Message].

Emphasis on the Nation to Adhere to Imamat

O companies of mankind! Allah, Almighty and Majestic, has indeed perfected your religion through his *imamah* (leadership). So, whoever does not take him as an *imam* and those who succeed him from amongst my offspring from his loins until the Day of Judgment and Presentation before Allah, Almighty and Majestic indeed they are the ones whose deeds have failed in this world and in the Hereafter, and in the Fire, they are eternal, the punishment will not be lightened for them, nor will they be granted any respite.

O companies of mankind! This is Ali; the most supportive of ye to me, the most rightful of ye to [succeed] me, the closest of ye to me, and the most esteemed and precious of ye to me; both Allah Almighty and Majestic and I are contented and pleased with him. No ayah of contentment in the Qur'an was [ever] sent down except [it was] about him, and Allah did not address _those who believe_ except that He started with him, no verse of praise in the Qur'an was [ever] sent down except that which was about him, Allah did not attest Paradise in [the surah of] has there been on mankind...except for him, nor did He send it down for other than him, and He did not admire anyone with it other than him.

O companies of mankind! He is the succourer of Allah's religion, the disputer [in support] of Allah's messenger, and he is indeed the Pious (*Taqiyy*), the Pure (*Naqiyy*), the Guide (*Hadi*), and the Guided (*Mahdi*). Your Prophet is the best Prophet, your *wasiy* is the best *wasiy,* and his sons are the best of the *awsiya*

O companies of mankind! The offspring of every Prophet is from his loins, whereas my offspring is from the loins of the Commander of the Faithful (*Amir al-Mo'mineen*) Ali.

O companies of mankind! Iblees caused Adam to be dismissed from Paradise through envy, so do not envy him for your deeds will be nullified and your feet will slip away, for Adam was lowered to the earth due to a single fault, while he was the Chosen One of Allah, Almighty and Exalted, and what about ye, and ye being what ye are, and some of ye are the enemies of Allah?

O Indeed no one loathes Ali except for the wicked, no one supports Ali and support his *wilayah* except for the pious, and none believes in him except for a sincere believer. And– by Allah – it was about Ali that descended the surah of al-Asr; In the Name of Allah, the all-beneficent, the all-merciful. By Time, indeed man is at a loss except for Ali who believed, and contented to the Truth and to Perseverance.

O companies of mankind! Indeed, I have taken Allah as a witness, conveyed my message and there is none upon the messenger save a clear conveying.

O companies of mankind! Fear Allah as He should be feared and die not except when ye are *Muslims*.

Warning about the Plots of the Usurpers

O companies of mankind! Believe in Allah and His Messenger and the light that has been sent down with him before we blot out the faces and turn them backwards, or curse them as we cursed the People of the Sabbath. By Allah He did not imply anyone in this *ayah* except for a group from amongst my *sahabah* (Companions) whom I know by their names and their lineages, and indeed I have been ordered [by the Almighty] to overlook them. So, let everyone act according to what one finds in his heart of love or hate for Ali.

O companies of mankind! The light from Allah, Almighty and Majestic, is entwined within me, and then within Ali Ibn Abitaleb, then within his descendants Until al-Qaim al-Mahdi [the Upholder, the Guided] who will re-establish the right/rule of Allah, and any right that is ours, for Allah, Almighty and Exalted, has made us a proof upon the negligent, the obstinate, the opponents, the traitors, the sinners, the wrongdoers, and the usurpers from amongst all the worlds.

O companies of mankind! I warn ye that I am Allah's messenger, [while other] messengers have passed before me; so, should I die or I am slain will ye turn back on your heels? And he who turns back on his heels will never harm Allah in the least, and Allah will reward the thankful the

The Doctor & Sheikh's Debate

perseverant. O Indeed it is Ali who has been described by perseverance and gratitude, then after him are my offspring through his loins.

O companies of mankind! Deem not your embracing of Islam a favour onto me, rather do not even count it as a favour unto Allah, for He would nullify your deeds, and will wrath against ye, and will subject ye with tribulations of flame of fire and molten brass, indeed your Lord is in ambush.

O companies of mankind! Indeed, there will be after me leaders who invite to the Fire, and on the Day of Resurrection they will not be succoured.

O companies of mankind! Indeed, both Allah and I abjure them and bear absolutely no responsibility for any of their deeds, actions, or sayings.

O companies of mankind! They, their supporters, their followers, and their devotees are in the lowest depth of the Fire and indeed miserable is the abode of the arrogant. **Indeed, they are the signatories of the document, so let each one ye [O signatories of the document] look into his document.** The narrator commented: this reference the Prophet made about the document went by most of the people unnoticed, except for a few of them.

O companies of mankind! I bequeath [the issue of succession] as divine leadership (*imamah*) and as an inheritance in my posterity until the Day of Resurrection. Indeed, I have conveyed that which I have been commanded to convey [by the Almighty]; as a proof and evidence upon every one present or absent, upon everyone who witnessed or did not witness [this sermon], and [anyone who] is born or is yet to be born; so, let those who are present here inform the absent, and let the parent inform the offspring until the Day of Resurrection. Verily, they will make the *imamah* after me a possession and a usurpation, O Verily the curse of Allah be upon the usurpers and the usurping [transgressors]; and then those who will do the un-occupying will make themselves unoccupied for ye [to deal with ye at length] O ye two weights, and there will be unleashed upon ye flames of fire and molten brass, and ye will not receive help.

O companies of mankind! Allah, Almighty and Exalted, will not leave ye in the state ye are in until He distinguishes the corrupt from the good, and Allah will
not inform ye of the Unseen.

O companies of mankind! Indeed, there shall be no a city except that Allah will destroy it – for its belying – before the Day of Resurrection, and He will give its governance to Imam Mahdi, and surely Allah honours His promise.

O companies of mankind! Indeed, most of the former generations before ye went astray, and indeed Allah destroyed the former generations, and He will destroy the latter. Almighty Allah said, Did We not destroy the former generations, and then will follow them with the latter, that is how We deal with the guilty, Woe that day unto the beliers.

O companies of mankind! Indeed, Allah has commanded me and He has prohibited me, and I certainly commanded Ali and prohibited him by His command. Thus, the knowledge of [all] the commandments and the prohibitions are with him, so listen to his commands and ye will be safe [from going astray], obey him and ye will be guided, stop at his prohibition ye will be led to righteousness, comply with his course and do not let the diverse paths scatter ye from his path.

The Devotees and the Enemies of Ahl Al Bayt

O companies of mankind! I am Allah's Straight Path (*alsirat al-mustaqeem*) that He ordered ye to follow, and after me it is Ali, and then [after him are] my offspring from his loins – the Leaders of Guidance – they guide to the Truth and do justice by it. In the Name of Allah the Beneficent the Merciful, All praise belongs to Allah, Lord of all the worlds, the beneficent, the merciful, Master of the Day of Retribution, You alone do we worship, and to You alone do we turn for help, guide us on the Straight Path, the Path of those whom You have blessed, not of those whom You are wrathful, nor of those who are astray. [This surah] was sent down about me and – by Allah – it was sent down about them (the *imams*), it encompasses [all of] them, 100 and it is specific only to them. Those are the authorities and devotees of Allah who have no fear and nor do they grieve; O surely the party of Allah are victorious.

O Indeed it is their enemies who are the fools, the perverse, and the brothers of the devils inspiring each other with flashy words deceptively.

O Indeed their [the imams'] supporters and devotees are those whom Allah mentions in His Book, saying, Almighty and Majestic is He, You shall not find a people who believe in Allah and the latter day befriending those who act in opposition to Allah and His Messenger, even though they were their (own) fathers, or their sons, or their brothers, or their clan; they are those into whose hearts He has impressed faith, and whom He has strengthened with an inspiration from Him: and He will cause them to enter gardens beneath which rivers flow, abiding therein forever; Allah is well-pleased with them and they are well-pleased with Him, they are Allah's party: O surely the party of Allah are the successful ones.

O Indeed their [the imams'] supporters and devotees are the believers whom Allah, Almighty and Exalted, describes them as, those who have faith and do not taint their faith with wrongdoing; to them belongs the true security, and they are the rightly guided.

O Indeed their supporters and devotees are those who have attained faith and then have never doubted.

O Indeed their supporters and devotees are those who enter Paradise in peace and security, the angels meet them with greetings saying, Peace be upon ye! Well ye Have fared; so, enter in, to dwell forever.

O Indeed their supporters and devotees are those for whom is The Paradise; they are provided therein without any reckoning. O Indeed their enemies are those who will roast intensely in a

Blaze. O Indeed their enemies are those who will hear the Hell blaring as it seethes and they will see it roaring.

O Indeed their enemies are those about whom Allah said, every time that a nation enters [Hell], it will curse its sister [nation], until when they all gather together in it, the last of them will say about the first of them, 'Our Lord, it was they who led us astray; so, give them a double punishment of the Fire'. He will say, 'It is double for each [of ye], but ye do not know'.

O Indeed their enemies are those about whom Allah, Almighty and Majestic, says, whenever a group is thrown in [Hell], its keepers ask them, 'Did there not come to ye any warner?' They will say, 'Yes, a warner did come to us, but we cried lies, saying, 'Allah did not send down anything; ye are only in great error'. And they will say, 'Had we listened or applied reason, we would not have been among inmates of the Blaze'. Thus, they will admit their sin, so far-removed [from Allah's mercy] are the inmates of the Blaze!

O Indeed their [the imams'] supporters and devotees are those who fear their Lord in secret; for them there is forgiveness and great reward O companies of mankind! What a difference there is between the Blaze and great reward.

O companies of mankind! Our enemy is he whom Allah has condemned and cursed, and our devotee is any one whom Allah has praised and loved. O companies of mankind! Indeed, I am the Warner _alnadheer_ and Ali is the Bearer of Good Tidings _albasheer_.

O companies of mankind! Indeed, I am the one who warns _mundhir_ and Ali is the Guide _had_. O companies of mankind! Indeed, I am a Prophet and Ali is a *wasiy*.

O companies of mankind! Indeed, I am a Messenger, while Ali is the Leader (*imam*) and the *wasiy* after me, and the leaders (*imams*) after him are his sons. O Indeed I am their father but they are from his loins.

The Glad-Tiding of Reappearance of Imam Mahdi

O Indeed the seal of the *imams* from amongst us is *al-Qaim al-Mahdi* [the Upholder, the Guided].

O Indeed he is the one who prevails over the religion. O Indeed he is the avenger against the oppressors. O Indeed he is the conqueror of the fortresses and their destroyer. O Indeed he is the winner over all tribes of the polytheists and their guide [to the truth].

O Indeed he is the avenger of the blood of every one of Allah's devotees. O Indeed he is the Succourer of Allah's religion. O Indeed he is the scooper of the deep ocean [of knowledge]. O Indeed he will mark every owner of distinction by his distinction and every owner of ignorance by his ignorance. O Indeed he is Allah's Choice and His Chosen One. O Indeed he is the inheritor of all knowledge, encompassing every perception.

O Indeed he is the communicator on behalf of his Lord –Almighty and Majestic – and he is the elevator of the teachings of His verses. O Indeed he is the rightful guide, the one of strong infallible opinion who is not prone to errors and puts things right. O Indeed he is the delegated to [by the Almighty].

O Indeed he is the one whom past generations have given glad tidings of. O Indeed he is the remaining proof (*hujjah*) and there shall be no *hujjah* after him, and there is no right other than that that is with him, and there is no light except that That is with him.

O Indeed none can overcome him and there is no victor over him. O Indeed he is the authority of Allah on His earth, His judge over His creation, and His trustee over His secret and His evident.

Preparation for Seeking Allegiance (mentioning of Ahl Al Bayt)

O companies of mankind! Indeed, I have clarified for ye and made ye understand, and this Ali will teach ye and make ye understand after me. O Indeed I will, at the conclusion of my sermon, ask ye to shake hands with me to swear your allegiance to him, assenting and recognising him [and his authority], and then to shake hands with him, after [ye have shaken hands with] me.

O Indeed I have sworn allegiance to Allah and Ali has indeed sworn allegiance to me, and I, on behalf of Allah, Almighty and Majestic, require ye to swear the oath of allegiance to him indeed those who swear allegiance to you, do but swear allegiance to Allah: the hand of Allah is above their hands. So, whosoever breaks his oath breaks it only to his own detriment, and whoever fulfils the covenant he has made with Allah, He will give him a great reward.

The Nation's Reference for the Permissible and the Prohibited

O companies of mankind! Indeed, the Hajj and the Umrah are amongst Allah's sacraments, so whoever performs the hajj to the House, or performs the Umrah then there is no blame upon him to circuit between them. Should anyone volunteer a good deed, then Allah is indeed appreciative, all-knowing.

O companies of mankind! Perform the hajj to the House, for no household arrives at it except that they will be enriched and receive glad tidings, and none refrain from it save they will be without posterity and impoverished.

O companies of mankind! No believer stands at the *site* save that Allah forgives him his past sins until his present time, and when he finishes his hajj let him begin his deeds afresh [with no record of sin in his book of deeds].

O companies of mankind! The Hujjaj (pilgrims) are assisted, and their expenses will be reimbursed, for Allah does not waste the reward of the faithful. O companies of mankind! Perform the hajj of the House with perfect religion and thorough understanding and learning, and do not leave the sites except with repentance and a [resolute] determination to abstain from any sin.

O companies of mankind! _Maintain the Prayers and give the Zakah just as Allah, Almighty and Majestic, commanded ye, so if some time was gone-by and ye were negligent or forgetting, then Ali is your *waliy* (patron/authority) and he will elucidate for ye, for he is the one whom Allah, Almighty and Majestic, appointed him for ye after me as the trustee of His creation. He is from me and I am from him, and he and the ones who succeed him from amongst my progeny will teach ye what ye ask about, and they will elucidate to ye what ye do not know.

O Indeed the halal and the haram issues are more than I can list and define, and then for me to go on to command to the halal and forbid the haram in one session.

However, I am commanded [by the Almighty] to take the oath of allegiance from ye and to make a covenant with ye that ye assent to what I have brought from Allah, Almighty and Majestic, about Ali the Commander of the Faithful (*Amir al-Mo'mineen*) and the *awsiya'* (successors) after him, those who are from me and from him, which is the *imamah* (divine leadership) that is upheld and established in them – the seal of which is al-Mahdi – until the day he stands before Allah who determines and decrees.

O companies of mankind! Every halal I have guided ye to, and every haram I have forbidden ye from, indeed I will never go back on, nor will I change or modify. O so make sure ye remember that, keep it, adhere and enjoin to it, and never change it nor modify it. O Indeed I repeat the word, O do uphold the prayers, give the Zakah, enjoin good, and forbid evil.

O Indeed the pinnacle of enjoining good is to adhere to my speech, and to convey it to he who is not present, and enjoin him, on my behalf, to accept it, agree to it, and assent it, and prohibit him from opposing it, for it is a commandment from Allah, Almighty and Majestic, and from me. There is no enjoining good and forbidding evil except with a *ma'soom imam* (infallible leader).

O companies of mankind! The Qur'an teaches ye that the *imams* after him are his descendants, and I informed ye and made ye know that they are from me and from him, as Allah says in His Book and He made it a lasting word among his posterity_, 126 and I say, "Ye will never go astray so long as ye adhere to them both".

O companies of mankind! [I urge ye to adhere] to piety, to piety (*taqwa*), and be wary of the Hour, just as Allah, Almighty and Majestic, said, indeed the quake of the Hour is a mighty thing.

Remember death, the resurrection, the reckoning, the balances, being held to account before the Lord of Worlds, and [remember] the reward, and the punishment. So, he who comes forward with the good deed he will be rewarded for it, and he who comes with the evil deed he will not have a share in paradise.

Formal Seeking of Allegiance

O companies of mankind! Ye are more than ye could shake hands with me all at the same time, and Allah, Almighty and Majestic, has commanded me to seek from ye verbal confirmation and recognition for what I have made binding obligation [of allegiance] for Ali Amir al-Mo'mineen, [as my successor], and for those who succeed him of the *imams* who are from me and from him, as I have informed ye that my offspring are from his loins.

So, all together say in one voice: "We hear, obey, approve of, and are bound by what you have conveyed from our Lord and your Lord with regards to our *imam* Ali Amir al-Mo'mineen, and those *imams* who are born from his loins. We swear the oath of allegiance to you in this regard with our hearts, with our souls, with our tongues, and with our hands. Upon that we will live, upon it we will die, and upon it we will resurrect. We will not change, we will not alter, we will not doubt, we will not deny, we will not hesitate, we will not renege against the covenant, nor will we break the pledge.

You have advised us with Allah's admonition about Ali Amir al-Mo'mineen (the Commander of the Faithful) and the *imams* whom you mentioned to be your offspring from his descendants after him; Hasan, Husayn and those Allah appointed after them two.

The covenant and the pledge for them are taken from us; from our hearts, our souls, our tongues, our consciences, and our hands. He who realises it [by being present] he does that with his handshake, otherwise he [would] indeed confirm and admit it by his tongue, and we do not seek to alter that, and may Allah not see from us any change or conversion. We fulfil that on your behalf to the close and the far from amongst our offspring and our families, and we take Allah as our witness on that, and surely Allah suffices for a witness, and you are a witness on us for that".

O companies of mankind! What do ye say? Indeed, Allah knows every voice and the hidden [thought] of every soul, so whoever is guided is guided for his own sake, and whoever goes astray goes astray to his own detriment, and whoever pledges allegiance [to Ali] he has indeed pledged allegiance to Allah, the hand of Allah is above their hands. **O companies of mankind! So, swear the oath of allegiance to Allah and swear it to me, and swear the oath of allegiance to Ali Amir al-Mo'mineen, Hasan, Husayn, and the imams from their offspring in this world and in the Hereafter the lasting Word**; Allah will destroy he who betrays, and He will have mercy on he who remains loyal. So, whoever breaks his oath breaks it only to his own detriment, and whoever fulfils the covenant he has made with Allah, He will give him a great reward.

O companies of mankind! Say that which I have just told ye and greet Ali as Amir al-Mo'mineen (the Commander of the Faithful), and ye say we hear and obey, Our Lord, grant us Your forgiveness, and unto You is the return, and ye should say All praise belongs to Allah who guided us unto this, and we would have never been guided had not Allah guided us, indeed our Lord's messengers came with the truth.

O companies of mankind! Indeed, the merits and virtues of Ali Ibn Abitaleb in the sight of Allah, Almighty and Majestic – which He has revealed in the Qur'an– are more than I can list them in one session, so whoever informs ye of them [quoting me] and described them to ye, believe him. O companies of mankind! He who obeys Allah, His messenger, Ali, and the *imams* whom I mentioned, he has indeed triumphed a great triumph O companies of mankind! Those who rush to swear allegiance to him and his authority and to greet him as Amir al-Mo'mineen are indeed the ones who are triumphant in the Gardens of Bliss.

O companies of mankind! Ye say that word with which Allah will be pleased with ye, for if ye disbelieve, together with all who are on the earth this will not harm Allah in the least.

O Allah! Forgive the believers through what I have conveyed and commanded, and wrath against the obstinate disbelievers, and all praise belongs to Allah the Lord of the worlds.

List of Some of the Chain of Transmissions Mostly Used in the Software

Aloosi Baqdadi, Shahabu Din Mahmood, Tafsir Ruh Al Ma'ani, 1891 A.D

Abulfateh Muhammad Ibn Umar Maroof Be Fakhr Razi, Al Melal Va Al Nehal, 1227 A.D

Asir Jazri, Az Al Din Ibn, Asad Al Qabah Fi Ma'arefah Al Sahabah, 1251 A.D

Ahmad Ibn Hanabal, Musnad, 877 A.D

Ahmad Sa'albi, Abu Es-haq, Al Kashf Va Al Bayan, Maroof Be Tafsir Saalbi, 1048 A.D

Esfahani, Raqib, Mufradat Al Faze Al Quran, 1046 A.D

Undolosi, Qassi Muhammad Abdul Haq Ibn Qaleb Atiyah, Al Muharar Al Vajiz Fi Tafsir Al Ketab Al Aziz, 1167 A.D

Bukhari, Muhammad Ibn Ismael, Sahih Bukhari, 877 A.D

Belazari, Ahmad Ibn Yahya, Ansa Bul Ashraf, 900 A.D

Tamimi, Ahmad Ibn Ali, Musnad Abuyo La Musali, 928 A.D

Al Jazari, Muhammad Ibn Asir, Jamel Ul Sul, 1227 A.D

Hakem Neyshabouri, Muhammad Ibn Abdullah, Al Mustadrak Ala Ass Sahihin, 1026 A.D

Hanbali Dameshqi, Ibn Al Emad, Shazarat Al Zahab Fi Akhbar Man Zahab, 1710 A.D

Hanafi, Obeydulalh Ibn Abdullah Ibn Ahmad Maruf Be Hakem Al Haskaani, Shavahed Al Tanzil Le Qavaed ul Tafzil, from the 11th century

Khatib Baqdadi, Abubakr Ahmad Ibn Ali, Tarikh Baqdad u Medina Tus Salam, 1084 A.D

Al Zahabi, Muhammad Ibn Ahmad Ibn Usman, Siyare A'alaam Un Nabala, 1369 A.D

Zamakhshari, Jaralah Mahmood Ibn Umar, Al Kashaf, 1159 A.D

Surat, Abu Isa Muhammad Ibn Isa Ibn, Sunan Tarmazi, 918 A.D

Suyuti, Abubakr Abdul Rahman Ibn Muhammad Jalalu Din, Asbabol Nozom, 1532 A.D

Suyuti Abubakr Abdul Rahman Ibn Muhammad Jalalu Din, Jameul Ahadith, 1532 A.D

Al Shokani, Muhammad Ibn Ali, Fath ul Qadir Al Jame Beyne Fani Al Raviyat Va Al Dariya Fi Elmut Tafsir, 1871 A.D

Tabarani, Hafez Suleyman Ibn Ahmad, Al Mujam Al Kabir, 981 A.D

Tabarani, Abu Jafar Muhammad Ibn Jarir, Tarikh Al Umam Va Al Molook, 931 A.D

Tabarani, Abu Jafar Muhammad Ibn Jarir, Jameul Bayan Fir Tafsir Al Quran Maroof be Tafsir Tabari, 931 A.D

Tabari, Muheb Al Din Abul Abbas Ahmad Ibn Abdullah, Zakhaer Al Uqba Fi Manaqib Za Vel Qurba, 1315 A.D

A'sqalani, Ibn Hejr, Al Esabah Fi Tamiiz el Sehabah, 1473 A.D

Al Asqalani Maroof be Ibn Hajar, Shahabudin Ahmad Ibn Ali Muhammad, Al Maqal Al A.D Alamiyah Bezaavede Al Masanid Ass Samaniya, 1473 A.D

Qartabi, Muhammad Ibn Ahmad, Al Jame ul Ahkam ul Quran (Tafsir Al Qurtabi), 1292 A.D

Qazvini, Muhammad Ibn Yazid Marof Be Ibn Majaah, Sunan Ibn Maajah, 1421 A.D

Qonduzi Hanafi, Suleyman Ibn Ibrahim, Yanabi Al Maodah Laza Vel Qarbi, 1913 A.D

Kasir Dameshghi, Ismael Ibn, Tafsir Al Quran Al Azim Maroof be Tafsir Ibn Kasir, 1395 A.D

Kasir, Ismael Ibn Amar Ibn, Jame ul Masanid Va Al Sunan, 1395 A.D

Muhammad Ibn Umar Maroof be Fakhr Razi, Tafsir Kabir, 1227 A.D

Nesaei, Ahmad Ibn Shoayb, Khasaes Amir Al Mumenin Ali Ibn Abitaleb Karam Al Lah Vajha, 924 A.D

Neyshabouri, Abul Hossien Muslem Ibn Hajaj, Sahih Muslem, 882 A.D

Hendi, Alaedin Al Mutaqi Hesamudin, Kanzal Amaal Fi Senin Al Qaval va Alfaal, 1596 A.D

Heysami Makki, Ahmad Ibn, Al Savaeq Al Maharraqa Fer Rade Ala Ahl Al Bedah Va Al Zandaqah, 1595 A.D

www.ingramcontent.com/pod-product-compliance
Lightning Source LLC
Chambersburg PA
CBHW081152070526
44583CB00021B/2805